THE Virgin BOOK OF Football Records 3

JIM DREWETT AND ALEX LEITH

Virgin

First published in Great Britain in 1998 by Virgin Books,
an imprint of Virgin Publishing Ltd,
Thames Wharf Studios, Rainville Road, London W6 9HT

This revised and updated edition published in 1998

A catalogue record for this book is available from the British Library

ISBN 1 85227 7777

Printed in Great Britain by Jarrold Books

Design and repro: Prima Creative Services

We are enormously proud to welcome you to the third edition of the Virgin Book of Football Records, improved and updated to include the 1997/8 season and, of course, France 98. But we feel we must warn you: this book is so jam-packed with facts and figures, quotes and quirks, the weird, the wacky and the wonderful that once you pick it up you might find it very, very hard to put down again.

The Virgin Book of Football Records is not just a book of records, although it does tell you all the best '-ests' in the history of the game: the biggest crowds, the fastest goals, the quickest sendings-off, the silliest haircuts. As well as all these superlatives, this book gives you the facts about all the essential players, teams, competitions and pundits in the history of the game - and a good deal more besides. You don't believe us? Open up the book and have a browse. You may be there some time.

WHERE TO START

In the Virgin Book of Football Records we've pooled together the most significant facts in football, as well as throwing in some of the more bizarre, quaint and quirky ones (like the referee who scored against Plymouth Argyle in 1968, or the two Leicester City players who conspired to score the only joint own goal ever recorded in 1954).

The problem, when we were deciding what to put in and what not, was where to start... and more to the point where to stop? We had to make decisions about which clubs, players and countries to cover, knowing that although most people probably couldn't give a hoot, for others the omission of Albania's pre-war international record might be too much to bear.

The basic starting point we eventually agreed upon was that we'd include every current English and Scottish league club, as well as the most famous and most successful clubs from around the world. Then we added the top players from the English and Scottish leagues and the world's finest internationals (from John Aldridge to Gianfranco Zola) as well as the great players of the past (from Ivor Allchurch to Dino Zoff). We also managed to stick in a collection of managers, pundits, administrators and commentators... the people whose faces we see every week on the telly but whose often great and glorious footballing past has been forgotten after years of dodgy suits, sheepskin jackets and Colemanballs-style blunders.

COUNTRIES AND WILD CARDS

There are entries on the countries that loom large on the footballing map, the Brazils, the Italys and the Germanys, and some whose moments of glory might have been a little rarer but are equally memorable. Even San Marino hold a record... as Stuart Pearce will tell you.

From the FA Cup to the Copa Libertadores, from the World Cup to the European Championship, we've covered all the major international and club competitions in world football, plus individual awards like Footballer of the Year, Goal of the Month and the classic Golden Boot awards for the game's top scorers.

And finally we topped off this list with a bunch of 'wild card' entries featuring anything from dogs (find out about the one who actually ran on and scored the winner) to superstitions (did you know about Birmingham City's gypsy curse?) Put it all together and you've got a book jam-packed with enough football facts, figures and fun to qualify you to take over as manager of Lincoln City!

THE STATISTICS

To help you digest all this information, there are a number of regular elements you'll come across in the book. For English and Scottish clubs we've started each entry with a breakdown of the year they were founded, their ground and capacity, their largest ever crowd, previous names, most popular nickname and regular colours. There's also a roll of honour for their glorious triumphs, and for major clubs we've included their post war league record. For international clubs the entries follow a slightly different format: for instance we've given the number of national league wins they've landed.

For players the entries include information, wherever possible, on their place and date of birth (and death), height, playing position and club (league only) and international career with dates, appearances and goals.

And for countries we've covered their first international and World Cup finals matches, most capped player and highest goalscorer, best win and worst defeat, and regular colours, as well as their World Cup record where relevant.

All the information should be accurate up to the end of the 1997/98 season although we did manage to catch some late-breaking records before the presses started rolling... like Brian Laudrup's amazing wages at Chelsea.

HOW YOU CAN HELP

No doubt some of you will be outraged that we've missed out a top fact about your club's record-breaking reserve team or award-winning groundsman. So if there's a stat missing or incorrect and you're sick as a parrot then we're truly sorry, but at the end of the day we were giving 110 per cent and you can't ask for any more than that...

Help us make the next edition even better: tell us what you think we've missed and should include by writing to us c/o Virgin Publishing, Thames Wharf Studios, Rainville Road, London W6 9HT. We can't guarantee to agree with you but we'll certainly take every suggestion, fact and comment into account when we update the book.

Jim Drewett & Alex Leith
July 1998

ABANDONED MATCHES

ENGLAND'S SHORTEST match took place in Buenos Aires against Argentina on 17th May 1953. The match was abandoned after 23 minutes with the score at 0–0 when a monsoon struck and torrential rain made the pitch unplayable. The 15th February 1995 match against Ireland, abandoned because of crowd trouble, lasted for 27 minutes.

● SCOTLAND's first international abandonment took place against Austria on 8th May 1963. With 79 minutes played, two Austrians had been sent off and the remainder carried on kicking lumps out of their Scottish counterparts, so referee Jim Finney abandoned the game with Scotland winning 4–1.

● THE SHORTEST English game on record saw Stoke playing Wolves in a monstrous blizzard in 1894. Only 400 hardy souls braved the elements, and they were mightily relieved when referee Mr Helme called off proceedings after just three minutes.

● IN SOUTH AMERICA abandoned matches are as common as beans and salsa. On 25th June 1975, for instance, a match between Chile and Uruguay was called off after the referee sent off 19 players (10 Chileans and 9 Uruguayans)!

● PERHAPS the most bizarre match abandonment occurred on 12th December 1891. Ten minutes into the second half of a niggly game between arch rivals Burnley and Blackburn Rovers a player from each side was sent off after they came to blows. But in support of their team-mate the entire Blackburn team, except for goalkeeper Herbie Arthur, marched off the pitch in protest. With ten men against one the referee re-started the game and Burnley scored... only for Arthur to quite rightly appeal for offside. When the keeper delayed taking the ensuing free-kick the referee gave up and abandoned the match.

● DURING THE 1997/98 season no fewer than three Premiership matches were abandoned due to floodlight failure: Derby v Wimbledon, West Ham v Crystal Palace and Wimbledon v Arsenal.

ABERDEEN

Year founded: 1903
Ground: Pittodrie Stadium (21,634)
Highest ever crowd: 45,061, 13th March 1954 v Hearts (Scottish Cup rd 4)
Nickname: The Dons
Colours: Red shirts, red shorts and red socks

ABERDEEN's finest hour came in 1983 when they became only the third Scottish club ever to win a European trophy, by beating Real Madrid 2–1 to lift the European Cup Winners' Cup. Ten days later they beat Rangers in the Scottish Cup to claim a unique 'double', something which then manager Alex Ferguson is now accustomed to doing most seasons at Manchester United.

● ONE of few clubs to threaten Rangers' and Celtic's domination of Scottish football, Aberdeen won a First Division title in 1955. Then 25 years later they did it again becoming Premier Division champions three times in 1980, 1984 and 1985 under Alex Ferguson.

● ORIGINALLY NICKNAMED The Whites and then The Wasps after their early strips (all white and black and gold). Because some of the founder members of the club were professors at Aberdeen University they are now known as 'The Dons' (and they play in red).

● THE CLUB's best victory was back on 9th February 1923, when they beat Peterhead 13–0. The club's heaviest defeat was at the hands of mighty Celtic, who beat them 8–0 in a league match they'd rather forget on 30th January 1965. Aberdeen's most capped player is strapping defender Alex McLeish who made 77 appearances for Scotland between 1980–93. Scottish international Willie Miller made more league appearances for the club than any other player, an amazing 556 games between 1973–90.

● IN 1995 the club paid Oldham just over £1 million for Paul Bernard, their record transfer. The biggest fee they received was £1.75 million from Coventry City for Eoin Jess in 1996.

● JOE HARPER is The Dons' record goalscorer, with 199 during his two spells at the club (1969–72 and 1976–81), while Benny Yorston netted the most in one season (38 in 1929/30).

● ABERDEEN's Pittodrie Stadium has a tradition of historic 'firsts'. In the 1920s it became the site of the first ever 'dug-outs', requested by then coach Donald Coleman so he could study his players' footwork. And in 1978 Pittodrie (believed to mean 'dungheap' in Gaelic) became Britain's first ever all-seater stadium.

● IT IS also Britain's most northerly league football ground and, only 300 yards from the North Sea, very often the coldest. While many fans were unhappy about the banning of alcohol and bottles from football grounds in 1980, at Aberdeen they complained about not being allowed to take their thermos flasks in!

Roll of Honour

Division 1 champions 1955
Premier Division champions 1980, 1984, 1985
Scottish Cup 1947, 1970, 1982, 1983, 1984, 1986, 1990
League Cup 1956, 1977, 1986, 1990, 1996
European Cup Winners' Cup 1983

Did You Know?

AC Milan was founded in 1899 by a group of English ex-pats. At first the club members were more interested on the chock of willow on leather than thumping a bladder around. It was originally called Milan Cricket and Football Club and didn't change its name to AC (Associazione Calcio) Milan until 1938.

George Weah, the first Liberian to play for AC Milan, looks up at the club's overflowing trophy cabinet

AC MILAN

Year founded: 1899
Ground: Giuseppe Meazza [San Siro] (85,847 – shared with Inter Milan)
League wins: 15
Colours: Red-and-black-striped shirts, white shorts and socks

WHEN the famous Italian club was founded by an Englishman in 1899 it was known as the Milan Cricket and Football Club. Even now the English 'Milan' is used instead of the Italian 'Milano'.

● IN 1906 Milan became the first club in Italy to use nets behind their goals.

● AC MILAN have by far and away the best European record of any club in recent times, appearing in five finals since 1989 and winning the famous trophy three times (1989 v Steaua Bucharest, 1990 v Benfica and 1994 v Barcelona). They were also losing finalists against Marseille in 1993 and Ajax in 1995.

● ONLY JUVENTUS (25) have won more Italian league titles than AC Milan (15), but in the 1990s they have dominated Serie A, winning it in 1992, 1993, 1994 and 1996.

● AC MILAN hold the record for the longest unbeaten run in Italian football. They went 58 matches without losing in a 17-month streak between October 1992 and March 1993. The run was finally broken by Parma who beat them with a goal by Faustino Asprilla.

Roll of Honour

Serie A champions 1901, 1906, 1907, 1951, 1955, 1957, 1959, 1962, 1968, 1979, 1988, 1992, 1993, 1994, 1996
Italian Cup 1967, 1972, 1973, 1977
European Champions Cup 1963, 1969, 1989, 1990, 1994
European Cup Winners' Cup 1968, 1973
European Super Cup 1989, 1990, 1994
World Club Cup 1969, 1989, 1990

TONY ADAMS

Born: London 10.10.66
Height: 6ft 3ins Position: Defender
Club career:
1983– Arsenal 421 (33)
International record:
1987– England 55 (4)

NOW AGED 32, Tony Adams is believed to have become Arsenal's youngest ever captain at 21 when he took over from Kenny Sansom in 1988. He has retained the captain's armband pretty much ever since and, at the end of the 1997/98 season, became the second Arsenal skipper in history to lift both the League and FA Cup trophies in one season (Pat Rice being the first in 1970/71).

● In all Adams has lifted eight major trophies at the club – three league championships (1988/89, 1990/91 and 1997/98), two FA Cups (1993 and 1998) two League Cups (1987 and 1993) and the European Cup Winners Cup (1994).

● IN A career highlighted by honours, Adams can also boast winning the PFA Young Player of the Year Award in 1987 as well as the Arsenal Player of the Year Award three times (1987, 1990 and 1994).

● IN 1990, his career and life hit their lowest point when he was jailed for drink-driving, just before Christmas. And in 1996 Adams admitted he was an alcoholic, a problem he has tackled with characteristic determination.

● WHEN HE MADE his debut for England against Spain in Madrid on 18th February 1987, Adams became the first player born after the 1966 World Cup win to pull on the England shirt. He has gone on to play in two European Champioinships (1988 and 1996) and one World Cup (1998).

Tony Adams: making an ass of his critics

AGE

'WING WIZARD' Sir Stanley Matthews was the first 50-year-old to play in the top flight when he turned out for First Division Stoke City against Fulham in 1965, five days after his birthday. He was not, however, the oldest player ever to play a league match.

● THAT particular honour – which will surely never be beaten – fell to Neil McBain, the New Brighton manager, who had to go in goal for his team's Division Three (North) match against Hartlepools United during an injury crisis in 1947. He was 52 (and let in three goals).

● The oldest international in British football was Billy Meredith, who played for Wales against England in 1920 at the ripe age of 45.

● On February 11th 1998, Liverpool striking sensation Michael Owen became the youngest England player this century when he pulled on the white shirt for the first time against Chile aged just 18 years and 59 days.

● THE YOUNGEST player to appear in an FA Cup Final was Paul Allen, who was just 17 and 256 days when he tearfully picked up a winners' medal with West Ham in 1980 after beating Arsenal 1–0. The oldest FA Cup finalist was Walter Hampson, who was 41 years and 8 months when he turned out for for Newcastle against Aston Villa in 1924.

● The oldest footballer currently playing organised football in Britain is Fred Rosner. At an incredible 74, left back Fred is 40 years older than anyone else in the North London Sunday League where he plays for Downham FC at Hackney Marshes.

AIRDRIEONIANS

Year founded: 1878
Ground: Excelsior Stadium (10,215)
Previous names: Excelsior
Highest ever crowd: 24,000, 8th March 1952 v Hearts (Scottish Cup qtr-final)
Nickname: The Diamonds
Colours: White shirts (with red diamond), white shorts, red socks

AIRDRIE, like all Scottish clubs, have lived in the shadow of the Old Firm clubs of Celtic and Rangers in nearby Glasgow. In May 1994 they accepted a £5.5 million offer from Safeway and moved out of their ageing Broomfield Park ground to share with Clyde. However, at the start of the 1998/99 season they returned home to a brand new 10,000 capacity stadium in the town.

● THE WORLD's first ever penalty was taken at Airdrie in March 1891, three days after the new rule had been adopted. Unfortunately for the home club, it was awarded against them, and was duly converted by Andrew Mitchell of Royal Albert.

● AIRDRIE's record victory was established more than a century ago when they beat Dundee Wanderers 15-1 in 1894, a Scottish League record. More recently, on 24 October 1959, they suffered their worst ever defeat – 1-11 to Hibernian, also a Scottish record for worst home defeat.

● DESPITE his unfortunate name, the most capped player for Airdrieonians, Jimmy Crapnell – nine Scotland appearances – was actually quite good.

● THE CLUB's finest hour came in 1924 when, featuring future Chelsea and Newcastle star Hughie Gallacher, they won the Scottish Cup, a feat they nearly repeated in 1995, eventually losing 1–0 in the final to Celtic.

Roll of Honour

Scottish Cup 1924

AJAX AMSTERDAM

Year founded: 1900
Ground: Amsterdam Arena (51,300)
League wins: 27
Colours: White shirts with a broad red stripe, white shorts and socks

NAMED AFTER mythological Greek hero Ajax, the famous Amsterdam club is the most successful in Dutch footballing history, winning the league 27 times and the cup 13 times.

● IN 1992 Ajax became only the second team after Juventus to have won all three major European trophies (European Cup, UEFA Cup and European Cup Winners' Cup) when they beat Torino in the UEFA Cup Final.

● WITH OUTSTANDING players like Johan Cruyff, Rudi Krol and Johan Neeskens in the side, in the 1970s Ajax became the first club to play Total Football – a system of inter-changing positions which the club still uses.

● AJAX WERE the first Dutch club to reach the European Cup Final in 1969, but lost 4–1 to AC Milan. They made up for the disappointment two years later by winning the cup three years on the trot in 1971 (2–0 v Panathinaikos of Greece), 1972 (2–0 v Inter Milan) and 1973 (1–0 v Juventus). However, they were not the first Dutch team to win the European Cup. That honour fell to arch-rivals Feyenoord who beat Celtic 2–1 in 1970.

● AT THE START of the 1996/97 season the club moved into the brand new all-seater stadium, the Amsterdam Arena, the first football stadium in Europe with a retractable roof. During that 1996/97 campaign Ajax' defender Marcio Santos set a new Dutch record by getting sent off just 17 seconds after coming on as a substitute against PSV Eindhoven.

Roll of Honour

Dutch League champions 1918, 1919, 1931, 1932, 1934, 1937, 1939, 1947, 1957, 1960, 1966, 1967, 1968, 1970, 1972, 1973, 1977, 1979, 1980, 1982, 1983, 1985, 1990, 1994, 1995, 1996 1998
Dutch Cup 1917, 1943, 1961, 1967, 1970, 1971, 1972, 1979, 1983, 1986, 1987, 1993, 1998
European Champions Cup 1971, 1972, 1973, 1995
European Cup Winners' Cup 1987
UEFA Cup 1992
European Super Cup 1972, 1973
World Club Cup 1972, 1996

A

ALBION ROVERS

Year founded: 1882
Ground: Cliftonhill, Coatbridge (1,200)
Highest ever crowd: 27,381, 8th February 1936 v Rangers (Scottish Cup rd 2)
Nickname: The Wee Rovers
Colours: Yellow shirts (with red trim), red and yellow shorts, yellow socks

ALBION ROVERS enjoyed their record win more than 100 years ago when they defeated Airdriehill 12–0 in 1887. Unfortunately memories of their worst ever defeat are somewhat clearer, an 11–1 loss to Partick Thistle in the Scottish Cup of 1993.

● THOUGH it rarely happens these days, the term 'capacity crowd' has little meaning at Albion Rovers since Cliftonhill has the smallest capacity of any league ground in Britain at just 1,200. This may be enough to hold the 300 who regularly attend, but no fewer than 12,000 recently signed a petition against ground sharing with near neighbours Airdrie.

● MURDY WALLS holds the league appearance record for the club. He played in 399 matches between 1921 and 1936. Record international caps holder is Jock White who got one of his two caps for Scotland while with Rovers.

● NOT known for their prolific goalscoring (they're the third lowest-scoring Scottish league team in history), incredibly Albion Rovers' all-time scorer Bunty Weir achieved his feat in just three seasons – 105 goals between 1928 and 1931.

● THE CLUB, nicknamed the Wee Rovers, have played at Cliftonhill since 1919. The track around the pitch has also been used for greyhound, stock car and speedway racing.

Roll of Honour

Div 2 champions 1934
Second Division champions 1989

JOHN ALDRIDGE

Born: Liverpool 18.9.58
Height: 5ft 11ins Position: Striker
Club career:
1979–84 Newport County 170 (69)
1984–87 Oxford United 114 (72)
1987–89 Liverpool 83 (50)
1989–91 Real Sociedad 63 (33)
1991– Tranmere Rovers 242 (138)
International record:
1986– Republic of Ireland 69 (19)

JOHN ALDRIDGE is the highest scorer in the history of English football. In total he has scored 475 goals in all competitions for Newport (88), Oxford (90), Liverpool (63), Real Sociedad (40), Tranmere Rovers (175) and the Republic of Ireland (19), to beat Jimmy Greaves' record of 467.

● ALDRIDGE is the second highest scorer in the history of the Republic of Ireland with 19 goals (behind Frank Stapelton on 20) even though he had to wait until the age of 28 to make his international debut against Wales in 1986.

● WITH HIS 69 caps for the Republic of Ireland, goalscorer extraordinaire Aldridge is Tranmere Rovers' Most Capped Player ever. Twenty nine of those were gained while playing for the club.

● ALDRIDGE finished top scorer in the Second Division in 1984/85, scoring 30 league goals in 42 matches for Second Division Champions Oxford United (which is still a club record), his highest ever haul in a season.

IVOR ALLCHURCH

Born: Swansea 16.10.1929
Position: Forward
Club career:
1948–58 Swansea City 330 (124)
1958–62 Newcastle United 143 (46)
1962–65 Cardiff City 103 (39)
1965–67 Swansea City 116 (42)
International record:
1951–66 Wales 68 (23)

SCORING an incredible 251 goals in 692 league appearances for various clubs in the 1950s and 60s, Ivor Allchurch was the 'Golden Boy' of Welsh football.

● HIS GOALS and inspirational play at inside forward took Wales to the 1958 World Cup Finals in Sweden for the first and only time in their history. With Allchurch on top form, Wales reached the quarter-finals and were only beaten 1–0, a late Pele goal seeing through eventual winners Brazil.

● IN A 16-year career Allchurch won 68 caps, scoring 23 international goals for Wales. He held the goalscoring record for Wales, with Trevor Ford, until Ian Rush got his 24th against Belgium on 31st March 1993.

ALLOA

Year founded: 1883
Ground: Recreation Park (3,148)
Highest ever crowd: 13,000, 26th February 1939 v Dunfermline Athletic (Scottish Cup rd 3)
Previous name: Alloa Athletic
Nickname: The Wasps
Colours: Gold shirt (with black trim), black shorts, gold socks

NICKNAMED The Wasps because of their gold and black strip, Alloa have been starved of success almost since the day they were formed, way back in 1883.

● OVER the past 10 years the club has been the 12th least successful Scottish league club and their only real moment of glory was winning the Division Two Championship in 1922.

● ALLOA have rarely had a star-studded team and their most capped player is Jock Hepburn who played, yes you guessed it, one game for Scotland.

● THE WASPS' worst defeats came in matches against Dundee in 1947 and Third Lanark in 1953. They lost 10–0 on both occasions, although in 1933 they did beat Forfar Athletic 9–2 to record their highest win.

● GLASGOW giants Rangers play their reserve team matches at Recreation Park, and regularly get crowds of four times the 500 or so who turn up for Alloa matches.

John Aldridge's 375 league goals make him the highest-scoring player in current English football

● ONE END of the ground is called the Railway End, where a line once passed so close to the terrace that stray shots sometimes ended up in goods wagons and were promptly ferried to Perth.

Roll of Honour

Division 2 champions 1922

AMATEUR FOOTBALL

In 1885 the Football Association allowed football clubs to pay players for their services. Some clubs, however, decided to remain 'amateur', playing purely for the love of the game.

The most famous of these amateur sides were the Corinthian Casuals, who were once the best club side in the world and twice, back in the 1880s, provided all the players in the England team. The team became a byword for fair play and, based in Tolworth, Surrey, they still play in the Isis League, Division Three. Players who are booked or sent off are likely to be thrown out of the club. Legend has it that at one point in their history if a penalty was awarded against them their goalkeeper would stand to one side as the club would consider it 'unsporting' of him to save the spot-kick.

● In 1974 the distinction between 'amateur' and 'professional' clubs was scrapped altogether by the FA. Now clubs can choose whether or not they want to pay their players, and most cup shocks these days are caused by semi-professional teams (like Sutton and Woking) rather than amateur ones.

● THE LAST amateur player ever to earn a full England cap was Bernard Joy of Arsenal who played against Belgium in 1936.

● THE last amateur to play in an FA Cup Final was Bill Slater, who got a late call up to the Blackpool side that lost 2–0 to Newcastle in 1951. He later captained Wolves to victory in the 1960 final, but this time as a professional.

ANDERLECHT

Year founded: 1908
Ground: Constant Vanden Stock, Brussels (29,000)
League wins: 24
Colours: White shirts with mauve trimming, white shorts and white socks

OFFICIALLY known as Royal Sporting Club Anderlecht, the club was formed in 1908 but didn't emerge as a major force until the 1950s after many years in the Belgian Third Division. Much of their new-found success was down to the coaching of former Blackburn goalkeeper Bill Gormlie and money provided by millionaire brewer Constant Vanden Stock, after whom the club stadium is named.

● ANDERLECHT have the best record of any Belgian team, winning the league no less than 24 times. The club also became the first Belgian club ever to win a European trophy with a 4–2 victory in the 1976 Cup Winners' Cup over West Ham United.

● ANDERLECHT's worst ever result was against Manchester United in 1956, when they lost 10–0 at Old Trafford in the first round of the European Cup. This is also Manchester United's best ever result.

● THE CLUB was so successful in the 1960s that on more than one occasion the whole Belgian national squad consisted entirely of players from Anderlecht.

Did You Know?

Arbroath's 36-0 record British scoreline vs Bon Accord in the Scottish Cup was on exactly the same day in exactly the same competition as the second highest score ever recorded in the country, Dundee Harps beating Aberdeen Rovers 35-0.

Roll of Honour

Belgian League champions 1947, 1949, 1950, 1951, 1954, 1955, 1956, 1959, 1962, 1964, 1965, 1966, 1967, 1968, 1972, 1974, 1981, 1985, 1986, 1987, 1991, 1993, 1994, 1995
Belgian Cup 1965, 1972, 1973, 1975, 1976, 1988, 1989, 1994
European Cup Winners' Cup 1976, 1978
UEFA Cup 1983
European Super Cup 1976, 1978

ARBROATH

Year founded: 1878
Ground: Gayfield Park (6,488)
Highest ever crowd: 13,510, 23rd February 1952 v Rangers
Nickname: The Red Lichties
Colours: Maroon shirts, white shorts and white socks

THOUGH their history is not a glorious one in terms of trophy-winning, Arbroath can at least bask in the glory of having achieved the highest ever score in competitive British match. On 12th September 1885 they thrashed Aberdeen side Bon Accord 36–0 in the Scottish Cup. Striker John Petrie's 13 goals in this match remains a British scoring record.

● ANOTHER record held by Arbroath is that they are the closest club in Britain to the sea! Just 50 yards from the icy North Sea, Gayfield Park is often the coldest and most miserable place in the country to watch football.

● THE club's nickname, The Red Lichties, is thought to originate from the red light which was once sited near the ground and used to guide ships into Arbroath harbour.

OSVALDO ARDILES

Born: Cordoba, Argentina 3.8.52
Position: Midfield
Club career:
Instituto Cordoba (Argentina)
Huracan (Argentina)
1978–88 Tottenham Hotspur 238 (16)
1982 Paris St. Germain (loan) 14 (1)
1988 Blackburn Rovers 5 (0)
1989 QPR 5
International record:
1975–82 Argentina 42 (8)

THE MOST successful South American import ever seen in English football, Osvaldo 'Ossie' Ardiles delighted his adopted country with his skill on the pitch and his charm and intelligence off it in the late 1970s and early 80s.

● AFTER WINNING the World Cup with Argentina in 1978 (Ardiles won 42 caps in all), the midfield star was sensationally signed by Keith Burkinshaw for £300,000 to play – with his international team-mate and friend Ricky Villa – for 'Tottingham Hotspur'.

● THE WHITE HART Lane crowd gave them a ticker tape reception and Ardiles went on to play 238 games in his two spells at Spurs (the Falklands War interrupting his Tottenham career), scoring 16 goals and helping them win the FA Cup in 1981 and the UEFA Cup in 1984.

● IN 1994 the little Argentinian later returned to Tottenham as manager but his attacking philosophies, although exciting, meant Tottenham were letting in just as many goals as, if not more, than they were scoring and he was replaced by Gerry Francis. In 1996 he became manager of Japanese J-League team Shimuzu S-Pulse.

● WHEN Spurs reached the FA Cup Final in 1981 Ardiles was the subject of the club's official cup song which included the unforgettable line: 'Ossie's going to Wembley, his knees have gone all trembly'.

ARGENTINA

First international: Argentina 3 Uruguay 2 (Montevideo, 1901)
First World Cup appearance: Argentina 1 France 0 (Uruguay, 1930)
Highest capped player: Oscar Ruggeri (98)
Highest goalscorer: Gabriel Batistuta (43)
Best win: 12–0 v Ecuador, 1942
Worst defeat: 1–6 v Czechoslovakia, 1958
Colours: Sky-blue-and-white-striped shirts, black shorts

ARGENTINA is the oldest footballing nation outside Britain. In 1865 the Buenos Aires Football Club was founded for British residents in the Argentine capital, but football soon caught on everywhere and in 1891 a full championship was first played – five years before any other country outside Britain.

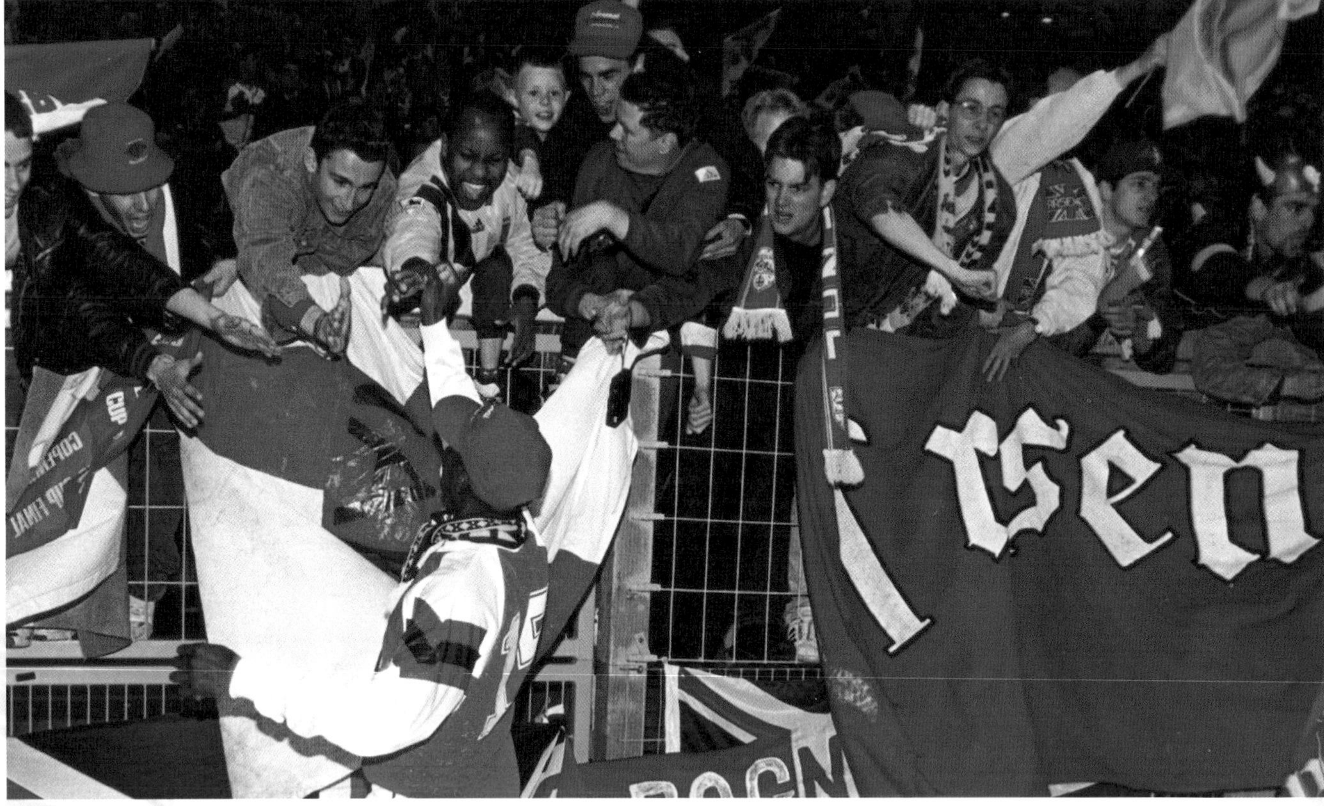

'1-0 to the Arsenal' (just for a change!). Arsenal fans celebrate their 1-0 European Cup Winners' Cup victory over Parma in 1994, the club's first European triumph since winning the Fairs Cup in 1970

● SINCE the early days, Argentina's fiercest rivals have been Uruguay and the match between the two countries is the 'most played international fixture'. The neighbouring nations have played each other no less than 184 times since 1901 (England and Scotland, by comparison, have only played 108 times since 1872).

● IN 1901 Argentina and Uruguay (who else!) met in the first ever representative international match to be played outside Britain (which Argentina won 3–2).

● THE ARGENTINIANS have appeared in four World Cup Finals (1930, 1978, 1986 and 1990), including the first ever final in 1930 when they lost to 4–2 to Uruguay. Only Brazil (five), Italy (five) and Germany (six) have appeared in more finals.

● WITH 43 GOALS, including five at France '98, Gabriel Batistuta is Argentina's all-time leading scorer, having overtaken his former team-mate Diego Maradona's total of 33. Batistuta's last goal in France was a penalty against England which put the South Americans 1–0 up; they eventually won the game on penalties only to lose out to Holland in the quarter-finals. Claudio Lopez's goal in that match was the Argentinians' 100th in World Cup finals. Only Brazil, Germany and Italy have scored more.

Roll of Honour

World Cup 1978, 1986
South American Championship 1910, 1921, 1925, 1927, 1929, 1937, 1941, 1945, 1946, 1947, 1955, 1957, 1991, 1993

WORLD CUP RECORD

1930 Runners-up	1970 Did not qualify
1934 Round 1	1974 Round 2
1938 Did not enter	1978 Winners
1950 Did not enter	1982 Round 2
1954 Did not enter	1986 Winners
1958 Round 1	1990 Runners-up
1962 Round 1	1994 Round 2
1966 Quarter-finals	1998 Quarter-finals

ARSENAL

Year founded: 1886
Ground: Highbury Stadium (38,500)
Previous names: Dial Square, Royal Arsenal, Woolwich Arsenal, The Arsenal
Highest ever crowd: 73,295, 9th March 1935 v Sunderland (Div 1)
Nickname: The Gunners
Colours: Red shirts with white sleeves, white shorts, red socks

IN 1998, Arsenal, managed by French manager Arsene Wenger, became the second club ever to win a second League and Cup 'double', having pipped Manchester United to the post in the Carling Premiership and beaten Newcastle United 2-0 in the FA Cup Final with goals from Mark Overmars and Nicholas Anelka.

● Wenger, who formed a team largely made up of English defenders and French and Dutch midfielders and attackers (plus Ray Parlour), thus became the first foreign manager ever to win the English League Championship.

● The club had originally won the double in 1971, beating Leeds to the League title and defeating Liverpool 2-1 in the FA Cup final, under the astute management of Bertie Mee, who called on such stars as Charlie George, Ray Kennedy, Bob Wilson and a certain George Graham.

● ARSENAL are nicknamed the Gunners (and more lately the Gooners) because of their old connections with the Royal Arsenal, an important local munitions factory in the late 1800s and early 1900s.

● Current manager Arsene Wenger is the first foreign coach to win the English league title. Initial rumours that he was only appointed because of his highly appropriate Christian name were quickly dispelled by the team's performance on the pitch.

● During the glorious 'double'-winning season of 1997/98, crowd favourite Ian Wright broke the club goalscoring record. The second goal of his hat-trick against Bolton on 13th September 1997 saw him equal Cliff Bastin's record of 178 goals for the club, the third saw him break it. Unfortunately he lifted his shirt to reveal a Nike sponsored 'Just done it, 179' t-shirt a goal early!

● AMAZINGLY, Arsenal's biggest win and worst defeat were against the same team. Back in 1896 the Gunners were thrashed 8–0 by Loughborough Town in a Division Two game. Just four years later, however, they got more than their own back by piling 12 goals past the Town goalkeeper without reply.

● FORMER skipper Kenny Sansom has won more international caps than any other Arsenal player. The steady left-back appeared for England on no fewer than 86 occasions between 1979 and 1988.

● SANSOM's defensive partner, Irish central defender David O'Leary, holds the record for the most appearances for the Gunners. He played an incredible 558 games for Arsenal between 1975–93.

A

● IN 1935 Arsenal became the first London club to win the league title and, having won it again in 1933, 1934 and 1935, they became only the second ever side to win the title three years in succession. The first was Huddersfield Town (1924, 1925 and 1926).

● THE WORST point in the club's history was their relegation in 1913 – they only managed one home win all season, which is an all-time record.

● A WORKMAN's horse, which died in an accident during construction of Arsenal's Highbury Stadium, was buried there and then under what is now the North Bank stand. It is said to bring the club good luck.

● THE CORRIDORS of their North ondon stadium are also said to be haunted by the ghost of their former manager, Herbert Chapman.

● ARSENAL Tube Station on the Piccadilly Line is the only train station in Britain to be named after a football club. It used to be called Gillespie Road.

● ARSENAL'S most successful manager is George Graham (six trophies in eight years).

● IN THE summer of 1995 Arsenal forked out £7.5 million to Inter Milan for Dutch international striker Dennis Bergkamp, a national record at the time. This topped their previous record (£2.5 million to Crystal Palace for Ian Wright) by £5 million.

● FAMOUS FANS who support the Gunners include talkshow host Clive Anderson, Fever Pitch author Nick Hornby and actor Tom Watt. Watt, who played the part of Lofty in Eastenders, has written a history book about the club entitled 'the North Bank'.

Roll of Honour

Div 1 champions 1931, 1933, 1934, 1935, 1948, 1953, 1971, 1989, 1991
FA Cup 1930, 1936, 1950, 1971, 1979, 1993
League Cup 1987, 1993
Double 1971
European Fairs Cup 1970
European Cup Winners' Cup 1994

Arsenal's Post-War Record

47 DI 13th	64 DI 8th	81 DI 3rd
48 DI 1st	65 DI 13th	82 DI 5th
49 DI 5th	66 DI 14th	83 DI 10th
50 DI 6th	67 DI 7th	84 DI 6th
51 DI 5th	68 DI 9th	85 DI 7th
52 DI 3rd	69 DI 4th	86 DI 7th
53 DI 1st	70 DI 12th	87 DI 4th
54 DI 12th	71 DI 1st	88 DI 6th
55 DI 9th	72 DI 5th	89 DI 1st
56 DI 5th	73 DI 2nd	90 DI 4th
57 DI 5th	74 DI 10th	91 DI 1st
58 DI 12th	75 DI 16th	92 DI 4th
59 DI 3rd	76 DI 17th	93 PR 10th
60 DI 13th	77 DI 8th	94 PR 4th
61 DI 11th	78 DI 5th	95 PR 12th
62 DI 10th	79 DI 7th	96 PR 5th
63 DI 7th	80 DI 4th	97 PR 3rd
		98 PR 1st

Did You Know?

Of all the clubs currently in the Premiership, Arsenal have spent the longest unbroken run in the top flight. The Gunners have occupied the top division every year since 1919, a record run of 79 years. They were last relegated after their disastrous season in 1913 when they finished bottom of Division One having only won three matches all season.

ARTIFICIAL TURF

THE FIRST ARTIFICIAL PITCH in the world was built in, and named after, the Houston Astrodome in Texas in the 1960s – hence the name astroturf.

● IN 1976 the first World Cup international to be played on astroturf saw Canada drawing 1–1 with the USA in Vancouver.

● QUEENS PARK RANGERS were the first British club to lay down a so-called 'plastic pitch' for the start of the 1981/82 season. Opposing players complained of the extra bounce of the ball, which gave an advantage to QPR because they were more used to it.

● IN THE 1980s Oldham Athletic, Luton Town, Preston North End and Stirling Albion all followed QPR's lead, but by 1994 Preston were the last club still playing on plastic, finally scrapping their Deepdale astroturf when the Football League banned artificial pitches before the 1994/95 season, because it was deemed an unfair advantage to the home team.

● THE TURF USED in the first ever indoor World Cup finals game between Switzerland and the USA at the Detroit Silverdome in 1994 was not artificial. It was grown in hexagonal sections in the stadium's car park and then assembled inside the dome a few days before kick off.

Arsenal's Double-winning side of 1971 laugh at something Ray Kennedy says about Bob Wilson

FAUSTINO ASPRILLA

Born: Tulua, Colombia 10.11.69
Height: 5ft 9ins Position: Striker
Club career:
1990–92 Nacional De Medellin (Colombia) 61 (23)
1992–96 Parma 84 (25)
1996–98 Newcastle United 48 (9)
1998– Parma 3 (0)
International record:
1993– Columbia 39 (15)

ASPRILLA, the first Colombian ever to play in the Football League, was Newcastle United's record signing when he arrived from Parma in February 1997, costing the Geordie club £6.7 million.

● NICKNAMED 'Pulpo' (Octopus) by his friends in Colombia because of the way his arms and legs flail rubber-like when he's in pursuit of the ball, Asprilla was named Colombian Footballer of the Year at the tender age of 22 before he was signed by Italian club Parma.

● AFTER leaving his homeland (where he won the Colombian title with Nacional) Asprilla made an immediate impact with Parma, eventually scoring 25 goals in a total of 84 league games and helping the club win the Italian Cup, European Cup Winners' Cup and the UEFA Cup.

● HIS trademark somersault in the air after scoring became a regular sight on TV, although he became as well-known in Italy for his off-field brushes with the law and the paparazzi as for anything he did on the pitch. On one eventful trip back home to Colombia he fired a gun in a crowded bar, an action which eventually saw him in court and heavily fined.

● DURING NEWCASTLE'S UEFA Cup run in 1996/97, Asprilla was the victim of the most bizarre bookable offence ever seen at St. James' Park. After scoring his side's first goal against Metz he took off his shirt, ran to the corner flag, put the shirt on the flag, and raised it to the joyous crowd.

A

ASTON VILLA

Year founded: 1874
Ground: Villa Park (40,310)
Highest ever crowd: 76,588, 2nd March 1946 v Derby County (FA Cup rd 6)
Nickname: The Villans
Colours: Claret and blue shirts, white shorts and claret socks

ONE OF England's most famous and illustrious clubs, Aston Villa have won the League Championship no fewer than seven times, the last being in 1981.

● VILLA have scored more league goals than any other club in the history of the football league, bulging the old onion bag a total of 6,549 times since they were a founder member of the Football League in 1888.

● IN 1897 the club became only the second club ever to do the League and FA Cup 'double' (Preston North End was the first in 1889) under legendary manager George Ramsay. Only five other clubs have ever achieved this honour.

● THANKS TO HIS record with Aston Villa, Ramsay is still the most successful manager in the history of the FA Cup, guiding his team to no less than six FA Cup wins (all in all Aston Villa have the third highest number of FA Cup wins in history with seven). Ramsay is also the second most successful league manager ever after guiding the Villa to 12 major trophies (only Liverpool's Bob Paisley won more).

'It'll be all Dwight on the night': Aston Villa's Trinidad and Tobago star Dwight Yorke hopes one day he can fire The Villains to an eighth title win

● ON TOP of all that, Ramsay is the second-longest serving manager in the history of English football, occupying the hotseat at Villa Park for an astonishing 42 years between 1884 and 1926. Only West Brom's Fred Everiss has managed a club longer with his 46 years at the Hawthorns.

● A FOUNDER member of the Football league in 1888, Villa have spent the second highest number of seasons in the top flight (88 compared to Everton's 95).

● VILLA last won the League Championship in the 1980/81 season, during which manager Ron Saunders called on the services of just 14 players. The following season they beat Bayern Munich 1–0 to become only the fourth English team to win the European Cup.

● ASTON VILLA have had more sets of brothers on their books at the same time than any other British league club. Amos and Frank Moss got the ball rolling when they were both at the club between 1946 and 1954. Then there was now-Arsenal boss Bruce Rioch and his brother Neil (1969–73) and current Villa manager Brian Little and brother Alan (1974).

● WHEN VILLA won the first ever League Cup in 1961 (beating Rotherham United 3-2 on aggregate) they became the first club to have won all three major English trophies.

● THE CLUB'S record score is the 12-2 they recorded against Accrington Stanley in Division 1 in 1892. No team has ever scored more than 12 goals in a match in the top flight.

● ASTON VILLA have supplied more full England internationals than any other club, with a total of 57 Villans players making it into the national team including current players Gareth Southgate and Ugo Ehiogu.

● VETERAN IRISH former defender Paul McGrath, however, is their most capped player, picking up 45 caps for the Republic whilst at Villa Park.

● WHEN LOCAL LAD Stan Collymore signed for the Birmingham club for £7 million from Liverpool in May 1997 he became the club's record signing. His first season was a huge disappointment, however, with Stan the Man netting just 6 league goals.

● THE MOST the club has ever received for a player is the cool £5.5 million that Bari handed over for England midfielder David Platt in 1991.

● WITH ROOM to squeeze in 40,310 fans, Villa Park has the fourth highest capacity of a football ground in England. The famous Holte End, however, with its 13,501 seats, has one of the highest capacities of any single stand in Europe.

● VOLUBLE punk violinist Nigel Kennedy is surely the most bizarre football fan in the world – unfortunately for Aston Villa supporters he happens to follow their team.

Roll of Honour

Div 1 champions 1894, 1896, 1897, 1899, 1900, 1910, 1981
Div 2 champions 1938, 1960
Div 3 champions 1972
FA Cup 1887, 1895, 1897, 1905, 1913, 1920, 1957
Double 1897
League Cup 1961, 1975, 1977, 1994, 1996
European Cup 1982

Aston Villa's Post-War Record

47 DI 8th	64 DI 19th	81 DI 1st
48 DI 6th	65 DI 16th	82 DI 11th
49 DI 10th	66 DI 16th	83 DI 6th
50 DI 12th	67 DI 21st	84 DI 10th
51 DI 15th	68 D2 16th	85 DI 10th
52 DI 6th	69 D2 18th	86 DI 16th
53 DI 11th	70 D2 21st	87 DI 22nd
54 DI 13th	71 D3 4th	88 D2 2nd
55 DI 6th	72 D3 1st	89 DI 17th
56 DI 20th	73 D2 3rd	90 DI 2nd
57 DI 10th	74 D2 14th	91 DI 17th
58 DI 14th	75 D2 2nd	92 DI 7th
59 DI 21st	76 DI 16th	93 PR 2nd
60 D2 1st	77 DI 4th	94 PR 10th
61 DI 9th	78 DI 8th	95 PR 18th
62 DI 7th	79 DI 8th	96 PR 4th
63 DI 15th	80 DI 7th	97 PR 5th
		98 PR 7th

RON ATKINSON

Born: Liverpool 18.3.39

RON ATKINSON first made waves in football as a sturdy midfielder at Oxford United nicknamed 'the Tank' for his stocky tough-tackling style.

● AT OXFORD he became the first player to captain a team to promotion all the way from the Southern League to the (old) Second Division, before hanging up his boots in 1971.

Left: Big Ron in a rare tight-lipped moment

● Since then 'Big Ron', as he is affectionately nicknamed, has managed Cambridge United, West Bromwich Albion (twice), Manchester United, Atletico Madrid, Sheffield Wednesday (twice), Aston Villa and Coventry City. And apart from sporting a serious tan and wearing sunglasses whatever the weather, his hallmark has been to produce fast, attacking sides which play attractive football.

● Atkinson has won the Manager of the Month Award no fewer than 17 times in his career, putting him fourth in the all-time list. He is also the fourth-most successful manager in the League Cup competition (winning the trophy with Sheffield Wednesday in 1991 and Aston Villa in 1994).

● Atkinson, who is the oldest manager in the Premiership, is famous for his quotability and for having coined such terms as 'early doors' and 'the back stick'.

● HE ONCE told a post-match press conference: 'It was a game of two halves, and we were crap in both of them.'

AUSTRALIA

First World Cup appearance: Australia 0 East Germany 2 (West Germany, 1974)
Best win: 13–0 v Solomon Islands, 1997
Colours: Yellow and green shirts, black shorts, black socks

Australia have only ever qualified for the World Cup Finals once. In 1974 they reached the tournament stage in West Germany but lost to both East and West Germany, then drew with Chile to finish bottom of their group.

● The closest they have come since was when, under the coaching of ex-England manager Terry Venables, the Socceroos narrowly missed out on qualification for France '98. Having drawn 1-1 in the away leg of the play-off against Iran, the Australians then went 2-0 up in front of more than 100,000 fans at the Melbourne Cricket Ground, only for Iran to score two late goals themselves and go through on away goals.

● The most famous Australian players ever are probably Craig Johnston (who played more than 200 times for Liverpool between 1981 and 1988, and later invented the Predator boot), Aston Villa goalkeeper Mark Bosnich, Leeds starlet Harry Kewell and West Ham's Stan Lazaridis.

AUSTRIA

First international: Austria 5 Hungary 0 (friendly, Vienna, 1902)
First World Cup appearance: Austria 3 France 2 (Italy, 1934)
Highest capped player: Gerhard Hanappi (93)
Highest goalscorer: Toni Polster (36)
Best win: 9-0 v Malta, 1977
Worst defeat: 1-11 v England, 1908
Colours: White shirts, black shorts, white socks

Austria played in the first international match in continental Europe, beating Hungary 5-0 in Vienna on 12th October 1902. Encouraged by that result Austria went on to play the Magyars an incredible 46 times in their first 61 internationals.

● Austria's golden period was between 1931 and 1934 when the so-called Wunderteam, managed by the legendary Hugo Meisl and trained by Scotsman Jimmy Hogan, lost just two out of 30 games. This glorious run ended at the 1934 World Cup when the well-fancied Austrians lost 1-0 to hosts Italy in the semi-final.

● In 1954 Austria won the highest-scoring match in the history of the World Cup finals, defeating hosts Switzerland in a 7-5 goalfest. Amazingly, the Austrians recovered from being 3-0 down after 23 minutes to lead 5-3 ten minutes later!

● Austria's most embarrassing defeat - and arguably the most humiliating reverse of any international side - was in 1990, when they lost 1-0 to the Faroe Islands in a European Championship qualifier.

● Current striker Toni Polster is Austria's highest ever international scorer with 38 goals, including a last-gasp equaliser against Cameroon during France '98. Despite pulling back goals in injury time in all three of their matches the physical Austrian side were eliminated from the competition in the preliminary stages.

WORLD CUP RECORD

1930 Did not enter	1970 Did not qualify
1934 Fourth place	1974 Did not qualify
1938 Did not enter	1978 Round 2
1950 Did not enter	1982 Round 2
1954 Third place	1986 Did not qualify
1958 Round 1	1990 Round 1
1962 Did not enter	1994 Did not qualify
1966 Did not qualify	1998 Round 1

A Ron Atkinson Double Bill

'I don't care if he's black or white or yellow with purple spots, if he can do a job for West Bromwich Albion he's in the team.'
(Tackling the race issue head-on in 1972)

'He is without doubt the greatest sweeper in the world, I'd say, at a guess.'
(World Cup 1990)

For years Villa fans have been saluting Australian international Mark Bosnich's wallaby-style saves

A

AYR UNITED

Year founded: 1910
Ground: Somerset Park (13,918)
Highest ever crowd: 25,225, 13th September 1969 v Rangers (Div 1)
Nickname: The Honest Men
Colours: White shirts with black sleeves, black shorts, white socks

AYR UNITED enjoyed their most successful period in the 1960s and 70s under Ally MacLeod when they enjoyed a prolonged spell in the top flight. MacLeod, of course, later went on to manage Scotland and triumphantly led them to the 1978 World Cup Finals in Argentina... only to return in disgrace after losing to Peru and drawing with Iraq.

● DESPITE being the 4th lowest-scoring team in Scottish history (averaging less than a goal a game), Ayr United were the first team in the history of the Scottish League Cup to register a score in double figures when, in 1952, they beat Dumbarton 11–1.

● TO BALANCE out that proud record, however, Ayr have lost 9–0 three times in their history: to Rangers in 1929, Hearts in 1931 and Third Lanark in 1954.

● AYR UNITED'S Jimmy Smith is Britain's highest-ever league scorer in one season, notching up an incredible 66 in the 1927/28 season (coincidentally the same season that Dixie Dean recorded his English record 60 goals for Everton).

● AYR's record transfer fee received was £300,000 from Liverpool for Steve Nicol in 1981.

● AYR UNITED owe their nickname 'the Honest Men' to great Scottish poet Robert Burns who wrote in one of his works that Ayr was 'for honest men and bonnie lassies'.

Roll of Honour

Div 2 champions 1912, 1913, 1928, 1937, 1959, 1966
Second Division champions 1988, 1997

B

ROBERTO BAGGIO

Born: Vicenza 18.2.67
Height: 5ft 7ins Position: Forward
Club career:
1982–85 Vicenza 36 (13)
1985–90 Fiorentina 94 (39)
1990–95 Juventus 141 (78)
1995–96 AC Milan 50 (12)
1997–98 Bologna 31 (22)
International record:
1989– Italy 52 (27)

DESPITE possessing quite breathtaking talent and awesome skill, Roberto Baggio will probably be best remembered for missing the most important penalty in World Cup history. With the score at 3-2 to Brazil in the 1994 World Cup Final penalty shoot-out, Baggio stepped up knowing he had to score... and skied it over the bar.

● At France 98, however, Baggio – now without ponytail – went some way to making up for that terrible moment by stepping up to score twice from the penalty spot (once against Chile and once against France in the quarter-final penalty shoot-out).

● Baggio had made his debut for then Serie B team Vicenza in 1982, aged just 15. After two years he moved to Fiorentina and in 1993 sparked riots in the city of Florence by signing for arch rivals Juventus in 1990. At £7.7 million he had become the world's most expensive player.

● AT JUVENTUS he starred, scoring 14 goals in 33 matches in his first season, being voted European and World Footballer of the Year in 1993 as Juve won the UEFA Cup, and eventually guiding them to their first Serie A Championship win for five years in 1995.

● AFTER the win, though, the devout Buddhist was sensationally signed for £10 million to Juve's arch-rivals, AC Milan, where he struggled to make his mark – spending more time on the substitutes bench than in his opponents' penalty box – before being signed by Bologna.

● DESPITE this loss of form, however, and his penalty miss, Roberto Baggio is undoubtedly one of the players of the 1990s. As David Platt once said: 'As footballers go, he's a genius.'

ALAN BALL

Born: Farnworth 12.5.45
Height: 5ft 7ins Position: Midfield
Club career:
1960–61 Bolton Wanderers
1961–66 Blackpool 116 (4)
1966–71 Everton 208 (66)
1971–76 Arsenal 177 (45)
1976–80 Southampton 132 (9)
1980–81 Blackpool (Plyr-man) 30 (5)
1981–83 Southampton 63 (2)
1983 Bristol Rovers 17 (2)
International record:
1965–75 England 72 (8)

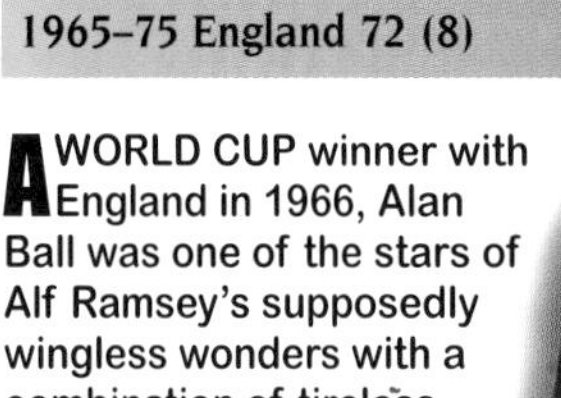

A WORLD CUP winner with England in 1966, Alan Ball was one of the stars of Alf Ramsey's supposedly wingless wonders with a combination of tireless running and superb creative play.

● JUST 21 when he played so magnificently in the World Cup Final, Ball went on to win 72 caps for England, having made his debut against Yugoslavia on 9th May 1965, just three days before his 20th birthday.

● ONE OF football's hottest properties in the 1969s and 70s, Ball broke the record transfer fee of both Everton (£110,000) and Arsenal (£220,000) when he joined them in 1966 and 1971 respectively.

● WHILE at Everton he won a League Championship Winner's medal in 1970 and he was a losing FA Cup finalist twice (1968 with Everton and 1972 with Arsenal).

● PAULO DI CANIO take note, Ball was the first man to play in groovy white boots way back in the 1960s when he was strutting his stuff for Everton.

● AS A MANAGER, Ball has so far taken the helm at Portsmouth (twice), Stoke City, Exeter City, Southampton and Manchester City (where he oversaw the club's disastrous relegation from the Premiership in 1996).

BALLS

SINCE stipulations were agreed in 1872, balls have always been the same size (circumference 27–28") and weight (not more than 453g or less than 396g at the start of a match). But before plastic materials were brought in, during the 1950s the balls would get waterlogged and get heavier as the game progressed, sometimes actually doubling in weight.

● THE RECORD of keeping a regulation football off the ground without the use of hands ('keepy uppy') is held by Brazilian Ricardinho Neves who juggled for 19 hours, 5 minutes and 31 seconds in July 1994.

● IN THE 1946 FA Cup Final, the referee stated before the match that there was a one-in-a-million chance of the ball bursting. Maybe he nipped off to the bookies to lay down a bet. When Derby's Jack 'Hotshot' Stamps took a hefty whack at it 30 seconds from time, exactly that happened. Remarkably

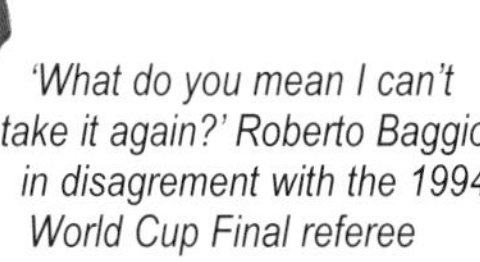

'What do you mean I can't take it again?' Roberto Baggio in disagreement with the 1994 World Cup Final referee

enough, the ball burst again in the 1947 final between Charlton and Burnley.

● IN THE 1930s, arch rivals Argentina and Uruguay couldn't agree on whose ball would be used during the World Cup Final... so they played one half with each. The Argentinian ball was used in the first half and Argentina went in at half time 1–0 up. In the second half they switched, however, and Uruguay ran out 4–2 winners.

● In 1990 a particularly skilful Czech player Jan Skorkovsky ran the entire 26 mile Prague City marathon while juggling the ball with his feet and not letting it touch the ground.

● DURING THE 1960s, Wolves player Peter Knowles was so happy with a goal he scored at Fratton Park that he kicked the ball out of the ground. His celebrations backfired on him later, though, when he was told he had to cough up £7.10 for a new one.

GORDON BANKS

Born: Sheffield 20.12.37
Height: 6ft 1in   Position: Goalkeeper
Club career:
1955–59 Chesterfield 23
1959–67 Leicester City 293
1967–72 Stoke City 194
International record:
1963–72 England 73

'BANKS of England' as he was known (because he had the 'safest hands in the country'), was probably England's greatest ever goalkeeper. He made 73 appearances between the sticks for his country and kept an incredible 35 clean sheets.

● GORDON BANKS is also the unofficial holder of the 'Greatest Save Ever' title, and it is for this one moment that he will always be remembered. How he managed to get across his goal and turn Pele's downward header over the bar in the 1970 World Cup match against Brazil is still a mystery to most people, despite a million action replays.

● THE second most capped England goalkeeper after Peter Shilton, Banks was a World Cup winner in 1966 and up until he was beaten by a Eusebio penalty he had kept a remarkable seven clean sheets in a row (another England record).

● DOMESTICALLY Banks was a double FA Cup runner-up with Leicester in 1961 and 1963, and won the League Cup twice, with Leicester in 1964 and then with Stoke in 1972. He was awarded the OBE in 1970 and was Footballer of the Year in 1972.

● BANKS's English career was sadly ended in 1972 when he lost the sight of one eye in a car crash, although he continued to play in the NASL (North American Soccer League) with Fort Lauderdale Strikers.

Funny Old Game

Alan Ball is one of only five men ever sent off while playing for England. The others are Alan Mullery, Trevor Cherry, Ray Wilkins and, of course, David Beckham

BARCELONA

Year founded: 1899
Ground: Nou Camp (115,000)
League wins: 15
Colours: Blue-and-red-striped shirts, blue shorts, blue socks

WITH a staggering 110,000 members, Barcelona is the biggest football club in the world and many people in the Catalan region of Spain (for which Barcelona is effectively the national team) believe the club has God on its side... Pope John Paul II was enrolled as member 108,000!

● HOLDING 115,000, the Nou Camp Stadium is the second biggest stadium in Europe (only Benfica's Stadium of Light in Lisbon holds more).

● Equal with arch rivals Real Madrid, Barcelona have won a record eight major European trophies. They have won the European Cup once (1982), the European Cup Winners' Cup four times (1979, 1982, 1989, 1997) and the Fairs Cup three times (1958, 1960 and 1966).

● On top of that Barca have played more games in European competitions than any other club. In total they have played 291 matches, nine more than second-placed Real.

● Barcelona were the first team ever to knock Real Madrid out of the European Cup. After the Madrid club had stormed to victory in the first five European Cup competitions between 1956 and 1960, in 1961 Barca beat them in the semi-finals... only to lose the final 3-2 to Benfica. They had to wait until 1992 for their first and only European Cup triumph to date (when they beat Sampdoria 1-0 at Wembley).

Roll of Honour

Spanish League champions 1929, 1945, 1948, 1949, 1952, 1953, 1959, 1960, 1974, 1985, 1991, 1992, 1993, 1994, 1998
Spanish Cup 1910, 1912, 1913, 1920, 1922, 1925, 1926, 1928, 1942, 1951, 1952, 1953, 1957, 1959, 1963, 1968, 1971, 1978, 1981, 1983, 1988, 1990, 1997, 1998
European Cup 1992
European Cup Winners' Cup 1979, 1982, 1989, 1997
Fairs Cup 1958, 1960, 1966
European Super Cup 1992, 1998

FRANCO BARESI

Born: Travagliato 8.5.60
Height: 5ft 8ins   Position: Defender
Club career:
1978–   AC Milan 469 (5)
International record:
1982–94 Italy 81 (1)

FRANCESCHINO Baresi only ever played for one club, and at AC Milan he is known simply as 'God'.

● BARESI HAS made more appearances for AC Milan than any other player, turning out for them more than 600 times in all competitions. His elder brother, Giuseppe, also a defender, played for arch-rivals Inter, and they played against each other more than 20 times.

● AN ASTONISHINGLY skillful defender and one of the greatest readers of the game in its history, Baresi was capped 81 times by Italy before retiring from international football in 1994. If he had not been kept out of the side until 1987 by the legendary Gaetano Scirea he might have been Italy's most capped player ever.

● WITH HIS ability to come forward with the ball, Baresi transformed the sweeper's role in the Italian League from a purely defensive role into 'il Libero'.

● BARESI won three European Cups, six Serie A titles, three European Super Cups and two World Club Cups with Milan. He never won the World Cup, though, and along with Roberto Baggio missed a penalty in the 1994 World Cup Final shoot-out. He captained Italy to third place in 1990.

At last! Barcelona lift the European Cup for the first time, at Wembley in 1992

JOHN BARNES

Born: Kingston, Jamaica 7.11.63
Height: 5ft 11ins Position: Midfield
Club career:
1981–87 Watford 233 (65)
1987– Liverpool 314 (84)
1997– Newcastle United 26 (6)
International record:
1982–95 England 79 (11)

ONE OF the outstanding players of his generation, John Barnes has played more than 300 games for Liverpool and almost 80 for England... although he has only ever showed flashes of his club form for his country.

● BARNES, nevertheless, is the scorer of one of England's greatest goals ever. In 1984, aged just 20, he ran at and single-handedly beat the entire Brazilian defence in the great Maracana Stadium in Rio and slotted the ball past the keeper. It was a great moment, but one that Barnes had to live up to forever afterwards.

● AT LIVERPOOL his career was more consistent, winning the league title twice (1987/88 and 1989/90) and the FA Cup twice (1989 and 1992) as well as the Coca-Cola Cup in 1995.

● IN 1987 Barnes moved to Anfield from Watford for £900,000 and, with Peter Beardsley, instantly made a huge impact. He might have been making that impact at AC Milan. Rumours abound that when the great Italian club signed his Watford colleague Luther Blissett in 1986, they thought it was Barnes they were buying!

● THE SON of a Jamaican footballing international (his father was a centre-half), Barnes made his England debut at 19 (against Northern Ireland on 28th May 1983) and was voted Player of the Year by both the PFA and the Football Writers Association in 1988. He has more recently taken over from Barry Venison as television's worst-dressed football pundit.

John Barnes: the most accurate volleyer of Lucozade cans in English football

BARNET

Year founded: 1888
Ground: Underhill Stadium (4,057)
Previous name: Barnet Alston FC
Highest ever crowd: 11,026, 1952 v Wycombe Wanderers (FA Amateur Cup rd 4)
Nickname: The Bees
Colours: Amber and black striped shirts, black shorts, amber and black socks

NORTH LONDON outfit Barnet were the last but two non-league club to be elected to the football league, gaining election to the Football League from the GM Vauxhall Conference in 1991.

● THEIR tiny ground, Underhill, has the smallest capacity in the whole of the English league, accommodating a measly 3,924 fans. Mind you, up until 1926 there were no offices at the ground and the club had to hold meetings in the Red Lion pub on Barnet Hill.

● LIVELY striker Andy Clarke's £350,000 move from Barnet to Wimbledon in 1991 is the biggest transfer from the Vauxhall Conference to the Football League, taking place just before The Bees (as they are known because of their colours) were elected to the League.

● BARNET's most famous son is cheeky cockney Barry Fry who managed the club in the 1980s and early 1990s. Fry loved the club so much he once re-mortgaged his house to pay its debts and, legend has it, he was once caught cutting the grass on the pitch in the middle of the night by moonlight.

● LEGENDARY England sharp-shooter Jimmy Greaves appeared for the Bees at the end of his playing career in the mid-1970s, but Barnet are one of only seven English league clubs who have never supplied a full international for any country.

Roll of Honour

FA Amateur Cup 1946
GM Vauxhall Conference winners 1991

BARNSLEY

Year founded: 1887
Ground: Oakwell (18,806)
Previous name: Barnsley St. Peters
Highest ever crowd: 40,255, 15th February 1936 v Stoke (FA Cup rd 4)
Nickname: The Tykes
Colours: Red shirts, white shorts, white socks

UP UNTIL THE 1997/98 season, despite a proud footballing tradition Barnsley had never experienced life in the top flight. And despite a memorable second half of the campaign their first ever stay in the Premiership only lasted for one short season.

● THEY DID win the FA Cup in 1912, however, and earned themselves the nickname 'Battling Barnsley' in the process because it was such a hard campaign. In all the cup run took in 12 games and included no less than six 0–0 draws, ending in a 3–1 final win over Birmingham City at Bramall Lane, Sheffield.

● THE Yorkshire club have always played at their current ground, Oakwell, since they bought the land in 1888. The landowner who sold it told them they could have it 'so long as you behave yourselves'. Originally there were no changing rooms and the team had to change in the Dove Inn which to this day stands near the ground.

● WHEN Viv Anderson was appointed player/manager of the club in 1993 he became the first black manager in the history of the English game, just as he had been the first black player ever to play for England.

Roll of Honour

Div 3 (N) champions 1934, 1939, 1955
FA Cup 1912

KEN BATES

Born: 4.12.31

KEN BATES, the Chelsea chairman for the last 15 years, is arguably the most controversial behind-the-scenes figure in the Premier League. In 1985 he sensationally tried to erect electric fences at Stamford Bridge to keep the Sheddites off the pitch, but was thwarted by the local council who didn't think it was such a good idea.

● BATES bought Chelsea for the princely sum of £1 in 1982, but also had to take on the massive debts the London club had accrued over the years. His finest moment came in 1992 when, after years of legal wranglings, he finally secured the ownership of Stamford Bridge from the clutches of an eager-to-develop property company.

● He has now overseen the transformation of the ground into one of the most modern all-seater stadiums in the country, and his 'Chelsea Village' complex also includes a hotel, luxury flats, restaurants and a Chelsea megastore.

● AS A BUDDING player, Bates had a trial at Arsenal, but a club foot held him back from a full playing career and eventually he went into farming where he made his fortune... hence his affectionate Chelsea nickname 'Farmer Bates'.

GABRIEL BATISTUTA

Born: Avellaneda, Argentina 1.2.69
Height: 6ft 2ins Position: Striker
Club career:
1988–89 Newells Old Boys 16 (4)
1989–90 River Plate 7 (4)
1990–91 Boca Juniors 29 (13)
1991– Fiorentina 213 (124)
International record:
Argentina 1991- 64 (43)

Long-haired Gabriel Batistuta is Argentina's leading all-time scorer with 43 goals, many of them spectacular piledrivers from outside the penalty box. His best run of goals came in 1991, when his six strikes in six matches helped Argentina lift the South American Championship for the first time since 1959.

● After beginning his career with three Argentinian clubs, Batistuta moved to Fiorentina in 1991. His one honour with the 'Viola' came in 1996 when Fiorentina beat Atalanta 3-0 on aggregate to win the Italian Cup, with Batistuta scoring in both legs.

● At the beginning of the 1994/95 season Batistuta scored in every one of Fiorentina's first eleven matches, breaking the Serie A record held by Bologna's Ezio Pasciutti who scored in ten successive games at the start of the 1962/63 season. Batistuta's tally of 26 goals that year made him Serie A's top scorer.

● Batistuta – who is nicknamed 'Bati-Gol' – was equal second highest goalscorer at France 98 with five goals. His hat-trick against Jamaica also made him the first man ever to score hat-tricks at consecutive World Cup tournaments (at USA 94 he scored three times against Greece).

DAVID BATTY

Born: Leeds 2.12.68
Height: 5ft 8ins Position: Midfield
Club career:
1987–93 Leeds United 211 (4)
1993–96 Blackburn Rovers 54 (1)
1996– Newcastle United 75 (3)
International record:
1991– England 35 (0)

David Batty picked England's crucial last spot-kick in the France '98 World Cup second round match against Argentina to take his first ever penalty in competitive football. Unfortunately his shot was saved and England went out of the competition. Luckily for the tenacious tough-tackling midfielder the country had a different scapegoat to blame for the defeat.

● Batty actually made his England debut way back in 1991 (playing in the 1992 European Championships) but lost his place in the side after injury and was rarely picked by Terry Venables. Glenn Hoddle, however, made him a regular in the side, realising that his reluctance to lose the ball made him a perfect defensive midfielder in international football.

● Batty may have missed out on international silverware (goldware?) but he is no stranger to lifting domestic trophies. After joining Newcastle in 1996 he just missed completing a unique three-club Championship treble at the end of the 1995/96 season, having already won the title with Leeds in 1992 and Blackburn in 1995.

● Batty is the only player to have played in the European Cup for three different English teams, though he has never come close to winning the trophy. What he will be most remembered for in European comeptitions is being hit on the chin by his team-mate Graeme Le Saux whilst playing for Blackburn in Moscow.

JIM BAXTER

Born: Hill o'Beath, Fife 29.9.39
Position: Midfield
Club career:
1957–60 Raith Rovers
1960–65 Rangers
1965–67 Sunderland 87 (10)
1967–69 Nottingham Forest 48 (3)
1969–70 Rangers
International record:
1961–68 Scotland 34 (3)

LEGENDARY Scottish international, Baxter became a cult hero in the 1960s for his skilful and unorthodox attacking style and his self-confessed love of the high life.

● BAXTER started his football life as a part-timer with Crossgates Primrose before moving to Raith Rovers and onto Glasgow Rangers for £20,000 in 1960, the year before he made his debut for Scotland against Northern Ireland.

● BEFORE moving south in 1965 to play for Sunderland and then Nottingham Forest, Baxter helped Rangers to three Scottish League Championships and three Scottish Cup wins, but it was his antics for Scotland, particularly against England, for which he is be best remembered.

● HIS GREATEST day came in 1967 when he starred in Scotland's 3–2 victory over recent World Cup winners England, at Wembley, crowning the Scots 'unofficial World Champions'.

● IN THE end Baxter's love of a drink meant the nickname of 'Slim Jim' no longer applied, and in 1970 he retired to open a pub. He recently said of Everton's controversial Duncan Ferguson: 'Big Fergie likes a few pints, loves to stay out late and chase the birds, and give a bit of lip in training. In my book he's got all the perfect ingredients of a great footballer.'

BAYERN MUNICH

Year founded: 1900
Ground: Olympiastadion (64,000)
League wins: 14
Colours: Red-and-blue-striped shirts, white shorts and white socks

THE MOST famous and successful German club of recent years, amazingly Bayern Munich weren't even included in the inaugural Bundesliga when it was formed in 1963/64, their recent record was so poor. By 1969, however, they had won it for the first time and with 14 league titles under their belt now, they have won more German championships than any other club.

● IN 1967 Bayern became only the second German club to win a European trophy when they beat Glasgow Rangers 1–0 to take the European Cup Winners' Cup, announcing their presence as a force to be reckoned with in Europe.

● IN 1974 Bayern then became the first German club to win the European Cup, by beating Atletico Madrid 4–0 in a replay (the only replay ever in a European Cup final), and went on to complete a hat-trick of wins (1975 2–0 v Leeds United and 1976 1–0 v St. Etienne). The outstanding team was based around three truly world class players: the great Sepp Maier in goal, 'Der Bomber' Gerd Müller in attack, and the legendary Franz Beckenbauer as sweeper, a role he had invented for himself.

● IN THE 1990s Beckenbauer returned to the club to try and bring back the glory years as Bayern hadn't won a European trophy since he was in the team in 1976. So when Jürgen Klinsmann fired them to UEFA Cup victory against Bordeaux in 1996 (beating Nottingham Forest along the way) it was a proud moment indeed for 'Der Kaiser'.

Roll of Honour

Bundesliga champions 1932, 1969, 1972, 1973, 1974, 1980, 1981, 1985, 1986, 1987, 1989, 1990, 1994, 1997
German Cup 1957, 1966, 1967, 1969, 1971, 1982, 1984, 1986
European Cup 1974, 1975, 1976
European Cup Winners' Cup 1967
UEFA Cup 1996
World Club Cup 1976

Jürgen Klinsmann is startled to see he's still pictured in Bayern Munich kit

Don't quote me

'John Hollins was a mistake. He has a very strong wife, maybe I should have made her manager.'

Chelsea chairman Ken Bates after sacking John Hollins in 1988

PETER BEARDSLEY

Born: Newcastle 18.1.61	
Height: 5ft 8ins	Position: Forward
Club career:	
1979–82	Carlisle United 102 (22)
1982	Vancouver Whitecaps (Canada)
1982–83	Manchester United 0 (0)
1983–87	Newcastle United 147 (61)
1987–91	Liverpool 131 (46)
1991–93	Everton 81 (25)
1993–	Newcastle United 94 (38)
1997–98	Bolton Wanderers 17(2)
1998	Manchester City (loan) 8(0)
1998	Fulham (loan) 8(1)
International record:	
1986–	England: 59 (9)

ONE OF the truly great players of the 1980s and 1990s, Peter Beardsley sometimes looks like he could keep going forever.

● NO stranger to silverware, winning two league titles with Liverpool (1987/88 and 1989/90) and one FA Cup (1989), Beardsley would dearly have liked to help Newcastle to start restocking their trophy cabinet.

● ONCE on the books of Manchester United without ever playing a game, it was at St. James' Park that Beardsley first made a name for himself as a sweetly-skilled, terrier-like forward before moving to Liverpool in July 1987 for £1.9 million.

● IN 1991 he became one of only a handful of players who have turned out for both Liverpool and Everton, and his tireless running and sizzling skill made him a huge favourite with both sets of fans. Indeed, he is the only player ever to score for both sides in Merseyside derbies.

● WHILE notching up his 59 caps and nine goals for England, Beardsley shone brightest when playing up front alongside Gary Lineker, and the pair flourished in both the 1986 and 1990 World Cups. Beardsley was frequently the creator of Lineker's goals as England reached the quarter-finals and semi-finals respectively.

● WHEN HE DOES finally hang up his boots, Beardsley is likely to go into management. When Kenny Dalglish arrived at Newcastle United in 1997 he immediately installed his former Liverpool colleague as youth team coach.

FRANZ BECKENBAUER

Born: Munich 11.9.45	
Position: Defender	
Club career:	
1962–76	Bayern Munich
1976–83	New York Cosmos
1983–84	SV Hamburg
International record:	
1965–74	(West) Germany 103 (13)

THE LEGENDARY sweeper Franz Beckenbauer – 'Der Kaiser' as he was known – is Germany's second highest capped player, with 103 international appearances... but mere statistics cannot quantify the influence he had both on Germany and on football in general.

Franz Beckenbauer looks over to see if anything interesting is happening in Belgium... there isn't

● The man who effectively created the attacking 'sweeper' role and mastered it like no other before or since, Beckenbauer tasted glory with both Bayern Munich (captaining them to three European Cups in a row between 1974–76) and West Germany (winning the World Cup in 1974 as German captain after reaching the final in 1966 and the semi-final in 1970).

● WITH BOTH the desire and the ability to turn defence into attack, Beckenbauer was the father of the modern day sweeper, gliding effortlessly out of the back four to mount attacks for both club and country. His consistency earned him European Footballer of the Year awards in both 1972 and 1976.

● EVEN WHEN he moved to the North American Soccer League in the 1970s he was successful, winning the NASL Soccer Bowl three times with New York Cosmos in 1977, 1978 and 1980.

● THEN, when Germany won the 1990 World Cup against Argentina in Rome, Beckenbauer became the first man to coach and captain champions of the world, having taken control of the national team in 1986.

DAVID BECKHAM

Born: Leytonstone 2.5.75	
Height: 6ft 0ins	Position: Midfield
Club career:	
	Preston (loan) 5 (2)
1995–	Manchester United 109 (24)
International record	
1996–	England 18 (1)

WHEN DAVID BECKHAM petulantly kicked Argentine midfielder Diego Simeone in the second round of France '98 he become only the fifth ever English player to be sent off and ensured a second successive season of cat-calls and boos from away fans in the Premiership. It wasn't a very good end to what had so far been a rather mixed season for the young Cockney Red, who had previously only known success in his career.

● A PRODUCT of Manchester United's famous youth policy, swashbuckling midfielder Beckham was voted the PFA's Young Player of the Year in 1997 at the end of the season during which he scored the longest range goal ever seen in the Premiership. His shot from inside his own half against Wimbledon on the first day of the season instantly transformed him from a promising youngster to a household name. Beckham ended the season with his second Championship title to go with his FA Cup-winning medal from 1996/97

● GLENN HODDLE installed him in his England team as soon as he took over from Terry Venables as England boss and Beckham was the only player to feature in all eight of England's qualifying matches for France '98. The manager left him out, however, for England's first match in France '98 against Tunisia, worried that his temperament wouldn't be up to such a big tournament. Beckham soon won back his place, scoring a wonderful free-kick against Columbia that sealed England's qualification to the second round, only to drench his copy-book against Argentina.

● WITH HIS good looks and bleached hair Beckham has become used to featuring on the front pages of newspapers as much as the back, especially after announcing his engagement to Victoria Adams, aka Posh Spice.

BELGIUM

First international: Belgium 3 France 3 (Brussels, 1904)
First World Cup appearance: Belgium 0 USA 3 (Uruguay, 1930)
Highest capped player: Jan Ceulemans (96 caps)
Highest goalscorer: Bernard Voorhoof/ Paul Vam Himst (30 goals)
Best win: Belgium 9 Zambia 0, 1994

Worst defeat: Belgium 2 England Amateurs 11, 1909
Colours: Red shirts, red shorts and red socks

THE SECOND oldest footballing nation – along with Sweden – outside Great Britain, Belgium had a league up and running in 1895, but as a footballing nation they have always lived in the shadow of their illustrious neighbours Holland and Germany.

● THEY have had their moments, though, and perhaps the greatest was in 1920 when Belgium became the first non-English-speaking nation to win the Olympic Games, held that year in their home city of Antwerp. This was before the World Cup had been invented, so naturally the Belgians proclaimed themselves World Champions.

● THEN, ON 1st November 1923, Belgium became the first non-British team to avoid defeat against England when the sides drew 2-2 in a friendly in Antwerp.

● IN 2000 Belgium will jointly host the European Championship finals with Holland, the first time the finals have been shared.

● BELGIUM'S finest World Cup hour came in 1986 when they reached the semi-finals, only to be knocked out 2-0 by Argentina, inspired by two-goal Diego Maradona, this time using the feet of God. More recently they failed to set the world alight at France '98, failing to reach the second round after negative draws with Holland (0-0) Mexico (2-2) and, disastrously, South Korea (1-1). Not many viewers from outside the country were sad to see the back of them.

WORLD CUP RECORD

1930	Round 1	1974-78	Did not qualify
1934	Round 1	1982	Round 2
1938	Round 1	1986	Fourth place
1950	Did not enter	1990	Round 2
1954	Round 1	1994	Round 2
1958-66	Did not qualify	1998	Round 1
1970	Round 1		

BENFICA

Year founded: 1904
Ground: Estadio Da Luz (Stadium of Light) (130,000)
League wins: 30
Colours: Red shirts, white shorts and red socks

BENFICA are by far and away the most successful club in Portugal with a staggering 30 league wins compared to Sporting Lisbon's 17 and FC Porto's 17.

● THE CLUB's magnificent Estadio Da Luz (Stadium of Light) is the biggest ground in Europe, officially seating 130,000 fans (although you won't find many sitting down when arch-rivals Sporting are visiting). The stadium needs to be that big too, because the club has a membership of 122,000.

● THE Portuguese giants were the first club, other than Real Madrid, to win the European Cup when, back in 1961, they beat Barcelona 3–2 in the Swiss city of Berne. They won the trophy again the following year against the mighty Real Madrid, with the Benfica side featuring a certain young player called Eusebio.

● IN 13 glorious seasons at Benfica the great Eusebio inspired the club to seven league titles up until 1969 and in 1992 a statue of the great man was unveiled at the entrance of the Estadio Da Luz.

● In 1997, former Rangers, Liverpool and Southampton manager Graeme Souness took charge at the club and immediately imported some English blood in the form of full back Scott Minto and striker Brian Deane.

Roll of Honour

Portuguese League winners 1936, 1937,1938,1942, 1943, 1945, 1950, 1955, 1957, 1960, 1961, 1963, 1964, 1965, 1967, 1968, 1969, 1971, 1972, 1973, 1975, 1976, 1977, 1981, 1983, 1984, 1987, 1989, 1991, 1994
Portuguese Cup 1930, 1931, 1935, 1940, 1943, 1944, 1949, 1951, 1952, 1953, 1955, 1957, 1959, 1962, 1964, 1969, 1970, 1972, 1980, 1981, 1983, 1985, 1986, 1987, 1993
European Cup 1961, 1962

DENNIS BERGKAMP

Born: Amsterdam 18.5.69
Height: 6ft 0ins Position: Striker
Club career:
1986–92 Ajax Amsterdam 185 (103)
1992–95 Inter Milan 52 (11)
1995– Arsenal 90 (39)
International record:
1990– Holland 64 (36)

DENNIS BERGKAMP is now Holland's leading goalscorer of all time, having beaten Faas Wilkes' record of 35 international strikes with his stunning quarter-final goal against Argentina at France 98.

● A 'DOUBLE' WINNER with Arsenal in 1997/98 and both Footballer of the Year and Player of the Year for that season, the only thing that can stop him, it seems, is his fear of flying which means he can only play in matches he can reach by coach or train.

● BERGKAMP BEGAN his career at Ajax where he inherited the mantle of Marco Van Basten and scored an incredible 103 goals in 185 league games. In 1992 he moved to Inter Milan for £8 million where he had such a terrible time that the players' competition of 'donkey of the week' was renamed 'Bergkamp of the week'. Despite this he did win a UEFA Cup winners medal to add to the Cup Winners' Cup one he won with Ajax in 1987.

● WHEN Arsenal snapped him up for £7.5 million, the player who had supported Tottenham as a child growing up in Amsterdam (the player he most admired was Glenn Hoddle and he kicked around in the park in a Spurs shirt) became Arsenal's most expensive ever signing.

Dennis Bergkamp can even control the ball with the waistband of his shorts

SILVIO BERLUSCONI

Born: Milan 1936

SILVIO BERLUSCONI has been the Italian Prime Minister (1994–95) and is head of a massive media network in Italy and beyond called Fininvest... but he is best known to football fans as the multi-millionaire owner of AC Milan.

● WHEN Berlusconi ran for Prime Minister in Italy in 1994, the name of his party – Forza Italia – was a well known football slogan, which roughly translates as 'Come on Italy!' He won the election.

● BERLUSCONI has pumped billions of lire into AC Milan, making them the richest club in the world, able to buy virtually any player they want. His money has helped finance the transfers of such stars as Gullit, Rijkaard, Van Basten, Lentini, Papin, Weah, Savicevic and Desailly, and has brought countless trophies, including three European Cups, to the club.

● WHEN Berlusconi arrived at the club in 1986 they were hugely in debt and facing bankruptcy. He immediately made the club part of his business empire and spent some £20 million. Within a year AC Milan had won the Italian Scudetto.

BERWICK RANGERS

Year formed: 1881
Ground: Shielfield Park (4,131)
Highest ever crowd: 13,365, 28th January 1967 v Rangers (Scottish Cup rd 1)
Nickname: The Borderers
Colours: Black and gold striped shirts, black shorts, black and gold socks

BERWICK Rangers started as a member of the Northumberland Football Association but joined the Scottish League in 1951, making them the only English team playing in the Scottish league. Their proximity to the border explains their nickname.

● THE CLUB's trophy room is not exactly bulging with silverware, and they are one of only 10 Scottish clubs who have never supplied a full international. The one real moment of glory came in 1979 when they were crowned Second Division champions, but the moment most die-hard supporters still talk about is the 1–0 giant-killing of Rangers in the Scottish Cup in 1967 (where Berwick recorded their record gate of 13,365).

● THE CLUB's record victory was on Christmas Day 1965, when they beat Forfar Athletic 8–1 and their heaviest defeat was a 9–1 trouncing by Hamilton Academical in 1980.

Roll of Honour

Second Division champions 1979

GEORGE BEST

Born: Belfast 22.5.46
Height: 5ft 9ins Position: Forward
Club career:

1963–75	Manchester United 361 (137)
1975–76	Stockport County (loan) 3 (2)
1976	Cork Celtic
1976	Los Angeles Aztecs
1976–78	Fulham 42 (8)
1978–79	Fort Lauderdale Strikers (USA)
1979–80	Hibernian 27 (4)
1980–83	San Jose Earthquakes (USA)
1983–84	Bournemouth 5 (0)

International record:

1964–78	Northern Ireland 37 (9)

POSSIBLY the greatest footballer that the British game has ever seen, George Best was quite simply a footballing genius. After making his debut for United aged just 17, the gifted Northern Irishman went on to dazzle with a combination of breathtaking skills, superb tackling and the ability to score goals from nowhere.

● BEST went on to play 361 league games for United, firing them to the league title in 1965 and 1967 and to European Cup glory in 1968 (he scored the vital second goal at Wembley in the 4–1 win over Benfica, which made United the first English club to win the trophy). In 1968 he was also named European Footballer of the Year. If it hadn't been for his much publicised love of the high life, particularly champagne and beautiful women, who knows what he might have achieved.

● HE still holds United's 'goals in a game' record. On 7th February 1970 he returned from suspension (for kicking the ball out of a referee's hands) for the FA Cup 5th round tie at Northampton and scored six goals in the 8–2 win. 'I was so embarrassed that I played the last 20 minutes at left back,' he said years later.

● BEST was part of United's 'Holy Trinity', combining with Bobby Charlton and Denis Law. Yet he never appeared in an FA Cup Final and never reached the final stages of a World Cup or European Championships competition (although he is equal 10th top goalscorer for Northern Ireland, albeit with just nine goals).

● THE FIRST footballer to truly cash in on his playing success, Best opened a chain of shops and put his name to everything from clothes to nightclubs. But as his problems with alcohol worsened, he became something of a footballing nomad. In 1977 he set an unusual record, playing in all four countries of the British Isles in 10 days. He played for Northern Ireland in Belfast, for Fulham at home to Crystal Palace and then away to Cardiff and St. Mirren (the latter a friendly).

'There was a knock on my hotel room door and it was the porter with a bottle of champagne. I'd just won at the casino and there was a huge pile of money on the bed, and next to it was the current Miss World in a negligee. He looked at the champagne, and the money, and the girl, and he said to me "George, where did it all go wrong?"' **—George Best 1996**

BETTING

Bets have been placed on the outcome of football matches ever since the first FA Cup Final in 1872. The bookies made Royal Engineers the 4/7 favourites, but they went on to lose 1-0 to Wanderers.

● In 1986 Nursing Sister Margaret Francis and ten colleagues from Roundway Psychiatric Hospital, Devizes became the first million-pound pools winners, scooping £1,017, 890. The winning numbers had been selected by their patients.

● In 1992 Brian McGregor of Hexham, Northumberland claimed the biggest football pay-out ever – a massive £3.83 billion for a 50p bet with Ladbrokes – after correctly predicting the scores of 61 matches. Ladbrokes didn't pay up and McGregor was fined £20 by Hexham magistrates for attempted fraud after altering his betting slip once he knew the results.

● The Canadian Ontario Lottery Corporation made the biggest boob in the history of football betting in 1995 when they advertised four afternoon English matches as evening kick-offs, allowing fans to place bets when they already knew the results. The Corporation had to pay out £365,000 to the lucky punters.

● Perhaps the strangest bet ever placed was by a Reading postman who put a fiver at odds of 50,000-1 on Mr Blobby to replace Graham Taylor as England manager. He lost when the job went to 'Mr Bubbly' (Terry Venables) instead.

BILLY BINGHAM

Born: Belfast 5.8.31

THE FATHER figure of football in Northern Ireland, Billy Bingham holds the record for the longest-serving British international manager, having been in charge of Northern Ireland for a total of 15 years, including one spell of 13 years (1980–93).

● A MASTER tactician, he is also his country's most successful manager by a mile, appearing in two World Cup tournaments, in 1982 and 1986. His greatest moment was when Northern Ireland beat hosts Spain 1–0 on 25th June 1982 (thanks to a Gerry Armstrong goal) to qualify for the second round of the competition.

● AS A PLAYER Bingham achieved success with Northern Ireland on the pitch as well. A tricky winger, he was part of the team which reached the quarter-finals of the competition in 1958, and in all he won a total of 56 caps.

● BUT DESPITE international success, he was not known as the greatest of club managers. He was in charge at Southport, Plymouth Argyle and Mansfield Town as well as taking the reins at Everton for four trophyless years in the mid-1970s. His only other spell in charge was a brief one running the national team of Greece.

BIRMINGHAM CITY

Year founded: 1875
Ground: St. Andrews (25,812)
Previous names: Small Heath Alliance, Small Heath, Birmingham
Highest ever crowd: 66,844, 11th February 1939 v Everton (FA Cup rd 5)
Nickname: The Blues
Colours: Blue and white shirts, white shorts, blue socks

CURRENTLY living in the shadow of near neighbours and arch-rivals Aston Villa, despite some recent success Birmingham City are still trying to shake off the label of 'sleeping giant'. The return of favourite son Trevor Francis to the club as manager in 1996 was part of the plan to change all that, masterminded by the first ever female football club managing director, Karren Brady, who was just 25 when she was appointed by multi-millionaire owner David Sullivan in 1992.

● FRANCIS became Britain's first £1 million player when he moved from City to Brian Clough's Nottingham Forest in February 1979, a true star who the club never replaced as they plummeted down through the divisions. Amazingly, Francis's fee remained the highest the club had received for a player until striker Steve Claridge signed for Leicester City for £1.2 million in 1996.

● BARRY FRY, who Francis replaced as manager, signed 41 players in his high profile spell at the club. But failing to bring the Premiership status that the club so desperately desires, his head was soon on the chopping block. Fry's dismissal was not the first time City have treated a manager in a somewhat ruthless fashion. In 1977 Willie Bell was sacked after just 16 days of the new season.

● WITH THEIR best league finish being 6th in the old First Division in 1956, the club has always come second-best to their near neighbours and even in 1897, when they bought their first stand, it came second-hand from Aston Villa! These days the newly redeveloped ground is somewhat more spectacular.

● THE LACK of silverware at St. Andrews (except for the Division Two Championship on five occasions, the League Cup in 1963 and the Auto Windscreens Shield in 1995) might be explained by a curse said to have been put on the site when gypsies were evicted by the club in the last century. During a particularly bad run of form in the 1980s, boss Ron Saunders had the bottom of the players' boots painted red to ward off evil spirits lurking in the turf.

● DESPITE the curse, Birmingham were actually the first English club to reach a European final – the Fairs Cup final in 1960 (losing to Barcelona).

Roll of Honour

Second Division champions 1893, 1921, 1948, 1955, 1995
League Cup 1963
Auto Windscreens Shield 1995
Leyland Daf Cup 1991

BLACKBURN ROVERS

Year founded: 1875
Ground: Ewood Park (31,367)
Highest ever crowd: 61,783, 2nd March 1929 v Bolton (FA Cup rd 6)
Colours: Blue and white halved shirts, white shorts, white socks

BEST remembered in recent years for their dramatic renaissance and 1994/95 Premiership win thanks to the millions of

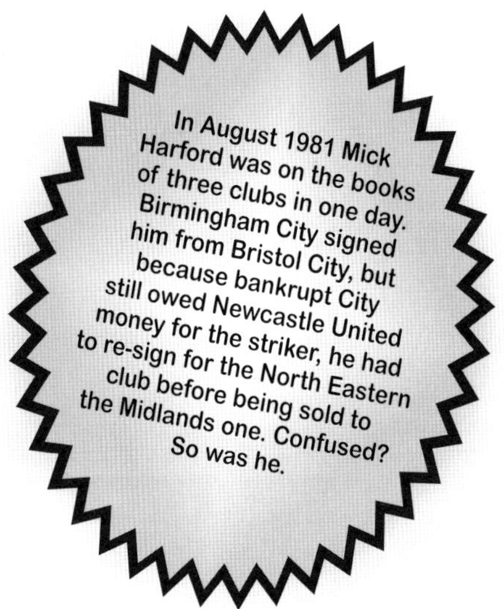

Below: Alan Shearer lifts the Premiership trophy in 1995, Blackburn Rovers' first title victory since 1914

steel magnate Jack Walker, in fact historically Rovers are one of English football's most successful clubs.

● TWICE league champions before the recent Premiership triumph (in 1912 and 1914) and six times FA Cup winners (the last time being in 1928), Rovers are only now beginning to relive the glory days. In fact, of all the current English league clubs, Blackburn was the first to win the FA Cup, in 1884, and they still hold the record for the longest unbeaten run in FA Cup history – 24 matches in the process of winning the cup three times on the trot between December 1883 and November 1886.

● IN 1884 THEY beat Rossendale in the FA Cup 11–0, their biggest winning margin. Their biggest defeat was in 1933, when they lost 8–0 to Arsenal.

● DEREK FAZACKERLEY made the most appearances for Blackburn, playing in no fewer than 596 games between 1970–86, and the club's most capped player is legendary Rovers' stalwart Bob Crompton, who played 41 times for England between 1902–14.

● IN 1891 they played arguably the strangest game ever, against hated local rivals Burnley. After two mass brawls Rovers ended up with only goalkeeper Herby Arthur on the pitch after the rest of his team refused to carry on. Legend has it that Arthur appealed successfully for offside and then refused to take the free kick because he had no one to pass to... forcing the referee to abandon the game.

● THE CLUB was originally the Blackburn Grammar School Old Boys team, and they lost their first FA Cup final in 1882 to upper-crust rivals Old Etonians.

● IN 1954/55 the club beat its 'goals in a season' record, scoring 114 times, which outweighs the record number the club has conceded in a season – the 104 they let in in 1932/33.

● THE CLUB'S most prolific goalscorer in recent years was Alan Shearer, who notched an incredible 122 goals in 138 games for the club. Shearer smashed the English transfer record, putting £15 million in the Jack Walker coffers when he moved 'home' to Newcastle in the summer of 1996.

Roll of Honour

Premier League champions 1995
Div 1 champions 1912. 1914
Div 2 champions 1939
Div 3 champions 1975
FA Cup 1884, 1885, 1886, 1890, 1891, 1928

Blackburn's Post-War Record

47 D1 17th	64 D1 7th	81 D2 4th
48 D1 21st	65 D1 10th	82 D2 10th
49 D2 14th	66 D1 22nd	83 D2 11th
50 D2 16th	67 D2 4th	84 D2 6th
51 D2 6th	68 D2 8th	85 D2 5th
52 D2 14th	69 D2 19th	86 D2 19th
53 D2 9th	70 D2 8th	87 D2 12th
54 D2 3rd	71 D2 21st	88 D2 5th
55 D2 6th	72 D3 10th	89 D2 5rd
56 D2 4th	73 D3 3rd	90 D2 5th
57 D2 4th	74 D3 13th	91 D2 19th
58 D2 2nd	75 D3 1st	92 D2 6th
59 D1 10th	76 D2 15th	93 PR 4th
60 D1 17th	77 D2 12th	94 PR 2nd
61 D1 8th	78 D2 5th	95 PR 1st
62 D1 16th	79 D2 22nd	96 PR 7th
63 D1 11th	80 D3 2nd	97 PR 13th
		98 PR 6th

BLACKPOOL

Year founded: 1887
Ground: Bloomfield Road (10,337)
Previous name: Blackpool St. Johns
Highest ever crowd: 39,098, 17th September 1955 v Wolverhampton Wanderers (Div 1)
Nickname: The Seasiders
Colours: Tangerine shirts, white shorts and tangerine socks

THE GLORY days may have deserted Blackpool in recent years, but the club is still one of England's most famous. Their greatest day occurred on 2nd May 1953 when, inspired by the legendary Stanley Matthews, the club won the FA Cup, beating Bolton Wanderers 4–3. Although Stan Mortenson scored a hat-trick, the game will always be known as 'The Matthews Final', with the whole country rejoicing that the 38-year-old 'Wizard of Dribble' had at last won an FA Cup Winners' medal.

● IT HASN'T all been cup success down at Bloomfield Road though, and the club actually went eight years (13 games) without winning an FA Cup match between 1960–68, the second worst run in the competition's history (equal with Rochdale – but not as bad as Leeds United's 16).

● AN APPRENTICE at the club at the time of the Matthews Final, the great Jimmy Armfield holds the record for league appearances at Blackpool. He played 568 between 1952–71 and says that the 1953 match was his inspiration to become a pro. Armfield is also

Stanley Matthews is held aloft by his teammates after inspiring Blackpool's 4–3 Cup Final win over Bolton in 1953

Blackpool's most capped player, having played for England 43 times

● ON 10th September 1960, Blackpool's match against Bolton Wanderers was the first league game ever to be televised.

● THE SEASIDERS' biggest victory was in 1948, when they beat Preston 7–0. They have been beaten by as much as 1–10 twice against Small Heath in 1901 and Huddersfield in 1930.

Roll of Honour

Div 2 champions 1930
FA Cup 1953

DANNY BLANCHFLOWER

Born: Belfast 10.2.26 Died: 9.12.93
Height: 5ft 10ins Position: Midfield
Club career:
1945–49 Glentoran
1949–51 Barnsley 68 (2)
1951–54 Aston Villa 148 (10)
1954–64 Tottenham Hotspur 337 (15)
International record:
1950–63 Northern Ireland 56 (2)

AN INSPIRATIONAL figure both on and off the pitch, playmaking midfielder Danny Blanchflower led Tottenham Hotspur to their greatest ever achievement, the 1961 League and FA Cup double (making Spurs the first club to do the 'double' this century). Footballer of the Year twice (1958 and 1961), Blanchflower also inspired Spurs to FA Cup success in 1962 and then on to European Cup Winners' Cup glory in 1963.

● FOR Northern Ireland he was again the driving force behind his country's finest hour, captaining them to the quarter-finals of the World Cup in Sweden in 1958, only to be walloped 4–0 by France. In all he played 56 times for his country.

● BLANCHFLOWER – a serious and stubborn man – holds the distinction of being one of the few people ever to refuse to go on the TV show 'This Is Your Life'.

● AFTER a successful spell as a journalist and a less successful flirtation with management at Chelsea and then Northern Ireland, he retired in 1979 and died in 1993 after a long illness.

SEPP BLATTER

Born: 10.3.36

Swiss football administrator Sepp Blatter, the President of FIFA, is the most powerful man in world football. He stepped up from the post of General Secretary in July 1998, replacing Brazilian Joao Havelange.

● FORMER General Secretary of the Swiss Ice Hockey Association, he was once a Swiss amateur footballer, a handy athlete and later a serving colonel in the Swiss Army.

Spurs' Double-winning captain Danny Blanchflower swaps the FA Cup for three marbles and a champion conker

● BEFORE his appointment to FIFA in 1982 and his subsequent rise to a position of such power in the world game, Blatter was chosen as president of the newly formed World Friends of the Suspender Belt Society in 1971.

● IN HIS role travelling the world as a football administrator, Blatter has picked up a number of other unusual titles and honours. He is a member of the Olympic Order, a Knight of the Kingdom of Pahang in Malaysia and an Honorary Citizen of Texas... all of which no doubt come in very handy.

STEVE BLOOMER

Born: Cradley Heath 20.1.1874
Died: 1938
Height: 5ft 7ins Position: Forward
Club career:
1896–1906 Derby County
1906–10 Middlesbrough
1910–14 Derby County
International record:
1895–1907 England 23 (28)

ENGLAND's most prolific striker before the First World War, Bloomer became top scorer for his country with an astonishing 28 goals in just 23 games. He remained top scorer until he was overtaken by both Tom Finney and Nat Lofthouse in 1958.

● WITH THE best strike rate of any England forward, Bloomer scored in each of his first 10 internationals and is still the sixth highest-scoring England international.

● A SLIGHTLY-BUILT player, Bloomer played for Derby County and Middlesbrough and is still Derby's top scorer ever with 292 league goals.

● BLOOMER was the First Division's top scorer on four occasions during his career.

BOCA JUNIORS

Year founded: 1905
Ground: Bombonera, Buenos Aires (58,740)
League wins: 19
Colours: Blue shirts with a yellow hoop, blue shorts and blue socks

ALONG with fellow Buenos Aires residents River Plate, Boca Juniors are Argentina's most famous team. Although founded by an Irishman called Patrick MacCarthy in 1905, most of the club's first players were Italian. Boca Juniors became the first team to win the brand new Argentine Professional League Championship in 1931.

● IN 1981 Barcelona paid Boca a world record £3 million for Diego Maradona, who returned to the club in 1995 sporting possibly the silliest haircut (dyed blue and yellow) in the history of the game.

● BOCA Juniors won the Copa Libertadores (the South American equivalent of the European Cup) in 1977 and 1978 despite not having any World Cup internationals in the team. Outside South America their greatest success was winning the World Club Cup against Borussia Moenchengladbach of Germany in 1977.

● IN 1971 BOCA Juniors were involved in one of the most violent game of football ever in the Copa Libertadores against Sporting Cristal of Peru. After a bad tackle the match erupted into a mass punch up and nineteen players were sent off (and later jailed for 30 days, except three who were so badly injured they had to go to hospital). The match was abandoned.

Roll of Honour

Argentine champions 1919, 1920, 1923, 1926, 1930, 1931, 1934, 1935, 1940, 1943, 1944, 1954, 1962, 1964, 1965, 1969, 1976, 1981, 1991, 1993
Copa Libertadores 1977, 1978
World Club Cup 1977

BOLTON WANDERERS

Year founded: 1874
Ground: The Reebok Stadium (25,000)
Previous names: Christ Church
Highest ever crowd: 69,912,
18th February 1953 v Manchester City
(FA Cup rd 5)
Nickname: The Trotters
Colours: White shirts, navy blue shorts, blue socks

BOLTON WANDERERS are one of the founder members of the Football League. Known as the Wanderers because they didn't have a permanent home until they moved to former rubbish tip Burden Park in 1895, in August 1997 they moved to the Reebok Stadium, winner of the Institute of Structural Engineers Special Award for Design in 1998.

● ONCE KNOWN AS The Reds, they even wore white shirts with red spots once because it was believed this strip made the players seem bigger.

● THEIR FINEST hours came in winning the FA Cup in 1923, 1926 and 1929, and an incredible total of just 17 loyal players appeared in all three matches.

● BURNDEN PARK – featured in LS Lowry's famous painting 'Going to the Match' – was the scene of the first major English footballing disaster in 1946 when 33 people were killed after a barrier collapsed during a cup tie with Stoke City.

● THE CLUB's top scorer (255 goals between 1946–61) is legendary striker Nat Lofthouse who only ever played for Bolton and is also their record international appearances holder, with 33 for England.

● During the 1996/97 campaign, in the process of becoming First Division Champions, Bolton came within a whisker of becoming the first team in league history to gain 100 points and score 100 goals in a season. They managed the 99th and 100th goals in their last game against Tranmere but a last minute equaliser from Rovers' Lee Jones made it 2-2 and meant they finished on 98 points not 100.

Roll of Honour

First Division champions 1997
Div 2 champions 1909, 1978
Div 3 champions 1973
FA Cup 1923, 1926, 1929, 1958

BORUSSIA DORTMUND

Year founded: 1909
Ground: Westfalenstadion (42,800)
League wins: 5
Colours: Yellow shirts, black shorts, yellow and black socks

IN 1997 Borussia Dortmund became the third German team in football history to win the European Cup, with a 3–1 win over hot favourites Juventus in the final in Munich.

● THE CLUB'S only previous European triumph was in winning the 1966 European Cup Winners' Cup Final when they beat Liverpool 2–1.

● IN THEIR flourescent yellow shirts, Dortmund have stood out as Germany's top club side in recent years after a long spell in the relative wilderness. Their Bundesliga triumph in 1995 was their first since 1963 but they won it again in 1996 to record their fifth win in all and send them into the Champions League and eventual European Cup triumph.

Roll of Honour

Bundesliga champions 1956, 1957, 1963, 1995, 1966
German Cup 1965, 1989
European Cup 1997
European Cup Winners' Cup 1966

BOSMAN RULING

NAMED AFTER little known Belgian first division player Jean Marc Bosman, the 1995 ruling by the European Court of Justice that footballers fall under the same free trade legislation as any other European workers has turned the football transfer system on its head. Effectively the ruling means that if a player is out of contract at a club, that club can no longer demand a transfer fee if the player leaves to play for a team in another European country.

● BOSMAN TOOK his case to the European court after his club in Belgium, RFC Liege, refused him a transfer to French Second Division side Dunkerque.

● FIFA HAS ALREADY been forced to adopt this ruling to cover transfers between all countries all over the world, not just Europe, and from July 1998 a new FA ruling means that any out-of-contract players over the age of 24 can now move freely from one club to another within England.

● PLAYERS WHO have benefited from the ruling include Paul Lambert (Motherwell to Borussia Dortmund), John Collins (Celtic to Monaco), Gianluca Vialli (Juventus to Chelsea) and Patrick Kluivert (Ajax to AC Milan).

BOURNEMOUTH

Year founded: 1899
Ground: Dean Court (10,770)
Previous names: Boscombe St. Johns, Boscombe, Bournemouth & Boscombe Athletic
Highest ever crowd: 28,799, 2nd March 1957 v Manchester United (FA Cup rd 6)
Nickname: The Cherries
Colours: Red and black striped shirts, black shorts, black socks

Apart from overcoming severe financial problems and staying afloat in 1996/97, Bournemouth's finest moments have occurred in the FA Cup, their greatest achievement coming when they reached the Sixth Round in 1957 while floundering in the Third Division. This famous run was notable for a 1–0 victory against Wolverhampton Wanderers but they were eventually knocked out in the quarter-finals by Manchester United in front of their highest ever crowd at Dean Court.

● ON 20th November 1971 demon Bournemouth striker Ted MacDougall scored nine times in an FA Cup First Round tie at home to fellow seasiders Margate, making him the highest ever scorer in an FA Cup tie. Bournemouth eventually won the match 11–0, the club's highest ever score.

Roll of Honour

Div 3 champions 1987

BRADFORD CITY

Year founded: 1903
Ground: Valley Parade (18,018)
Highest ever crowd: 39,146,
11th March 1911 v Burnley (FA Cup rd 4)
Nickname: The Bantams
Colours: Claret-and-amber-striped shirts, black shirts and socks

BRADFORD City were a rugby league club before they switched to football in 1903. Keen to establish football in a strong rugby area, the Football League granted their application before they had even assembled a team. The club's finest hour was in 1911, when they beat Newcastle United 1–0 in a replay at Old Trafford to win the FA Cup, a feat the club has never repeated.

● SADLY Bradford City will be remembered for the tragic fire in which 56 people lost their lives on 11th May 1985 – the old main stand which burnt down was due to be demolished the very next day.

● CITY SCORED 128 goals during the 1928/29 season, a record for a 42 game campaign shared with Aston Villa.

Roll of Honour

Div 2 champions 1908
Div 3 (N) champions 1929
Div 3 champions 1985
FA Cup 1911

Did You Know?

The world's top scorer of all time is Brazilian striker Artur Friedenreich, who netted 1,329 goals in a career which lasted from 1909 to 1935. He played for club sides Germania, Ipiranga, Americano, Paulistano, Sao Paulo and Flamengo, as well as the Brazilian national team, for whom he scored nine goals in 17 appearances.

LIAM BRADY

Born: Dublin 13.2.56
Height: 5ft 8ins Position: Midfield
Club career:
1973–80 Arsenal 253 (43)
Juventus 57 (13)
Sampdoria 57 (6)
Inter Milan 58 (5)
Ascoli 17 (0)
1987–90 West Ham United 89 (9)
International record:
1974–90 Republic of Ireland 72 (9)

LIAM BRADY was known as 'Chippy', not because of his ability to delicately loft the ball but thanks to his penchant for a traditional British food made from slices of potato.

● THREE times Arsenal's Player of the Year (1976, 1978 and 1979) and PFA Player of the Year (1979), Brady starred in the Gunners' midfield in the 1970s – winning the FA Cup in 1979 – before moving to Italian giants Juventus for £514,000.

● ONE OF three brothers who all played for English or Irish league clubs, Brady won two league titles with Juventus and was regarded by the Italians (he went on to play for Sampdoria, Inter and Ascoli) as one of the greatest ever imports from the British league.

● WINNING 72 caps and scoring nine goals for the Republic of Ireland, Brady is the Republic's third most capped player of all time.

● IN 1990 he retired after a short time at West Ham, returning to football in 1991 for unsuccessful managerial spells at Celtic and Brighton. He is now head of Youth Development at Arsenal.

BRAZIL

First international: Argentina 3 Brazil 0 (Buenos Aires, 1914)
First World Cup appearance: Brazil 1 Yugoslavia 2 (Uruguay, 1930)
Highest capped player: Djalma Santos (100)
Highest goalscorer: Pele (77)
Best win: 9–0 v Colombia, 1957
Worst defeat: 6–1 v Argentina, 1940
Colours: Yellow shirts, blue shorts, white socks

THE most successful international team in the history of football, the very word 'Brazil' is synonymous with flamboyant, attacking football, played with a smile and accompanied by a thumping samba beat.

● Brazil is the only country to have won the World Cup four times. They beat Sweden 5–2 in 1958, Czechoslovakia 3–1 in 1962, Italy 4–1 in 1970 and Italy again (3–2 on penalties) in 1994.

● Defeat in the 1998 final by France consigned them to the runners-up spot for the second time in their history. It was, however, the first time they had lost a World Cup Final. In 1950, when they finished second to Uruguay, the deciding match (often wrongly described as a final) was actually the last game of a four team final round in which all the teams played each other.

● Brazil is the only country to have appeared in every World Cup finals tournament, a total of 16. They have also scored more goals in the World Cup final stages than any other nation – 171 in total – and most of them were corkers, too.

● In 1970, when Brazil beat the Italians 4–1 in Mexico to win their third out of the last four World Cup tournaments, they got to keep the Jules Rimet trophy. Unfortunately it was soon stolen from the Brazilian FA and hasn't been seen since.

● Brazil's coach for the 1998 World Cup, Mario Zagallo, is the most successful man in international football. Zagallo was the first man to win the World Cup as both a player (he was Brazil's left back when they won the tournament in both 1958 and 1962) and as a coach (he was in charge of the 1970 team). He was also on the coaching staff in 1994 when Brazil became the first side ever to win the World Cup by means of a penalty shoot-out, beating Italy at the Rose Bowl in Pasadena, Los Angeles.

● Surprisingly their record in the South American Championship is very poor. They have only won the competition five times since its inauguration in 1916, and only twice in the last 50 years.

Roll of Honour

World Cup 1958, 1962, 1970, 1994
South American champions 1919, 1922, 1949, 1989, 1997

WORLD CUP RECORD

1930	Round 1	1970	Winners
1934	Round 1	1974	Fourth place
1938	Semi-finals	1978	Third place
1950	Runners-up	1982	Round 2
1954	Quarter-finals	1986	Quarter-finals
1958	Winners	1990	Round 2
1962	Winners	1994	Winners
1966	Round 1	1998	Runners-up

Brazil players in a position their opponents normally adopt – down on their knees

BRECHIN CITY

Year founded: 1906
Ground: Glebe Park (3,980)
Highest ever crowd: 8,122, 3rd February 1973 v Aberdeen (Scottish Cup rd 3)
Colours: Shirt, shorts and socks red with white trimmings

AT THE start of every season, survival is the aim of Brechin City, who have never won a major trophy and whose two Second Division title wins in 1983 and 1990 are their greatest achievements. Brechin has a population of just 6,500, which means it is the smallest town in Britain to have a league team... so even with a ground capacity of just 3,980 there's always plenty of room.

● BRECHIN's record signing is Sandy Ross, who cost £16,000 from Berwick Rangers in 1991, and no player has ever won international honours while at Brechin City.

● BRECHIN RECORDED their record defeat no fewer than three times in the 1937/38 season, losing 10–0 to Airdrie, Albion Rovers and Cowdenbeath in Division Two.

● GLEBE PARK has a famous hedge running along one side of the ground. So revered is this by the club and its supporters that when the club's new stand was built in 1991 it was erected behind one of the goals and not opposite the main stand!

Roll of Honour

Second Division champions 1983, 1990
C Division champions 1954

Did You Know?

Brazil have played in more World Cup finals matches than any other team – a total of 80 (Germany are next on 78)

BILLY BREMNER

Born: Stirling 9.12.42 Died: 7.12.97
Height: 5ft 4ins Position: Midfield
Club career:
1959–76 Leeds United 586 (90)
1976–77 Hull City 61 (6)
1979–81 Doncaster Rovers 5 (0)
International record:
1965–74 Scotland 54 (3)

LEEDS' and Scotland's terrier-like captain, Billy Bremner, who sadly died in December 1997, won two league titles (1968/69 and 1973/74), the FA Cup (1972), League Cup (1969) and Fairs Cup (1969) with Leeds United under the late, great Don Revie.

● FEROCIOUSLY passionate and committed, Bremner played 54 times for Scotland and skippered them in the 1974 World Cup Finals in Germany when they failed to qualify for the second round despite being undefeated. Although his goals were few and far between, they tended to be vital ones.

● HE WAS voted Footballer of the Year in 1970, but in 1974 he and Kevin Keegan became the first Britons to be sent off at Wembley when they were dismissed for fighting in the Charity Shield. Both players tore off their shirts as they trudged off and were later banned for five weeks.

Bremner leads Leeds to their first ever League Championship in 1969

BRENTFORD

Year founded: 1889
Ground: Griffin Park (12,783)
Highest ever crowd: 39,626, 5th March 1938 v Preston (FA Cup rd 6)
Nickname: The Bees
Colours: Red and white striped shirts, black shorts, black socks

ONE OF TWO London clubs known as the Bees (Barnet is the other), Brentford enjoyed their heyday in the 1930s with the high point coming when they finished 5th in the First Division in 1935/36. Since then they have been Division Three and Four champions and reached the Freight Rover Trophy Final at Wembley in 1985.

● IN 1930 The Bees became the only league club ever to win every one of their home league games in a season (21). And in 1955 they finished the season having won 16 games, lost 16, scored 82 goals, conceded 82, and earned 46 points from 46 games!

● PERHAPS their history would have been more glorious if Rod Stewart, an apprentice at Griffin Park in the early 1960s, hadn't decided to pursue a career as a pop star instead!

Roll of Honour

Div 2 champions 1935
Div 3 champions 1992
Div 3 (S) champions 1933
Div 4 champions 1963

BRIGHTON & HOVE ALBION

Year founded: 1901
Ground: Withdean Stadium (6,000)
Previous name: Brighton & Hove United
Highest ever crowd: 36,747, 27th December 1958 v Fulham (Div 2)
Nickname: The Seagulls
Colours: Blue-and-white-striped shirts, blue shorts, white socks

ALBION ARE one of select band of clubs to reach the FA Cup Final and be relegated from the top flight in the same season (a group joined by Middlesbrough at the end of the 1996/97 season). Victory over Manchester United in the 1983 final might have softened the blow, but they lost 4–0 in a Wembley replay after coming desperately close in the first match.

● BRIGHTON escaped relegation to the Vauxhall Conference on the very last day of the 1996/97 season – at the expense of Hereford United – in one of football's greatest ever escapes. At one stage they were 12 points adrift at the bottom of the table after having three points deducted for crowd trouble.

● ERNIE 'TUG' WILSON has made the most appearances for the Seagulls, playing no less than 509 games between 1902–36. Wilson was twice on the verge of turning out for 100 games in a row but was foiled both times by injury while on 99!

Roll of Honour

Div 3 (S) champions 1958
Div 4 champions 1965

Did You Know?

Between 1966 and 1967 Bristol City were very confident about their starting 11. So confident, in fact, that for 53 consecutive league and FA Cup matches they didn't use a single substitute.

BRISTOL CITY

Year founded: 1894
Ground: Ashton Gate (20,000)
Previous name: Bristol South End
Highest ever crowd: 43,335, 16th February 1935 v Preston (FA Cup rd 5)
Nickname: The Robins
Colours: Red shirts, white shorts, red-and-white socks

WITH a vast potential support, it is perhaps surprising that Bristol City haven't been more successful. Their only real sniff of glory came when they finished second in the First Division in 1907 and reached the FA Cup Final in 1909 (losing to Manchester United 1-0). Historians might point to the 1934 Welsh Cup and 1986 Freight Rover Trophy wins as major glory moments, but the club's fans have been starved of success for years. At least they had something to cheer about in May 1998, when they were promoted to the First Division.

● As recently as the early 1980s Bristol City were resident in the top flight, but their decline was astonishing, plummeting from the First to the Fourth Divisions in just three years (making them the first ever club to suffer three consecutive drops).

● Andy Cole was both the club's most expensive purchase and most lucrative sale. He cost £500,000 from Arsenal in June 1992 but moved to Newcastle nine months later for £1,750,000... a very nice little earner.

Roll of Honour

Div 2 champions 1906
Div 3 (S) champions 1923, 1927, 1955
Welsh Cup winners: 1934 Freight Rover Trophy winners: 1986 Anglo-Scottish Cup winners: 1978

BRISTOL ROVERS

Year founded: 1883
Ground: Memorial Ground (9,200)
Previous names: Black Arabs, Eastville Rovers, Bristol Eastville Rovers
Highest ever crowd: 38,472, 30th January 1960 v Preston (FA Cup rd 4)
Nickname: The Pirates
Colours: Blue-and-white-quartered shirts, white shorts, blue socks

ROVERS BY NAME and rovers by nature, between 1986–97 fans of the blue half of Bristol had to travel to nearby Bath to watch their club, having had to quit their traditional home at Eastville. They now play their games at rugby union team Bristol FC's Memorial Ground.

● WHILE still at Eastville – back in 1928 in fact – Bristol Rovers player Ronnie Dix became the youngest player to score in the league. He scored his goal against Norwich in only his second game at the tender age of 15 years and 180 days.

● TWO opposing strikers have set goal-scoring records against unfortunate Bristol Rovers. In 1936 Luton's Tommy Payne set the league record for goals in a game when he scored no fewer than 10 times in his side's 12-0 win. Then in 1955 Blackburn's Tommy Briggs scored seven times in his club's 8-3 victory over Rovers, a second division record.

● IN 1973/74 Rovers went an amazing 26 matches unbeaten – a club record – only losing to Wrexham on 2nd February 1974.

● THE Memorial Ground has the smallest pitch in the English league at 101 x 68 yards, not surprising as it was designed for rugby (Rovers share a ground with Bristol RFU).

Roll of Honour

Div 3 (S) champions 1953
Div 3 champions 1990

TREVOR BROOKING

Born: Barking 2.1.48
Height: 6ft 0ins Position: Midfield
Club career:
1967–84 West Ham United 528 (88)
International record:
1974–82 England 47 (5)

WEST HAM born and bred, cultured midfielder Trevor Brooking joined the Hammers as an apprentice in 1965... and he never played for another professional club.

● HE WAS in the West Ham side that won the FA Cup in 1975 (beating Fulham 2–0) and the Second Division title in 1981, but his greatest day at club level came at Wembley in 1980, when he scored the only goal of the FA Cup Final to give The Hammers a shock 1–0 win over Arsenal. Amazingly for a man known for his sweet feet, he scored with a header... only the third headed goal of his career.

● BROOKING won 47 caps for England, finishing his career in the 1982 World Cup in Spain, when England were knocked out in the 2nd round without losing a game. In fact, England only ever lost seven times when Brooking was in the team from 1974–82.

● After finishing his playing career Brooking moved into journalism, becoming an integral part of BBC's radio and TV football team.

Trevor Brooking – West Ham's most cultured ever player?

CRAIG BROWN

Born: Lanarkshire 1.7.40

Craig Brown, Scotland manager since 1993, has twice been on the brink of being the first man to guide the Scots to the second round of a major tournament. At Euro 96 only a late Patrick Kluivert shot through David Seaman's legs denied Scotland a place in the quarter finals. In France 98 the soft spoken gaffer guided his team to a narrow but glorious defeat in the opening game against Brazil, an inspired 1-1 draw with Norway and, alas, a 3-0 drubbing by Morocco.

● AFTER PLAYING for Falkirk, Dundee and Rangers, Brown began his managerial career as assistant coach at Motherwell. He moved to Clyde, guiding them to two First Division Championships and producing future stars like Steve Archibald, Pat Nevin, and Ian Ferguson.

● IN 1989 he took Scotland's Under-16 team to the World Youth Cup final, and three years later his Scottish Under-21 team came third in Europe. His brother Jock is a former football commentator and now general manager at Celtic.

STEVE BRUCE

Born: Newcastle 31.12.60
Height: 6ft 0ins Position: Central defender
Club career:
1979–84 Gillingham 205 (29)
1984–87 Norwich 141 (14)
1987–96 Manchester United 309 (36)
1996– Birmingham City 72 (2)
1998– Sheffield United

ONE OF the best players never to win an England cap, stalwart central defender Steve Bruce captained Manchester United to three Premiership titles (1992/93, 1993/94 and 1995/96).

● HE ALSO WON two FA Cup winners' medals in 1990 and 1994 before moving to Birmingham City and then on to Sheffield United as player-manager.

● A RUGGED, uncompromising defender, Bruce has picked up more than 100 stitches in a career where he's never been afraid to put his head in where it hurts.

● BOUGHT for £800,000 by Alex Ferguson from Norwich in 1987, Bruce had already picked up a League Cup winners' medal with The Canaries. At Norwich he had the distinction of scoring on his debut... unfortunately it was an own goal! On his United debut at Portsmouth he broke his nose.

● AT UNITED he became a prolific scorer, and in the 1990/91 season grabbed 19 goals, but after Eric Cantona took over penalty-taking duties his figures dropped dramatically.

BULGARIA

First international: Austria 6 Bulgaria 0 (Vienna, 1924)
First World Cup appearance: Bulgaria 0 Argentina 1 (Chile, 1962)
Highest capped player: Hristo Bonev (96)
Highest goalscorer: Hristo Bonev (47)
Best win: 7–0 v Norway, 1957, and Malta, 1982
Worst defeat: 13–0 v Spain, 1933
Colours: White shirts, green shorts, white socks

BULGARIA's best World Cup performance was in the USA in 1994, when they sensationally knocked out Germany to reach the semi-finals, eventually being beaten by Italy to finish in fourth place. That same year, Hristo Stoichkov was the first Bulgarian to be named European Player of the Year, while he was playing for Spanish giants Barcelona.

● DESPITE qualifying for five World Cup tournaments before USA 94, until that tournament Bulgaria had never won a match in the finals themselves. When Nigeria beat them 3–0 in their opener it looked like much the same old story.

● MUCH WAS EXPECTED of the Eastern Europeans in France '98, despite the fact that they were an ageing team. However they failed to impress and, after a disappointing draw against Paraguay and a lame defeat by Nigeria they were thrashed 6-1 by Spain in the competition's heaviest defeat and went out of the competition.

WORLD CUP RECORD

1930 Did not enter	1970 Round 1
1934 Did not qualify	1974 Round 1
1938 Did not qualify	1978 Did not qualify
1950 Did not enter	1982 Did not qualify
1954 Did not qualify	1986 Round 2
1958 Did not qualify	1990 Did not qualify
1962 Round 1	1994 Round 1
1966 Round 1	1998 Round 1

BURNLEY

Year founded: 1882
Ground: Turf Moor (22,966)
Previous name: Burnley Rovers
Highest ever crowd: 54,775, 23rd February 1924 v Huddersfield (FA Cup rd 3)
Nickname: The Clarets
Colours: Claret shirts with sky blue sleeves, white shorts and socks

BURNLEY are a founder member of the league and have been top flight champions twice (1921 and 1960). Despite their current lowly plight they are still one of the greatest and most famous clubs in English football, with some of the most passionate fans in the game.

● IN 1914 Burnley appeared in the first Cup Final to be attended by a reigning monarch as George V watched them beat Liverpool 1–0 at Crystal Palace. They were also runners-up in 1947 and 1962.

● THE CLARETS won their first league title in 1921 despite losing their first three games. After that, however, they embarked on the longest unbeaten run ever put together in a single English league season (4th September 1920 to 26th March 1921), an astonishing 30 games without defeat.

● IN 1975 Burnley became the first top club in 55 years to be defeated on their own ground by non-league opposition, when they lost 1–0 in the FA Cup 3rd round to then lowly Wimbledon.

● IN THE 1970s and 80s Burnley fell through the divisions and only a last game of the season win in 1987 saved them from relegation to non-league football.

Roll of Honour

Div 1 champions 1921, 1960
Div 2 champions 1898, 1973
Div 3 champions 1982
Div 4 champions 1992
FA Cup 1914

BURY

Year founded: 1885
Ground: Gigg Lane (12,000 approx)
Highest ever crowd: 35,000, 9th January 1960 v Bolton (FA Cup rd 3)
Nickname: The Shakers
Colours: White shirts, royal blue shorts and socks

TWICE FA Cup winners (1900 and 1903), unfortunately Bury have never been able to match their early achievements. When they won the FA Cup in 1903, Bury recorded the highest FA Cup Final win when they beat Derby County 6–0, a record which still stands. During that cup run they didn't concede a single goal, although this feat had been achieved 14 years earlier when Preston North End won the cup.

● DURING THE big freeze winter of 1962/63 Bury's third round FA Cup tie with Birmingham was postponed a record 14 times. Birmingham eventually won the tie 2–0 two months after its scheduled date.

● BURY ARE the team with the shortest name in the Football League.

Roll of Honour

Div 2 champions 1895
Div 3 champions 1961
Second Division champions 1997
FA Cup 1900, 1903

SIR MATT BUSBY

Born: Orbiston, near Bellshill 26.5.1909
Died: 20.1.94

MANCHESTER United legend Sir Matt Busby was one of the greatest managers in the history of English football.

● THE longest-serving post-war manager of all time, Sir Matt retired in 1969 after 24 years in the Old Trafford hot seat. In that time he won two FA Cup Finals (1948 and 1963) and five League Championships (1952, 1956, 1957, 1965 and 1967).

● SIR MATT BUSBY was also the first ever manager to bring the European Cup to England when his Manchester United side beat Benfica 4–1 in the final of the competition at Wembley in 1968. He was knighted in the same year.

● WINNING the famous trophy had been his dream for years. Chances are he would have achieved the goal 10 years earlier but for one of the biggest tragedies to befall British football.

● THE MUNICH AIR DISASTER in 1958, in which eight Manchester United players from arguably the club's best ever side (nicknamed the Busby Babes because they were so young) lost their lives after an away match against Red Star Belgrade. Busby was one of 20 people who survived the crash (Bobby Charlton was also on the plane).

● BUSBY spent most of his playing career as a midfielder with Manchester United's two greatest rivals, Liverpool and Manchester City. He won one cap for Scotland v Wales in 1934.

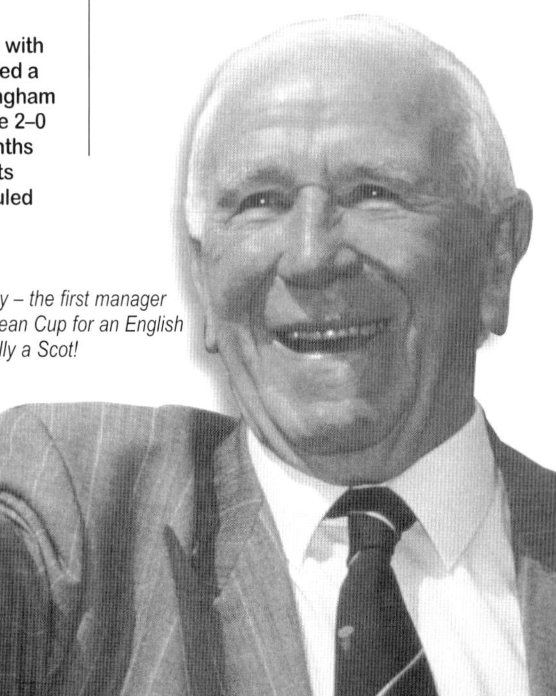

Sir Matt Busby – the first manager to win the European Cup for an English team – was actually a Scot!

CALEDONIAN THISTLE

Year founded: 1994
Ground: Telford Street Park, Inverness (5,600)
Highest ever crowd: 5,600, February 14th 1998 v Dundee United (Scottish Cup)
Colours: Blue shirts with white flashes, white shorts with blue flashes, blue socks

CALEDONIAN Thistle is the newest club in British league football, an amalgamation of Inverness Caledonian and Inverness Thistle. Both sides date back from before the turn of the century. They are also one of the most recent additions to the Scottish League, having amalgamated to join the new Scottish Third Division in 1994.

● INVERNESS Thistle enjoyed the shortest match ever played in Scottish football – in 1895 they scored a dodgy goal after just two minutes against Citadel, and the Citadel players walked off the pitch in disgust.

● THE WEATHER can be so bad up in the Scottish Highlands that one Thistle cup tie against Falkirk was postponed a record 29 times. The match, which should have been played on 6th January 1979, was eventually played on 22nd February. Falkirk won!

CAMBRIDGE UNITED

Year founded: 1919
Ground: Abbey Stadium (9,617)
Previous name: Abbey United
Highest ever crowd: 14,000, 1st May 1970 v Chelsea (friendly)
Nickname: The 'U's
Colours: Amber and black striped shirts, black shorts, amber and black socks

A CLUB which it would be fair to say has had more downs than ups in its history, in 1983/84 United played a record 31 matches without winning a game. They finished the season dropping into the Third Division.

● THEIR former managers include Ron Atkinson, who took the club from the Fourth to the Second Division between 1974–78, and John 'Long Ball' Beck, who is one of the most extroverted managers in the game. While at Cambridge he made the players have cold showers before games and kept the grass long in each corner of the pitch so long balls over opposing full backs were less likely to go out of play.

● FORMER club captain Steve Spriggs holds the record for league appearances – 416 between 1975–87.

● CAMBRIDGE United's highest ever goalscorer is Alan Biley, who sported a Rod Stewart haircut and netted 74 times between 1975–80.

Roll of Honour

Div 3 champions 1991
Div 4 champions 1977

CAMEROON

First World Cup appearance: Cameroon 0 Peru 0 (Spain, 1982)
Colours: Green shirts, red shorts, yellow socks

THE Indomitable Lions, as Cameroon are known, have qualified for four World Cup Finals tournaments – in 1982, 1990, 1994 and 1998 – which is more than any other African nation apart from Morocco (who have also qualified for four).

● Their best performance in the tournament came in Italia 90. In the opening game of the tournament they caused one of the biggest shocks in the history of international football when they beat World Champions (and eventual finalists) Argentina 1-0 despite finishing the game with nine men after two sendings off.

● Cameroon went on to become the first (and to date only) African country to reach the quarter finals of the tournament, and very nearly made it to the semis. They were 2-1 up against England with seven minutes on the clock before a couple of Gary Lineker penalties saved Bobby Robson's team.

● In 1998 in France they were denied a second round place in controversial circumstances after they had two goals disallowed against Chile, in a match they had to win but drew 1-1. During the match defender Rigobert Song became the first ever player during that match to be sent off in two consecutive World Cups.

● Roger Milla, who appeared three times in the World Cup Finals, became the oldest man to appear in the tournament in 1994, at the ripe old age of 42. His goal against Russia also made him the oldest ever World Cup finals scorer.

● Cameroon won the African Nations Cup in 1984 and 1988.

WORLD CUP RECORD

1930-66 Did not enter	1986 Did not qualify
1970 Did not qualify	1990 Quarter-finals
1974 Did not qualify	1994 Round 1
1978 Did not qualify	1998 Round 1
1982 Round 1	

SOL CAMPBELL

Born: Newham 18.9.74
Height: 6ft 2ins Position: Defender
Club career:
1992– Tottenham 168 (2)
International record:
1996– England 20 (0)

AN OUTSTANDING defender with maturity above and beyond his age, Tottenham's Sol Campbell is now a regular figure at the heart of the England defence who looked rock solid and capable at the back in France '98 and pretty good up front, too. If his headed goal against Argentina hadn't been disallowed for a foul by Shearer who knows how far England would have gone in the competition?

● CAMPBELL scored on his debut for Tottenham, coming on as a substitute against Chelsea in December 1992 and despite playing some of his football at White Hart Lane in midfield and even up front has settled into a defensive role at the club.

● A GRADUATE of the FA's National School of Excellence at Lilleshall, Campbell has represented England at schoolboy, youth, under-21 and B levels before making his debut for the full side in May 1996, one of the few players to represent England at every level. He was part of the England Youth team that won the European Youth Championships in 1993.

● HIS NAME Sol is short not – as many Tottenham fans believe – for Solomon but for Sulzeer.

Funny Old Game

In 1993, Cameroon's Roger Milla organised a tournament featuring different teams of 120 pygmies. He kept them under guard in the stadium. When asked why, a spokesman said, 'You don't know the pygmies. They are extremely difficult to keep in control.' When asked why they weren't fed properly he replied: 'They play better if they don't eat too much.'

The Cameroon team line-up and try to work out who the blokes standing on their right are

ERIC CANTONA

Born: Paris 24.5.66	
Height: 6ft 2ins	Position: Forward
Club career:	
1983–88	Auxerre 81 (23)
1988–89	Marseille 22 (5)
1989	Bordeaux 11 (6)
1989–90	Montpellier 33 (10)
1990–91	Marseille 18 (8)
1991–92	Nimes 17 (2)
1992–93	Leeds Utd 28 (9)
1993–97	Manchester United 143 (64)
International record:	
1987–	France 45 (19)

MAVERICK FRENCHMAN Eric Cantona shook Manchester United and the entire football world when he announced his retirement from the game at the end of the 1996/97 season.

● CANTONA is the most influential foreign player ever to grace the English game, winning the league championship five times in his six seasons this side of the Channel and landing the league and FA Cup 'double' twice.

● CANTONA became the first man to win back-to-back championships with different clubs, when in 1993 Manchester United won their first title for 26 years, twelve months after Leeds United. Manchester's maverick number 7 actually won a league title in four successive seasons – starting with Marseille in 1991 and ending with Manchester United in 1994.

● CANTONA was involved in one of the most controversial moments in English football history when he dived into the crowd to scissor-kick Crystal Palace 'fan' Matthew Simmons at Selhurst Park in January 1995.

● HE WAS banned for eight months, fined £10,000 by the FA (£20,000 by his club) and ordered to complete 120 hours of community service. He returned to the field in October 1995 to inspire United to another league and cup double, scoring the winning goal in the 1996 FA Cup Final, completing a six-month rehabilitation that had seen him booked just once, and picking up the English Footballer of the Year Award for the second time (1994 and 1996).

CAPS

LEGENDARY goalkeeper Peter Shilton holds the record number of international caps for a British player. He played for England no fewer than 125 times between 1971–90, despite the fact that his rival, Ray Clemence, played for England 61 times in that period.

● THE MOST capped player in world football is Saudi Arabia's Majed Abdullah who managed an incredible 147 caps for his country in a career that lasted from 1978–94.

● THE FIRST international caps were awarded by England in 1886, and to this day players do actually get a hand-made 'cap'.

● England caps are made by a company called Toye, Kenning & Spencer, who also make flags.

● THREE players have won caps for three different countries, including the great but not very patriotic Alfredo di Stefano, an Argentinian who also played for Spain and Colombia.

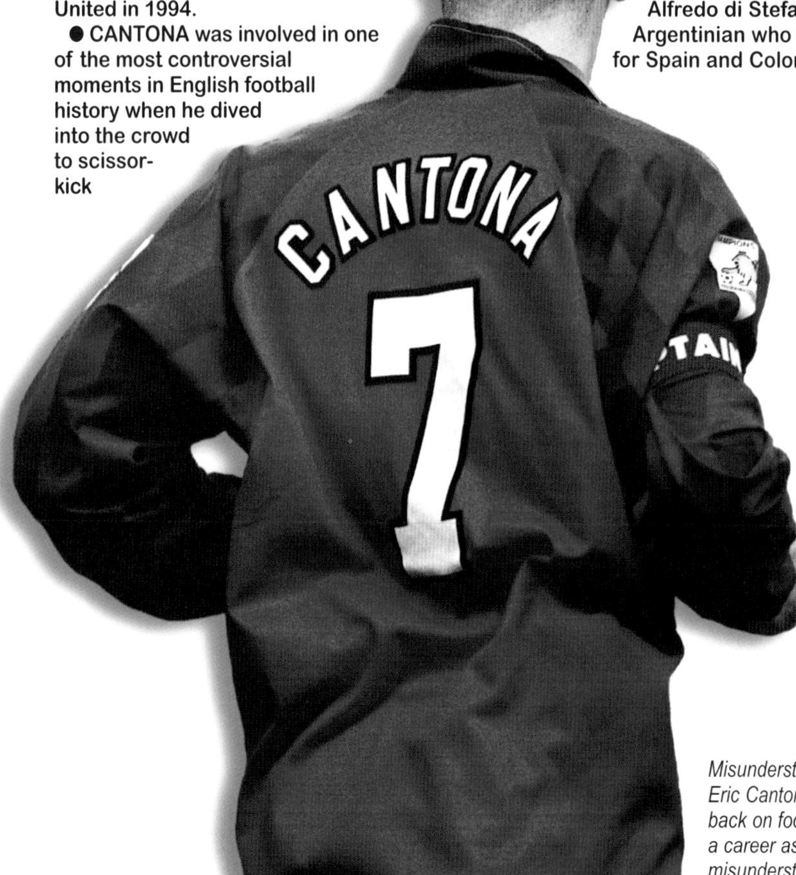

Misunderstood footballer Eric Cantona turns his back on football to pursue a career as a misunderstood actor

CAPTAINCY

There is nothing in the rules of football which states that a team must have a captain. However, teams have been captained since the 17th Century when – at top public schools like Eton and Harrow where the game first thrived – it was the captain's job to oversee the behaviour of his team and ensure sporting behaviour.

● ANDY FEELEY was only 17 years old when manager Frank Lord made him Hereford's captain in the 1979/80 season, making him the youngest captain recorded in British football.

● THE GREAT Bobby Moore proudly captained the England team a record 91 times between 1962–73, pulling on the skipper's armband just once more than Billy Wright (1946–59).

Don't Quote Me

'God can tell Heaven's XI to start getting changed, the captain has arrived.'

The Sun on Bobby Moore's death, 24.2.93

CARDIFF CITY

Year founded:	1899
Ground:	Ninian Park (14,601)
Previous names:	Riverside, Riverside Albion
Highest ever crowd:	57,893, 22nd April 1953 v Arsenal (Div 1)
Nickname:	The Bluebirds
Colours:	Blue shirts, white shorts, white socks

CARDIFF CITY are the only club ever to take the FA Cup out of England. In 1927 the Welsh club beat Arsenal 1-0 which sparked scenes of jubilation that are still talked about today. The Bluebirds side that day consisted of four Irishmen, three Scots and an Englishman as well as three Welshmen.

● Three years earlier, in 1924, Cardiff came within a whisker of becoming the first non-English champions of the Football League. They lost out on 'goal average' to Herbert Chapman's Huddersfield side, missing out on the title by 0.024 of a goal.

● Cardiff were involved in one of the most remarkable coincidences in the history of football when they were drawn away to Leeds United in the third round of the FA Cup three years running in 1955, 56 and 57. Even more remarkably the Bluebirds won each match by the same scoreline... 2–1.

Roll of Honour

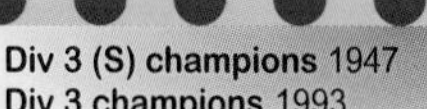

Div 3 (S) champions 1947
Div 3 champions 1993
FA Cup 1927

Steve McManaman and Gary Kelly are red carded during a regional heat of Come Dancing

CARDS

THE YELLOW AND RED CARD system was invented by English referee Ken Aston who thought of the idea while waiting at a set of traffic lights. They were first used in the Mexico World Cup of 1970 when the hosts played USSR in the opening game... five yellows were shown but no reds.

● FIRST INTRODUCED in the English league on 2nd October 1976, David Wagstaffe of Blackburn Rovers has the dubious honour of being shown the first ever red card in Britain. The system was withdrawn in 1981 as referees were getting 'too flashy' and then re-introduced in 1987 because they were deemed 'crowd friendly'.

● VINNIE JONES is the proud record holder of the fastest ever booking in English football. On 15th February 1992, while playing for Chelsea, he was yellow carded after just three seconds of the FA Cup tie against Sheffield United. Surprisingly enough he was later sent off.

● THE QUICKEST sending-off in League history befell Crewe's Mark Smith, who lasted just 19 seconds of the match against Darlington on 12th March 1994 before seeing red. He probably didn't even have to bother with the early bath.

CARLISLE UNITED

Year founded: 1903
Ground: Brunton Park (17,500)
Previous name: Shaddongate United
Highest ever crowd: 27,603, 7th February 1970 v Middlesbrough (FA Cup rd 5)
Nickname: The Blues
Colours: Blue shirts, white shorts, blue socks

CARLISLE's proudest moment came when, having won promotion to the First Division in 1974, they sat at the top of the table in August. Their success, however, was short-lived and they were relegated at the end of the season.

● CARLISLE's travelling supporters have to spend more on travel than any other fans as Brunton Park is also the most isolated British League ground. The nearest other league club is Newcastle United, a total of 58 miles away.

● Between 1961 and 1965 Carlisle United inhabited a different division for five seasons in a row. Promoted from division four at the end of the 1961/62 season, they stayed up for only one season before being relegated. The following season they were promoted again and they followed that success by winning the third division title and reaching the heady heights of division two.

● The club is currently run by maverick chairman Michael Knighton who once famously claimed he had seen a UFO and has even had a go at picking the team.

Roll of Honour

Div 3 champions 1965, 1995

ROBERTO CARLOS

Born: Garca (Brazil) 10.4.73
Height: 5ft 7ins Position: Defender
Club career:
1991-93 Uniao Sao Joao (Brazil)
1993-95 Palmeiras (Brazil) 45 (4)
1995-96 Inter Milan 30 (5)
1996- Real Madrid 37 (4)
International record:
1995- Brazil 52 (2)

Runner-up to Ronaldo as FIFA World Player of the Year in 1997, Roberto Carlos probably possesses the most powerful left-foot in world football. When he was with Inter Milan one shot was measured at a blistering 150 km/h.

● The crop-haired Brazilian left-back is one of the game's deadliest deadball specialists and scores a high proportion of his goals from free kicks. His 40-yard swerving exocet against France at the 1997 Tournoi was hailed by Glenn Hoddle as one of the greatest goals ever. 'I don't think I have ever seen a ball bent as much,' said the England boss.

● Roberto Carlos joined Inter Milan from Palmeiras for £4.5 million in 1995. He scored the winning goal on his league debut against Vicenza, but didn't settle in Italy and moved to Real Madrid the following season, becoming the first Brazilian to play for the Spanish giants. In May 1998 Roberto Carlos played for Real in the Champions' Cup Final against Juventus.

THE TOP 5 SILLIEST FRANCE 98 HAIRCUTS

The entire Romanian team
(Bleached hair, red faces)
Taribo West (Nigeria)
(10 new uses for green string)
Carlos Valderrama
(Still frizzy after all these years)
Emmanuel Petit
('Winning was cool, man, you know?')
Zvonimar Boban
('Number 10 at the back, please')

CELTIC

Year founded: 1888
Ground: Celtic Park (45,000)
Highest ever crowd: 92,000, 1st January 1938 v Rangers (Div 1)
Nickname: The Bhoys
Colours: Green-and-white hoops, white shorts and socks

THE FIRST BRITISH team ever to win the European Cup, Celtic are one of the world's most famous clubs.

● In winning the Scottish league for the 37th time in 1997/98, Celtic denied Rangers the pleasure of beating their famous record of nine titles in a row. Ten in a row for their arch enemies would have been a fate worse than death for most Celtic fans.

● It was under legendary manager Jock Stein in the 1960s and early 1970s that Celtic recorded their famous nine title victories in a row. The side included such great players as Jim Craig, Billy McNeill, Tommy Gemmell and Jimmy Johnstone. This is a world record (also held by CSKA Sofia of Bulgaria, MTKA Budapest of Romania and Rangers).

● THE GREATEST ever Celtic side, nicknamed the 'Lisbon Lions' and managed by the late, great Stein, became the first British club to win the European Cup when they beat Inter Milan 2–1 in Portugal in 1967. They remain the only Scottish club to win Europe's premier club event.

● INTER WERE then the masters of the defensive system nicknamed 'catenaccio' or 'big chain', but Celtic managed to force their way through. Stein was a great motivating force, and got the side's spirit going by getting them to sing the Celtic song before the match – much to the Italians' bemusement – and sitting in Inter Milan manager Helenio Herrera's seat and refusing to budge. Gemmell and Chalmers got the goals, after Inter had gone ahead from the penalty spot after eight minutes. Such were the celebrations that some Celtic fans are said to have never returned from Lisbon.

● THAT 1966/67 Celtic season was the most successful in British club history, the club winning every competition they entered... the Scottish League, Scottish Cup and Scottish League Cup as well as the European Cup.

● CENTRAL DEFENDER and skipper of the Lisbon Lions side was Billy McNeill, who went on to become the Bhoys' manager and made a record 486 appearances for the club between 1957–75. He was one of four of the Lisbon Lions to manage the team.

● CELTIC'S Jimmy McGrory, with 398 League goals between 1922 and 1938, is the highest ever scorer in Scottish football. If you add his Scottish Cup goals and those he scored whilst playing at Clydebank his total rises above 500, an unparallelled feat in the country, and one which will probably never be beaten.

● WITH A CAPACITY of 60,000, after several years of dramatic redevelopment Celtic Park now boasts the biggest capacity of any club ground in Britain. The actual pitch is the largest in the Scottish Premier League at 8,625 square yards.

● CELTIC ARE the most successful team ever in the Scottish Cup, with a total of 30 wins in the final. They have also appeared more than any other team in the final, with a total of 47 appearances.

● 1997/98 WAS CELTIC'S 101st season in the top flight in Scotland, more than any other club apart from Rangers who have appeared in the same number.

● CELTIC HOLD the record for the longest unbeaten run in Scottish football, with 62 matches undefeated from 13th November 1915 to 21st April 1917 when Kilmarnock finally beat them 2–0 at Parkhead.

Roll of Honour

Div 1 champions 1893, 1984, 1896, 1898, 1905, 1906, 1907, 1908, 1909, 1910, 1914, 1915, 1916, 1917, 1919, 1922, 1926, 1936, 1938, 1954, 1966, 1967, 1968, 1969, 1970, 1971, 1972, 1973, 1974
Premier Division champions 1977, 1979, 1981, 1982, 1986, 1988, 1998
Scottish Cup 1892, 1899, 1900, 1904, 1907, 1908, 1911, 1912, 1914, 1923, 1925, 1927, 1931, 1933, 1937, 1951, 1954, 1965, 1967, 1969, 1971, 1972, 1974, 1975, 1977, 1980, 1985, 1988, 1989, 1995
League Cup 1957, 1958, 1966, 1967, 1968, 1969, 1970, 1975, 1983, 1998
European Cup 1967

Celtic's Post-War Record

47 DI 7th	64 DI 3rd	81 PR 1st
48 DI 12th	65 DI 8th	82 PR 1st
49 DI 6th	66 DI 1st	83 PR 2nd
50 DI 5th	67 DI 1st	84 PR 2nd
51 DI 7th	68 DI 1st	85 PR 2nd
52 DI 9th	69 DI 1st	86 PR 1st
53 DI 8th	70 DI 1st	87 PR 2nd
54 DI 1st	71 DI 1st	88 PR 1st
55 DI 2nd	72 DI 1st	89 PR 3rd
56 DI 5th	73 DI 1st	90 PR 5th
57 DI 5th	74 DI 1st	91 PR 3rd
58 DI 3rd	75 DI 3rd	92 PR 3rd
59 DI 6th	76 PR 2nd	93 PR 3rd
60 DI 9th	77 PR 1st	94 PR 4th
61 DI 4th	78 PR 5th	95 PR 4th
62 DI 3rd	79 PR 1st	96 PR 2nd
63 DI 4th	80 PR 2nd	97 PR 2nd
		98 PR 1st

Celtic's Billy McNeill is presented with the European Cup in 1967, the only Scottish club ever to win the trophy

'You'll never walk alone,' the Kop's anthem at Liverpool, was the first pop song to make it onto the football terraces.

Julio Iglesias
(Real Madrid)
Eddie Large
(Manchester City)
Des O'Connor
(Northampton Town)
Rod Stewart
(Brentford)
Stan Boardman
(Liverpool)

CHANTS

FOOTBALL fans have sung at games since Victorian times, but 'modern' terrace chanting started at Liverpool in the mid-1960s when the Kop started singing songs by The Beatles and other contemporary pop groups. These included Gerry and the Pacemakers' 'You'll Never Walk Alone', which is still sung in the stands all over the country.

● A survey in 1996 by Total Football magazine discovered that the four clubs with the loudest-singing fans in the Premiership were Leeds United, Newcastle United, West Ham and Arsenal. Poor old Wimbledon were the quietest.

● THE MOST common chant at football grounds from Newcastle to Mansfield goes: 'We're by far the greatest team the world has ever seen'. Brazilian fans at the World Cup in 1970, who were best qualified to sing it, didn't.

HERBERT CHAPMAN

Born: Sheffield 19.1.1878
Died: 6.1.34

HERBERT CHAPMAN is Arsenal's greatest ever manager. He won one FA Cup and two League Championships in his nine years at the club, before dying of pneumonia while watching the third team in action in 1934. His Arsenal team went on to win three consecutive titles.

● The side he built were dubbed 'Lucky Arsenal' but there was a lot more to it than luck. Chapman was a visionary ahead of his time. The first manager to use a centre back to bolster the defence after the change in the offside law in 1925, he also experimented with white balls, rubber studs, players' numbers and floodlighting before they became an accepted part of the game.

● CHAPMAN managed Leeds City and Huddersfield Town before he joined Arsenal. His four-year spell at Huddersfield was the most successful era in the club's history – they won one FA Cup and two consecutive Championships under his management, with a third following the year after he left.

CHARITY SHIELD

SINCE 1928 the Charity Shield has been an annual fixture, played usually between the League Champions and the FA Cup Winners. Between 1908–28 it was played between the League Champions and the Southern League Champions, or between a select team of amateurs against a select team of professionals.

● IN 1967 Spurs keeper Pat Jennings scored a goal from his own area against Manchester United, the longest-distance goal in the competition.

● IN THE first Charity Shield to be played at Wembley in 1974, champions Leeds met cup winners Liverpool. Kevin Keegan and Billy Bremner were sent off for fighting, the first British players to be dismissed at Wembley.

● THE highest-scoring Charity Shield took place in 1911 when Manchester United beat Swindon Town 8–4.

Wembley Charity Shield Matches

1974	Liverpool 1 Leeds 1 (trophy shared)
1975	Derby 2 West Ham 0
1976	Liverpool 1 Southampton 0
1977	Liverpool 0 Manchester United 0 (trophy shared)
1978	Nottingham Forest 5 Ipswich 0
1979	Liverpool 3 Arsenal 1
1980	Liverpool 1 West Ham 0
1981	Aston Villa 2 Spurs 2 (trophy shared)
1982	Liverpool 1 Spurs 0
1983	Manchester United 2 Liverpool 0
1984	Everton 1 Liverpool 0
1985	Everton 2 Manchester United 0
1986	Everton 1 Liverpool 1 (trophy shared)
1987	Everton 1 Coventry 0
1988	Liverpool 2 Wimbledon 1
1989	Liverpool 1 Arsenal 0
1990	Liverpool 1 Manchester United 1 (trophy shared)
1991	Arsenal 0 Spurs 0 (trophy shared)
1992	Leeds 4 Liverpool 3
1993	Manchester United 1 Arsenal 1 (United won on penalties)
1994	Manchester United 2 Blackburn 0
1995	Everton 1 Blackburn 0
1996	Manchester United 4 Newcastle 0
1997	Manchester United 1 Chelsea 1 (United won on penalties)

JOHN CHARLES

Born: Swansea 27.12.31
Height 6ft 2ins Position: Forward/defender
Club career:

1949–57	Leeds United 297 (150)
1957–62	Juventus 154 (93)
1962	Leeds United 11 (3)
1962–63	Roma 10 (6)
1963–66	Cardiff City 66 (19)

International record:
1950–65 Wales 38 (15)

WHEN John Charles won his first Welsh cap against Northern Ireland in March 1950, aged 18 years and 71 days, he became the youngest man to pull on the famous red jersey (a record beaten by Ryan Giggs in 1991). Charles was one of the stars of Wales' greatest side, which qualified for the 1958 World Cup in Sweden, where they beat Hungary and only lost 1–0 to the eventual winners Brazil. He won 38 caps for Wales.

● HIS 38-goal tally in the 1956/57 season, which put him at the top of the First Division chart, is still a Leeds record. He was soon bought up by Juventus for £65,000, a British transfer record at the time.

● UNLIKE many Brits who followed, Charles was a great success in Italy, where he scored 93 times in 155 games and helped bring three Italian Championships and two Italian Cups to Turin.

● NICKNAMED the 'Gentle Giant' in Italy, Charles was never booked or sent off in a career that brought 270 goals in 538 appearances.

CHARLTON ATHLETIC

Year founded: 1905
Ground: The Valley (15,000)
Highest ever crowd: 75,031, 12th February 1938 v Aston Villa (FA Cup rd 5)
Nickname: The Addicks
Colours: Red shirts, white shorts, red socks

CHARLTON ATHLETIC have three nicknames: The Robins, The Valiants and, most popularly, The Addicks. They were first called The Addicks after a chippy owner whose shop was used by the club for post-match meals in the early 1900s.

● CHARLTON's stadium, the Valley, had the biggest capacity in England in the early 1970s, with room for 67,000 fans. But the Addicks had to vacate it in 1985 to share Selhurst Park with Crystal Palace and then Upton Park with West Ham before returning to a much smaller Valley in 1992.

● FANS OF Charlton formed a political party to persuade the club to return to its traditional home when Greenwich Council opposed the renovation of the stadium. The Valley Party polled an impressive 14,838 votes in the council elections, which was bigger than their average crowd that season.

● CHARLTON were the first team to play in the FA Cup Final after being beaten in an earlier round. In 1946 they lost 2–1 at Fulham but had previously won 3–1 at home so went through on aggregate. They lost the final 4–1 to Derby County, with defender Bert Turner the first man in a Cup final to score for both sides (an own goal 5 minutes from the end and a strike for Charlton a minute later). At 36 years 312 days he was also the oldest ever scorer in the final. Charlton got to the final the next year, this time lifting the Cup after a 1–0 victory over Burnley.

● SAM BARTRAM, who many consider one of the finest goalkeepers ever, played a record 582 games for the club between 1934–56.

Roll of Honour

Div 3 (S) champions 1929, 1935
FA Cup 1947

Did You Know?

Charlton Athletic were the victors in the only ever English league match to finish with a 7–6 scoreline, beating Huddersfield Town on 21st December 1957 after being 5–1 down and reduced to 10 men.

SIR BOBBY CHARLTON

Born: Ashington 11.10.37
Height: 5ft 9ins Position: Midfield
Club career:
1954–73 Manchester United 754 (247)
1974–75 Preston North End 38 (8)
International record:
1958–70 England: 106 (49)

THE MOST famous English footballer ever, Sir Bobby Charlton won everything the game had to offer including 106 England caps, a World Cup winners medal and the European Cup. He is the highest ever international goalscorer for England, with a total of 49.

● EUROPEAN Footballer of the Year in 1966 after the World Cup, Sir Bobby made a big impact on the game of football right from the very start, scoring twice on his Manchester United debut against Charlton Athletic in 1956.

● HE WON the league championship three times, most crucially in 1967 as it set United up for the greatest day in their history when they won the European Cup, beating Benfica 4–1 at Wembley. Charlton scored twice.

● SIR BOBBY left Manchester United in 1973, having scored 247 goals in 754 games, a club record.

JACK CHARLTON

Born: Ashington 8.5.35
Height: 6ft 1in Position: Defender
Club career:
1953–73 Leeds United 629 (71)
International record:
1965–70 England 35 (6)

THE GIRAFFE, as Jack Charlton was affectionately known, made a record 629 appearances for Leeds United, his only club, winning the League Championship, the FA Cup and the Fairs Cup while at Elland Road.

● CHARLTON also played a key role in England's World Cup winning side of 1966 and in all won 35 caps for his country. He was made Footballer of the Year in 1967.

● HE MOVED into management in 1973, and, following spells at Middlesbrough, Sheffield Wednesday and Newcastle, became the most successful manager in the history of the Republic of Ireland, the first man to take them to a major championship final.

● APPOINTED in 1986, Charlton led Ireland to the 1988 European Championship and two World Cup finals, guiding the team to the quarter-finals in Italia 90.

Bobby Charlton had one of the fullest heads of hair in the League in the 1958 Cup Final against Bolton. Unfortunately he played better when he was as bald as a coot, because Bolton won this match 2–0

CHEATING

THE FIRST recorded incidence of match fixing saw the great Wales international Billy Meredith banned for a season for offering Aston Villa's skipper Alec Leake £10 to throw a game against Manchester City in 1905/06. Leake refused the money and Villa won 3–2.

● BETWEEN 1963–66 over 30 players were involved in the biggest match fixing scandal in British history. Ringleader James Gauld, a Scottish forward, set up a syndicate to rig matches for betting purposes, bringing in £4,000 a month... ten times the average wage for a player.

● IN DECEMBER 1962 Santos of Brazil were playing a friendly match against Sheffield Wednesday when they were found to be playing with 12 men!

● IN A VITAL 1976 Copa Libertadores cup match in Argentina, Independiente were losing 1–0 at home to River Plate when some 'bright' home fans had the idea that by getting the match suspended a replay would be ordered, so they sabotaged the floodlights – causing the longest delay in a cup match on record (87 minutes) with 20 minutes to go. The referee wanted to suspend the match but was persuaded to wait for an electrician to fix the fault!

● THE most famous piece of cheating was when Diego Maradona fisted a ball into the net against England in the quarter-finals of the 1986 World Cup. After the match Maradona said the goal had been scored by 'the Hand of God, and the head of Diego'.

Gianluca Vialli's former career as a piggy back racer can come in very handy in the Premiership

Did You Know?

Chelsea were the first club in Football League history to concede goals to seven different players in one match. Leeds were their conquerers in 1967/68 - one of the goals was an own goal by the hapless Marvin Hinton.

CHELSEA

Year founded: 1905
Ground: Stamford Bridge (41,000)
Highest ever crowd: 82,905, 12th October 1935 v Arsenal (Div 1)
Nickname: The Blues
Colours: Royal blue shirts, royal blue shorts and white socks

CHELSEA ARE the only London team apart from Arsenal and Tottenham ever to win the league title, their one and only triumph coming in 1955.

● THIS TRIUMPH was achieved with the lowest points total of any title-winning team in the post-war period. The Blues' tally of 52 points, though, provided them a four-point buffer from second-place Wolves.

● Chelsea's 2-0 FA Cup win over Middlesbrough in the 1997 FA Cup Final gave the club its first major trophy in 26 years. They won the League Cup the following season, amazingly beating Middlesbrough 2-0 again which prompted chants of 'can we play you every year?' from the Blues' faithful.

● NEW GAFFER Gianluca Vialli, who replaced the sacked Ruud Gullit in February 1998, capped an incredibly successful start to his managerial career when he helped Chelsea become the first English club to win the European Cup Winners' Cup for the second time. The Blues' 1-0 win over Stuttgart, thanks to a first-touch goal by Gianfranco Zola, meant the bald Italian had won two major trophies in just three months.

● THE CLUB CAN virtually field a team of famous fans: John Major is an occasional visitor to Stamford Bridge, film director Sir Richard Attenborough is the club's Life Vice-President, Blur frontman Damon Albarn is a keen supporter, as is comedian David Baddiel. Then, of course, there's David Mellor. The former Heritage Secretary allegedly dressed in The Blues' kit while romping with an actress – a sex scandal that hit the tabloid headlines and led to his resignation as a minister.

● CHELSEA's most humiliating experience was in 1931, on a freezing rainy October afternoon in Blackpool. The 6,000 hardy souls who'd braved the elements to watch the match jeered them for being Southern softies as five Chelsea players failed to finish the game because of the cold, leaving only six Blues on the pitch. Blackpool won 4–0.

● CHELSEA took part in the first unresolved FA Cup final at Wembley – a 2–2 draw with Leeds in 1970. They won the replay 2–1 at Old Trafford to become the only team to win the FA Cup away from Wembley in the post-war era. The following year they went on to win the Cup Winners' Cup – again after a replay – beating Real Madrid 2–1 in Athens. It was the last replay in a final of the competition.

● PETER OSGOOD scored in every round of the FA Cup in 1970, and remains the last player to achieve this feat.

● BOBBY TAMBLING is Chelsea's leading scorer. Between 1958–70 he notched up 164 league goals. Jimmy Greaves scored the most goals in one season – an amazing 41 in 1961.

● IN THE early 1990s Chelsea had three successive managers who had all scored FA Cup-winning goals. Ian Porterfield scored the only goal for Sunderland in the 1973 Final, Dave Webb – briefly manager at The Bridge in 1993 – provided the winning goal for The Blues in 1970, and Glenn Hoddle's penalty was a match-winner for Tottenham in 1982.

● CHELSEA strolled to the Second Division championship with a record 99 points in 1989. The Blues were only beaten on five occasions – a record for a 46-match Second Division campaign.

● IN 1986 Chelsea became the first

Chelsea's Post-War Record

47 D1 15th	64 D1 5th	81 D2 12th
48 D1 18th	65 D1 3rd	82 D2 12th
49 D1 13th	66 D1 5th	83 D2 18th
50 D1 13th	67 D1 9th	84 D2 1st
51 D1 20th	68 D1 6th	85 D1 6th
52 D1 19th	69 D1 5th	86 D1 6th
53 D1 19th	70 D1 3rd	87 D1 14th
54 D1 8th	71 D1 6th	88 D1 18th
55 D1 1st	72 D1 7th	89 D2 1st
56 D1 16th	73 D1 12th	90 D1 5th
57 D1 12th	74 D1 17th	91 D1 11th
58 D1 11th	75 D1 21st	92 D1 14th
59 D1 14th	76 D2 11th	93 PR 11th
60 D1 18th	77 D2 2nd	94 PR 14th
61 D1 12th	78 D1 16th	95 PR 11th
62 D1 22nd	79 D1 22nd	96 PR 11th
63 D2 2nd	80 D2 4th	97 PR 6th
		98 PR 4th

Chesea fans salute the Blues' first FA Cup win back in 1970

winners of the now defunct Full Members' Cup, beating Manchester City 5–4 at Wembley in an entertaining final.

Roll of Honour

Div 1 champions 1955
Div 2 champions 1984, 1989
FA Cup 1970, 1997
League Cup 1965
European Cup Winners' Cup 1971

CHESTER CITY

Year founded: 1884
Ground: Deva Stadium (6,000)
Previous name: Chester
Highest ever crowd: 20,500, 16th January 1952 v Chelsea (FA Cup rd 3)
Nickname: The Blues
Colours: Blue-and-white-striped shirts, blue shorts and socks

IN 1936 Chester thrashed York City 12–0 in the Third Division (North), their biggest win in a history not exactly awash with glorious achievements. Their record defeat was an 11–2 drubbing by Oldham Athletic, also in the Third Division (North), in January 1952.

● LEGENDARY Welsh striker Ian Rush cost Liverpool £300,000 when they bought him from Chester. It seems a snip, but it is still Chester's record sale.

● GARY TALBOT scored three times in three minutes for The Blues against Crewe in November 1964, one of the quickest hat-tricks in the history of the game.

● ON NEW YEAR's Day 1966 Chester suffered one of the most unfortunate coincidences in the history of the game when both their full-backs – Ray and Bryn Jones (no relation) – broke their left legs.

● RAY GILL holds the record for league appearances for Chester, having played 408 games for them in 1951-62. Chester's Deva Stadium has the third smallest capacity in the football league, holding a maximum of only 6,000 fans.

CHESTERFIELD

Year founded: 1866
Ground: Recreation Ground (8,880)
Highest ever crowd: 30,968, 7th April 1939 v Newcastle (Div 2)
Nickname: The Spirites
Colours: Blue shirts, white shorts, blue socks

IN 1996/97 Chesterfield were one refereeing decision away from becoming the first club from outside the top two divisions to reach the FA Cup Final. If referee David Elleray hadn't ruled out Jonathon Howards's goal (TV replays showed the ball had crossed the line) they would have been 3–1 up in the FA Cup semi-final against Middlesbrough with 22 minutes to go. As it was the game went to a replay and they ended up losing 3–0.

● IN A COCA-COLA CUP match in October 1993, Chesterfield included the fresh-faced Kevin Davies in their side: at 16 years 104 days he was the youngest player ever to appear in the competition.

● OVER THE YEARS The Spirites have become known as being a bit of a goalkeeping academy. Great goalkeepers who have played for Chesterfield include Gordon Banks and Sam Hardy.

Roll of Honour

Div 3 (N) champions 1931, 1936
Div 4 champions 1970, 1985

CHILE

First international: Argentina 3 Chile 1, Buenos Aires 1910
First World Cup appearance: Chile 3, Mexico 0 (Uruguay, 1930)
Highest capped player: Leonel Sanchez (85)
Highest goalscorer: Carlos Caszely (29)
Best win: 7–1 v Bolivia, 1926, and Ecuador, 1955
Worst defeat: 0–6 v Argentina, 1923, and Peru, 1995
Colours: Red shirts, blue shorts and white socks

CHILE didn't have a very good start to their history in international football. It took them 23 games before they recorded their first win. But when they won, they certainly won, beating Bolivia 7–1, which still matches their highest ever victory.

● CHILE hosted the 1962 World Cup Finals, and produced their best performance in the competition, reaching the semi-finals before going out to eventual winners Brazil.

● THEIR TIE against Italy in the qualifying stages of the tournament is one of the bloodiest games in soccer history, dubbed 'the Battle of Santiago'. One Italian had his nose broken, two were sent off, there was a mass brawl and the match nearly had to be abandoned. Chile eventually won 2–0.

WORLD CUP RECORD

1930	First round	1970	Did not qualify
1934	Did not enter	1974	First round
1938	Did not enter	1978	Did not qualify
1950	First round	1982	First round
1954	Did not enter	1986	Did not qualify
1958	Did not qualify	1990	Did not qualify
1962	Third place	1994	Did not enter
1966	First round	1998	Second round

CLEAN SHEETS

ON 31st JANUARY 1987, when Adrian Sprott scored for Hamilton Academical against Rangers in the Scottish Premier League, it ended a run of 14 clean sheets by goalkeeper Chris Woods, which had lasted 1,196 minutes, a British record.

● THE WORLD record for clean sheets is held by Abel Resino of Atletico Madrid who went for 1,275 minutes before he let one in from Enrique of Sporting Gijon during the 1990/91 season.

● GORDON BANKS kept a record six consecutive clean sheets for England in 1966. Ex-Italian keeper Dino Zoff, however, holds the international record having spent 1,143 minutes between the azzurro posts without conceding a goal between September 1972 and June 1974.

RAY CLEMENCE

Born: Skegness 5.8.48
Ht: 6ft 3ins Position: Goalkeeper
Club career:
1965–67 Scunthorpe Utd 48
1967–80 Liverpool 470
1980–87 Tottenham Hotspur 240
International record
1972–83 England 61

RAY CLEMENCE, Livepool's goalkeeper during the most successful period in their history, won three European Cups, five league titles, an FA Cup and a League Cup with the Anfield club. He was even awarded the MBE.

● A HIGHLY AGILE, super-consistent keeper who was like lightning off his line, Clemence held the appearances record for European club competitions – 124 – until it was beaten in 1998.

● CLEMENCE made 61 appearances for his country although this woud have been many more without Peter Shilton's giant presence (under England manager Ron Greenwood the pair took it in turns between the sticks).

● In 1990 Clemence moved to Spurs for £300,000 where he played more than 240 league games. Then in 1996 he became manager of Barnet, a post from which he retired to take up a coaching position with Glenn Hoddle's new England regime.

BRIAN CLOUGH

Born: Middlesbrough 21.3.35

BRIAN CLOUGH is the second longest-serving post-war league manager, having held the reins at Nottingham Forest for 18 years between 1975–93. It was the most successful period in the club's history, during which they won two European Cups, one League Championship and four League Cups.

● BEFORE moving to Forest, Clough won the League Championship with unfancied Derby County in 1972. So in 1978 he became the first manager since Herbert Chapman to win the title with two separate clubs, a feat repeated by Kenny Dalglish in 1995.

● He earned his managerial spurs at Hartlepool, and also had unsuccessful spells at Leeds United and Brighton and Hove Albion.

● Clough was a prolific goalscorer as a player, scoring 254 goals for Middlesbrough and Sunderland (a post war record for both clubs) before injury forced him out of the game. Indeed, he was the quickest player in league history to amass 200 goals, doing so in just 219 games. He also won two caps for England.

Brian Clough, who once said: 'if God had meant football to be played in the air he'd have put grass on the clouds'

CLOUGHIE ON...

Dalglish
'He had a huge arse. It came down below his knees and that's where he got his strength from.'

Coaching
'I told Roy McFarland to go and have his bloody hair cut – that's coaching at the top level.'

Hooliganism
'Football hooligans? Well there are 92 club Chairmen, for a start.'

Footballer's IQ's
'Show me a talented player who's thick and I'll show you a player who has problems.'

Long Ball Football
'If God had wanted football played in the air he wouldn't have put grass on the ground.'

CLYDE

Year founded: 1878
Ground: Broadwood Stadium, Cumbernauld (8,008)
Highest ever crowd: 52,000, 21st November 1908 v Rangers (Div 1)
Nickname: The Bully Wee
Colours: White shirts, black shorts, black socks

THE BULLY WEE as they are known (either because in the past they were always 'bullying' big boys Rangers and Celtic or because of an old sea shanty that mentions the river Clyde) were homeless between 1986 and 1996. They shared with Partick Thistle (Scotland's first ever ground share) and then Hamilton before they moved into their brand new Broadwood Stadium.

● BEFORE THE South Stand was opened in 1996 it was Scotland's breeziest ground, thanks to its two touchline stands and open ends.

● CLYDE's record win was over Cowdenbeath in 1951: an 11–1 walkover. Their worst defeat came in 1879, when they lost 11–0 to Dumbarton, and again the following year, when they were humiliated by Rangers by the same margin.

● CLYDE HAVE won eight divisional titles outside the top flight, more than any other Scottish club. However they are also Scotland's most relegated club, suffering the heartbreak of failure 11 times.

● THE CLUB's most lucrative sale was Pat Nevin, who went to Chelsea in July 1983 for £95,000.

Roll of Honour

Div 2 champions 1905, 1952, 1957, 1962, 1973
Second Division champions: 1978, 1982, 1993
Scottish Cup 1939, 1955, 1958

CLYDEBANK

Year founded: 1965
Ground: Boghead Park (shared with Dumbarton) (5,503)
Highest ever crowd: 14,900, 10th February 1965 v Hibernian (Scottish Cup rd 1)
Nickname: The Bankies
Colours: Red and white striped shirts, black shorts, blue socks

CLYDEBANK won the Second Division championship in 1976 and were First Division runners-up in 1977, becoming the first Scottish club to be promoted in successive seasons.

● JIM FALLON has played more times for The Bankies than any other player, with 620 appearances between 1968–86. Pop superstars Wet Wet Wet sponsored the club in 1993. Their name is spelt out on the floodlights.

● DAVIE COOPER, who tragically died of a brain haemorrhage in March 1995, was the club's most famous discovery. He returned to Clydebank as player-coach after starring for Rangers, Motherwell and Scotland. The biggest transfer fee the club has received is the £175,000 they were paid by Airdrie for the services of Owen Coyle.

● CLYDEBANK are currently ground-sharing with Dumbarton at Boghead Park. A projected move to Dublin for 1998/99 was scuppered when FIFA passed a ruling in June 1998 that clubs cannot play their home matches in foreign countries.

Roll of Honour

Second Division champions 1976

COLCHESTER UNITED

Year founded: 1937
Ground: Layer Road (7,190)
Highest ever crowd: 19,072, 27th November 1948 v Reading (FA Cup rd 1)
Nickname: The 'U's
Colours: Blue-and-white-striped shirts, white shorts, white socks

THE 'U's finest moment was in 1971 when, as a Fourth Division side, they overcame a star-studded Leeds side, top of Division One, 3–2 in the FA Cup 5th round at Layer Road. At one point they led 3–0! However, Everton beat the minnows 5–0 in the quarter-finals.

● THEIR greatest comeback was more recent – 3–0 down in 18 minutes against Scunthorpe United in February 1995, they eventually ran out 4–3 winners.

● IN 1990 Colchester sank to their lowest ebb when they suffered relegation to the Vauxhall Conference, but they recovered and were promoted again in 1992.

● IN 1948 Colchester reached the FA Cup Fifth Round as a non-league side, beating first division Huddersfield before going out to Blackpool, the eventual runners-up. In 1997 they reached the Auto Windscreens Shield final, cruelly losing to Carlisle on penalties at Wembley.

ANDY COLE

Born: Nottingham 15.10.71
Height: 5ft 11ins Position: Striker
Club career:
1990–92 Arsenal 1 (0)
1991–92 Fulham (loan) 13 (3)
1992–93 Bristol City 41 (20)
1993–95 Newcastle United 70 (55)
1995– Manchester United 103 (44)
International record:
1995– England 2 (0)

ANDY COLE's £6 million pound move from Newcastle to Manchester United in 1995 made him the most expensive player in British football at the time. On 4th March that year he became the highest scorer in a single Premier League match when, during United's 9-0 rout of Ipswich Town, he scored five times.

● HIS 34 Premier League goals in 1993/94 for Newcastle United is the second highest 'goals in a season' tally in Newcastle's long and illustrious history. He made his England debut against Uruguay in March 1995 but failed to make much of an impression (despite hitting the bar) and has rarely figured since.

● COLE STARTED out at Arsenal, but only made one league appearance before being transferred to Bristol City for £500,000 in March 1992, a record fee or the club.

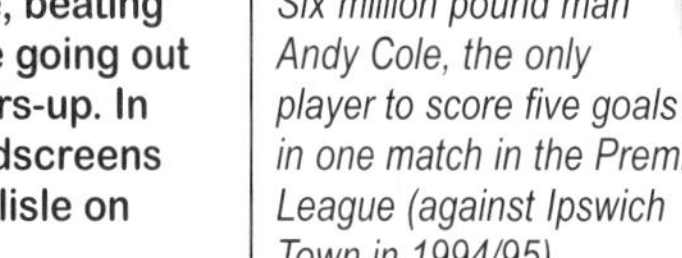
Six million pound man Andy Cole, the only player to score five goals in one match in the Premier League (against Ipswich Town in 1994/95)

JOHN COLLINS

Born: Galashiels 31.1.68
Height: 5ft 7ins Position: Midfield
Club career:
1985–90 Hibernian 163 (15)
1990–96 Celtic 225 (43)
1996– Monaco 28 (6)
International record:
1988– Scotland 52 (11)

JOHN COLLINS became one of the first British players to benefit from the Bosman ruling when he made a shock signing for Monaco in the summer of 1996 after playing for six years at Celtic. He became a mainstay in the Monte Carlo-based side as Newcastle found to their dismay in the 1996/97 UEFA Cup quarter final.

● THE GOALSCORING midfielder is something of a free-kick specialist, as he showed before his move to French football by scoring from two almost identical long range set pieces in consecutive Ibrox derbies in 1994/95.

● DURING the France 98 World Cup Collins passed the 50 cap mark for Scotland and his penalty equaliser against Brazil was the Scots' most memorable moment of another ultimately disappointing tournament.

STAN COLLYMORE

Born: Stone 22.1.71
Height: 6ft 2ins Position: Striker
Club career:
1991–93 Crystal Palace 20 (1)
1993 Southend United 30 (15)
1993–95 Nottingham Forest 65 (41)
1995–97 Liverpool 61 (26)
1997– Aston Villa 25 (6)
International record:
1995– England 2 (0)

STAN COLLYMORE was Britain's most expensive player when he moved from Nottingham Forest to Liverpool in the summer of 1995, for £8.5 million.

● TWO YEARS later, though, he was on the move to Aston Villa for a club record £7 million after a turbulent if not totally unsuccessful spell at Anfield.

● His first season at his hometown club, however, proved to be something of a disaster. He only scored six Premiership goals throughout the season, with Villa fans and pundits claiming he looked distracted and disinterested. This could have been due to his high profile and ultimately disastrous relationship with sexy TV babe Ulrika Jonsson.

● It was a sharp contrast to his first season at Liverpool where he scored on his debut and formed half of the Premiership's most prolific strikeforce in 1995/96 with Robbie Fowler. Before Liverpool and Nottingham Forest he had played for Crystal Palace and Southend United.

● COLLYMORE made his England debut in 1995 under Terry Venables but, despite making Hoddle's squad for a 1997 friendly against Mexico, he is some way down the queue for the England centre forward role.

COLOMBIA

First international: Mexico 3 Colombia 1 (Panama City, 1938)
First World Cup appearance: Uruguay 2 Colombia 1, (Chile, 1962)
Best win: 5–0 v Argentina, 1994
Worst defeat: 9–1 v Argentina, 1945
Colours: Yellow shirts, blue shorts, red socks

COLOMBIAN national football – and club football – has been riddled with scandal and mismanagement.

● THE NATIONAL team didn't play a game until 1938 and didn't organise an international match at all between 1949–57.

● PELE said that Colombia were his favourites to win the 1994 World Cup in the USA, which was perhaps the worst football prediction ever made. When they got there the team performed very poorly, leading to allegations of match fixing.

● ON RETURNING home, their defender, Andreas Escobar, was shot, apparently for having scored an own goal in the match against the USA.

● THEY DIDN'T FARE much better in France '98, going out in the first round after a 2-0 defeat by England, having lost their top striker Faustino Asprilla after he'd argued with national coach Hernan Gomez after being substituted in an earlier game.

COLOURS

A RECENT psychological study showed that red was the best colour for teams to wear as it created the most fear in opponents.

● THE MOST successful post-war colour combination in the FA Cup Final has been red shirts and white shorts, which has adorned the winning team on nine occasions. The least successful is white shirts and white shorts, which has seen seven losing sides.

● IN THE LAST century players wore different coloured caps, socks and armbands (but not shirts) to distinguish between the two sides.

● IN THE 1962 clash between Coventry City and Southend United the referee stopped the game after three minutes because both sides were wearing blue. He made the Sky Blues go back into the dressing rooms and change into red.

● MANCHESTER UNITED became the first team to emerge for the second half of an English league match in a completely different strip when they changed from the dreaded grey to blue and white in a league game at Southampton in April 1996. 3–0 down at half-time, United still lost 3–1, but at least they did 'win' the second half 1–0!

● Probably the most unpopular kit ever was England's indigo blue (popularly seen as 'grey') kit sported for the heartbreaking Euro 96 semi-final against Germany. The kit caused an outcry among those who insisted England's second strip should always be 1966 red.

COPA LIBERTADORES

THE COPA LIBERTADORES is the South American equivalent of the European Champions Cup, played annually between the championship winners of all the countries in the continent. Argentine club Independiente are the most successful in the competition, winning the trophy four times in succession between 1972–75 and seven times in total.

● TOP SCORER in the Copa Libertadores is Uruguayan club Penarol's Albert Spencer, who netted over 50 goals in the competition, helping his side to win the first two tournaments in 1960 and 1961.

● AN INCREDIBLE 105,000 spectators watched São Paolo beat Newell's Old Boys of Argentina on penalties in the Rio play-off of the competition in 1992, the biggest attendance ever at such a match.

● ARGENTINA are the most successful country: their clubs have won the competition 17 times, compared with Uruguay's eight and Brazil's seven.

WORLD CUP RECORD

1930–54	Did not enter
1958	Did not qualify
1962	Round 1
1966–86	Did not qualify
1990	Round 2
1994	Round 1
1998	Round 1

Carlos Valderrama, sporting football's frizziest haircut, didn't think much of his team's 1994 World Cup challenge

COVENTRY CITY

Year founded: 1883
Ground: Highfield Road (23,662)
Highest ever crowd: 51,455, 29th April 1967 v Wolverhampton Wanderers (Div 2)
Previous name: Singers FC
Nickname: The Sky Blues
Colours: Sky blue shirts, shorts and socks

THE CLUB was formed by workers at Singer's bicycle factory and first played under the title Singers FC. Coventry City made an inauspicious start to their Football League career, losing 5–0 at home to Tottenham Hotspur in Division Two in 1919.

● COVENTRY's Highfield Road Stadium was bombed by German aeroplanes in the blitz of 14th November 1940. Although it took three direct hits, the bombs landed on the pitch and the stands miraculously survived major damage.

● ONLY ARSENAL, Liverpool and Everton have been in the top division longer than Coventry, who, despite more than a handful of relegation scares, have been in the top flight since 1967.

● COVENTRY were pioneers of publicity in the 1960s, when manager Jimmy Hill sold football to the public with a new sky blue strip (hence the nickname Sky Blues), special sky blue trains, a sky blue stand, a sky blue shop, sky blue caterers and a sky blue radio station.

● IN OCTOBER 1965 the club relayed live action from their match at Cardiff on to a huge screen at Highfield Road – the first club to do so. A crowd of 10,295 watched as The Sky Blues won 2–1. It was billed as the first game ever to be staged in two separate grounds: 12,639 people watched the game in Cardiff.

● JIMMY HILL turned Highfield Road into England's first all-seater stadium, mainly to reduce hooliganism. It was never popular with supporters, and seats were removed from the Kop End in 1985, allowing room for 9,000 standing spectators. Highfield Road returned to all-seater status after the Taylor Report in 1994.

● COVENTRY CITY hold the record for the highest victory score achieved with depleted numbers. In November 1958, before the introduction of substitutes, they lost their goalkeeper through injury but still went on to beat Aldershot 7-1.

● COVENTRY's most capped players are Dave Clements (48 games for Northern Ireland) and Ronnie Rees (39 for Wales). City star Reg Matthews played for England while the club were in the Third Division, one of only a handful of players to do so.

● IN THE 1919/20 season Coventry went 11 games without scoring and had to wait until Christmas Day for their first point. They called on the services of a record 42 players that season.

● THEIR BEST FA Cup season was 1987, when they beat Spurs 3–2 to win the trophy. Their worst was in 1962, when they lost at home to non-league King's Lynn, and 1989, when they were eliminated by non-league Sutton.

● IN MARCH 1995 Peter Ndlovu scored all Coventry's goals away to Liverpool in their 3–2 win. He became the first visiting player to score a hat-trick at Anfield for an astonishing 33 years.

Roll of Honour

Div 2 champions 1967
Div 3 champions 1964
Div 3 (S) champions 1936, 1959
FA Cup 1987

Coventry's Post-War Record

47 D2 8th	64 D3 1st	81 D1 16th
48 D2 10th	65 D2 10th	82 D1 14th
49 D2 16th	66 D2 3rd	83 D1 19th
50 D2 12th	67 D2 1st	84 D1 19th
51 D2 7th	68 D1 20th	85 D1 18th
52 D2 21st	69 D1 20th	86 D1 17th
53 D3 6th	70 D1 6th	87 D1 10th
54 D3 14th	71 D1 10th	88 D1 10th
55 D3 9th	72 D1 18th	89 D1 7th
56 D3 8th	73 D1 19th	90 D1 12th
57 D3 16th	74 D1 16th	91 D1 16th
58 D3 19th	75 D1 14th	92 D1 19th
59 D4 2nd	76 D1 14th	93 PR 15th
60 D3 4th	77 D1 19th	94 PR 11th
61 D3 15th	78 D1 7th	95 PR 16th
62 D3 14th	79 D1 10th	96 PR 16th
63 D3 4th	80 D1 15th	97 PR 17th
		98 PR 11th

Coventry City's Keith Houchen celebrates the goal that sent The Sky Blues on their way to their first and only FA Cup win in 1987

COWDENBEATH

Year founded: 1881
Ground: Central Park (4,370)
Highest ever crowd: 25,586,
21st September 1949 v Rangers
(League Cup quarter-final)
Colours: Royal blue and white shirts and shorts with blue socks.

ONE OF Cowdenbeath's biggest successes was winning the Division Two title in 1939, a season during which they scored a remarkable 120 goals. They picked a bad year. Hitler invaded Poland and football activities were suspended for the duration of the war. In the reorganisation afterwards they found themselves back in the same old division again.

● RAB WALLS notched a record 53 goals for them during that fabulous 1938/39 season.

● COWDEN, as they are imaginatively nicknamed, knocked 12 goals without reply past St. Johnstone in 1928, recording their biggest victory. In 1951 they went down 11–1 to Clyde, their worst performance.

● CENTRAL PARK is an international venue that has held four World Championships – in stock car racing.

Roll of Honour

Division 2 champions 1914, 1915, 1939

CREWE ALEXANDRA

Year founded: 1877
Ground: Gresty Road (5,759)
Highest ever crowd: 20,000
30th January 1960 v Spurs
(FA Cup rd 4)
Nickname: The Railwaymen
Colours: Red shirts, red shorts, white socks

BASED in a town more famous for its railway station than its football club, unsurprisingly Crewe Alexandra FC are known as the Railwaymen. The club was actually founded by railway workers in 1877 and, until their promotion to Division One via the play-offs in 1997, had shunted around the lower divisions.

●Crewe's manager Dario Gradi – awarded an MBE in 1998 – is the longest serving gaffer in the English Leagues, having been in charge at Crewe since 1983. Gradi has become well known for developing talent, and the likes of David Platt, Liverpool's Rob Jones and Danny Murphy have all come off the Gresty Road production line.

●Crewe have been beaten ten times in the FA Cup by non-league opponents, more than any other existing Football league club apart from Exeter City. The closest the club have ever come to winning a trophy was way back in 1888 when they reached the semi-finals of the FA Cup, only to be defeated 4-0 by Preston North End.

● IN 1996/97 Crewe, (where former England star David Platt started his career) and Liverpool formed the League's first ever 'alliance' between teams 'for the mutual benefit of both clubs'.

CROATIA

First international: Hungary 1
Croatia 0 (Budapest, 1940)
Best win: 6–0 v Bulgaria, 1942
Worst defeat: 1–5 v Germany, 1941
Colours: Red-and-white-chequered shirts, white shorts, blue socks

CROATIA'S first ever World Cup tournament was a glorious one. They reached the semi-finals of France 98, where they lost narrowly to eventual winners France, and won the third place play-off match against Holland.

● To top off a remarkable tournament, Croatia's star striker Davor Suker won the 'golden boot' as top scorer with six goals.

● Croatia's 1–0 defeat of Slovenia in June 1991 was their fifth win on the trot, matching their best ever winning sequence. But it took them 48 years to put it together. From 1944 to 1990 the country was swallowed up by Yugoslavia and played no matches in its own national colours.

● Croatia's previous matches were all played during WW2 after the country was declared an independent state during occupation of Yugoslavia by the Axis forces.

● Before the France 98 World Cup the greatest result of Croatia's history was their 2–1 win over Italy in Palermo during the Euro 96 qualifiers in 1994. This made them the only team to beat Italy on Italian soil in normal play (Argentina beat them on penalties in the 1990 World Cup).

CROWDS

THE BIGGEST crowd in football history saw 199,589 turn up to the newly built Maracana Stadium in Rio in 1950 to see Brazil play Uruguay in the final game of the World Cup. Most of the fans left disappointed; Brazil lost the game 2–1.

● The biggest crowd ever to witness a football match in Britain was for the first ever FA Cup Final at Wembley in 1923. The official attendance for the match between Bolton and West Ham is 126,047 although there were at least 30,000 more inside the ground who had got in without paying. The biggest official crowd for a British match was the 146,547 who paid to see Scotland v England at Hampden Park on 17th April 1937.

● In January 1947, 83,260 crammed into Maine Road (Old Trafford had been bombed) to see Manchester United play Arsenal – the biggest ever crowd in English league football. The figure is dwarfed, however, by the 143,470 who went to see Rangers play Hibernian in 1948, the biggest figure ever to see a British club match apart from a cup final.

Zvonimir Boban proudly wears cash-strapped Croatia's new kit, made from one of his mum's tablecloths

Funny Old Game

The lowest crowd ever for a Football League record match occurred in 1921. Having had their ground closed down because of crowd trouble, already relegated Stockport County were forced to switch their last, meaningless match against Leicester City to Old Trafford... and only 13 people turned up! What the record books don't show is that there were already 2,500 people in the ground who'd been watching a United reserve match played first.

JOHAN CRUYFF

Born: Amsterdam 25.4.47
Position: Midfield
Club career:
1963–73 Ajax Amsterdam
1973–78 Barcelona
1978–80 Los Angeles Aztecs
1980–81 Washington Diplomats
International record:
1966–78 Holland 48 (33)

CRYUFF was the greatest Dutch footballer of all time, captaining his country to the 1974 World Cup Final and winning the European Cup with Ajax three times in a row at the start of the 1970s. He was undoubtedly the best player in the world at the time, and became the first man to win the European Footballer of the Year award three times, in 1971, 1973 and 1974.

● BARCELONA were so impressed they paid a world record £922,000 fee for Cryuff in 1973. It was worth it: he helped the club win the championship in his first season.

● HE EVENTUALLY moved back to Barcelona as coach, and became their most successful manager, winning the Championship four times in a row between 1991–94 and winning the club the European Cup for the first time ever, with a 1–0 win over Sampdoria at Wembley in 1992.

● CRUYFF, who suffered a heart attack in 1997, is Holland's third highest goalscorer ever with 33 goals.

Johan Cruyff goes down in the box to win a first-minute penalty for Holland in the 1974 World Cup Final against West Germany

CRYSTAL PALACE

Year founded: 1905
Ground: Selhurst Park (26,400)
Highest ever crowd: 51,482, 11th May 1979 v Burnley (Div 2)
Nickname: The Eagles
Colours: Red-and-blue-striped shirts, red shorts, red socks

CRYSTAL PALACE are the only club to have been relegated three times from the Premiership (in 1994, 1996 and 1998). This is some feat considering the league has only been up and running for six seasons. They can rightfully claim to be the top flight's undisputed 'yo yo' team.

● THE VERY first Palace team, made up of staff working at the Great Exhibition, reached the semi-final of the first ever FA Cup competition in 1871.

● LITTLE centre forward Johnny 'Budgie' Byrne won an England cap when he played in Division Three with Palace in 1962. Winger Peter Taylor achieved the same feat in 1977.

● PALACE'S BIGGEST ever win was over Barrow, 9–0, in 1959. They lost by the same scoreline to Burnley in 1909 and Liverpool in 1990.

● THE GREATEST moment in their history came when they held Manchester United 3–3 in the FA Cup Final in 1990, with Ian Wright scoring two goals from off the substitutes' bench. Unfortunately for The Eagles, they were beaten 1–0 in the replay.

● PETER SIMPSON is the club's star scorer, with 153 goals between 1930–36. He netted a club record 46 in his first full season, 1930/31.

● THE CLUB's best ever sale was Chris Armstrong to Spurs in 1995 for £4.5 million. They paid Sunderland £1.8 million for Marco Gabbiadini in September 1991.

● JIM CANNON played a record 571 games for the club between 1973–88. Fans, fed up with a side that promised much and achieved little, used to sing: 'When Jim goes up, to lift the FA Cup, we'll be dead, we'll be dead'.

Roll of Honour

Div 1 champions 1994
Div 2 champions 1979
Div 3 (S) champions 1921

CSKA SOFIA

Year founded: 1948
Ground: Bulgarska Armia (30,000)
League wins: 28
Colours: Red shirts, red shorts and red socks

CSKA SOFIA, the Bulgarian army team, are the most successful club in the country, having won eight more titles than local rivals Levski Sofia (the Ministry team). CSKA have only once finished outside the top five in the Bulgarian League, in 1964, when they dropped to lowly 11th place.

● CSKA SOFIA have won a post war European record of 28 league titles, including nine in a row between 1954–62 (under the name CDNA Sofia) equalling the world record also held by Glasgow clubs Celtic and Rangers.

● THE Bulgarian national team was traditionally picked from the ranks of the CSKA squad before players were allowed to go abroad in recent years, which had good and bad effect on the team's results.

Roll of Honour

League champions 1948, 1951, 1952, 1954, 1955, 1956, 1957, 1958, 1959, 1960, 1961, 1962, 1966, 1969, 1971, 1972, 1973, 1975, 1976, 1980, 1981, 1982, 1983, 1987, 1989, 1990, 1992, 1997
Bulgarian Cup 1981, 1983, 1987, 1988, 1989, 1993

STAN CULLIS

Born: Ellesmere Port 25.10.16

STAN CULLIS was best known for masterminding Wolverhampton Wanderers' championship treble in the 1950s, the best ever period of success at the club.

● CULLIS, who spent 30 years at the club as player and manager, invented a kick and rush version of football which was extremely effective and very unpopular outside Wolverhampton. Cullis drove his side to league titles in 1954 (their first), 1958 and 1959. In 1960 Burnley pipped them for the title by one point to prevent a Wanderers hat-trick.

● IN 1949 they won the FA Cup beating Leicester City 3–1 and a second Cup followed in 1960 when they beat Blackburn 3–0.

● CULLIS even claimed that Wolves were World Champions in the mid-1950s when Spartak Moscow and Honved came to Molineux and were beaten.

CUP WINNERS' CUP

THE EUROPEAN Cup Winners' Cup has been running since 1960/61, pitting together the cup winners of all European countries. The first winners were Fiorentina, who beat Glasgow Rangers 4–1 on aggregate over two legs.

● THE FIRST British club to win were Tottenham Hotspur, who beat Atletico Madrid 5–1 in 1963, becoming the first British club to win a major European tournament.

● IN 1981 Welsh Cup winners Newport County (then in the English Fourth Division) caused the biggest shock by knocking out holders Valencia in the 2nd round.

● BARCELONA, with four victories (in 1979, 1982, 1989 and 1997) have won the cup more times than any other team.

CUP WINNERS' CUP FINALS

1961	Fiorentina 2 Rangers 0 (1st leg)
	Fiorentina 2 (4) Rangers 1 (1) (2nd leg)
1962	Atletico Madrid 1 Fiorentina 1
	Atletico Madrid 3 Fiorentina 0 (replay)
1963	Tottenham Hotspur 5 Atletico Madrid 1
1964	Sporting CP 3 MTK Budapest 3
	Sporting CP 1 MTK Budapest 0 (replay)
1965	West Ham United 2
	TSV 1860 Munchen 0
1966	Borussia Dortmund 2 Liverpool 1
1967	Bayern Munich 1 Rangers 0
1968	AC Milan 2 Hamburg 0
1969	Slovan Bratislava 3 Barcelona 2
1970	Manchester City 2 Gornik Zabrze 1
1971	Chelsea 1 Real Madrid 1
	Chelsea 2 Real Madrid 1 (replay)
1972	Rangers 3 Dynamo Moscow 2
1973	AC Milan 1 Leeds United 0
1974	FC Magdeburg 2 AC Milan 0
1975	Dynamo Kiev 3 Ferencvaros 0
1976	Anderlecht 4 West Ham United 2
1977	Hamburg 2 Anderlecht 0
1978	Anderlecht 4 FK Austria 0
1979	Barcelona 4 Fortuna Dusseldorf 3
1980	Valencia 0 Arsenal 0 (5-4 on penalties)
1981	Dynamo Tblisi 2 Carl Zeiss Jena 1
1982	Barcelona 2 Standard CL 1
1983	Aberdeen 2 Real Madrid 1
1984	Juventus 2 FC Porto 1
1985	Everton 3 Rapid Vienna 1
1986	Dynamo Kiev 3 Atletico Madrid 0
1987	Ajax 1 Lokomotiv Leipzig 0
1988	Mechelen 1 Ajax 0
1989	Barcelona 2 Sampdoria 0
1990	Sampdoria 2 Anderlecht 0
1991	Manchester United 2 Barcelona 1
1992	Werder Bremen 2 Monaco 0
1993	Parma 3 Royal Antwerp 1
1994	Arsenal 1 Parma 0
1995	Real Zaragoza 2 Arsenal 1
1996	Paris St. Germain 1 Rapid Vienna 0
1997	Barcelona 1 Paris St, Germain 0
1998	Chelsea 1 VFB Stuttgart 0

CZECH REPUBLIC

First international: Czechoslovakia 7 Yugoslavia 0 (1920)
First World Cup appearance: Czechoslovakia 2 Romania 1 (Italy, 1934)
Highest capped player: Zdenek Nehoda (90)
Highest goalscorer: Antonîn Puc (34)
Best win: 7–0 v Yugoslavia, (1920)
Worst defeat: 3–8 v Hungary, 1937
Colours: Red shirts, white shorts, blue socks

THE CZECH REPUBLIC (formerly Czechoslovakia) played their first game in 1994 after the country had split from Slovakia in 1993.

● THE MOST humiliating defeat in the Czechs' history took place in the qualifiers for Euro 96 in 1995. They lost 1–0 to Luxembourg, who had only won one other match in the last 16 years, and that against Malta. However, they redeemed themselves by reaching the final of the tournament, becoming the first team in the history of international football to lose on the 'Golden Goal' rule as Germany beat them 2–1 at Wembley.

● THE CZECHS have reached the final of the World Cup twice, but lost both times. In 1934 they went down to Italy in Rome, and in 1962 Brazil beat them 3–1 in Chile.

● THEIR biggest triumph came in the 1976 European Championships when they beat West Germany in the final. The match finished 2–2 and the Czechs won 5–3 on penalties to become the fifth side to win the fifth tournament. They also won the Olympic Games in Moscow in 1980 as well as finishing runners-up in the 1920 and 1964 games.

WORLD CUP RECORD

1930	Did not enter		
1934	Runners-up	1970	Round 1
1938	Quarter-finals	1974	Did not qualify
1950	Did not enter	1978	Did not qualify
1954	Round 1	1982	Round 1
1958	Round 1	1986	Did not qualify
1962	Runners-up	1990	Quarter-finals
1966	Did not qualify	1994	Did not qualify
		1998	Did not qualify

KENNY DALGLISH

Born: Glasgow 4.3.51
Height: 5ft 8in Position: Forward
Club career:
1967–77 Celtic 204 (112)
1977–90 Liverpool 354 (118)
International record:
1972–87 Scotland 102 (30)

DALGLISH WAS the first player ever to score more than a century of goals in both the Scottish (for Celtic) and English (for Liverpool) leagues. He moved between the clubs for a then British record £440,000 in 1977.

● HE WAS Footballer of the Year twice, in 1979 (Football Writers') and in 1983 (PFA) , a year after scoring the only goal in the European Cup Final as Liverpool beat FC Bruges. He won nine Championships and two FA Cups as a player with The Reds.

● HE GAINED 102 Scottish caps, scoring an equal (with Denis Law) record 30 goals in the process, before becoming player-manager of Liverpool in 1985. He was the first manager to win the 'double' in his first season.

● KING KENNY led Liverpool to three championships in his five seasons as manager before stunning football with his decision to quit the game in 1991, returning to manage Blackburn eight months later. In 1995 he steered the Lancashire club to their first championship win in 81 years, becoming only the third manager to win the title with two different clubs. He quit the game again a year later but returned in February 1997 after Kevin Keegan's shock resignation to take the helm at Newcastle United. He clipped the wings of the flyaway Magpies with his defensive tactics, but nevertheless guided United to a Champions League place in 1997 and to an FA Cup Final in 1998.

Liverpool's Kenny Dalglish, the first and only player/manager to win The Double

DARLINGTON

Year founded: 1883
Ground: Feethams (7,046)
Highest ever crowd: 21,023, 14th November 1960 v Bolton (League Cup rd 3)
Nickname: The Quakers
Colours: White shirts, black shorts and white socks

THE MAIN entrance to Darlington's ground is an ornamental gateway which, according to club historian Frank Tweddle, is the only set of twin towers the club's supporters are ever likely to see.

● SINCE 1927 Darlington have been in the bottom two divisions, apart from 1989/90, when they went out of the league. The change did them good. They won the Vauxhall Conference the next year and then won the Fourth Division title in 1991.

● DARLINGTON are one of seven league clubs who have never supplied a full international.

● IN 1971 Darlington's manager, Len Richley, was sacked just 12 days after the beginning of the season, an equal record with Denis Butler (Port Vale), Mick Jones (Peterborough) and Peter Reid (Manchester City).

● DAVID BROWN is The Quakers' record league goalscorer, with 39 goals back in 1924/25, the club's most successful season.

● DARLINGTON's record win was a 9–2 thrashing of Lincoln City in 1928. The worst day in the club's history, meanwhile, was on 25th January 1964 when The Quakers were stuffed 10–0 by Doncaster.

Roll of Honour

Div 3 (N) champions 1925
Div 4 champions 1991
Vauxhall Conference champions 1990

BARRY DAVIES

Born: 24.10.40

BARRY DAVIES is one of the two top football commentators for the BBC, where he has worked since 1969. His friendly rivalry with John Motson is legendary, reaching a peak when he was chosen to commentate on the 1994 World Cup Final and the 1995 FA Cup Final.

● HIS FIRST TV commentary was made in 1966 for ITV, when his voice informed the nation of events in the Chelsea v AC Milan Fairs Cup match. He was later part of ITV's 1966 World Cup commentary team.

● REMARKABLY, Cranbrook School in Kent, where Davies was educated, has also produced two other sports commentators of the highest calibre: Brian Moore and Peter West.

● DAVIES GOT HIS break in television after doing a trial commentary on a schoolboys match for ITV. To give himself an edge over the other candidates he visited both schools the day before the game and learnt all the players' names and nicknames.

Dixie Dean, sporting the highest-riding shorts in the history of the game, scored 60 goals in the 1927/28 season for Everton

DIXIE DEAN

Born: Liverpool 22.1.07 Died: 1.3.80
Height: 5ft 10ins Position: Forward
Club career:
1923–25 Tranmere Rovers 29 (27)
1925–37 Everton 399 (349)
1938–39 Notts County 9 (3)
International record:
1927–33 England 16 (18)

DIXIE DEAN scored 60 goals for Everton in 1927/28, an all-time league record that is unlikely to be emulated. He netted a hat-trick in the last match against Arsenal after scoring four and two in his previous two games to overhaul Middlesbrough's George Camsell, who managed 59 the previous season.

● HE SCORED a total of 349 goals for Everton between 1925–37, easily the club record, and unlikely to be equalled.

● HE WAS only picked 16 times for England, which seems short-sighted as he scored 18 goals in those games, including 12 in his first five appearances.

● HE HATED his nickname 'Dixie', preferring to be called by his real name Bill. 'Bill Dean' doesn't have the same ring to it, somehow.

DEATHS

THE FIRST recorded death in a football match came in 1892 when James Dunlop died of tetanus after suffering a cut on the pitch during a game.

● ONE OF THE NASTIEST ever football deaths befell poor Thomas Grice of Aston in 1897. He was killed on the pitch when he stumbled to the ground and his belt buckle punctured his stomach.

● JOHN THOMPSON, Celtic's brilliant young international goalkeeper, died after a collision with Rangers forward Sam English after both men went for a 50-50 ball in the 1931 Old Firm derby. The goalie fractured his skull, and passed away after five hours in hospital.

● IN 1962 a fan ran onto the pitch during a game in South America and stabbed the referee to death. An opposing fan was so enraged that he shot the man who killed the ref. Then there was a crowd stampede which killed the man who shot the man who stabbed the ref, who swallowed the spider.

● EIGHT PLAYERS were taken to hospital during the Army Cup Final of 1948 at Aldershot after being struck by lightning which had probably been attracted by the referee's whistle. Two of them never made it out again.

DEBUTS

WREXHAM new-boy Bernard Evans made the best start to a debut ever when he scored after 25 seconds against Bradford City.

● GOALKEEPER Tony Coton, on the other hand, was 83 seconds into his debut with Birmingham City when he saved a penalty with the first touch of his league career.

● HALIFAX TOWN weren't very pleased with their debutant keeper Stanley Milton in 1934. He let in 13 goals in Stockport's biggest ever win and Halifax's worst defeat.

● CHELSEA's George Hilsdon was pleased with his league debut back in 1906. He thumped in five goals. He was later the model for the weather vane on the West Stand at Stamford Bridge.

● THE OLDEST England debutant was Leslie Compton, who made his international debut on 5th November 1950 against Wales, aged 38! He played one more match for his country.

Did You Know?

When Cameron Cambell Buchanan made his debut for Wolves against West Brom in a Wartime League match in September 1942 he became the youngest senior footballer ever. He was just 14 years and 57 days old.

ALESSANDRO DEL PIERO

Born: Italy 9.11.74
Position: Forward
Club career:
1991–93 Padova 14 (1)
1993– Juventus 122 (48)
International record:
1995– Italy 22 (8)

With 19 goals in the Champions League, young Alessandro del Piero is the highest ever scorer since the European Cup was re-vamped. He has never finished, however, on the trophy-winning side, having played in the losing Juventus team in the 1997 and '98 finals and missed out on a place in the victorious 1996 side. He did, however, score in the 1997 final after coming on as substitute against Borussia Dortmund.

● Del Piero displaced fellow Veneto striker Roberto Baggio from the Juventus side in 1995, and their rivalry has been intense ever since. During France '98 the two gifted forwards were both fighting for the creative attacking role in the team. Del Piero spent more time on the pitch than Baggio but, carrying an injury, was not so effective.

● In fact Del Piero has never impressed in major international tournaments. Just like the rest of the Italian team he was a major disappointment at both Euro 96 and France 98. Del Piero failed to score and Italy failed to qualify for the second round on both occasions.

● However the young striker, who is quick, agile, skilful and possesses an eye for goal (especially at free-kicks) has time on side and will certainly soon add much more to a list of trophies that includes three Italian titles, one Italian Cup, a Super Cup and a World Club Championship.

DENILSON

Born: Sao Bernando do Campo, Brazil 24.8.77
Height: 5ft 11ins
Position: Midfielder
Club Career:
1995–98 Sao Paulo (Brazil)
1998– Real Betis (Spain)
International Career:
1996- Brazil 14 (5)

Brazilian midfielder Denilson is the world's most expensive player. His £21.5 million move from Sao Paulo to Real Betis of Spain smashed the previous record of £18 million paid by Inter Milan to Barcelona for Ronaldo in 1997.

● Denilson made his debut for Sao Paulo, aged 18, in 1995. The super-quick youngster was soon earning rave reviews, and in November 1996 Brazilian coach Mario Zagallo gave Denilson his international debut against Cameroon. In the following year's Copa America Denilson played a key role, helping Brazil to only their second win since 1949.

● Despite displaying flashes of brilliance,the France 98 World Cup was a disappointing tournament for Denilson whose only appearances were from the substitutes bench.

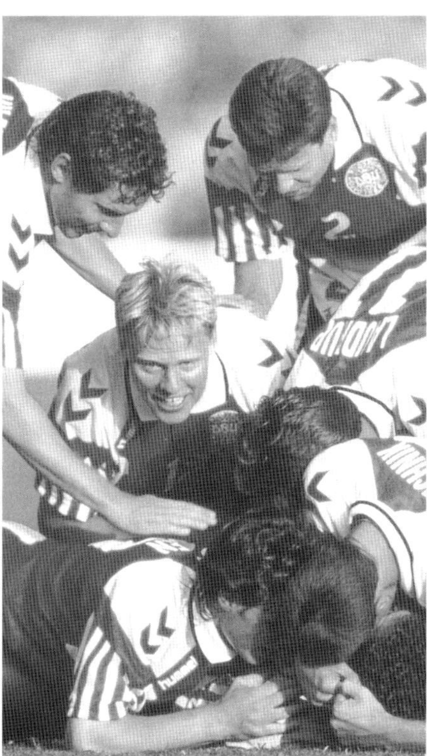

Danish players collapse in surprise as John Jensen opens the scoring for Denmark in their 2–0 win over Germany in the 1992 European Championship Final

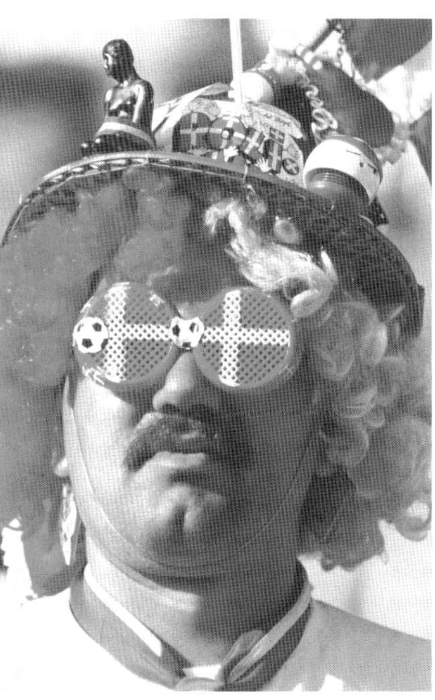

Denmark won the 1992 European Championships… unfortunately this fan couldn't see a thing

DENMARK

First international: Denmark 9 France 0 (London Olympics 1908)
First World Cup appearance: Denmark 1 Scotland 0 (Mexico, 1986)
Highest capped player: Morten Olsen (102)
Highest Appearance maker: Peter Schmeichel (105)
Highest goalscorer: Poul Nielsen (52)
Best win: 17–1 v France, 1908
Worst defeat: 8–0 v Germany, 1937
Colours: Red shirts, white shorts, red socks

DENMARK were the most successful team outside the British Isles in the early part of the century. They won their first two matches (both against France in the Olympic Games) 9–0 and 17–1. In the second game Sophus Nielsen scored ten goals, which is still a record in international football.

● THE COUNTRY's greatest success came in the 1992 European Championship in Sweden. They beat Germany 2–0 in the final to become the only team to win a major international tournament after being knocked out in the qualifiers.

● DENMARK were given the last-gasp reprieve when Yugoslavia dropped out of the competition due to the civil war in that country. They are thus the only country ever to have won a tournament after being eliminated from it in the qualifiers.

● At France 98, after a shaky start, they surprised everybody outside Jutland by getting to the quarter-finals, and giving World Champions Brazil a fright or two before going down 3–2.

WORLD CUP RECORD

1930–54	Did not enter	1986	Round 2
1958	Did not qualify	1990	Did not qualify
1962	Did not enter	1994	Did not qualify
1966–82	Did not qualify	1998	Quarter-finals

DERBIES

A NAME GIVEN originally to games of such popularity that they rivalled the Epsom Derby, probably the most intense 'local derby' in British football is that between Scottish rivals Rangers and Celtic.

● ALSO VYING for that title would be Liverpool v Everton, Arsenal v Spurs, Manchester United v Manchester City, Newcastle v Sunderland and titanic European contests like Inter v AC Milan, Lazio v Roma and Real v Atletico Madrid. To the fans these matches are as important, if not more so, than any cup final.

● ARGUABLY the most dramatic 'derby' moment in a Manchester United v Manchester City match was in 1974, in which City won the game and all but doomed United to relegation to the Second Division. The scorer of the goal (with a cheeky back-heel) was former United idol Denis Law, whose celebrations afterwards were a trifle muted.

● PROBABLY the most important goal in an English derby game came at Tottenham's White Hart Lane in 1971, when Ray Kennedy scored in the 89th minute to silence the home crowd and give Arsenal the League Championship. Arsenal went on to do The Double.

● TWO MERSEYSIDE derbies have been played at Wembley to contest the FA Cup Final: in 1986 and 1989. Liverpool won both games (3–1 and 3–2), with Ian Rush bagging two goals in each game. In Scotland, Rangers and Celtic have contested the Scottish Cup Final no fewer than 23 times (in 1909 the cup was awarded to neither team after fans rioted during the replay).

● FOR 38 YEARS, between 1930–68, the Faroe Islands only ever played their North Atlantic neighbours the Shetland Islands. In arguably the least glamorous international derby of the lot, the Faroes recorded eight wins out of 13 matches, the Shetlands coming out on top on just four occasions.

DERBY COUNTY

Year founded: 1884
Ground: Pride Park (30,000)
Highest ever crowd: 41,826, 20th September 1969 v Tottenham Hotspur (Div 1)
Nickname: The Rams
Colours: White shirts, black shorts, black socks

DERBY was formed in 1884 by members of the Derbyshire County Cricket Club who thought a football club would boost finances for the summer game. The team first wore the cricket club's colours of amber, chocolate and pale blue.

● IN AUGUST 1997 the club moved into a brand new stadium in Pride Park on the outskirts of town. When they moved in at the Baseball Ground in 1895 they had to oust a band of gypsies who were said to have left a curse on the place, and fans have been blaming bad results on the Romanies ever since.

● DERBY were founder members of the Football League and have been one of its leading sides, if one of the unluckiest. They have got as far as the FA Cup semi-finals 13 times but have only won the competition once, in the first post-war FA Cup Final, when they beat Charlton 4–1 after extra time (before the match their captain had sought out a gypsy camp to have the old curse lifted). They have been FA Cup runners-up three times (1898, 1899 and 1903).

● IN 1945/46 a record crowd of 80,407 flocked to Maine Road for the FA Cup semi-final between Derby County and Birmingham City, a record for a midweek match between two English clubs outside Wembley. The massive attendance caused the government to be so worried about absenteeism from work, however, that they banned midweek afternoon matches.

● BRIAN CLOUGH made the club a runaway success in 1969 when he guided them to promotion to the First Division and then the league title in 1972. That League Championship was the most open ever, with four teams in with a shout up until the last day. The players were actually on holiday in Majorca when they heard the news of their victory.

● WHEN Clough left Derby his championship-winning captain Dave Mackay took over as manager. Remarkably he won the title for The Rams again in 1975, the first man to captain then manage a side to championship success within four seasons.

● THINGS, however, soon went pear-shaped. By 1984, their centenary year, Derby were in the Third Division and out of money. It was publisher Robert Maxwell who saved them from extinction, although fans, upset at the lack of money invested in the team, used to sing 'He's fat, he's round, he's never at the ground' of their chairman.

● NEW OWNER Lionel Pickering spent £12 million on players after the club were relegated from Division One in 1991. The spree failed to win them instant promotion, although they finally reached the top flight again in 1996, finishing runners-up in the First Division.

● DERBY's record victory came in their first UEFA Cup match in 1976. They beat Finn Harps (of Ireland) 12–0. Their worst defeat was more than a century ago when, in 1890, they lost 11–2 to Everton.

● Derby's most embarrassing defeat was a shocking 1–6 drubbing at home to non-league Boston United in the 2nd round of the FA Cup on 12th December 1955.

● THE CLUB's best ever goalscorer was one of the true greats of the early part of

Rangers v Celtic derbies were too intense for poor old Paolo Di Canio... so he moved to Sheffield Wednesday

Derby County's 1972 championship-winning side: the only club to win the title while sitting on a beach in Majorca

the century, Steve Bloomer, who netted 331 league and cup goals for Derby in two spells at the club, and was also a prolific striker for England.

Roll of Honour

Div 1 champions 1972, 1975
Div 2 champions 1912, 1915, 1969, 1987
Div 3 (N) champions 1957
FA Cup 1946

MARCEL DESAILLY

Born: Ghana 7.9.68
Height: 6ft 1in Position: Defender
Club career:
1986–92 Nantes 162 (5)
1992–94 Olympique Marseille 47 (1)
1994–98 AC Milan 133 (6)
1998– Chelsea
International record:
1992– France 49 (2)

A World Cup winner, awesome French defender Marcel Desailly was one of the outstanding players of the France 98 tournament and is currently one of the best defenders in the world.

● Desailly is the only player to have won consecutive European Cups with different clubs. In 1993 the Ghanaian-born defender was a lynchpin of the Marseille side which beat Milan 1–0 in the final in Munich. Milan were so impressed they immediately bought him. The following season Desailly won another European Cup winners medal and scored the last goal in Milan's 4–0 thrashing of Barcelona in Athens.

● Desailly was a member of the Olympique Marseille side which won the French league in 1993, only to be stripped of their title when it was revealed one of their players had paid opponents to take things easy during a crucial French league match just before the final. Marseille were relegated and forced to sell their top players, including Desailly.

● And after a four year spell at Milan, just before the World Cup Desailly signed for Chelsea in a £4.5 million deal.

Derby's Post-War Record

47 D1 14th	65 D2 9th	83 D2 13th
48 D1 4th	66 D2 8th	84 D2 20th
49 D1 3rd	67 D2 17th	85 D3 7th
50 D1 11th	68 D2 18th	86 D3 3rd
51 D1 11th	69 D2 1st	87 D2 1st
52 D1 17th	70 D1 4th	88 D1 15th
53 D1 22nd	71 D1 9th	89 D1 5th
54 D2 18th	72 D1 1st	90 D1 16th
55 D2 22nd	73 D1 7th	91 D1 20th
56 D3 2nd	74 D1 3rd	92 D2 3rd
57 D3 1st	75 D1 1st	93 D1 8th
58 D2 16th	76 D1 4th	94 D1 6th
59 D2 7th	77 D1 15th	95 D1 9th
60 D2 18th	78 D1 12th	96 D1 2nd
61 D2 12th	79 D1 19th	97 D1 12th
62 D2 16th	80 D1 21st	98 PR 9th
63 D2 18th	81 D2 6th	
64 D2 13th	82 D2 16th	

DISASTERS

THE WORST ever disaster in football occurred in the Lenin Stadium in Moscow on 20th October 1982, when 340 people died in a crush on the icy terraces during a UEFA Cup tie between Spartak Moscow and Dutch club Haarlem. Full details of this disaster did not emerge until 1989 when the Iron Curtain came down.

● PREVIOUSLY, the worst soccer tragedy occurred in Lima, Peru in 1964, when 318 died as fans rioted during a match between Peru and Argentina.

● THE WORST disaster in English football saw 96 Liverpool fans die at Hillsborough, Sheffield, when they were crushed at the start of the 1989 FA Cup semi-final between Liverpool and Nottingham Forest.

● ENGLISH TEAMS were banned from European competition in 1985 after 39 Juventus fans were crushed to death when a wall collapsed as they tried to flee from surging Liverpool supporters before the European Cup Final at the Heysel Stadium in Belgium.

● THE MOST recent major football disaster occurred in Guatemala on 16th October 1996 when 81 fans were crushed to death and 147 were injured at the Mateo Flores Stadium in Guatemala City. The tragedy occurred an hour before the kick off of a World Cup qualifier between Guatemala and Costa Rica, when overcrowding resulted in a devastating crush against the perimeter fencing. The disaster is believed to have been the result of a massive ticket forgery scam which enabled 60,000 fans to gain entry into a stadium with a capacity of 45,000.

THE TEN MOST SUCCESSFUL EUROPEAN CLUBS

(Trophies won)

1 Real Madrid (9)
2 Barcelona (8)
3 AC Milan (7)
4= Ajax (6)
Juventus (6)
Liverpool (6)
7= Bayern Munich (5)
Inter Milan (5)
9= Anderlecht (3)
Tottenham Hotspur (3)

ROBERTO DI MATTEO

Born: Schaffhausen 29.5.70
Ht: 5ft 9ins Position: Midfield
Club career:
1988–91 Schaffhausen (Switzerland) 50 (2)
1991–92 Zurich (Switzerland) 34 (6)
1992–93 Aarau (Switzerland) 32 (1)
1993–96 Lazio
1996– Chelsea 66 (11)
International career:
1994– Italy 34 (2)

ITALIAN INTERNATIONAL Roberto Di Matteo capped a brilliant first season in English football with Chelsea by scoring the fastest goal ever in an FA Cup Final at Wembley. His 35-yard stonker against Middlesbrough in May 1997 came after just 42 seconds, beating the previous record held by Jackie Milburn, who scored after 45 seconds for Newcastle in the 1955 final against Manchester City.

● HE BECAME the first current Italian international to sign for an English club when he joined Ruud Gullit's Chelsea in the summer of 1996 for £4.9 million from Paul Gascoigne's old club Lazio. So popular was Di Matteo at his old club that the transfer caused a riot in Rome.

● DI MATTEO was actually born and brought up in Switzerland by his Italian parents and was wanted for the Swiss national team by then national team boss Roy Hodgson. The player had his heart set on playing for the Azzurri, however, and on November 16th 1994 his dream came true when he was picked for the team to play Croatia in a European Championship qualifier in Palermo. Unfortunately the team lost – Italy's first ever defeat on home soil in a competitive match – but he became a regular in the team, despite watching most of his country's World Cup 98 campaign from the bench.

ALFREDO DI STEFANO

Born: Buenos Aires 4.7.26
Height: 5ft 9ins Position: Forward
Club career:
1943–49 River Plate
1949–53 Millionarios (Colombia)
1953–64 Real Madrid
1964 Español (Spain)
International record:
1947–48 Argentina 8 (5)
1957–61 Spain 31 (23)

ALFREDO DI STEFANO, architect of Real Madrid's domination of European football in the late 1950s and early 60s, is considered by many to be the greatest footballer of all time.

● REAL WON the European Cup five times in a row between 1956–60. Di Stefano scored in each final, including a hat-trick in the 1960 7–3 win against Eintracht Frankfurt.

● HE IS ONE of only three men to have scored a hat-trick in the European Cup Final. The others are Real's Puskas in 1962 (who also scored the other four of Real's goals in 1960) and Milan's Prati in 1969.

● DI STEFANO was born in Argentina, and made his international debut for his home country, but also won caps for Colombia and Spain, making him one of a handful of players to appear for three different countries.

● HE WAS once kidnapped while on tour with Real Madrid in Venezuela, the terrorists finally releasing him after three days.

● Di Stefano is the highest scorer in the history of the European Cup with 49 goals.

Roberto Di Matteo, a Ferrari at the heart of Chelsea's midfield, sports the longest socks in the Premiership

TOMMY DOCHERTY

Born: Glasgow 24.4.28

THE DOC was one of the most outspoken managers in the game. As one of his former players Jimmy Nicholl states 'He could start an argument in an empty house'.

● HE WAS also one of the most footloose. He was manager of nine different football league clubs, more than any other man. The clubs in question are Chelsea (1962), Rotherham (1967), QPR (1968 and 1979), Astin Villa (1968), Hull City (1971), Manchester United (1972), Derby County (1977), Preston North End (1981) and Wolves (1984).

● HE HAS ALSO been manager of Scotland (for 14 months between 1971–72) and managed Portuguese giants Porto (1970), as well as Australian clubs Sydney Olympic (1980) and South Melbourne (1982), and non-league Altrincham (1987). As he puts it himself: 'I've had more clubs than Jack Nicklaus'.

● THE HIGHLIGHT of his managerial career was guiding Manchester United to a 2–1 Cup Final victory over Liverpool in 1977.

DOGS

THE MOST FAMOUS dog in football was Pickles, the collie who discovered the stolen Jules Rimet World Cup trophy in his front garden in Norwood, South London on Sunday, 20th March 1966 and became a national hero. Alas he was strangled by his lead running after a cat in the same year.

● IN 1970 Brentford goalkeeper Chic Brodie was stretchered off during a match against Colchester after colliding with a dog that had run onto the pitch. His knee was badly damaged and he never played professional football again.

● A POLICE DOG saved Torquay from relegation from the football league in their last match of the 1986/87 season... by biting one of their defenders. Torquay, needing to stay up, were 2–1 down to Crewe with eight minutes remaining when police dog Ginger sank his teeth into Jim McNichol. The game was stopped for five minutes while he received treatment. Torquay's Paul Dobson scored an equaliser deep in the injury time allowed for the stoppage, and Lincoln lost their league status instead of Torquay.

● IN THE 1985 Staffordshire Sunday Cup a dog did actually score a goal for Knave of Clubs against Newcastle Town, intercepting a shot that was going wide and bundling it over the line! The referee had no option but to give the goal.

D

DONCASTER ROVERS

Year founded: 1879
Ground: Belle Vue (7,994)
Highest ever crowd: 37,149,
2nd October 1948 v Hull City (Div 3)
Colours: Red shirts, white shorts
and red socks

SITUATED at the heart of the British coal mining industry, Doncaster Rovers – like the area which surrounds them – have struggled in recent years, suffering relegation to the Vauxhall Conference in May 1998. Rovers' last taste of any sort of glory was way back in 1969 when they won the Fourth Division title.

● IN THE 1950s Rovers reached the 5th round of the FA Cup four times, partly because they had the great Harry Gregg in goal. Gregg was later sold to Manchester United for £23,500, then a world record for a goalkeeper.

● IN THE 1970s, however, at least the turf (if not the team) at Belle Vue was the best in the land. It was so good – partly due to the fact that the base was built from ash carted to the ground from nearby coalfields – that Wembley offered to buy the entire pitch. The offer was declined.

● DONCASTER'S tally of 33 wins from 42 matches in the 1946/47 season in Division Three (North) remains an English record.

Roll of Honour

Div 3 (N) champions 1935, 1947, 1950
Div 4 champions 1966, 1969

DOUBLES

AT THE end of the 1995/96 season Manchester United became the first team ever to win The Double (League Championship and FA Cup) twice – a feat matched by Arsenal two seasons later.

● THE FIRST TEAM ever to win The Double was Preston North End, back in 1888/89. They did it in some style: they didn't lose a match in the Championship or concede a goal in the FA Cup all season.

● THE FIRST TEAM to win The Double this century was Tottenham Hotspur, who clinched the most elusive club honour in English football by beating Leicester 2–0 in the FA Cup Final in 1961.

● ASTON VILLA (1897) and Liverpool (1986) are the only other teams who have achieved The Double.

● In 1998 Arsenal became only the second-ever team to win the 'Double double', having beaten Newcastle in the FA Cup Final and outpaced Manchester United in the League to emulate their 1971 success. But their achievement pales in front of United's, as Alex Ferguson's men completed the feat within three seasons (winning it in 1994 and 1996). The race for the first 'treble Double' is on...

TED DRAKE

Born: Southampton 6.8.12 Died: 31.5.95
Height: 5ft 10ins Position: Striker
Club career:
1931–34 Southampton 72 (48)
1934–45 Arsenal 168 (124)
International record:
1935–38 England 5 (6)

FORMER ARSENAL and England centre-forward Ted Drake (who also played cricket for Hampshire) holds the record for goals in a season for the Gunners, hammering in 42 in 1934/35.

● IN DECEMBER 1935 Drake equalled the League record of seven goals in a game for Arsenal against Aston Villa (still a Division One record). The amazing thing about the record was that Drake was carrying a serious knee injury and only had eight shots at goal. Seven went in and one hit the bar!

● IN THE 1950s, when manager at Chelsea, he set up one of the country's first youth schemes resulting in his team - known as Drake's Ducklings - winning Chelsea's only Championship in 1955.

● He was also assistant manager at Barcelona between January and July 1970 and later a full-time scout for Fulham until the mid-80s.

● DRAKE WAS one of the members of the inaugural pools panel, which sat for the first time during the big freeze of 1963.

DRAWS

NORWICH are the all-time draw specialists of the Football League, finishing their 1978/79 First Division campaign with 23 draws out of 42 matches (winning seven and losing twelve).

● ABERDEEN hold the record for most drawn games in a season in the Scottish Premier League: 21 out of 44 games in 1993/94. They lost just six and finished the season as runners-up to Rangers.

● IN THE 4th qualifying round of the FA Cup in 1971/72 Alvechurch and Oxford City drew five times before Alvechurch finally won 1–0 in the fifth replay. Their total playing time of 11 hours is an FA Cup record.

● ON TWO occasions in the Football League two sides have drawn 6–6. It first happened in 1930 when Leicester entertained Arsenal. The score was the same (in a torrential downpour) when Charlton faced Middlesbrough in 1960: a certain Brian Clough got a hat-trick that day for the away side. More recently Ossie Ardiles's Newcastle United side came away from Tranmere with a 6–6 draw in the Zenith Data Systems Cup in 1991 (although they finally lost the match on penalties).

DRUGS

The first player to be kicked out of the World Cup for taking drugs was Haiti's Ernst Jean-Joseph, who was sent home from the 1974 competition in West Germany after failing a dope test. Four years later Scotland's Willie Johnston tested positive after the defeat against Peru. The winger protested that he had taken pills for his hay fever, but few believed him, and he was ordered to pack his bags and suspended from international football for a year. The disgraced Johnston never played for Scotland again.

● The biggest World Cup drugs scandal, however, involved Diego Maradona at the 1994 tournament. The Argentinian star tested positive for a banned substance after inspiring his side to a magnificent 4-0 victory over Greece. He was kicked out of the competition and banned from football. Maradona had previously been given a worldwide 15-month ban after being charged with cocaine abuse in Italy in 1991.

● Drug-testing was introduced to English football in 1992. Players who have fallen foul of the testers include Chris Armstrong (while at Crystal Palace), Shane Nicholson (West Brom), Jamie Stuart (released by Charlton after testing positive for cocaine in 1997) and Roger Stanislaus (sacked by Orient for taking a performance-enhancing substance). Most famously, Paul Merson admitted that he was addicted to cocaine (and alcohol, and gambling) in 1994 when he was still at Arsenal.

Did You Know?

Ted Drake was the first man ever to win the League Championship both as a player (with Arsenal in 1934, 1935 and 1936) and as a manager (with Chelsea in 1955).

Eric Cantona decides to audition for Escape to Victory, even though the classic footie film was made 15 years earlier

DION DUBLIN

Born: Leicester 22.04.69
Height: 6ft 0ins Position: Striker
Club career:
1987–88 Norwich City 0 (0)
1988–92 Cambridge United 156 (53)
1992–94 Manchester United 12 (2)
1994– Coventry City 135 (58)
International career:
1998– England 3 (0)

MARVIN HAGLER lookalike Dion Dublin became Coventry City's most expensive ever signing when the club bought him for £1.9 million from Manchester United in 1994.

● DUBLIN scored on his Coventry City debut, going on to net eight times in his first eight games for The Sky Blues. Manager Phil Neal made him captain almost straight away.

● DUBLIN can play either as a powerful centre forward or as a centre half. He started his career at Norwich in the back four (though they never gave him a first-team game) and has been used in that position more recently at Highfield Road. This versatility gave Dublin a chance to be in Glenn Hoddle's France 98 squad but he was heart-breakingly left out of the final 22 having made the initial 28.

● STRANGELY ENOUGH, he actually made his debut for Manchester United in the city of Dublin, on 27th July 1992.

● During the 1997/98 season Dublin made his England debut against Chile and finished the season as the Premiership's equal top scorer with 18 goals (shared with Michael Owen and Chris Sutton).

DUMBARTON

Year founded: 1872
Ground: Boghead Park (5,503)
Highest ever crowd: 18,000, 2nd March 1957 v Raith Rovers (Scottish Cup qtr-final)
Nickname: The Sons
Colours: Gold shirt and shorts, gold and black socks

DUMBARTON were once one of the top sides in Scotland, are founder members of the League and were twice Champions in the first three years.

● IN 1888 they marked their record victory, thrashing Kirkintilloch 13–1. Their record defeats – they have been walloped 11–1 twice, by Albion and Ayr – came more recently, in 1926 and 1952.

● DUMBARTON settled in their Boghead Park Stadium in 1879 and have been there ever since, making them the longest residents at their present ground in Scotland and the second longest in Britain (and thus the world) after Stoke City.

● DUMBARTON SETTLED in their Boghead park Stadium in 1879 and have been there ever since, making them the longest residents at their present ground of any league clubs in Britain.

Roll of Honour

League champions 1891 (shared with Rangers), 1892
Div 2 champions 1911, 1972
Second Division champions 1992
Scottish Cup 1883

Dion Dublin belies his brutish Marvin Hagler looks with some surprisingly subtle footwork

DUNDEE

Year founded: 1893
Ground: Dens Park (16,871)
Highest ever crowd: 43,024, 1953 v Rangers (Scottish Cup)
Nickname: The Dee
Colours: Dark blue shirts, white shorts, blue and white socks

JUST ONCE the scene of a Scottish Championship triumph (1962), Dundee's Dens Park Stadium lies just 100 yards from Dundee United's Tannadice Park, making the two clubs easily the closest neighbours in British football.

● IN 1910 Dundee won their first trophy – the Scottish Cup – but not until their second replay with Clyde. Remarkably it was the third time the Scottish Cup Final had taken three matches to decide.

● THE CLUB's worst ever defeat came in 1895 when they lost 11-0 to Celtic, a record scoreline for Scotland's top flight. Things have improved recently, however, and in 1997/98 they achieved promotion to the brand new Scottish Premiership by topping the First Division.

● DUNDEE's best ever side, including the likes of Alan Gilzean (later of Spurs) and Ian Ure (later of Arsenal and Manchester United), won the Scottish Championship in 1962. Gilzean's stay at the club saw him hit a record 113 goals for the club. The manager of that team was Bob Shankly, brother of the more famous Bill.

Roll of Honour

Div 1 champions 1962
First Division champions 1979, 1992, 1998
Div 2 champions 1947
Scottish Cup 1910
League Cup 1952, 1953, 1974

DUNDEE UNITED

Year founded: 1909
Ground: Tannadice Park (14,209)
Previous name: Dundee Hibernian
Highest ever crowd: 28,000, 16th November 1966 v Barcelona (Fairs Cup)
Nickname: The Terrors
Colours: Orange shirts, black shorts, orange socks

WITH A recent history that has eclipsed their near neighbours Dundee, in the 1980s manager Jim McLean transformed Dundee United from being the city's second best side to a recognised force in Europe. They reached the European Cup semi-finals in 1984 and the UEFA Cup Final in 1987.

● THE TERRORS have a history of falling short on big occasions, losing two cup finals within five days in 1987 (Scottish and UEFA). They didn't manage to win the Scottish Cup until as recently as 1994, when they beat Rangers 1–0 in the final.

Dundee United's David Narey, who has played more European matches than any other Scottish player, has a right old knees-up with Aberdeen's Hans Gillhaus

Dundee Utd's Post-War Record

47 D2 10th	65 D1 9th	83 PR 1st
48 D2 15th	66 D1 5th	84 PR 3rd
49 D2 8th	67 D1 9th	85 PR 3rd
50 D2 7th	68 D1 11th	86 PR 3rd
51 D2 4th	69 D1 5th	87 PR 3rd
52 D2 4th	70 D1 5th	88 PR 5th
53 D2 8th	71 D1 6th	89 PR 4th
54 D2 15th	72 D1 9th	90 PR 4th
55 D2 13th	73 D1 7th	91 PR 4th
56 D2 8th	74 D1 8th	92 PR 4th
57 D2 13th	75 D1 4th	93 PR 4th
58 D2 9th	76 PR 8th	94 PR 6th
59 D2 17th	77 PR 4th	95 PR 10th
60 D2 2nd	78 PR 3rd	96 D1 1st
61 D1 9th	79 PR 3rd	97 PR 3rd
62 D1 10th	80 PR 4th	98 PR 7th
63 D1 7th	81 PR 5th	
64 D1 8th	82 PR 4th	

They had previously been runners-up on six occasions in the last 20 years.

● FORMERLY Dundee Hibernian (becoming United in 1923), the club is nicknamed The Terrors because of the lion in the club's badge.

● DAVE NAREY made an astonishing 612 appearances for the club between 1973–94. He played in no less than 76 European matches for Dundee United... a record for a Scottish player. Maurice Malpas is the club's most capped player, having played 55 games for Scotland.

● UNITED's biggest ever sale was for big Duncan Ferguson, when Rangers paid £4 million for him in 1993, two years before he moved 'down south' to Everton.

● IN 1994/95 Dundee United were relegated from the Premier League for the first time since 1960. Fortunately for them they managed to make it back the next season, though not without a tough struggle (finally achieving promotion through a play-off).

● THE CLUB's record victory was 14–0 over Nithsdale Wanderers in 1931, and the worst defeat 12–1 to Motherwell in 1954.

● IN THE 1955/56 season John Coyle scored 41 goals, a club record, although United's highest scorer is Peter McKay, who notched 158 goals in his time at the club.

● ALWAYS forward-thinking, in 1956 Dundee United became the first club in Scotland to have its own pools system in operation. And, aware of the growing importance of the commercial side of football, United became the first Scottish club to have a glass-fronted lounge for sponsors... in 1971!

● TV PRESENTER Lorraine Kelly admits to being a die-hard Dundee United fan.

● DESPITE being just 100 yards apart, Dundee United's Tannadice Stadium and Dundee's Dens Park are not the closest football stadiums in the world. That record is held by Hungarian teams MTK and BKV Elore of Budapest... their grounds back onto each other!

Roll of Honour

Premier League champions 1983
Div 2 champions 1925, 1929
Scottish Cup 1994
League Cup 1980, 1981

DUNFERMLINE ATHLETIC

Year founded: 1885
Ground: East End Park (12,000)
Highest ever crowd: 27,816, 30th April 1968 v Celtic (Div 1)
Nickname: The Pars
Colours: Black and white striped shirts, black shorts, white socks

PARTLY under the management of the great Jock Stein, Dunfermline enjoyed their heyday in the 1960s when they beat both Celtic and Hearts in Scottish Cup Finals (1961 and 1968). After a slump in the 1970s and 80s, recent years have seen an upturn in the club's fortunes with promotion back to the Premier League achieved in 1996.

● IN 1962/63 they tasted European glory by knocking Everton out of the Fairs Cup, and in 1968/69 reached the semi-finals of the Cup Winners' Cup, only losing narrowly to Slovan Bratislava of Czechoslovakia. In all the club enjoyed seven seasons of European competition in that golden era.

● THE CLUB's record victory was a stonking 11–2 win over Stenhousemuir in 1930. In 1889 they drew with Hibernian in the Scottish Cup 3rd round, only to collapse in the replay and record their worst ever defeat – a humiliating 11–1 loss.

● IN 1935 the East Terrace at East End Park was upgraded, using wood from the ocean liner Mauretania, which was being broken up in a nearby shipyard.

Roll of Honour

Div 1 champions: 1989
Div 2 champions 1926
Second Division champions 1986
Scottish Cup 1961, 1968

The Most Relegated Scottish Clubs (from any division)

1 Clyde 11
2 Greenock Morton 10
3= Falkirk 9
Raith Rovers 9
Stirling Albion 9
4= Ayr United 8
Dunfermline Athletic 8
5 Airdrieonians 7
6= Albion Rovers 6
Alloa Athletic 6
Dundee United 6
Kilmarnock 6
Queen of the South 6
St. Johnstone 6

DYNAMO MOSCOW

Founded: 1887
Stadium: Dinamo Stadium (50,000)
League wins: 11
Colours: Blue shirts, blue shorts and blue socks

THE CLUB was formed in 1887 by the English Charnock brothers. After the revolution they became the official Electrics team (hence the name), after which they became the official police team (hence their current nickname The Policemen).

● DYNAMO MOSCOW were the first Soviet side to play matches outside the Iron Curtain. Particularly notable was their tour of the UK in 1945. At a time when the British teams believed they were vastly superior to any foreign opposition, Dynamo drew with Chelsea and Rangers, and beat Cardiff 10–1 and Arsenal 4–3.

● At the Stamford Bridge encounter many Chelsea fans gained admission illegally after breaking down the main gates: the crowd of 100,000 is an unofficial club record as there was no way to verify it.

● DYNAMO were always fearsome opponents in Europe, especially at home, and became the first Soviet side to reach a major final in 1972, although they were defeated 3–2 by Glasgow Rangers in the Cup Winners' Cup.

● IN 1963 Dynamo's famous goalkeeper Lev Yashin, known as The Black Spider in Russia, became the first Soviet player to win the European Player of the Year Award.

Roll of Honour

League wins 1936, 1937, 1940, 1945, 1949, 1954, 1955, 1957, 1959, 1963, 1976
Cup wins 1937, 1953, 1967, 1970, 1977, 1984

EAST FIFE

Year founded: 1903
Ground: Name TBA (2,000)
Highest ever crowd: 22,515, 2nd January 1950 v Raith Rovers (Div 1)
Nickname: The Fifers
Colours: Amber shirts, amber shorts and amber socks

EAST FIFE became the first and only ever Scottish Second Division club to win the Scottish Cup when, in 1938, they beat Kilmarnock 4–2 in a replay after a 1–1 draw.

● IN 1998 the club moved into a brand new 2,000 capacity all-seater stadium but, as we went to print, the new ground had not been named.

● THE highest aggregate score in the Scottish League was recorded on 11th December 1937 when East Fife trounced Edinburgh City 13-2. This is, of course, the club's biggest ever win.

● EAST FIFE striker Henry Morris must be the unluckiest international player on record. In 1949 he scored a hat-trick for Scotland against Northern Ireland in his first game for the national team... but was never capped again!

● EAST FIFE once recorded the biggest tongue-twisting result in the history of football. At the end of the match the score was East Fife 5 Forfar 4... well you try saying it out loud!

Roll of Honour

Div 2 champions 1948
Scottish Cup 1938
League Cup 1948, 1950, 1954

EAST STIRLINGSHIRE

Year founded: 1880
Ground: Firs Park, Falkirk (1,880)
Highest ever crowd: 12,000, 13th February 1921 v Partick Thistle (Scottish Cup rd 3)
Nickname: The Shire
Colours: Black shirts with white hoops, black shorts, black socks

EAST STIRLINGSHIRE is Scotland's second smallest club after Albion Rovers, with a ground capacity at Firs Park of just 1,880 (a number that is particularly memorable as that was the year the club was founded!). In 1964 they actually spent a season away from their present home, but shareholders won a legal battle to bring the club back.

● DIVISION TWO champions in 1932, the club's record victory was way back in 1882 – an 11–2 thumping of Vale of Bannock. In 1936 the tables were turned, however, when they were slaughtered 12–1 by Dundee United, their worst defeat.

● THE SHIRE, as they are nicknamed for obvious reasons, suffered arguably the unluckiest away trip in 1981, when they travelled to Montrose to play in a Scottish League Cup tie. Three separate coaches broke down and the players had to complete their journey in a fleet of taxis. When they did eventually get there they lost 1–0!

Roll of Honour

Div 2 champions 1932
C Division Champions 19348

Did You Know?

In 1948 East Fife, then in the Second Division, became the first side to win the Scottish League Cup, beating Falkirk 4–1 in a replay. And in 1954 they became the first club to win the competition three times, beating Partick Thistle 3–2 in the final.

DUNCAN EDWARDS

Born: Dudley 1.10.36 Died: 21.2.58
Height: 5ft 11ins Position: Midfielder
Club career:
1953–58 Manchester United 175 (21)
International record:
1955–58 England 18 (5)

DUNCAN EDWARDS is the youngest player to have appeared for Manchester United, with a First Division debut at the age of 16 years and 285 days on Easter Monday in 1953.

● IN 1955, he became the youngest player this century to win a full England cap, making his debut against Scotland at Wembley aged 18 years and 183 days (a record beaten in February 1998 by Michael Owen).

● IN 1956 Edwards was the youngest member of the 'Busby Babes' Manchester United side which won the first of two successive league championships. In 1957 he played his one FA Cup final, but finished on the losing side to Aston Villa.

● EDWARDS was the most complete footballer of his generation. Powerful in the tackle, strong in the air and the possessor of a full range of ball skills, he was seen by many as a future England captain. Bobby Charlton once said: 'If I had to play for my life and could take one player with me, it would be Duncan Edwards.'

● TWO WEEKS after the Munich air crash on 6th February 1958 Edwards died in hospital. He was the last of eight Manchester United players to die as a result of the accident.

Tragic 'Busy Babe' Duncan Edwards is still sadly missed today

MARTIN EDWARDS

Born: Adlington Hall, Cheshire 24.7.45

SINCE MULTI-MILLIONAIRE Chairman Martin Edwards has presided over Manchester United, they have become the country's most successful side.

● EDWARDS took over when his father Louis (who had made his fortune as a butcher before ploughing much of his money into United) suffered a fatal heart attack in 1979.

● AFTER SACKING managers Dave Sexton and Ron Atkinson, Edwards famously stood by Alex Ferguson when many were calling for his head in the late 1980s. Three League titles, three FA Cups, a European Cup Winners' Cup and a League Cup later that's looking like a pretty wise decision.

● WITH the club now turning over an astonishing £88 million a year, major shareholder Edwards is certainly not getting any poorer. He's not as popular at Old Trafford as you might think, though, with many fans blaming him for what they see as excessive ticket pricing and exploitation of their support with constantly changing team strips.

ENGLAND

First international: England 0 Scotland 0 (Glasgow, 1872)
First World Cup appearance: England 2 Chile 0 (Brazil, 1950)
Highest capped player: Peter Shilton (125)
Highest goalscorer: Bobby Charlton (49)
Best win: 13–0 v Ireland, 1882
Worst defeat: 7–1 v Hungary, 1954
Colours: White shirts, blue shorts, white socks

ENGLAND's greatest moment came in 1966 when they hosted the World Cup and ended up winning the tournament. After a mediocre bore-draw start against Uruguay Alf Ramsey's 'Wingless Wonders' team went on to beat Mexico, France, Argentina, Portugal and West Germany, 4-2, in the final, to lift the Jules Rimet Trophy and make the whole country very happy indeed. Nobody's stopped talking about it since.

● ENGLAND'S THIRD goal in the final is the most disputed in the history of the game. It is impossible to tell for sure whether Geoff Hurst's shot bounced inside or outside the goal-line after it hit the crossbar. Russian linesman Bakhramov was sure however, and the goal stood. Hurst's three goal haul remains the only hat-trick ever scored in a World Cup Final.

● SINCE THEN England have never won the competition, although they have been tremendously unlucky, losing out to two of their traditional enemies. In 1970 they gave away a 2-0 quarter-final lead against West Germany after a trio of blunders by reserve keeper Peter Bonetti. In 1982 they finished the tournament unbeaten, but went out on goal difference, again to the Germans. Then in 1986 a hand-ball goal by Argentina's Maradona was the difference between the teams. In 1990 they came closest to glory, getting to the semi final of the World Cup, but went out on penalties after drawing 1-1 with West Germany, breaking the nation's heart. Just eight years later Glenn Hoddle's team befell the same fate at the hands of Argentina after a thrilling 2-2 draw that many rated the best match in the tournament.

● IT WAS by then a familiar story to England fans: two years earlier they were eliminated from Euro '96 - on penalties, by Germany. In fact England, along with Italy, are the team which has been eliminated the most times from major competitions after a spot-kick shoot-out.

● ENGLAND, along with Scotland, are the oldest international team. The two participated in the first ever official international match in London back in 1872, which finished 0-0. England have since played more international matches than any other team, and scored more goals.

● GREAT BRITAIN, which was an amalgamation of England and Scotland, were the first team to win the Olympic Games football tournament in 1908 and repeated the feat in 1912.

● IT WAS widely believed that, as England had invented the game, they were virtually invincible unless they met someone else from the British Isles. This belief was shattered when they were beaten by the United States in the 1950 World Cup, then defeated 6-3 at home and 7-1 away by Hungary in 1953 and 1954. Since then things haven't quite been the same.

● THE FASTEST ever England goal was scored by Tommy Lawton. He netted after just 17 seconds of a match against Portugal in 1947.

● ENGLAND'S YOUNGEST player this century and youngest ever goalscorer is Liverpool's Michael Owen. He made his debut against Chile in February 1998 aged just 18 years and 59 days and scored his first goal against Morocco in May of the same year aged 18 years and 166 days.

WORLD CUP RECORD

1930–38	Did not enter	1974	Did not qualify
1950	Round 1	1978	Did not qualify
1954	Quarter-finals	1982	Round 2
1958	Round 1	1986	Quarter-finals
1962	Quarter-finals	1990	Fourth place
1966	Winners	1994	Did not qualify
1970	Quarter-finals	1998	Round 2

EQUIPMENT

THE CRAZE for wearing odd coloured boots is nothing new. Alan Ball, for example, was famous for wearing flash white boots in the seventies. But you have to go back to before WW1 to find the first example: future Arsenal manager Herbert Chapman used to turn out in bright yellow boots.

● ARGUABLY the craziest player to brave a Scottish winter was Egyptian star Abdul Salim. He played for Celtic in the 1930s but incredibly refused to wear boots, wrapping his feet in bandages instead before he went out to play.

● THE WINTER of 1946/47 was the most severe in the history of the football league. More than 140 matches were postponed that year but many ice and snow-covered pitches were marked out with red paint so matches could go ahead.

● IN 1989 PORTSMOUTH FC were shocked to discover that one of the crossbars at Fratton Park was an inch too low. Over a century earlier in 1887 Crewe Alexandria lost 3–2 away to Swifts in a fourth round FA Cup replay, but after Crewe complained that one of the crossbars was two inches too low the FA ordered the match be replayed. Crewe won the second replay (played at the Derby Cricket Ground) 2–1. For the record the crossbar must be exactly 8ft (2.44 metres) from the ground.

Michael Owen already holds more records than any other current England player

EUROPEAN CHAMPIONSHIPS

GERMANY WON the European Championships for the third time at Wembley in 1996. They are the only nation to have won the competition on more than one occasion. The other years were 1972 and 1980.

● EURO 96 – the 10th edition of the tournament was the biggest so far, with more teams competing (16) more people attending matches (1.3 million) and bigger TV audiences (6.9 billion) than in any tournament before.

● EURO 2000 will take place in Holland and Belgium. It will the first time the tournament has been shared between two countries. Both countries qualify automatically as hosts.

● THE MOST astonishing result in European Championship history came in the qualifying rounds of the competition in 1984. Spain needed to beat Malta by 11 goals to qualify in front of Holland. There were suggestions that the Spaniards had put something in the half-time gazpacho when they scored nine second half goals to run out 12–1 winners.

European Championship Finals

1960	USSR 2 Yugoslavia 1 (Paris)
1964	Spain 2 USSR 1 (Madrid)
1968	Italy 2 Yugoslavia 0 (after 1–1 draw, Rome)
1972	West Germany 3 USSR 0 (Brussels)
1976	Czechoslovakia 2 West Germany 2 (Czechs won 5–3 on pens, Belgrade)
1980	West Germany 2 Belgium 1 (Rome)
1984	France 2 Spain 0 (Paris)
1988	Holland 2 USSR 0 (Munich)
1992	Denmark 2 Germany 0 (Gothenburg)
1996	Germany 2 Czech Republic 1 (London)

EUROPEAN CUP

THE MOST prestigious club event in world football was conceived by Gabriel Hanot, a former French international who became editor of the Paris-based sports newspaper L'Equipe. In the 1950s he was so irritated by the British media's claims that Wolverhampton Wanderers were the best team in Europe (after they had beaten Hungarian club Honved and Spartak Moscow in friendlies) that he launched a tournament pitting the league champions of the major European leagues against each other.

● SPANISH GIANTS Real Madrid have won the competition more times than any other club, with seven wins, and won the first ever final in Paris in 1956 (beating Reims 4–3).

● AFTER THAT victory Real went on to win the trophy for the next four years running and again in 1966 and 1998. Behind them are AC Milan (five wins) and Liverpool and Ajax Amsterdam (both four).

● THE FIRST BRITISH club to win the European Cup was Celtic in 1967 (beating Inter Milan 2–1 in Lisbon and the first English club to lift it was Manchester United in 1968 (after beating Benfica 4–1 at Wembley).

● LIVERPOOL are the most successful British club in the competition after winning the trophy four times in 1977, 1978, 1981 and 1985, although no English team has reached the final since the period when English clubs were banned from Europe in 1984 following the Heysel disaster.

Crazed Real Madrid players tried to run off with the trophy before the 1998 European Cup Final... fortunately they were aprehended and forced to play the game (which they won 1-0).

European Cup Winners

1956	Real Madrid v Reims 4–3
1957	Real Madrid v Fiorentina 2–0
1958	Real Madrid v AC Milan 3–2
1959	Real Madrid v Reims 2–0
1960	Real Madrid v Eintracht Frankfurt 7–3
1961	Benfica v Barcelona 3–2
1962	Benfica v Real Madrid 5–3
1963	AC Milan v Benfica 2–1
1964	Inter Milan v Real Madrid 3–1
1965	Inter Milan v Benfica 1–0
1966	Real Madrid v Partizan Belgrade 2–1
1967	Celtic v Inter Milan 2–1
1968	Manchester United v Benfica 4–1
1969	AC Milan v Ajax 4–1
1970	Feyenoord v Celtic 2–1
1971	Ajax v Panathinaikos 2–0
1972	Ajax v Inter Milan 2–0
1973	Ajax v Juventus 1–0
1974	Bayern Munich v Atletico Madrid 4–0 (replay after 1–1)
1975	Bayern Munich v Leeds Utd 2–0
1976	Bayern Munich v St. Etienne 1–0
1977	Liverpool v Borussia Moenchengladbach 3–1
1978	Liverpool v Club Brugge 1–0
1979	Nottingham Forest v Malmo 1–0
1980	Nottingham Forest v Hamburg 1–0
1981	Liverpool v Real Madrid 1–0
1982	Aston Villa v Bayern Munich 1–0
1983	Hamburg v Juventus 1–0
1984	Liverpool v Roma 1–1 (penalties)
1985	Juventus v Liverpool 1–0
1986	Steaua Bucharest v Barcelona 0–0 (penalties)
1987	Porto v Bayern Munich 2–1
1988	PSV Eindhoven v Benfica 0–0 (pens)
1989	AC Milan v Steaua Bucharest 4–0
1990	AC Milan v Benfica 1–0
1991	Red Star Belgrade v Marseille 0–0 (penalties)
1992	Barcelona v Sampdoria 1–0
1993	Marseille v AC Milan 1–0
1994	AC Milan v Barcelona 4–0
1995	Ajax v AC Milan 1–0
1996	Juventus v Ajax 1–1 (penalties)
1997	Borussia Dortmund v Juventus 3–1
1998	Real Madrid v Juventus 1–0

EUROPEAN FOOTBALLER OF THE YEAR

THE FIRST winner of the European Footballer of the Year (voted for by journalists from all over the continent) was 'Wing Wizard' Sir Stanley Matthews in 1956.

● NO PLAYER has ever won the award four times and only three players have been honoured three times. They are Johan Cruyff (1971, 1973 and 1974), Michel Platini (1983, 1984 and 1985) – the only player to win it three times in a row – and Marco Van Basten (1988, 1989 and 1992).

● THE LAST British player to be named European Footballer of the Year was Kevin Keegan when he played for German club Hamburg in 1979.

1956	Sir Stanley Matthews
1957	Alfredo di Stefano
1958	Raymond Kopa
1959	Alfredo di Stefano
1960	Luis Suarez
1961	Omar Sivori
1962	Josef Masopust
1963	Lev Yashin
1964	Denis Law
1965	Eusebio
1966	Bobby Charlton
1967	Florian Albert
1968	George Best
1969	Gianna Rivera
1970	Gerd Muller
1971	Johan Cruyff
1972	Franz Beckenbauer
1973	Johan Cruyff
1974	Johan Cruyff
1975	Oleg Blokhin
1976	Franz Beckenbauer
1977	Allan Simonsen
1978	Kevin Keegan
1979	Kevin Keegan
1980	Karl Heinz-Rummenigge
1981	Karl Heinz Rummenigge
1982	Paolo Rossi
1983	Michel Platini
1984	Michel Platini
1985	Michel Platini
1986	Igor Belanov
1987	Ruud Gullit
1988	Marco Van Basten
1989	Marco Van Basten
1990	Lothar Matthaus
1991	Jean-Pierre Papin
1992	Marco Van Basten
1993	Roberto Baggio
1994	Hristo Stoichkov
1995	George Weah
1996	Matthias Sammer
1997	Ronaldo

EUROPEAN GOLDEN BOOT

THE GOLDEN BOOT is awarded to the leading European league scorer of the season. The first winner was the legendary Eusebio who picked up the trophy after knocking in an incredible 43 goals for Benfica in 1968. The Black Panther outgunned his rivals again in 1973, at the age of 30, banging in 40 goals.

● THE FIRST BRITISH winner of the award was Ian Rush, in 1984, and the most recent was Ally McCoist, in 1991. Other notable recipients of the award include Marco Van Basten, Hristo Stoichkov and Austrian striker Hans Krankl.

● THE MOST CONTROVERSIAL winner was Rumania's Rodion Camataru, who scored 44 goals for Dynamo Bucharest in 1987. Eyebrows were raised when he stormed past the leading contenders with a sackful of goals in a series of end of season matches, and evidence produced in the post-Communist era suggests these games may not have been played in a wholly competitive spirit!

Portugal's best ever player and leading goalscorer Eusebio was rarely beaten for pace

Did You Know?

Eusebio scored Portugal's first World Cup hat-trick when he notched four in his country's 5–3 demolition of North Korea in 1966. The Koreans had been 3–0 up in the first half!

EUSEBIO

Born: Lourenço Marques, Mozambique 25.1.43
Position: Forward
Club career:
1961–74 Benfica 294 (316)
International record:
1961–73 Portugal 64 (41)

THE LEGENDARY Eusebio is Portugal's leading all-time scorer with 41 goals, and the most famous player to appear for his country.

● THE 'BLACK Panther', or the 'Black Pearl', as he was known, was top scorer at the 1966 World Cup, with nine goals, a haul which included four in one match against North Korea. Despite scoring in the semi-final against England, Eusebio left the pitch in tears, knowing that he would never win the World Cup medal his rich talents deserved.

● AS A YOUNG player Eusebio was the subject of the fiercest ever contract battle between two Portuguese clubs. Having made his debut in 1958 with Mozambique's Laurenço Marques, a nursery club of Sporting Lisbon, Eusebio was 'kidnapped' by Benfica on his arrival to Lisbon and hidden away in a fishing village on the Algarve until the argument between the two clubs died down.

● EUSEBIO was a member of the first side to beat legendary Real Madrid in a European Cup final. In 1962 Benfica trounced the Spanish aristocrats and five-time winners of the trophy 5–3 in the final, with Eusebio scoring two cannonball goals. A year earlier Benfica (without Eusebio) had beaten Barcelona 3–2 in the final.

ROY EVANS

Born: Bootle 4.10.48

ROY EVANS has only ever been involved with one club – Liverpool. Now boss at Anfield, Evans has been at the club since the age of 15.

● A PROMISING left-back who played for England Schoolboys, after a few years at Anfield it soon became clear that because of his lack of pace his first-team prospects would be limited. Then manager Bill Shankly saw his potential as a coach, and at 25 and after only nine first-team outings Evans retired from playing in 1974 to take charge of the Liverpool reserve team.

● AFTER SERVING as assistant manager to both Kenny Dalglish and Graeme Souness, Evans was appointed to the job he'd always dreamed of when Graeme Souness resigned in January 1994.

● AMID a clamour of 'Roy who?' exclamations, Evans slowly but surely got the stuttering Liverpool back on the rails. And in 1995 The Reds won their first trophy for three years when he guided them to the 1995 Coca-Cola Cup (beating Bolton 2–1).

EVERTON

Year founded: 1878
Ground: Goodison Park (40,209)
Previous name: St Domingo FC
Highest ever crowd: 78,299, 18th September 1948 v Liverpool (Div 1)
Nickname: The Toffees
Colours: Blue shirts, white shorts, black/blue hooped socks

AFTER STARTING out as a lowly church team, Everton soon emerged as one of the mightiest forces in British football and their roll of honour is impressive to say the least. In fact, no other club in England has spent as many seasons in the top flight as Everton, the Merseysiders inhabiting the top division for no fewer than 95 seasons.

● IN THAT time The Toffees, as they are known (after Ye Ancient Everton Toffee House which was right next to the pub where the club was founded), have won the league title nine times.

● EVERTON have appeared in more FA Cup semi-finals than any other club (23 compared to Manchester United's 21) and have won the cup on five occasions, the last being in 1995.

● THE CLUB's ground, Goodison Park, is just 840 yards away across Stanley Park from Liverpool's stadium, Anfield. They are not the two closest league grounds in England, however, as Nottingham's City and County grounds are even closer.

● THE CLUB'S record goalscorer is the legendary Dixie Dean who, between 1925 and 1937, banged in no fewer than 349 goals in 399 games. The prolific Dean still holds the league record for goals in a season when he scored 60 for Everton in the 1927/28 campaign (40 of them were scored with his head and nine came in the last three games).

● THE CLUB'S most capped player is Neville Southall, who made 91 appearances for Wales. He has also appeared more times for Everton than any other player, making 578 appearances between the sticks.

● IN 1915 Everton won the championship with the lowest ever points total, following the league's expansion to 20 teams. During that campaign they notched up just 46 points (when teams received two points for a win).

● IN 1930/31 they scored no fewer than 121 goals in the season (winning 26, losing 12 and drawing just four of their 42 matches) to win the Division Two title. In one four-game streak they scored an amazing 33 goals.

● IN THREE SUCCESSIVE seasons (1931, 1932 and 1933) the Toffeemen achieved the unique record of winning the Second Division Championship, First Division Championship and the FA Cup in turn.

● IN 1932/33 they were the first football team to wear the numbers 1 to 11 when they stepped out for their 3–0 FA Cup Final victory over Manchester City. The City players wore 12 to 22!

● IN 1958/59 Everton became the first club to experiment with undersoil heating at Goodison Park (itself the oldest of the current top flight football stadiums) at a cost of £70,000. Unfortunately it didn't work and eventually had to be scrapped.

● THE CLUB's most recent prolonged success came under Howard Kendall, who – with players like Peter Reid, Graeme Sharp, Andy Gray and Paul Bracewell – won the league (1985 and 1987), the FA Cup (1984) and the European Cup Winners' Cup (1985).

● Everton's worst ever defeat came at the hands of Tottenham on 11th October 1958, when Spurs hammered them 10–4. The Toffees' record victory was a 9–1 mauling of Manchester City, on 3rd September 1906, a score they also notched up against Plymouth on 2nd December 1930.

Everton's Duncan Ferguson gently asks Chelsea's Michael Duberry if he'd mind stepping aside

Everton's Post-War Record

47 D1 10th	64 D1 3rd	81 D1 15th
48 D1 14th	65 D1 4th	82 D1 8th
49 D1 18th	66 D1 11th	83 D1 7th
50 D1 18th	67 D1 6th	84 D1 7th
51 D1 22nd	68 D1 5th	85 D1 1st
52 D2 7th	69 D1 3rd	86 D1 2nd
53 D2 16th	70 D1 1st	87 D1 1st
54 D2 2nd	71 D1 14th	88 D1 4th
55 D1 11th	72 D1 15th	89 D1 8th
56 D1 15th	73 D1 17th	90 D1 6th
57 D1 15th	74 D1 7th	91 D1 9th
58 D1 16th	75 D1 4th	92 D1 12th
59 D1 16th	76 D1 11th	93 PR 13th
60 D1 16th	77 D1 9th	94 PR 17th
61 D1 5th	78 D1 3rd	95 PR 15th
62 D1 4th	79 D1 4th	96 PR 6th
63 D1 1st	80 D1 19th	97 PR 15th
		98 PR 17th

Roll of Honour

Div 1 champions 1891, 1915, 1928, 1932, 1939, 1963, 1970, 1985, 1987
Div 2 champions 1931
FA Cup 1906, 1933, 1966, 1984, 1995
European Cup Winners' Cup 1985

EXETER CITY

Year founded 1904
Ground: St. James Park (10,570)
Highest ever crowd: 20,984, 4th March 1931 v Sunderland (FA Cup rd 6 replay)
Nickname: The Grecians
Colours: Red-and-white-striped shirts, black shorts, red socks

WITH A highest position of 6th in the old Third Division in 1979/80, Exeter City have been permanent residents of the lower echelons of the football league for their entire history. They did beat Coventry City 8–1 once (their record win), but that came in 1926 when The Sky Blues were languishing in Division Three (South) themselves.

● THE CLUB's record defeat is 9–0, a result they have suffered twice: once at the hands of Notts County (1948) and once courtesy of Northampton Town (1958).

● IN THE FA Cup Exeter City's record is not exactly glorious. They did reach the 6th Round in 1931 when they took Sunderland to a replay, but since 1945 they have lost 11 times to non-league opponents. Only Halifax Town have a worse cup record against non-leaguers.

● DURING World War II US troops lived in the main stand at St. James Park and used the pitch for training.

Roll of Honour

Div 4 champions 1990
Div 3 (South) Cup 1934

EXTRA TIME

THE FIRST match to go into extra time was the 1875 FA Cup Final between Royal Engineers and Old Etonians. As is so often the case it wasn't enough to separate the sides – the score was 1–1 – and a replay was needed. Royal Engineers won the replay 2–0: both matches were played at Kennington Oval.

● THE FIRST World Cup Final to go to extra time was the 1934 tie between Italy and Czechoslovakia. It was 1–1 at the end of normal time but Italy ended up 2–1 winners.

● THE LONGEST game ever recorded – a 1962 Copa Libertadores match between Santos of Brazil and Penarol of Uruguay – featured extra time and so many stoppages that it finally ended at one o'clock in the morning with scores still level at 3–3!

● FIVE OUT OF the seven matches in the knockout stages of Euro 96 went to extra time... although incredibly only one (the final) was settled by a 'golden goal'.

● IN THE 1990 World Cup, eight out of the 15 knockout matches went to extra time, more than at any other World Cup finals tournament.

FA CUP

THE FA Cup is the oldest knockout competition in the world, dating back to 1871 when it was established under the control of the Football Association. The first ever round of the FA Cup saw the Civil Service lose 2–0 to Barnes, Crystal Palace draw 0–0 with Hitchin, Upton Park lose 3–0 to Clapham Rovers and Maidenhead beat Marlow 2–0 on 11th November 1871. Maidenhead and Marlow are the only two clubs to have played in the competition every year since it started.

● UNLIKE THE League Cup, the FA Challenge Cup – to give it's full title – has always retained the same name (although it is now known as the FA Cup sponsored by Littlewoods).

● THERE HAVE been four different FA Cup trophies, although the latest edition is an exact replica of its predecessor, which was gracefully retired in 1992 while in the possession of Tottenham Hotspur. The first trophy – known as the 'tin idol' – was stolen from a shop window in 1895 where it was on display after Aston Villa had won it. A successor was commissioned by red-faced Villa and the club were fined £25 for their negligence. Unfortunately no one thought to copyright the new design and before long every competition had its own replica 'FA Cup' trophy. So in 1910 the FA 'retired' the old trophy (it was presented to Lord Kinnaird on completing 21 years as FA President) and comissioned a new one from Fattorini and Sons sliversmiths in Bradford... and by coincidence it was won for the very first time by Bradford City in 1911.

● IN 1996 Manchester United won the FA Cup for the ninth time, more than any club, taking them past Tottenham's total of eight.

● United have also taken part in more FA Cup finals than any other team. The Reds have appeared in no fewer than 14 finals, compared with Arsenal's 13, Everton's 12 and Liverpool's 11. Everton, however, have appeared in more semi-finals than any other club, reaching the last four on 23 occasions (but only actually winning the cup five times).

● THE YOUNGEST ever captain in an FA Cup Final was David Nish, who was 21 and 212 days when he led Leicester City out of the Wembley tunnel to face Manchester City in 1969.

● Norman Whiteside is the youngest man ever to score in an FA Cup Final. He was only 18 years and 18 days old when he

Post-War Cup Finals

1946 Derby County 4 Charlton Athletic 1*
1947 Charlton Athletic 1 Burnley 0*
1948 Manchester United 4 Blackpool 2
1949 Wolverhampton Wanderers 3 Leicester City 1
1950 Arsenal 2 Liverpool 0
1951 Newcastle United 2 Blackpool 0
1952 Newcastle United 1 Arsenal 0
1953 Blackpool 4 Bolton Wanderers 3
1954 West Bromwich Albion 3 Preston North End 2
1955 Newcastle United 3 Manchester City 1
1956 Manchester City 3 Birmingham City 1
1957 Aston Villa 2 Manchester United 1
1958 Bolton Wanderers 2 Manchester United 0
1959 Nottingham Forest 2 Luton Town 1
1960 Wolverhampton Wanderers 3 Blackburn Rovers 0
1961 Tottenham Hotspur 2 Leicester City 0
1962 Tottenham Hotspur 3 Burnley 1
1963 Manchester United 3 Leicester City 1
1964 West Ham United 3 Preston North End 2
1965 Liverpool 2 Leeds United 1*
1966 Everton 3 Sheffield Wednesday 2
1967 Tottenham Hotspur 3 Burnley 1
1968 West Bromwich Albion 1 Everton 0*
1969 Manchester City 1 Leicester City 0
1970 Chelsea 2 Leeds United 2*
Chelsea 2 Leeds United 1 (replay)
1971 Arsenal 2 Liverpool 1*
1972 Leeds United 1 Arsenal 0
1973 Sunderland 1 Leeds United 0
1974 Liverpool 3 Newcastle United 0
1975 West Ham United 2 Fulham 0
1976 Southampton 1 Manchester United 0
1977 Manchester United 2 Liverpool 1
1978 Ipswich Town 1 Arsenal 0
1979 Arsenal 3 Manchester United 2
1980 West Ham United 1 Arsenal 0
1981 Tottenham Hotspur 1 Manchester City 1*
Tottenham Hotspur 3 Manchester City 2
1982 Tottenham Hotspur 1 Queens Park Rangers 1*
Tottenham Hotspur 1 Queens Park Rangers 0
1983 Manchester United 2 Brighton & Hove Albion 2*
Manchester United 4 Brighton & Hove Albion 0
1984 Everton 2 Watford 0
1985 Manchester United 1 Everton 0*
1986 Liverpool 3 Everton 1*
1987 Coventry City 3 Tottenham Hostspur 2*
1988 Wimbledon 1 Liverpool 0
1989 Liverpool 3 Everton 2*
1990 Manchester United 3 Crystal Palace 3*
Manchester United 1 Crystal Palace 0
1991 Tottenham Hotspur 2 Nottingham Forest 1*
1992 Liverpool 2 Sunderland 0
1993 Arsenal 1 Sheffield Wednesday 1*
Arsenal 2 Sheffield Wednesday 1*
1994 Manchester United 4 Chelsea 0
1995 Everton 1 Manchester United 0
1996 Manchester United 1 Liverpool 0
1997 Chelsea 2 Middlesbrough 0
1998 Arsenal 2 Newcastle United 0

*After extra time

Wimbledon – a non-league team only 11 years before – bring the FA Cup home and show it off to yet another bumper crowd

netted for Manchester United in the 4-0 Wembley replay win over Brighton in 1983. The longest FA Cup tie on record took six hours and eleven matches to complete. The fourth qualifying round contest between Oxford and Alvechurch in the 1970/71 season was eventually settled when Alvechurch won the sixth game 1-0. This, of course, could not happen now because since 1991 games that are level at the end of a replay are settled with a penalty shoot-out.

● THE FIRST player ever to be sent off in an FA Cup final was Manchester United's Kevin Moran in 1985, who received his marching orders from referee Peter Willis for a late tackle on Everton's Peter Reid. Despite this setback, United went on to win 1–0.

● The FA Cup's quickest dismissal came as recently as January 1997. Swindon's Ian Culverhouse was sent off in the 3rd round against Everton after just 58 seconds of the game.

● PRESTON North End's 26–0 demolition of Hyde back in 1887 remains the biggest ever winning margin in the FA Cup proper.

FALKIRK

Year founded: 1876
Ground: Brockville Park (9,706)
Highest ever crowd: 23,100, 21st February 1953 v Celtic (Scottish Cup rd 3)
Nickname: The Bairns
Colours: Dark blue shirt with white flashings, white shorts, red socks

FALKIRK have been at their Brockville Park stadium since 1882, longer than any club in Scotland apart from Dumbarton.

● A RAILWAY runs directly behind the stadium's open Hope Street End and legend has it that a ball kicked out of the ground once landed in a passing goods truck and was later found at Perth, 44 miles up the line. Brockville Park is only 800 yards away from East Stirlingshire's ground, Firs Park.

● FALKIRK, who were considerably richer in the past than they are now, became the first UK club to pay more than £5,000 for a player, when they bought West Ham striker Syd Puddefoot in 1922.

● FALKIRK splashed out a club record fee of £225,000 to Chelsea for Scottish winger Kevin McAllister in 1991.

● A MATCH against Clyde in 1962 finished 7–3 to Falkirk. All ten goals were scored by the same man... Falkirk's Hugh Maxwell.

● Falkirk's record victory was a 12–1 thrashing of Laurieston in the 2nd round of the Scottish Cup in March 1893. In April 1951, however, they were on the receiving end of an almost identical scoreline when Airdrieonians beat them 11–1.

Roll of Honour

Div 2 champions 1936, 1970, 1975
First Division champions 1991, 1994
Second Division champions 1980
Scottish Cup 1913, 1957

FAMILIES

THE MOST brothers to appear in one team in an FA Cup tie is three: in the 1st round local derby between Nottingham Forest and Notts County in 1878, Forest fielded two sets of three, the Cursham brothers and the Greeshalgh brothers.

● THE HIGHEST number of brothers ever to play in the football league is nine. Mrs Keetley was a very proud mum, especially of her third son Ted, who scored 160 goals for Doncaster Rovers between 1923–29, making him the club's top aggregate scorer.

● IN APRIL 1990 Hereford player-manager Ian Bowyer picked his son Gary to play alongside him. This was the first time a father and son had played in the same team since 1951.

● IN A Division Two match between Luton and QPR in 1980 brothers Martyn and Viv Busby both came on as substitutes... for opposite sides.

● WHEN SWINDON beat Exeter in a Division Three South match in 1946 the two scorers – Alfred and William Stephens – were twins.

● THE MOST famous modern footballing family is the Allens. During the 1990s no fewer than four members of the Allen family were playing in the football league. Clive Allen (former Crystal Palace and Tottenham striker and son of ex-Spurs player Les Allen) was playing at West Ham and Millwall, while his cousins, brothers Martin (West Ham) and Paul (Spurs and Southampton) and nephew Bradley (QPR and Charlton) were also keeping up the family's fine footballing traditions.

● The first brothers to play in a World Cup Final were not Bobby and Jack Charlton. 36 years earlier J. and M. Evaristo played for Argentina in the 1930 final against Uruguay... Argentina lost 4–2.

● Herbert and William Rowson were the first brothers to play in an FA Cup Final and the only pair to appear on opposing sides. In 1874 Herbert played for the Royal Engineers while William was in the Oxford University team, which won 2–0.

FANS

ONE of the most disappointed fans in the history of the game was Grimsby supporter Mike Rowell, who decided to cycle the 180 miles to Upton Park, West Ham to see his team play The Hammers in the 4th round of the FA Cup in 1996. When he finally arrived at the ground he found it was locked. The game had been postponed due to a frozen pitch.

● STILL, HE PROBABLY wasn't as disappointed as Wolves fan Christos Konospiris, 24, who saved up £800 for a flight to England from his native Australia to see Wolves in action on the last day of the season in May 1996. He turned up at Molineux in good time for kick-off only to find that the Wolves were playing away to Charlton, 130 miles away.

● BUT THE PRIZE for most dedicated air-miles-consuming fan goes to Newcastle nutter Graham Edmondson, who emigrated to Dallas, Texas in 1995, but still flies back to Geordie-land once a month to see his beloved Toon Army in action at St. James' Park. The flight alone costs him at least £600.

● GRIMSBY FANS,as we have already discovered, are perhaps the wackiest in the league. In the 1980s, many of them took inflatable plastic fish to the game,

Skinny striker Ian Ormondroyd meets some of his fans

which were nicknamed Harry the Haddock. The inflatable craze started at Manchester City when supporters began taking plastic bananas to the game. Around the same time Chelsea fans took sticks of celery to matches, which they threw around while singing a special celery song, the words of which are too rude to be printed here.

● IT IS unlikely that John Major was ever among the celery-throwers, but he is one of many politicians who support Chelsea. Indeed trendy Chelsea can probably boast the highest number of celebrity fans iincluding comedian David Baddeil,pop singer Damon Albarn, politicians David Mellor and Tony Banks and actor Phil Daniels.

● Most clubs have famous fans: singer Elton John actually took over his favourite club, Watford, on two separate occasions. Liam and Noel Gallagher of Oasis have such a thing for Manchester City that they looked into sponsoring the club.

FAROE ISLANDS

First international: Faroe Islands 0 Iceland 1 (friendly, Torshavn, 1930)
Colours: White shirts, blue shorts and white socks

WITH JUST 22 football pitches (only two of which are natural grass) and 3,914 registered players, the Faroe Islands are the smallest footballing nation ever to have won a competitive international.

● IN 1990 they beat Austria 1–0 in a European Championship qualifier (played in Denmark as they hadn't a grass pitch at the time), the biggest giant-killing act in internat-ional football's history. It was their first ever competitive international, although they had been playing friendlies since the 1930s.

● Since that famous result the Faroes have recorded victories only against fellow minnows San Marino and Malta.

ALEX FERGUSON

Born: Govan 31.12.41

MANCHESTER United manager Alex Ferguson became the first man to lead a team to two League Championship and FA Cup doubles when United pulled off the feat for the second time in three years in May 1996.

● Alex Ferguson is the most successful manager in the history of British football. He has won an unprecedented 19 major trophies with St Mirren and Aberdeen in Scotland and Manchester United in England.

● Ferguson is the only manager to have guided both English and Scottish clubs to success in Europe and in all three domestic competitions.

● It was as manager of Aberdeen from 1978 to 1986 that he made a name for himself as a manager, at the same time as breaking the Glasgow Old Firm domination of Scottish football. With the Dons he won three Premier Division titles, four Scottish Cups, one League Cup and a European Cup Winners Cup.

● From Aberdeen he moved to Old Trafford, and on November 6th 1996 Ferguson celebrated a decade as manager at Manchester United. He is now by far the longest serving manager in the Premiership.

DUNCAN FERGUSON

Born: Stirling 27.12.71
Height: 6ft 3ins Position: Forward
Club career:
1990–93 Dundee United 77 (28)
1993–94 Rangers 14 (2)
1994– Everton 103 (34)
International record:
1992– Scotland 7 (0)

IN 1993 Duncan Ferguson joined Rangers from Dundee United for a then British transfer record fee of £4 million. When he signed for Everton after a loan period at Goodison Park he set another British transfer record, by becoming the first player to be transferred twice between British clubs for a fee of £4 million or more.

● FERGUSON is the only British professional footballer to go to jail for assaulting a fellow pro during a match. On 11th October 1995 he was sentenced to three months in Barlinnie Prison for head-butting Raith Rovers full-back John McStay at Ibrox. It was not the first time 'Duncan Disorderly' had been on the wrong side of the law. In 1992 he was fined after head-butting a policeman, and two other assault convictions swiftly followed.

● DESPITE the prison sentence, 1995 was not all bad for Ferguson. In May he helped Everton win the FA Cup with a 1-0 win over Manchester United. This remains his only major honour to date. In 1997 he announced that he did not want to play for Scotland any more.

FIFA

FIFA, the Fédération Internationale de Football Association, is the most important administrative body in football. It organises World Cup tournaments and institutes law changes in the game.

● THERE ARE 202 members of FIFA, that's more counties than there are in the United Nations. The incumbent President of the organisation is Switzerland's Sepp Blatter, the latest in a distinguished line including Jules Rimet (1921-1954), Sir Stanley Rous (1961-1974) and Joao Havelange (1974-1998).

● LAW CHANGES FIFA have introduced into the World Cup include penalty shoot-outs, automatic red cards for tackles from behind, the use of stretchers to carry off players who have fallen over and the banning of the professional foul.

● BRITISH COUNTRIES have a long history of disputes with FIFA. They weren't involved with the setting up of the organisation in 1904 and pulled out briefly in 1918 and 1928.

TOM FINNEY

Born: Preston 5.4.22
Height: 5ft 7ins Position: Winger
Club career:
1946–60 Preston North End 433 (187)
International record:
1947–59 England 76 (30)

TOM FINNEY, a flying winger equally adept on both right and left wings, was the first player to be made Footballer of the Year twice. He won the award for the first time in 1954, after starring in his club's run to the FA Cup Final, and was honoured again in 1957.

● FINNEY is possibly the greatest English player never to win a major club prize. In 1953 Preston missed out on the League Championship on goal difference, the following year they lost to West Brom in the FA Cup Final, and in 1958 they again finished second in the league.

● NICKNAMED the 'Preston Plumber', Finney is North End's all-time leading goalscorer, notching 187 league goals between 1946–60. His 30 international goals place him fourth equal, with Nat Lofthouse, in the list of top England scorers.

TIM FLOWERS

Born: Kenilworth 3.2.67
Height: 6ft 2ins Position: Goalkeeper
Club career:
1984–86 Wolves 63
1986–93 Southampton 192
1987–88 Swindon (loan) 7
1993– Blackburn Rovers 166
International record:
1993– England 11

WHEN TIM FLOWERS moved from Southampton to Blackburn in November 1993 he became Britain's most expensive goalkeeper, until Nigel Martyn joined Leeds for £3 million in 1996.

● WHEN Blackburn won the Premiership title in 1994/95 Flowers conceded just 39 league goals, an average of less than one per game. Rovers manager, Kenny Dalglish, broke his normal rule of not singling individual players out for praise by announcing that Flowers was worth 'an extra 12 points a season'.

● FLOWERS, first picked for England in 1993 by Graham Taylor, has suffered from being behind David Seaman in the pecking order, the race for a place which inspired the famous female fans' banner 'Boys – we prefer Seaman to Flowers'. He has been picked for the squad for Euro '96 and France '98, but has yet to start a game in an international tournament.

● IN 1996 Flowers conceded possibly the weirdest goal in the Premiership's history, when a weak shot from Liverpool's Stan Collymore hit an Ewood Park divot and bounced over the Blackburn keeper's shoulder, before trickling over the line.

FOOTBALL ASSOCIATION

THE FA is the oldest football organisation in the world, founded in 1863 – the Football League was set up in 1888.

● THE FIRST laws the FA passed involved the outlawing of the use of hands and of kicking your opponents. Barnes and Richmond played the first game under the new laws in 1863.

● IN 1871 the president of the FA, Charles Alcock, remembered that at Harrow School there had been a very enjoyable knock-out competition, so he decided to institute it on a national level. The competition, named the FA Challenge Cup, has been running ever since, and is the most famous national club competition in the world.

● THE FA has traditionally been a highly conservative body, and through the years has kicked its heels on almost every innovation in the game, including the formation of an international football tournament, the use of substitutes and the use of floodlights.

FOOTBALLER OF THE YEAR

CONFUSINGLY there are two Footballer of the Year awards in England and Scotland, the PFA (Professional Footballers' Association) Footballer of the Year and the Football Writers' Footballer of the Year.

● THE FIRST winner of a Footballer of the Year title was Stanley Matthews, considered by the Football Writers' Association to have made the most valuable contribution to the 1947/48 season. Celtic's Billy McNeill became the first Scottish Player of the Year in 1965.

● THE FIRST Players' Player of the Year was Norman 'Bites Yer Legs' Hunter, who was honoured with the award by his shin-chomped colleagues in 1974.

● LIVERPOOL's Terry McDermott was the first player to hold both English awards simultaneously after his efforts helped Liverpool win the League Championship in 1980. This feat was matched by Arsenal's Dennis Bergkamp in 1998.

The 'Preston Plumber', Tom Finney, flushes out another chance... this time from a corner

PFA Footballer of the Year

1974	Norman Hunter (Leeds)
1975	Colin Todd (Derby)
1976	Pat Jennings (Tottenham)
1977	Andy Gray (Aston Villa)
1978	Peter Shilton (Nottingham Forest)
1979	Liam Brady (Arsenal)
1980	Terry McDermott (Liverpool)
1981	John Wark (Ipswich)
1982	Kevin Keegan (Southampton)
1983	Kenny Dalglish (Liverpool)
1984	Ian Rush (Liverpool)
1985	Peter Reid (Everton
1986	Gary Lineker (Everton)
1987	Clive Allen (Tottenham)
1988	John Barnes (Liverpool)
1989	Mark Hughes (Manchester United)
1990	David Platt (Aston Villa)
1991	Mark Hughes (Manchester United)
1992	Gary Pallister (Manchester United)
1993	Paul McGrath (Aston Villa)
1994	Eric Cantona (Manchester United)
1995	Alan Shearer (Blackburn Rovers)
1996	Les Ferdinand (Newcastle United)
1997	Alan Shearer (Newcastle United)
1998	Dennis Bergkamp (Arsenal)

Football Writers' Player of the Year (Since 1974)

1974	Ian Callaghan (Liverpool)
1975	Alan Mullery (Fulham)
1976	Kevin Keegan (Liverpool)
1977	Emlyn Hughes (Liverpool)
1978	Kenny Burns (Nottingham Forest)
1979	Kenny Dalglish (Liverpool)
1980	Terry McDermott (Liverpool)
1981	Frans Thijssen (Ipswich Town)
1982	Steve Perryman (Tottenham)
1983	Kenny Dalglish (Liverpool)
1984	Ian Rush (Liverpool)
1985	Neville Southall (Everton)
1986	Gary Lineker (Everton)
1987	Clive Allen (Tottenham)
1988	John Barnes (Liverpool)
1989	Steve Nicol (Liverpool)
1990	John Barnes (Liverpool)
1991	Gordon Strachan (Leeds)
1992	Gary Lineker (Tottenham)
1993	Chris Waddle (Sheffield Wednesday)
1994	Alan Shearer (Blackburn Rovers)
1995	Jürgen Klinsmann (Tottenham)
1996	Eric Cantona (Manchester United)
1997	Gianfranco Zola (Chelsea)
1998	Dennis Bergkamp (Arsenal)

FORFAR ATHLETIC

Year founded: 1885
Ground: Station Park (8,732)
Highest ever crowd: 10,780, 2nd February 1970 v Rangers (Scottish Cup rd 2)
Nickname: The Lions
Colours: Sky blue shirts, navy shorts, navy socks

FORFAR ATHLETIC's Station Park ground is inappropriately named as nowadays it finds itself 14 miles from the nearest train station, in Dundee, further than any club in Britain. Station Park has good claim to be the windiest ground in Britain. The roof of one of its stands has been blown off by gales on three separate occasions, in 1888, 1893 and 1921.

● A FUNDRAISING campaign by the club in 1956 included the creation of the world's largest bridie (meat and onion pie).

● IN 1984 Forfar set up their centenary year by winning the Second Division title with a record 63 points (when it was still two points for a win).

● THE SKY BLUES' record victory was in 1988, a 14–1 win over Lindertis in the first round of the Scottish Cup.

● ALEX BRASH has made the most appearances for the club – 376 between 1974–86. The most Forfar goals in one season were the 45 scored by Dave Kilgour in Division 2 in the 1929/30 campaign.

Roll of Honour

Second Division champions 1984
Third Division champions 1995
C Division champions 1949

ROBBIE FOWLER

Born: Liverpool 9.4.75
Height: 5ft 11ins Position: Forward
Club career:
1993– Liverpool 158 (92)
International record:
1996– England 7 (2)

Robbie Fowler burst onto the Premiership scene in 1993 and his phenomenal goal-scoring for Liverpool instantly made him one of the hottest young strikers in the country.

● In only his fourth senior game he equalled a Liverpool scoring record – shared by three other players including Ian Rush – by netting five goals against Fulham in the Coca Cola Cup. Then in August 1994 Fowler struck the fastest hat-trick in Premiership history, netting three goals inside five minutes against Arsenal at Anfield.

● In 1996 he became only the second player – after Ryan Giggs – to win the PFA Young Player of the Year trophy in consecutive seasons. And the following season, 1996/97, he scored his 100th goal for Liverpool, passed the 30 goals in a season mark for the third campaign in a row, and also scored his first goal for England (in the 2-0 friendly win over Mexico). He missed out on France '98, however, suffering a serious ankle injury against Everton towards the end of the 1997/98 season.

● AS WELL as scoring goals, though, Fowler has always courted controversy. In 1994 he was fined £1,000 by the FA for baring his backside to fans at Filbert Street and in March 1997 he was fined £900 by UEFA for 'a violation of the principles of sporting conduct' – revealing a vest supporting the striking Liverpool dockers in a Cup Winners Cup match at Anfield against Brann. Later on that month he showed another side of his character when he tried to get referee Gerald Ashby to overrule a penalty decision awarded when opponent David Seaman had apparently upended him in the box. He was later sent a congratulatary letter from FIFA General Secretary Sepp Blatter.

Liverpool's highest goalscorer stands next to the biggest wall in the world. Robbie Fowler has scored 83 goals in 138 league games for The Reds. The Great Wall of China is 2,550 miles long and is the only man-made structure that can be seen from the moon.

FRANCE

First international: Belgium 3 France 3 (Brussels, 1903)
First World Cup appearance: Belgium 4 Mexico 1 (Uruguay, 1930)
Highest capped player: Manuel Amaros (82)
Highest goalscorer: Michel Platini (41)
Best win: 8–0 v Iceland, 1957
Worst defeat: 1–17 v Denmark, 1908
Colours: Blue shirts, white shirts, red socks

In 1998 France won the World Cup for the first time ever, despite being the nation which conceived the tournament way back in 1930.

● FRANCE'S 3–0 victory over Brazil in the final at the Stade De France on 12th July 1998 was the culmination of the biggest ever World Cup. For the first time ever there were 32 teams involved in the tournament and a cumulative global television audience of 38 billion tuned in.

● DURING THE match midfielder Zinedine Zidane became the first man to score two goals in a final since Argentina's Mario Kempes twenty tears previously. Zidane was born in Marseilles the son of Algerian immigrants and, following the incredible victory celebrations across France sparked by the team which included French players from all different racial backgrounds, one journalist wrote: 'Zidane's two goals did more for the equal rights of citizens than a thousand speeches denouncing racism.'

● BEFORE 1998 France had never even reached the World Cup Final, losing at the semi-final stage on three occasions in 1958 (to Brazil), 1982 (to West Germany) and 1986 (to West Germany).

● During the 1958 World Cup campaign French striker Just Fontaine scored 13 goals in the tournament... a World Cup finals record. And Fontaine is still the second highest scorer of all time in World Cup finals tournaments (after Gerd Muller, 14).

● THE 1982 match (which they lost to West Germany on penalties) saw one of the worst unpunished fouls in football when German goalkeeper Schumacher broke Batiston's jaw and knocked out two of his front teeth in a brutal challenge. The referee gave a goal kick.

● THE FRENCH, however, did taste glory in the European Championship two years later, which they hosted. One of the best teams Europe has ever seen, inspired by the midfield genius of Michel Platini, won the title, beating Spain 2–0 in the final.

● PLATINI IS France's record goalscorer (41) and the country's most famous player of all time, and he also headed the France 98 organising committee. During the World Cup Final he responded to an appeal by the players for greater support by abandoning his usual shirt and tie for a French replica shirt.

● FRANCE BECAME the first side to play with 12 men on 11th November 1952 while playing Northern Ireland. In the first half injured Frenchman Bonifaci came back onto the pitch without realising he had been substituted. The error wasn't discovered until half-time, when France reverted back to 11-a-side and went on to win 3–1.

WORLD CUP RECORD

Year	Result	Year	Result
1930	Round 1	1970	Did not qualify
1934	Round 1	1974	Did not qualify
1938	Round 2	1978	Round 1
1950	Did not qualify	1982	Fourth place
1954	Round 1	1986	Third place
1958	Third place	1990	Did not qualify
1962	Did not qualify	1994	Did not qualify
1966	Round 1		

Ooh la la! France's highest goalscorer takes a tumble in the 1986 World Cup

TREVOR FRANCIS

Born: Plymouth 19.4.54
Height: 5ft 10ins Position: Forward
Club career:
1970–79 Birmingham City 280 (118)
1979–81 Nottingham Forest 70 (28)
1981–82 Manchester City 26 (12)
1982–86 Sampdoria (Italy) 68 (17)
1986–87 Atalanta (Italy) 21 (1)
1987–88 Rangers 18 (0)
1988–89 QPR 32 (12)
1989–94 Sheffield Wednesday 70 (5)
International record:
1977–86 England 52 (12)

TREVOR FRANCIS became the first million-pound player when Nottingham Forest manager Brian Clough bought him from Birmingham City for £1,150,500 in February 1979. He was also the first player to be transferred for more than a million pounds on three separate occasions.

● FRANCIS scored more goals as a 16-year-old in the First Division than any player before or since. He notched up 15 in his first 15 games for Birmingham City in 1970.

● FRANCIS had an illustrious career, scoring the winning goal in the 1979 European Cup final for Nottingham Forest against Malmo and going on to play for Manchester City, Sampdoria, Atalanta, Rangers and QPR, where he became player-manager.

● IN 1993, AS MANAGER of Sheffield Wednesday, Francis took Wednesday to both Wembley finals. But they were beaten in both the FA Cup and the League Cup by Arsenal (2–1 in both cases).

● IN 1996 Francis returned 'home' to become manager of his first club, Birmingham City. He has had a volatile relationship with the club's managing director Karren Brady, and resigned at one point during the 1997/98 season after his son was abused by a fan in the directors' lounge.

FRIENDLIES

THE FIRST official international friendly took place in 1872 between Scotland and England in Glasgow. The Scottish team was entirely composed of Queens Park players. Two thousand people packed into the West of Scotland Cricket Club to watch a 0–0 draw. Scotland made £38 profit from the game, enabling them to travel to England for the return match.

● ONE OF the most unfriendly friendlies took place between England and World Champions Italy at Arsenal in 1934, a game which was later nicknamed 'the Battle of Highbury'. After Monti left the field injured, the Italians played it rough and English captain Eddie Hapgood ended up with a broken nose. England ran out 3–2 winners.

● HIGHBURY was also the scene of another famous unfriendly friendly which witnessed the entire Benfica team being sent off after attacking the referee in a match they were losing 6–2 to Arsenal.

FULHAM

Year founded: 1879
Ground: Craven Cottage (19,000)
Previous names: Fulham St. Andrew's
Highest ever crowd: 49,335, 8th October 1938 v Millwall (Div 2)
Nickname: The Cottagers
Colours: White shirts, black shorts, white socks

Following a buyout by Harrods multi-millionaire Mohamed Al Fayed in the summer of 1997, Fulham are almost certainly the richest football club outside the top two divisions. During the 1997/98 season, having appointed Kevin Keegan as Director of Football, the club became the first from the Second Division to pay £1 million for a player (Paul Peschisolido from West Brom). A few months later they paid £2 million for Chris Coleman from Blackburn Rovers.

● FULHAM have inhabited a record number of different grounds for a league club. They played at no fewer than ten different venues before moving to Craven Cottage in 1896, where they have been ever since. The club was founded by two clergymen who wanted to add something to their congregation's lives.

● JOHNNY HAYNES played the most games for The Cottagers – 594 between 1952–70 – and was their most internationally honoured player, with 56 England caps.

● AFTER THE ABOLITION of the maximum wage in 1961, midfield star Johnny Haynes became the first £100 a week player in Britain.

● FULHAM is the only club in the country to have been managed by two different men with the same name. Bill Dodgins Snr. and Jnr. were father and son and both took the helm at Craven Cottage.

Roll of honour

Div 2 champions 1949
Div 3 (S) champions 1932

GALATASARAY

Year founded: 1905
Ground: Ali Sami Yen (40,000)
League wins: 11
Colours: Yellow shirts with red trim, yellow shorts and yellow socks.

THE MOST successful team in Turkey, Istanbul club Galatasaray have won 11 league titles and 11 Turkish cups (although hated rivals Fenerbahce have also won 11 titles they have only won four cups).

● GALATASARAY are followed by arguably the most passionate supporters in Europe. Just ask Manchester United. When United played there in the 1994 and 1995 they were greeted with 'Welcome to Hell' banners and screaming fans at the airport. In the 1994 game (which United drew, losing the tie on away goals) Eric Cantona lost his rag with the referee, sparking a near riot which the police seemed to enjoy, for which he was later banned for four European matches.

● AT THE of 1995/6 Galatasaray, who were managed just for that season by ex-Liverpool and Rangers boss Graeme Souness, had a record three British players on their books. Within weeks, however Barry Venison and Mike Marsh were back in England, and Dean Saunders soon followed.

● IN 1989 Galatasaray made the semi-finals of the European Cup, the furthest any Turkish side has ever got in the competition. They went out 5–1 on aggregate to Steaua Bucharest after beating Rapid Vienna, Neuchatel Xamax and Monaco. No Turkish club has ever won a European trophy.

HUGHIE GALLACHER

Born: Bellshill 2.2.1903 Died: 11.6.57
Height: 5ft 5ins Position: Forward
Club career:
1920–21 Queen of the South
1921-25 Airdrieonians 111 (90)
1925-30 Newcastle United 160 (133)
1930-35 Chelsea 132 (72)
1935-36 Derby County 51 (38)
1936-37 Notts County 45 (32)
1937-38 Grimsby Town 12 (3)
1938-39 Gateshead 31 (18)
International record:
1924–35 Scotland 20 (23)

WITH 23 goals for his country, Hughie Gallacher is Scotland's third top international goalscorer, behind Kenny Dalglish and Denis Law. Neither of those legendary figures, however, can remotely match Gallacher's strike rate of more than a goal per game.

● GALLACHER's finest hour was as a member of the Scottish side – dubbed the 'Wembley Wizards' – which thrashed England 5–1 in 1928. It was the last time Scotland scored more than three goals against the 'auld enemy'. The following year Gallacher equalled the Scottish scoring record by netting four times in a 7-3 rout of Northern Ireland.

● IN 1927 Gallacher captained the last Newcastle United side to win the league championship. Three years later he joined Chelsea for the then enormous sum of £10,000. His career tailed off in the late 1930s, and in 1957 he committed suicide on a railway line.

KEVIN GALLACHER

Born: Clydebank 23.11.66
Height: 5ft 8ins
Position: Striker
Club career:
1985-90 Dundee United 131 (27)
1990-93 Coventry City 100 (28)
1993- Blackburn Rovers 90 (25)
International record:
1988- Scotland 37 (8)

IT WAS LARGELY thanks to Kevin Gallacher's goals that Scotland made it to the 1998 World Cup finals. The nippy Blackburn striker was his country's top scorer in the qualifiers with six goals, including a decisive double against group winners Austria and the first goal at home to Latvia, the match which clinched Scotland's place in France.

● GALLACHER made his Scotland debut back in 1988 against Colombia, but it took him a while to adapt to international football, and he had to wait until his 16th appearance for his first goal – in a 3-0 win over Estonia in 1993.

● AFTER MAKING his name as a pacey attacker with Dundee United, Gallacher moved to Coventry in 1990. After three and a half seasons at Highfield Road he joined Blackburn Rovers. He has been a regular in the Rovers side ever since, but sadly a broken leg meant he only played one game in Blackburn's 1994/95 Premiership season.

● FOR A FORWARD, Gallacher is not a prolific scorer, and it took him until March 1997 to claim his first Premiership hat-trick in a 3-1 home win over Wimbledon. He is always a threat inside the box, however, and his partnership with England rebel Chris Sutton has developed into one of the most effective in the top division.

GARRINCHA

Born: Brazil 28.10.33 Died: 1983
Position: Forward
Club career:
1947–53 Pau Grande (Brazil)
1953–66 Botafogo (Brazil)
1966–67 Corinthians (Brazil)
AJ Barranquilla (Colombia)
Flamengo (Brazil)
Red Star Paris
International record:
1955–66 Brazil 51 (12)

BRAZIL STAR Garrincha overcame greater odds than any other player to become one of the quickest and most dangerous wingers of all time. He was born into poverty and contracted polio as a child, leaving him with a right leg so badly twisted doctors doubted he would ever walk properly again. Amazingly, he went on to play 51 time for his country and win two World Cups.

● IN 1962 Garrincha – his full name was Manoel Francisco dos Santos, though always known by his nickname which means Little Bird – became only the second player to be sent off in a World Cup semi-final.

● GARRINCHA was only allowed to play in the final after a personal plea by the Brazilian President, and he collected a second winner's medal as the reigning champions beat Czechoslovakia 3–1.

● IN 1983 Garrincha became one of football's most regretted casualties when he died prematurely of alcoholic poisoning.

PAUL GASCOIGNE

Born: Gateshead 25.5.67
Height: 5ft 10ins Position: Midfielder
Club career:
1985–88 Newcastle United 92 (21)
1988–92 Tottenham Hotspur 92 (19)
1992–95 Lazio 42 (6)
1995– Rangers 87 (35)
1998– Middlesbrough 7 (0)
International record:
1988– England 57 (10)

WHEN PAUL GASCOIGNE was dropped from Glenn Hoddle's final England 22 for France '98 such was the stature of the most gifted English player of his generation that a national debate ensued about whether or not the England manager was right. The incident was the latest chapter in a football career that had had more twists and turns than your average Alfred Hitchcock film.

● NO PLAYER'S movements – on and off the pitch – have been scrutinised more closely by the media than Gazza's - the Newcastle-born midfielder has achieved a status in the tabloids usually reserved for the more glamorous members of the royal family. Gazzamania first swept the country in the Italia '90 World Cup when the player's tears during the England-Germany semi-final neatly summed up the nation's disappointment, and his brilliant performance on the pitch helped fuel a wave of national optimism about the state of English football.

● ONCE DESCRIBED as 'daft as a brush' by former England manager Bobby Robson, Gazza's career unfortunately saw him on the front pages of the tabloids as often as the back as a result of his drink-influenced antics. Nor was he helped by a series of terrible – and often self-inflicted — leg and head injuries.

● NEVERTHELESS Gascoigne did manage some on-pitch honours to go with his off-pitch dishonour. In 1996 he became one of the select band of players to win the Cup in both Scotland (with Rangers) and England (with Spurs in 1991). And in 1997 he helped Rangers equal Celtic's record of nine successive Scottish Championships, winning two medals himself.

Don't Quote Me

'They say injuries come in threes. In my case it seems to be thirty-threes.'
Paul Gascoigne 1993

A man of smiles and tears – in this case the former as Gazza celebrates his Euro 96 goal for England against Scotland – the best goal of the tournament

GERMANY

First international:
Switzerland 5 Germany 3
(Basle, 1908)
First World Cup appearance
Germany 5 Belgium 2 (Italy, 1938)
Highest capped player:
Lothar Matthäus (126)
Highest goalscorer: Gerd Müller (68)
Best win: 16–0 v Tsarist Russia, 1912
Worst defeat: 0–6 v Austria, 1931
Colours: White shorts, black shorts
and white socks

Germany (formerly West Germany) have played in the World Cup Final more than any other team. They have reached the last game on six occasions, winning the trophy three times, in 1954, 1974 and 1990.

● THEY ARE ALSO the only team to win a World Cup final after going two goals down... recovering against the famous Hungary team of Puskas and co in 1954 to win 3–2.

● THE GERMANS have never lost the habit of coming from behind, and even in France 98, where their squad had an average age of over 30, they got to the quarter-finals after comebacks against Yugoslavia and Mexico. In the end, however, they were disposed of 3–0 by Croatia, their biggest World Cup defeat since 1958.

● GERMANY ARE the only country to have won the European Championship on more than one occasion, lifting the trophy three times (1972, 1980 and 1996). They have also been losing finalists twice (1976 and 1992).

● ONLY BRAZIL (with a total of 171) have scored more World Cup goals than Germany, who have notched a total of 162.

● AND ONLY BRAZIL have played in more World Cup tournament games – 80 as opposed to 78.

The Germans celebrate being the first (and possibly only if FIFA scrap the idea) international team ever to win a match by a 'golden goal' in the Euro 96 Final against the Czech Republic.

WORLD CUP RECORD

1930	Did not enter	1974	Winners
1934	Third place	1978	Round 2
1950	Did not enter	1982	Runners-up
1954	Winners	1986	Runners-up
1958	Fourth place	1990	Winners
1962	Quarter-finals	1994	Quarter-finals
1966	Runners-up	1998	Quarter-finals
1970	Third place		

GERSON

Born: Brazil, 1941
Position: Midfielder
Club career:
Botafogo (Brazil)
Flamengo (Brazil)
São Paulo (Brazil)
International record:
1960–71 Brazil 83 (14)

GERSON was the midfield playmaker in the legendary 1970 World Cup-winning Brazil side. His goal in the final against Italy was one of his country's most important ever. With the score standing at 1–1, Gerson smashed a 20-yard shot into the net to pave the way for Brazil's ultimately convincing 4–1 win.

● WITH 83 caps, Gerson – his full name is Gerson di Olivera Nunez – is the ninth most capped Brazilian player of all time. He enjoyed great success at club level too, winning Brazilian League championship medals with Botafogo in 1967 and 1968.

● ONE OF the heaviest smokers among players of his era, Gerson was reputed to smoke up to two packets of cigarettes a day while playing at his peak.

GIANT-KILLING

THE MOST FAMOUS and dramatic post-war giant-killing act in English football occurred at Edgar Street, in 1972 when then non-league Hereford beat mighty Newcastle United 2–1. After holding Newcastle to an incredible 2–2 draw at St. James' Park, Hereford were 1–0 down in the replay when, with seven minutes left, Ronnie Radford unleashed an unstoppable shot from 30 yards (which later won Goal of the Season), and in extra time Ricky George scored the winner.

● THE BIGGEST pre-war cup shock occurred when Third Division Walsall beat Arsenal 2–0 in 1933. Arsenal fans watching a reserve match at Highbury laughed when the score was announced... they thought it was a joke!

● THE HIGHEST SCORING giant-killing shocks in the FA Cup have been Boston United's 6–1 win away at Derby County in December 1955, Hereford's December 1957 6–1 win at home to QPR and Barnet's stonking of Newport County in November 1970 by the same score.

● THE BIGGEST giant-killing in international football occurred in 1990 when lowly Faroe Islands (pop. 48,000) stunned mighty Austria (pop. eight million) by beating them 1–0 in a European Championships qualifier... their first ever competitive international.

RYAN GIGGS

Born: Cardiff 29.11.73.
Height: 5ft 11ins Position: Winger
Club career:
1991– Manchester United 236 (49)
International record:
1991– Wales 21 (5)

WHEN Manchester United star Ryan Giggs came off the bench against Germany on October 16th 1991 he became the youngest player ever to appear for Wales... aged 17 years and 332 days, a record broken in June 1998 by namesake Ryan Green (17 yrs 226 days)

Ryan Giggs, the youngest ever Welsh cap, practises his legendary 'lazybones' overhead kick

● GIGGS MADE his debut for Manchester United in a First Division match against Everton on March 2nd of that same year, 1991, and in his second full season in the first team he was a member of the United side which won the League title for the first time in 26 years.

● IN 1996, at the age of 22, Giggs became the youngest player in the United side to have appeared in both double-winning sides (1994 and 1996). And in his short but glorious career so far he has won four league titles, two FA Cups and a League Cup.

● RYAN GIGGS is the only player to have played for two countries under different names. In 1989 he played for England schoolboys as Ryan Wilson, the surname being that of his father, a former Welsh rugby league player. In 1991 Giggs made his international debut for Wales against Germany. 'I only played for England schoolboys because I was at school in England,' he said.

KEITH GILLESPIE

Born: Larne, N. Ireland 18.2.75
Height: 5ft 10ins Position: Winger
Club career:
1994–95 Manchester United 9 (1)
1993–94 Wigan Athletic (loan) 8 (4)
1995– Newcastle United 106 (11)
International record:
1994– Northern Ireland 21 (1)

KEITH GILLESPIE only played nine games for Manchester United before joining Newcastle as the makeweight in Andy Cole's £6 million transfer to Old Trafford in 1995. Ironically, the only goal he scored for The Reds was against Newcastle.

● A winger with electric pace, Gillespie's finest performance for the Magpies was probably in the 3-2 win over Barcelona in the 1997/98 Champions League. He created two goals for Faustino Asprilla and repeatedly roasted Spanish international left back Sergi.

● In October 1994 Gillespie scored his first goal for Northern Ireland – a stunning 20-yard volley in a 2-1 victory over Austria in a Euro '96 qualifier.

● In 1996 Gillespie made the front pages when it was revealed he had accumulated gambling debts in the region of £60,000. He also found himself in the news in 1997 when he was allegedly involved in a fracas with team-mate Alan Shearer in a Dublin bar and had to go to hospital for stitches to a head wound.

GILLINGHAM

Year founded: 1893
Ground: Priestfield Stadium (10,600)
Previous name: New Brompton
Highest ever crowd: 23,002, 10th January 1948 v QPR (FA Cup rd 3)
Nickname: The Gills
Colours: Blue shirts, white shorts and white socks

AFTER NEARLY going into receivership in 1994, Kent club Gillingham recovered superbly to gain promotion into Division Two in the 1995/96 season. It was not the first time that Gillingham had looked close to collapse. In 1938 they dropped out of the league and were not re-elected until 1950.

● THE CLUB'S greatest moment came in 1964 when they won the Fourth Division Championship. At this time (between April 1963 and April 1965) Gillingham broke the record for the number of consecutive home matches without defeat (52)... until it was broken again in 1981 by Liverpool (who went undefeated at home for 85 games).

● GOALIE FRED FOX is the only player to be capped by England while playing for Gillingham... he earned one cap in 1925. The club's most capped player is Tony Cascarino who played three times for the Republic of Ireland while at the club.

● THE CLUB's record goalscorer is Tony Yeo, who netted 135 times between 1963–75.

Roll of Honour

Div 4 champions 1964

Did You Know?

Wolverhampton Wanderers were the last FA Cup holders to be knocked out by a non-league team when Crystal Palace beat them 4-2 in a 1909 1st round replay.

DAVID GINOLA

Born: Gassin, France 25.1.67
Height: 6ft 0ins Position: Forward
Club career:
1985–88 Toulon 81 (4)
1988–90 Racing Paris 61 (8)
1990–91 Brest 50 (10)
1991–95 Paris St. Germain 115 (32)
1995–97 Newcastle United 68 (6)
1997– Tottenham Hotspur 34 (6)
International record:
1993– France 15 (3)

KNOWN IN FRANCE as 'El Magnifico', in the summer of '95 Ginola signed for Newcastle for £2.5 million from Paris St Germain. While at the famous French club he won the French League and the French Cup (twice) and was voted French Player of The Year in 1994.

● HAVING fallen out with new Toon manager Kenny Dalglish, in the summer of 1997 Ginola moved to Spurs for £2 million where – almost single-handedly at times – he helped save Tottenham from the drop. It wasn't enough, however, to force his way into the French squad for the World Cup.

● IT WAS while playing for his country that Ginola suffered the lowest point of his career, giving the ball away in the last minute of a vital World Cup qualifier against Bulgaria, who went on to score and put France out of USA 94.

● GINOLA, a former law student, has an ambition to become a lawyer when he retires from football. 'I'd like to work in an office with friends and defend people,' he says.

GLENTORAN

Year founded: 1882
Ground: The Oval, Belfast (30,000)
League wins: 19
Colours: Green shirts, black shorts, green socks

NORTHERN IRELAND's second most successful club, Belfast based Glentoran have won the Irish League 19 times and the Irish Cup 16 times. Arch local rivals Linfield, however, have managed an astonishing 42 league wins and 37 cup victories.

● THE CLUB's most successful European campaign came in 1973/74 when they reached the quarter-finals of the Cup Winners' Cup. After beating Chemnia Ramnicu Valcea of Romania, and then Brann Bergen of Norway, they were beaten 7-0 on aggregate by German giants Borussia Moenchengladbach.

Roll of Honour

Irish League champions 1894, 1897, 1905, 1912, 1913, 1921, 1925, 1931, 1951, 1953, 1964, 1967, 1968, 1970, 1972, 1977, 1981, 1988, 1992
Irish Cup 1914, 1917, 1921, 1932, 1933, 1935, 1951, 1966, 1973, 1983, 1985, 1986, 1987, 1988, 1990, 1996, 1997, 1998

David Ginola, a great footballer with great hair...

GOAL OF THE MONTH

THE GOAL OF THE MONTH competition, launched by BBC's Match of the Day programme in 1970, has – like the programme which spawned it – become something of a national institution.

● The first winner of the first ever competition – in which the Match of the Day panel select the top three goals, in 1,2,3 order, from the best shown on BBC during each month – was Coventry City's Ernie Hunt in October 1970. In a match against Everton at Highfield Road, Hunt scored with a volley after Willie Carr flicked up the ball with both his heels from a free-kick. Carr's so-called 'donkey kick' was later judged to be illegal.

● Arsenal's Dennis Bergkamp is the only player to have made a clean sweep of the competition's top three places. In August 1997 the Dutchman won the award for a brilliant keepy-uppy strike against Leicester, came second with a long-range curler against the same team, and in third place was his mazy dribble against Southampton.

ANDY GORAM

Born: Bury 13.4.64	
Height: 5ft 11ins	Position: Goalkeeper
Club career:	
1981–87	Oldham Athletic 195
1987–91	Hibernian 138 (1)
1991–	Rangers 234
International record:	
1985–	Scotland 43

IT MUST HAVE come as quite a surprise to Andy Goram's schoolteachers to see him become Scotland's number one goalkeeper… until he left school he played as a centre-forward.

● IN 1988 Goram joined a tiny band of goalkeepers who have scored a goal. Playing for Hibs against Greenock Morton, he launched a huge kick downfield which bounced over his opposite number, David Wylie, and into the net.

● GORAM also belongs to another elite club – that of players who have appeared for their country at football and cricket. In 1989 he won the first of his three cricket caps for Scotland against the touring Australians.

● IN 1991 Goram became the most expensive goalkeeper in the history of Scottish football when he moved from Hibs to Rangers for £1 million.

● Goram stunned the football world in June '98 when he pulled out of Scotland's World Cup squad after allegations were made about his private life in a tabloid newspaper.

● Goram stunned the football world in June '98 when he pulled out of Scotland's World Cup squad after allegations were made about his private life in a tabloid newspaper.

Andy Goram – who has played both football and cricket for Scotland – is no stranger to the score-sheet (see above)

Did You Know?

Bobby Gould was the first Arsenal substitute to score for the club. He netted two goals after coming on against Leicester City on 10th August 1968.

IFK GOTHENBURG

Year founded: 1904
Ground: Gamla Ullevi (12,000)
League wins: 17
Colours: Blue-and-white-striped shirts, blue shorts and blue socks

SWEDEN's most successful club, Gothenburg (nicknamed The Angels) have won the Swedish league 17 times and the cup on four occasions.

● THE CLUB is most famous for its exploits further afield, however, and is the only Swedish team ever to win a European competition. Gothenburg have lifted the UEFA Cup on two occasions. In 1982 they defeated German club SV Hamburg in the two-legged final and in 1987 they beat Scottish club Dundee United.

● GOTHENBURG have never lost a European final, although they were beaten on penalties by Barcelona in the semi-final of the European Champions Cup in 1986.

Roll of honour

Swedish League champions 1908, 1910, 1918, 1935, 1942, 1958, 1969, 1982, 1983, 1984, 1987, 1990, 1991, 1993, 1994, 1995, 1996
Swedish Cup 1979, 1982, 1983, 1991
UEFA Cup 1982, 1987

BOBBY GOULD

Born: Coventry 12.6.46

BOBBY GOULD replaced Mike Smith as manager of Wales in 1995. His reign, so far, has not been very successful. In 1997 he watched from the sidelines as Wales suffered a humiliating 7–1 defeat by Holland in a World Cup qualifier, their heaviest loss since 1930. Like previous Welsh managers, Gould has found that you need more than a few star names (Giggs, Hughes and Southall) to create a decent international side.

● IN THE SAME year star striker Nathan Blake accused Gould of racism, after comments made in a training session and at half-time in the 3–1 home defeat by Holland. However, Gould denied the charge, and claimed his comments were misunderstood.

● GOULD'S GREATEST moment as a manager came with Wimbledon in 1988, when he led The Dons to a shock 1–0 win over Liverpool in the FA Cup Final.

● AS A PLAYER Gould was one of most widely-travelled of his generation, turning out for Coventry City, Arsenal, Wolves, West Brom, Bristol City, West Ham, Wolves again, Bristol Rovers and Hereford United. He scored Arsenal's solitary goal in the 1969 League Cup defeat by Swindon Town, when Swindon won 3–1 after extra time.

● HE CONTINUED his travels as a manager, taking charge of Bristol Rovers, Coventry City (twice), Wimbledon and West Brom. Explaining his decision to leave Coventry in 1993 Gould said, 'I've been racing Formula One in a Mini Metro.'

ANDY GRAY

Born: 30.11.55
Club career:
1973–76 Dundee United 62 (36)
1976–79 Aston Villa 113 (54)
1979–83 Wolverhampton Wanderers 133 (38)
1983–85 Everton 49 (14)
1985–87 Aston Villa 54 (5)
1987–88 Notts County (loan) 4
1987–88 West Bromwich Albion 32 (10)
1988–89 Rangers 13 (5)
International record:
1976–85 Scotland 20 (7)

AS ENTHUSIASTIC a striker on the pitch as he is today in the TV gantry for Sky Sports, Andy Gray netted a remarkable 224 goals for his eight clubs in the 1970s and 80s. In 1979 he became Britain's most expensive player when he moved from Aston Villa to Wolves for £1,469,000.

● HE WENT on to win the League Cup with Wolves in 1980 (scoring the winning Wembley goal), although his most successful spell came at Everton where he won the League Championship in 1984/85 and the FA Cup in 1984 when he scored in the 2–0 win over Watford.

● WHILE AT Aston Villa he became the first and only player ever to win the PFA Player of the Year and Young Player of the year awards in the same season (1977).

● GRAY NEVER quite translated his club form into the international arena, scoring just seven times for Scotland. In 1991 he gave up his job as assistant to Ron Atkinson at Aston Villa to work full-time for Sky Sports, where he has become famous for getting over-excited and drawing squiggly lines on video replays.

● NOW one of Britain's most popular sports broadcasters, he has won the Royal Television Society's Sports Broadcaster of the Year award and the Variety Club of Great Britain's Media Personality of the Year award, both in 1996, and the Cable TV Guide award for Best Sports Presenter in 1998. He has also co-writing an acclaimed football tactics book called 'Flat Back Four'.

JIMMY GREAVES

Born: London 20.2.40
Height: 5ft 8ins Position: Striker
Club career:
1957–61 Chelsea 157 (124)
1961–62 AC Milan 14 (9)
1962–70 Tottenham Hotspur 321 (220)
1970–71 West Ham United 38 (13)
International record:
1959–67 England 57 (44)

WITH 44 goals, Greaves is the third top scorer ever for England behind Bobby Charlton and Gary Lineker. He scored on his international debut in 1959 in a 4–1 defeat by Peru, and went on to net a record six hat-tricks for his country. In fact Greaves scored on his debut for every team he ever played for – club and country.

Jimmy Greaves – still Tottenham Hotspur's record goalscorer – shows his incredible powers of acceleration at the beginning of a Spurs v Blackpool match in 1962

● GREAVES began his career at Chelsea where he set a club record, which still stands, by scoring 43 goals in the 1960/61 season (including a post-war record six hat-tricks).

● AT 21 GREAVES became the youngest player to score 100 league goals. He scored his 200th aged 23 years and 290 days, amazingly exactly the same age at which Dixie Dean had reached the same figure with Everton.

● AFTER A BRIEF and unhappy spell in Italy he moved to Tottenham and contributed to the club's triumphs in the European Cup Winners' Cup in 1963 and the FA Cup in 1967. His tally of 220 league goals for Spurs remains a club record.

● ON 24th April 1963 Greaves became the first Tottenham player to be sent off for 35 years, when he was dispatched from the field in a match against OFK Belgrade.

● HE EXPERIENCED the lowest point of his career in 1966 when he was left out of England's World Cup-winning eleven. He was the only member of the squad not to attend the victory celebrations in a London hotel.

● HAVING FINISHED playing Greaves admitted that he was an alcoholic. He won his battle with the bottle, however, and in 1980 launched a new career as a television sports commentator.

GREENOCK MORTON

Year founded: 1874
Ground: Cappielow Park (14,267)
Highest ever crowd: 23,500, 1922 v Celtic (Div 1)
Previous name: Morton
Nickname: The Ton
Colours: Blue and white hooped shirts, blue shorts, blue socks

IN 1994 fans voted to change the name of Morton to Greenock Morton, Greenock being the name of the town which the club has inhabited since 1879.

● SET IN A true footballing heartland, the club's finest hour was in 1922 when they won the Scottish Cup for the first and only time in their history, beating Rangers 1–0.

● IN THE 1912/13 season every player to appear for Morton in the Scottish First Division scored at least once, including the goalkeeper who scored a penalty!

● THE CLUB has been relegated more times than any other in the Scottish league (10) except for Clyde (11).

● MORTON were the first club to form a limited company, in 1896, and also the first to install a commentary system for blind supporters in 1923.

Roll of Honour

First Division champions 1978, 1984, 1987
Div 2 champions 1950, 1964, 1967
Second Division champions 1995
Scottish Cup 1922

RON GREENWOOD

Born: Burnley 11.11.21

LATER MANAGER of England, in 1965 former Chelsea centre-half Ron Greenwood guided West Ham United to their first and only European triumph when they won the Cup Winners' Cup, beating TSV 1860 München of Germany 2–0 in the final at Wembley.

● A YEAR EARLIER, Greenwood had managed The Hammers (captained by Bobby Moore) to their first ever FA Cup win when they beat Preston North End 3–2 on the famous hallowed turf.

● IN 1977 he replaced Don Revie as England manager, a reign which lasted for 55 games (won 33, drew 12 and lost 10). Although in his reign England qualified for the 1982 World Cup in Spain (and were knocked out in the 2nd round despite being undefeated), it was a relatively barren era even though it coincided with the likes of Kevin Keegan and Trevor Brooking at their peak.

● CRITICISED for his indecisiveness, Greenwood couldn't decide who was his best goalkeeper and so alternated Ray Clemence and Peter Shilton, letting them take it in turns between the sticks.

GRIMSBY TOWN

Year founded: 1878
Ground: Blundell Park, Cleethorpes (8,870)
Previous name: Grimsby Pelham
Highest ever crowd: 31,657, 20th February 1937 v Wolverhampton Wanderers (FA Cup rd 5)
Nickname: The Mariners
Colours: Black-and-white-striped shirts, black shorts, white socks

THE MARINERS, as the team from the fishing port of Grimsby are known, have spent the majority of their existence in the lower reaches of the football league.

● FAMOUS MANAGERS at the club include the great Bill Shankly and Lawrie McMenemy, who led Grimsby Town to the Fourth Division title in 1971/72, a season in which they were the highest scorers in the football league.

● The club once fielded a father and son (J. and W. Butler) in the same game against Burnley in 1909. They are not the only club ever to have done this, however, the last being Ian and Gary Bowyer at Hereford in 1990.

● IN 1909 Grimsby goalkeeper Walter Scott saved a record three out of four penalties in an FA Cup match against Burnley... but his team still lost 2–0.

● BLUNDELL PARK is the closest English football ground to the sea... the North Sea is just 150 yards away. The ground isn't actually in the town of Grimsby, however, it's in Cleethorpes.

Roll of Honour

Div 2 champions 1901, 1934
Div 3 (N) champions 1926, 1956
Div 3 champions 1980
Div 4 champions 1972

BRUCE GROBBELAAR

Born: Durban, South Africa 6.10.57
Height: 6ft 1in Position: Goalkeeper
Club career:
1979–80 Crewe Alexandra 24 (1)
1980–93 Liverpool 440
1993– Stoke City (loan) 4
1994–96 Southampton 32
1996– Plymouth Argyle 36
International record:
Zimbabwe

THE MOST COLOURFUL goalkeeper of his generation, Bruce Grobbelaar arrived in England after serving in the Rhodesian army and then playing for Canadian club Vancouver Whitecaps. He played a season for Crewe Alexandra before joining Liverpool, where he developed a reputation as a brilliant, if erratic, shot stopper.

● GROBBELAAR has won more honours than any other goalkeeper in the history of the British game. At Liverpool he played in a team that won six championships, three FA Cups, three League Cups and the European Cup in 1984.

● In 1994 Grobelaar – whose name translates as 'clumsy' in his native language, Afrikaans – was accused of match fixing.

● However, after a second trial in 1997, the Zimbabwean and his co-defendants John Fashanu and Hans Segers were acquitted and Grobelaar returned to play football for Plymouth Argyle, Oxford United and Sheffield Wednesday.

Ruud Gullit, sporting the most famous dreadlocks in the history of the game, celebrates Dutch European Championship success in Munich, 1988

RUUD GULLIT

Born: Amsterdam 1.9. 62.
Height: 6ft 0ins Position: Midfielder
Club career:
1979–82 Haarlem 91(32)
1982–85 Feyenoord 85 (30)
1985–87 PSV Eindhoven 68 (46)
1987–93 AC Milan 117 (35)
1993–94 Sampdoria 31 (15)
1994 AC Milan 8 (3)
1994–95 Sampdoria 22 (9)
1995–98 Chelsea 43 (4)
International record:
1981–93 Holland 65 (16)

IN 1987, Ruud Gullit became the world's most expensive player when he moved from PSV Eindhoven of Holland to AC Milan of Italy for a staggering £6.5 million.

● IN THE same year he became only the third player – after Paolo Rossi and Michel Platini – to be voted both World and European Footballer of the Year in the same season. Gullit dedicated his double award to Nelson Mandela, then still imprisoned in South Africa.

● IN 1988 Gullit became the first Dutch captain to lift a major international trophy, when he led an outstanding side to victory in the 1988 European Championships.

● AFTER HELPING Milan win the Italian championship in 1988 Gullit was instrumental in the club's European Cup success the following year, scoring two goals in the 4–0 final win over Steaua Bucharest. In all he won three Serie A titles with Milan and two European Cups.

● When Chelsea beat Middlesbrough 2-0 to win the FA Cup in 1997 Gullit became the first non-British manager to win a major trophy with an English club. However, less than a year later he was sensationally sacked by the London club who claimed he was demanding excessive wages. Gianluca Vialli – one of his first signings for the Blues – was installed as manager.

Did You Know?

'Grobbelaar' is difficult to spell (remember: 2 b's, 2 a's) but that was no excuse for the Arab periodical Al Ahram to mis-spell it Bruce Webler in 1991.

GEORGHE HAGI

Born: Romania 5.2.65
Height: 5ft 9ins Position: Midfielder
Club career:
1982–83 FC Constanta (Romania) 18 (7)
1983–87 Sportul Studentesc (Rom) 108 (58)
1987–90 Steaua Bucharest (Rom) 97 (76)
1990–92 Real Madrid 64 (15)
1992–94 Brescia (Italy) 61 (14)
1994–96 Barcelona 16 (4
1996– Galatasaray
International record:
1983– Romania 113 (32)

The greatest Romanian player ever, Georghe Hagi retired from international football after the 1998 World Cup as his country's record appearance maker with 113 caps and record goalscorer with 32 goals.

● AS THE STAR player with Steaua Bucharest in the late 1980s he earned the nickname the 'Maradona of the Carpathians'.

● IN 1994 Hagi became the only international captain to see his side go out of two successive World Cups on penalties. At Italia 90 Romania lost on spot kicks to Ireland, and four years later they were eliminated in the same gut-wrenching manner by Sweden.

● HAGI IS the only Romanian player to have appeared for the two giants of the Spanish game, Real Madrid and Barcelona. He joined Real after the 1990 World Cup, and following a spell with Italian side Brescia returned to Spain with Barca in 1994. He then moved to Galatasaray in Turkey in 1996.

HAJDUK SPLIT

Year founded: 1911
Ground: Poljud Stadium (50,000)
League wins: 12 (3 Croatian, 9 Yugoslav)
Colours: Red-and-blue-striped shirts, blue shorts, blue socks

NOW PLAYING in the newly-formed Croatian league, in the 1970s Hajduk Split dominated Yugoslav football to such an extent that they won the domestic Cup four times on the trot between 1974–77, and the double in 1974/75.

● HAJDUK SPLIT won the domestic double in Croatia in 1994/95 amid a deal of controversy. They leapfrogged bitter rivals Croatia Zagreb to win the league at the last gasp, then went on to meet them in the two-legged cup final. There was a strong rumour doing the rounds that Hajduk had been allowed to win the league because Croatia Zagreb were banned from Europe, but they would in turn let their rivals win the Cup. The rumour was scuppered by a 4–1 aggregate win for Hajduk.

● THE CLUB'S nerve-jangling Yugoslav Cup win came in 1987 when they beat NK Rijeka 9–8 on penalties after a 1–1 draw, the first time the competition had been decided in this fashion.

● HAJDUK's most successful campaigns in Europe were both ended after close scraps against English clubs in the semi-finals. Leeds edged them out of the 1972/73 Cup Winners' Cup 1–0 on aggregate and Tottenham went to the final of the UEFA Cup in 1984 after beating the Croats on away goals.

Roll of Honour

League champions (Croatia) 1992, 1994, 1995
Croatian Cup 1993, 1995
League champions (Yugoslavia) 1927, 1929, 1950, 1952, 1955, 1971, 1974, 1975, 1979
Yugoslav Cup 1967, 1972, 1973, 1974, 1975, 1976, 1977, 1984, 1987, 1991

HALIFAX TOWN

Year founded: 1911
Ground: The Shay (7,449)
Highest ever crowd: 36,885, 15th February 1953 v Tottenham Hotspur (FA Cup rd 5)
Nickname: The Shaymen
Colours: Blue and white shirts, blue shorts, blue socks

HALIFAX TOWN won the Vauxhall Conference championship in 1998 to become the fourth team – after Lincoln City, Darlington and Colchester United – to regain Football League status after having been relegated from the dreaded 92nd spot. Town had been relegated from Division Three in 1993.

Gheorghe Hagi, the 'Maradona of the Carpathians' and Romania's most capped player, keeps his eye on the ball during the USA 94 World Cup

● It was a nice change for The Shaymen to lift a title, as their history has been somewhat less than success-filled. Indeed, the West Yorkshire club is one of a handful never to have won a Football League division.

● It was ironic, then, that the1980s terrace fashion for ridiculing inept opposition players with a 'hee-haw' donkey chant should have begun at the Shay Ground. The cry soon caught on elsewhere, with Arsenal's Tony Adams being a prime target.

● In 1934 Halifax were on the wrong end of the biggest thrashing in league football history, crashing 13-0 in a Division Three (North) match at Stockport County (Newport County equalled The Shaymen's unwanted record in 1946 against Newcastle).

Roll of Honour

Vauxhall Conference champions 1998

SIR JOHN HALL

Born: Seaton 21.3.33

SIR JOHN HALL became chairman of Newcastle United in 1992. His financial clout allowed manager Kevin Keegan and his successor, Kenny Dalglish, to build a side capable of challenging for the game's top honours. Sir John retired from the post in 1997 but returned in 1998 to steady the ship after club directors Douglas Hall (his son) and Freddy Shepherd found themselves embarassingly splashed all over the front page of the News of the World.

● IN HIS YOUTH Sir John was an accomplished defender, captaining East Northumberland. He never considered becoming a professional player, concentrating instead on his business career which included developing the huge Metro shopping centre outside Durham.

● SIR JOHN has a host of ideas for Newcastle's future. His most treasured ambition, though, seems unlikely to be realised. 'My eventual dream is to have 11 Geordies playing for Newcastle United and 11 in the reserves,' he says.

HAMILTON ACADEMICAL

Year founded: 1874
Ground: Firhill Park (shared with Partick Thistle) (20,676)
Highest ever crowd: 28,690, 3rd March 1937 v Hearts (Scottish Cup rd 3)
Nickname: The Accies
Colours: Red-and-white hoops, white shorts and socks

THE ACCIES' name is among the strangest in football. The club was named after a local school back in 1874.

● IN 1970 the struggling club resigned from the league and Clyde were about to take their place, but rebel directors won control of Hamilton and allowed The Accies to carry on.

● The only trophy the club have won in their 120-year existence is the B&Q Cup, which they picked up in 1992. It's a pinnacle, but more Ben Nevis than K2 as pinnacles go. They also got to the final of the Scottish Cup back in 1911 and 1935. The greatest moment in the club's recent history came when they beat the mighty Rangers at Ibrox in 1988.

● WHEN the Accies' John Brown scored a hat-trick against Berwick in 1980 he became the first full-back in British football to hit three goals in one game from open play.

Roll of Honour

First Division champions 1986, 1988
Div 2 champions 1904

SAM HAMMAM

Born: 17.7.56

UNTIL SELLING his controlling interest in Wimbledon to Norwegian millionaires Kjell Roekke and Bjoern Gjelsten for £26 million, Sam Hammam was Wimbledon's owner. The maverick Lebanese businessman still effectively runs the club, however, in his unique and passionate way.

● ORIGINALLY recommended to invest in a football club by his chauffeur, Hammam has overseen probably the most incredible rise of any football club in the world. When he arrived at the club in 1979 they had only just joined the football league and were in Division Four. Now they have been in the top flight for more than a decade (1986/87 was their first season) and have won the FA Cup (1988).

● NEVER AFRAID to fight his club's corner, Hammam said in 1992. 'We have to remain the English Bulldog SAS club. We have to sustain ourselves by sheer power and the attitude that we will kick ass.' The club's loyal band of supporters recently protested vociferously, however, at continually resurfacing rumours that he plans to move the club to Dublin.

ALAN HANSEN

Born: Alloa 13.6.55
Height: 6ft 1in Position: Defender
Club career:
1974–77 Partick Thistle 86 (6)
1977–91 Liverpool 434 (8)
International record:
1979–87 Scotland 26 (0)

DURING A GLORIOUS 13 year career at Liverpool, Alan Hansen won no fewer than eight championship titles, three European Cups, two FA Cups and four League Cups.

● HANSEN BEGAN his career at Partick Thistle with whom he won a First Division championship medal in 1976. At the end of the following season he joined Liverpool for £100,000, then a record fee received by Partick.

● A FIXTURE in the Liverpool defence in the late 1970s and throughout the 80s he also won three European Cup and two FA Cup Winners' medals.

● HANSEN was a part of the Liverpool back four which in 1978/79 conceded just 16 goals in 42 league games, to set a football league record for defensive meanness.

● THE LOWEST point of his career was in 1986 when he was not selected by Alex Ferguson for the Mexico World Cup. Without him, Scotland went out in the first round.

● SINCE RETIRING from the game in 1990, Hansen has developed a reputation as TV's most incisive football pundit.
His forte is pointing out the chain of tiny errors that lead to goals. But he's no Mystic Meg. After Manchester United lost to Aston Villa on the opening day of the 1995/96 season he dismissed The Reds' title chances, saying 'You don't win anything with kids.' Nine months later, United's 'kids' won the Double.

HARTLEPOOL UNITED

Year founded: 1908
Ground: The Victoria Ground (7,895)
Previous names: Hartlepools United until 1968, Hartlepool until 1977
Highest ever crowd: 17,426, 5th January 1957 v Manchester United (FA Cup rd 3)
Nickname: The Pool
Colours: Blue-and-white-striped shirts, blue-and-white shorts, blue socks

HARTLEPOOL UNITED have had to apply for re-election to the football league (after finishing bottom of the bottom division) a total of 14 times, more than any other club. Each time, however, they recorded enough votes to stay in.

● HARTLEPOOL can boast of being the first football club to be bombed. Their Victoria Ground was hit by bombs jettisoned by German Zeppelins on 17th November 1916. The aircraft were later shot down. The German government never answered the club's requests for £2,500 compensation.

● HARTLEPOOL were knocked out of the FA Cup four years running, between 1927–30, by non-league clubs. They have the worst FA Cup record of all established football league teams, having never reached the last 16.

● DURING THE 1992/93 season Hartlepool went a British record 13 league and cup matches without scoring a goal. Strangely the club's last goal before this run had knocked Premier League Crystal Palace out of the FA Cup.

Alan Hansen, pictured during his fairly successful Liverpool career, doing his famous Monty Python imitation

JOHN HARTSON

Born: Swansea 5.4.75
Height: 6ft 1in
Position: Striker
Club career:
1992–95 Luton Town 54 (11)
1995–97 Arsenal 53 (14)
1997– West Ham United 43 (20)
International record:
1996– Wales 14 (2)

JOHN HARTSON made his name at unfashionable Luton Town when he scored the first goal in the Kenilworth Road club's shock FA Cup fourth round win over Newcastle in 1994. The Hatters reached Wembley that year – albeit in the semi-finals, where they lost to Chelsea – with Hartson coming on as a second-half substitute.

● WHEN HE MOVED to Arsenal in January 1995 for £2.5 million Hartson became Britain's most expensive teenager (a record since surpassed by Lee Boywer when he left Charlton for Leeds in 1996 for £2.6 million). However, despite scoring Arsenal's consolation goal in the 1995 European Cup Winners' Cup final, he never settled at Highbury and moved on to West Ham in March 1997.

● AN INSTANT HERO at Upton Park, Hartson's strikes saved the Hammers from relegation in 1997 and the following year he notched up a career-best 15 Premiership goals. A couple of suspensions – he was sent off against Bolton and Derby – prevented him from scoring even more.

● HARTSON MADE his full Wales debut in the 3–1 defeat away to Bulgaria in 1995. Disciplinary problems have marred his international career, and in 1996 manager Bobby Gould quickly substituted the fiery striker after he took a swing at Dutch defender Philip Cocu in a match Wales lost 7–1.

HAT-TRICKS

THE FASTEST hat-trick ever scored in British football was hit by Blackpool's Jock Dodds on 28th February 1942. He notched three past the Tranmere Rovers keeper in an incredible two and a half minutes.

Did You Know?

Alan Shearer holds the Premiership hat-tricks record, scoring no fewer than five in the 1995/96 season... against Coventry (23rd September, Ewood Park), Forest (18th November, Ewood Park), West Ham (2nd December, Ewood Park), Bolton (3rd February, Ewood Park) and Tottenham (16th March, White Hart Lane).

● HIS FEAT was bettered by Maglioni of Argentinian giants Independiente on 18th March 1973, who hit three past Gimnasia y Esgrima in 1 minute 50 seconds, a world record.

● THE MOST hat-tricks scored by a British player in a season is the eight hit by Middlesbrough's George Camsell in 1926/27, which constituted 24 of his 59 goals.

● ON 9th NOVEMBER 1946 Liverpool's Jack Balmer hit three goals past the Arsenal goalkeeper to become the first man in football league history to score hat-tricks on three successive Saturdays. His others came against Portsmouth and Derby.

● IN 1931 Tom Keetley of Notts County scored three hat-tricks in successive away fixtures.

● GEOFF HURST is the only man ever to score a hat-trick in a World Cup final when he smashed home three for England at Wembley in 1966. The only man to score hat-tricks in consecutive hat-tricks in World Cup Finals is Argentina's Gabriel Batistuta who hit three against Greece in USA '94 and a further treble against Jamaica in France '98.

● ALAN SHEARER is the youngest ever scorer of a hat-trick in the top flight of English football, netting three times for Southampton against Arsenal on 9th April 1988 at the tender age of 17 years and 240 days. The previous youngest was Jimmy Greaves, who scored three times for Chelsea against Portsmouth on 25th December 1957 when he was 17 years and 10 months.

● DIXIE DEAN scored more top-flight hat-tricks than any other player, claiming no fewer than 34 in his career.

● THE FIRST PLAYER to score a triple hat-trick in English league football was Robert 'Bunny' Bell, who scored nine of Tranmere Rovers' goals in the 13–4 win over Oldham Athletic on 26th December 1935... and he missed a penalty!

JOÃO HAVELANGE

Born: Rio de Janeiro, Brazil 8.5.16

BEFORE HIS retirement before France '98, Joao Havelange was the second-longest-serving President of FIFA. He took office in 1974, succeeding England's Sir Stanley Rous. Only Jules Rimet (President from 1921 to 1954) held the position for a longer period of time.

● UNDER HAVELANGE the World Cup was expanded from 16 to 32 countries, providing more places for African and Asian nations.

● AT THE 1998 WORLD CUP five African countries (Cameroon, Morocco, Nigeria, South Africa and Tunisia) competed for the first time. Membership of FIFA in the Havelange era has grown to 202 countries.

● AN INTERNATIONAL water polo player in his youth, Havelange became known as a pragmatist who was able to find solutions to the most intractable of problems. After Israel were expelled from FIFA in 1976 for causing a rift with the Arab nations, Havelange successfully argued for the re-admittance of the Jewish state - as long as the country played World Cup qualifiers in the European section, rather than the Asian one.

JOHNNY HAYNES

Born: London 17.10.34
Height: 5ft 9ins Position: Midfielder
Club career:
1952–70 Fulham 594 (128)
Durban (South Africa)
International record:
1954–62 England 56 (18)

IN 1961, after the abolition of the maximum wage, fantastically gifted midfielder Johnny Haynes became the first £100-a-week player in England. A loyal one-club man, Haynes spent his entire League career with Fulham, with whom he failed to win a single major honour.

● HAYNES made his debut for England in 1954 against Northern Ireland, scoring in a 2–0 win. From 1960 until a serious car accident in 1962 he was England captain, a period which featured a run of six successive wins in which the national team scored the phenomenal total of 40 goals.

● IN 1970 Haynes left Fulham after 18 years, having played in a club record 594 league games. He ended his playing career in South Africa, where finally he won a championship medal with Durban City.

HEADERS

IN 1952 Aston Villa full back Peter Aldiss scored his first goal for the club on his 262nd appearance, a statistic which is remarkable enough on its own. The fact that the goal he scored was a header from 35 yards out, very possibly the longest headed goal of all time, gave him even more cause to celebrate.

● FORTY OF Dixie Dean's record 60 goals scored for Everton in 1927/28 came from his head, a record which is unlikely ever to be beaten.

● IN JANUARY 1935, Arsenal's Eddie Hapgood was recorded as having been the first man to score a penalty with his head! In fact his penalty had been saved by the Liverpool keeper, and Hapgood had headed in the rebound.

HEART OF MIDLOTHIAN

Year founded: 1874
Ground: Tynecastle Park, Edinburgh (18,300)
Highest ever crowd: 53,396, 13th February 1932 v Rangers (Scottish Cup rd 3)
Nickname: Hearts
Colours: Maroon shirts, white shorts, maroon socks with white tops

HEARTS' won their first trophy for 36 years when they lifted the Scottish Cup in 1998 after beating Rangers 2-1. It was their first Scottish Cup triumph since 1956 and capped a magnificent season when they challenged the Old Firm at the top of the Premier league table for virtually the entire campaign.

Johnny Haynes, Fulham's leading appearance maker and England's captain at the 1962 World Cup, leads out his club side at Craven Cottage

● HEARTS' romantic-sounding name derives from a former Edinburgh prison, which was immortalised in Sir Walter Scott's novel The Heart of Midlothian and destroyed 50 years before the club came into existence.

● THE WORD walkover doesn't do justice to Hearts' biggest victory. They beat Anchor 21–0 in the EFA Cup way back in 1880. The club's biggest defeat was a comparatively minor 8–1 drubbing dished out by Vale of Leithen in 1888.

● HEARTS WON the league with a record 132 goals in 1958, spurred on by Alfie Conn, Willie Bauld and Jimmy Wardhaugh (known as the Terrible Trio) and wingers Alex Young and Jimmy Crawford. They only conceded 29 goals that season, giving them the biggest goal difference in the Scottish league, an amazing 103. They only lost once in the league all season, but were knocked out of the Cup by the odd goal in seven by local rivals Hibs in the semis.

● IN 1965 Hearts came agonisingly close to winning the league championship – closer than any other runners-up in the history of Scottish football in fact. Kilmarnock beat them 2–0 at Tynecastle on the final day of

the season (shades of Arsenal 1989!) to win the title with a superior goal average of 0.042, despite having a markedly inferior goal difference.

● IN 1977 Hearts were relegated, alongside Kilmarnock, for the first time in their proud 103-year history. It was a topsy turvy season for the Edinburgh club, as they reached the semi-finals of both cup competitions – a unique treble. They were promoted again in 1980.

● HEARTS' HEARTS were broken again in 1986, when they looked likely to win The Double for the first time in their history, with the inspirational Sandy Jardine playing for them as sweeper. Having put together a 27-match unbeaten run they lost 2–0 to modest Dundee on the last day of the season. Celtic beat St. Mirren 5–0 and took the title on goal difference. Ironically, in view of what happened in 1965, Hearts would have won the title had it been decided on goal average. A week later Hearts lost again, 3–0 to Aberdeen in the final of the Scottish Cup.

● IN 1990 Hearts tried to end their long-standing rivalry with Hibs by buying the club and merging. The move was an attempt to break the dominance of Scottish football by the two Glasgow giants. Naturally fans of both teams, especially Hibs, were appalled and took to the streets to protest. Hearts eventually bowed to the pressure and pulled out of the deal.

● HALF-PINT COMEDIAN Ronnie Corbett had a trial for the club when he was a schoolboy, and you can probably guess why he was rejected. Corbett's cousin actually made the first team, however.

● HEARTS' record goalscorer in a single season is Barney Battles, who scored 44 times in the 1930/31 season. The overall club record goalscorer is Jimmy Wardhough with 206 between 1946–59, and the record appearance holder is Henry Smith, who played for the club 482 times between 1981–95.

Roll of Honour

Div 1 champions 1895, 1897, 1958, 1960
First Division champions 1980
Scottish Cup 1891, 1896, 1901, 1906, 1956, 1998
League Cup 1955, 1959, 1960, 1963

Hearts' Post-War Record

47 D1 4th	65 D1 2nd	83 D1 2nd
48 D1 9th	66 D1 7th	84 PR 5th
49 D1 8th	67 D1 11th	85 PR 7th
50 D1 3rd	68 D1 12th	86 PR 2nd
51 D1 4th	69 D1 8th	87 PR 5th
52 D1 4th	70 D1 4th	88 PR 2nd
53 D1 4th	71 D1 11th	89 PR 6th
54 D1 2nd	72 D1 6th	90 PR 3rd
55 D1 4th	73 D1 10th	91 PR 5th
56 D1 3rd	74 D1 6th	92 PR 2nd
57 D1 2nd	75 D1 8th	93 PR 5th
58 D1 1st	76 PR 5th	94 PR 7th
59 D1 2nd	77 PR 9th	95 PR 6th
60 D1 1st	78 D1 2nd	96 PR 3rd
61 D1 8th	79 PR 9th	97 PR 4th
62 D1 6th	80 D1 1st	98 PR 3rd
63 D1 5th	81 PR 10th	
64 D1 4th	82 D1 5th	

COLIN HENDRY

Born: Keith 7.12.65
Height: 6ft 1in
Position: Defender
Club record:
1983–87 Dundee 41 (2)
1987–89 Blackburn Rovers 102 (22)
1989–91 Manchester City 63 (5)
1991– Blackburn Rovers 234 (12)
International record:
1993– Scotland 32 (1)

SCOTLAND'S CAPTAIN at the 1998 World Cup, Colin Hendry is one of the most committed and determined defenders in football. He began his career with Scottish non-league side Islavale, before making his pro debut for Dundee in their 4-1 win over Hearts in January 1984.

● TRANSFERRED to Blackburn Rovers for £30,000 in March 1987, Hendry cost more than 20 times that amount when he moved on to Manchester City two and a half years later. The blond defender with the granite features soon returned to Ewood Park, though, as one of Kenny Dalglish's first signings.

● IN 1995 Hendry won a Premiership medal with Rovers, as they just pipped Manchester United for the title. Blackburn's fine defensive record that season (they conceded less than a goal a game in the league) was due in no small measure to the Scottish stopper's outstanding form.

● HENDRY made his Scotland debut in 1993 in a World Cup qualifier against Estonia in Tallinn, and he scored his first goal for his country in the same year against Malta. Hendry, whose girlfriend is a hairdresser, would have loved to have been the first man to skipper Scotland to the second round of a major competition but he just failed at both Euro '96 and France 98. When he retires from international football he says he will rejoin the 'Tartan Army' to follow the team around the world.

HEREFORD UNITED

Year founded: 1924
Ground: Edgar Street (8,843)
Highest ever crowd: 18,114, 4th January 1958 v Sheffield Wednesday (FA Cup rd 3)
Colours: White shirts, black shorts and white socks

HAVING suffered the nightmare of relegation from the Football League, Hereford started the 1997/98 season in the Vauxhall Conference. Before their sad exit at the hands of Brighton on the last day of the season, Hereford were the Football League club with the lowest percentage of wins. They had won just 32 per cent of their matches, slightly less than one in three.

● THE CLUB was, however, much more successful before they were elected to join the football league. They hold the record for consecutive appearances in the 1st round of the FA Cup for non-league teams, an amazing 17 seasons from 1956 to 1972.

● IT WAS IN 1972 that Hereford pulled off the most celebrated piece of giant-killing in English football history, when they beat First Division Newcastle 2–1 in the 3rd round of the FA Cup. They were the first non-league club in 23 years to achieve such a feat.

Roll of Honour

Div 3 champions 1976

Jim Leighton, veteran keeper pictured during his Hibs days, makes sure his sponsored gloves get in the picture

HIBERNIAN

Year founded: 1875
Ground: Easter Road, Edinburgh (16,218)
Highest ever crowd: 65,860,
2nd January 1950 v Hearts (Div 1)
Nickname: Hibs
Colours: Green shirts with white sleeves, white shorts, green socks

HIBS were the first ever British side to compete in the European Cup. Indeed, they reached the semi-finals of the first ever competition (which English league champions Chelsea did not enter) in 1955/56, when they lost to the French side Rheims.

● THE HIBERNIAN white-armed strip was introduced in 1938 to imitate the great Arsenal side of that era (with green instead of red).

● AFTER WINNING the league title in 1903 Hibernian had to wait till 1948 before they got their hands on the Scottish Championship trophy again. Tragically Willie McCartney, the manager who had assembled the greatest team in the club's history, died halfway through the season and so never got to taste the sweetness of success. The side included the Famous Five forward line of Eddie Turnbull, Willie Ormond, Bobby Johnstone, Gordon Smith and Lawrie Reilly, and went on to win two further titles, in 1951 and 1952, managed by Hugh Shaw.

● THEIR GOALKEEPER, Tommy Young, who was doing national service at the time in Germany, was flown home each week to play.

● TWO MEMBERS of that forward line are record holders for Hibs. Gordon Smith ended up as the top scorer in the club's history, with an incredible 364 goals. Lawrie Reilly is the club's most capped player, with 38. Arthur Duncan holds the record for league appearances with the club, having played in 446 matches.

● HIBS' trip to Stenhousemuir in 1951 was Scotland's first floodlit match. Hibs were also the first club in Scotland to install undersoil heating, which was a good idea, because it can get awful cold in Edinburgh.

● ON 24th OCTOBER 1959 Hibs travelled to Airdrie for a routine match in the First Division. They came away 11–1 winners, the record away win in British league football under their belts. Remarkably Airdrie conceded fewer goals than Hibs that season.

● IN 1961 Joe Baker, who holds the record for the most goals in a season for the club with 42, became the first man to represent England while playing for a Scottish club. He scored on his debut in a 2–1 win over Northern Ireland. He ended the season playing for Italian giants Torino.

● THE CLUB were managed by the great Jock Stein in 1964/65. On one famous occasion he arranged a friendly against European Champions Real Madrid on the same night as Hearts were playing in Europe to eclipse his local rivals' game. Hibs won 2–0.

● IN 1972 Hibs fell to the heaviest defeat this century in a Scottish Cup final when they were slaughtered 6–1 by Celtic. They got their revenge next season by beating The Bhoys 2–1 in the League Cup Final.

● NEW OWNERS at Hibs in the late 80s floated the club on the Stock Exchange. The plan failed and the club went £6 million in debt, which nearly led to a highly unpopular merger with bitter rivals Hearts.

● IN 1991 the club received £1 million from Rangers for Andy Goram, a club record and a record fee for a Scottish goalkeeper. Despite losing Goram Hibs won their first trophy in 19 years in 1992, when they beat Dunfermline 2–0 in the League Cup Final.

● HIBS' RECORD win was in 1881, a somewhat easy 22–1 destruction of 42nd Highlanders. Their worst ever defeat was a 10–0 humiliation by Rangers in 1898.

Roll of Honour

Div 1 champions 1903, 1948, 1951, 1952
First Division champions 1981
Div 2 champions 1894, 1895, 1933
Scottish Cup 1887, 1902
League Cup 1973, 1992

Hibs' Post-War Record

47 D1 2nd	64 D1 10th	81 D1 1st
48 D1 1st	65 D1 4th	82 PR 6th
49 D1 3rd	66 D1 6th	83 PR 7th
50 D1 2nd	67 D1 5th	84 PR 7th
51 D1 1st	68 D1 3rd	85 PR 8th
52 D1 1st	69 D1 12th	86 PR 8th
53 D1 2nd	70 D1 3rd	87 PR 9th
54 D1 5th	71 D1 12th	88 PR 7th
55 D1 5th	72 D1 4th	89 PR 5th
56 D1 4th	73 D1 3rd	90 PR 7th
57 D1 9th	74 D1 2nd	91 PR 9th
58 D1 9th	75 D1 2nd	92 PR 5th
59 D1 10th	76 PR 3rd	93 PR 7th
60 D1 7th	77 PR 6th	94 PR 5th
61 D1 7th	78 PR 4th	95 PR 3rd
62 D1 8th	79 PR 5th	96 PR 5th
63 D1 16th	80 PR 10th	97 PR 9th
		98 PR 10th

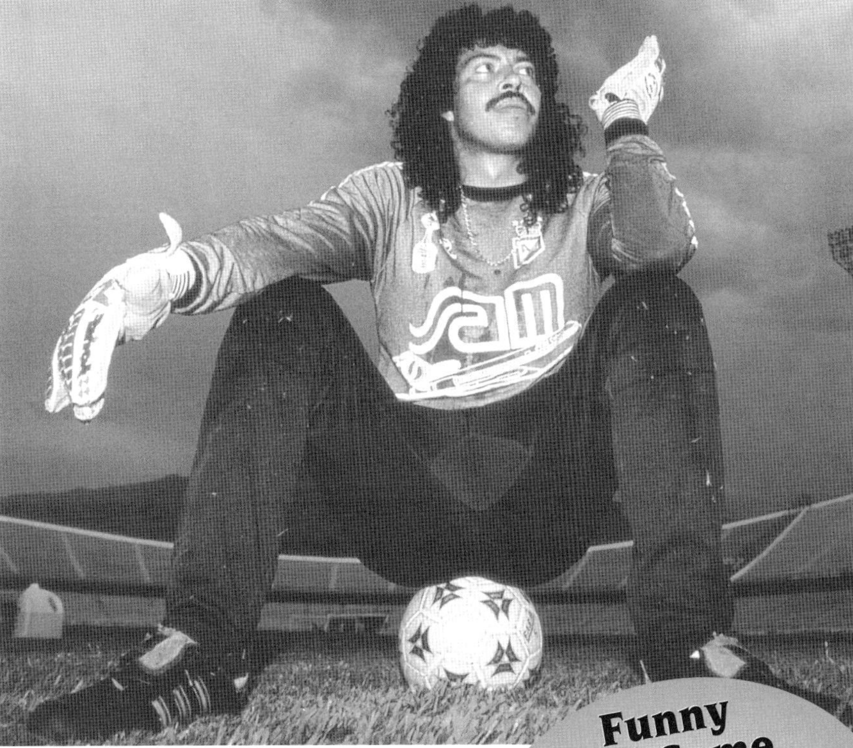

Following hot on the heels of the 'scorpion kick', Rene Higuita – Colombia's revolutionary goalkeeper – demonstrates his new 'sitting-on-the-ball' save

Funny Old Game

Higuita is not the only eccentric goalkeeper to emerge from South America. At the 1978 World Cup Peru's Argentinian-born goalie Ramon Quiroga was booked for a foul committed just inside the opposition half... his nickname was also 'El Loco'!

RENE HIGUITA

Born: Colombia 1966
Position: Goalkeeper
International record:
1987– Colombia: 60 (3)

COLOMBIAN keeper Rene Higuita made the most bizarre save ever seen in a friendly against England on 6th September 1995, which was immediately nicknamed the 'scorpion kick'. Jamie Redknapp lobbed in a weak shot that was looping towards the Colombian goal. Higuita, instead of clutching it to his chest, let it pass over his head, launched himself forward and kicked up his heels, knocking the ball back into midfield with the studs of his boots.

● HIGUITA, nicknamed 'El Loco' (the madman), is famous for his unconventional tactics. When Colombia played in the Italia 90 World Cup tournament, he redefined the role of the goalkeeper, often playing as a kind of sweeper well out of his box. He came to grief, however in the 2nd round against Cameroon, when Roger Milla dispossessed him 40 yards out and ran the ball into an unguarded net.

● HIGUITA's unconventional antics are not just confined to the football field. He was jailed for a short time in 1993 in Colombia for his role in a kidnapping.

● HIS THREE strikes for Colombia came between 1988–89 when he was the side's regular penalty-taker.

JIMMY HILL

Born: Balham 22.7.28

JIMMY HILL is best known for his TV punditry on the BBC. His unfettered, boyish enthusiasm makes him a bit of a fall guy for his colleagues Des Lynam and Alan Hansen, but he is well loved by the public and has become something of a national institution.

● HILL WAS a good but not great player: he scored 52 goals in 297 appearances for Fulham in the 1950s as an inside-forward. But the public took note when he became the youngest chairman of the Professional Footballers' Association, and it was largely down to his efforts that the maximum wage was abolished in 1961.

● THE CHIN, as he is affectionately known for obvious reasons, then turned his hand to management at Coventry City, and showed himself to be the most imaginative gaffer they had ever had. He had the team playing in a new sky blue kit, and made the colour a running theme throughout the club: there were sky blue trains, a sky blue stand, sky blue caterers and even a sky blue radio station. He guided the club, which had never before played top flight football, from the Fourth to the First Division.

● HILL IS ALSO a qualified referee, and in 1972 left the commentary box to serve as an emergency linesman in a vital match between Arsenal and Liverpool.

GLENN HODDLE

Born: Hayes 27.10.57
Height: 6ft 0ins Position: Midfielder
Club career:
1975–87 Tottenham Hotspur 377 (88)
1987–90 Monaco
1991–93 Swindon Town 64 (1)
1993–95 Chelsea 31 (1)
International record:
1979–88 England 53 (8)

ENGLAND manager Glenn Hoddle became the youngest ever England manager since Walter Winterbottom when he succeeded Terry Venables in the most coveted job in English football in 1996, aged just 38.

● Despite being the first manager to guide his team to a Wembley defeat in World Cup match (Italy beat England 1-0 in February 1997) his tactical acumen and intricate (though sometimes controversial) preparations helped the team reach France '98 and qualify to the second round of the tournament. However once in the final stages of the tournament Hoddle's team befell the fate of those of his two predecessors, losing on penalties – though this time to Argentina.

● As a player Hoddle made an immediate impact on international football. A talented midfielder with the ability to launch long inch-perfect defence-splitting passes at will, he scored on his England debut against Bulgaria in November 1979. But, mainly due to the safety-firsat tactics of long-term manager Ron Greenwood he never won as many caps as his outrageous talent deserved.

● Hoddle spent most of his career at Tottenham, who he left to join Monaco in 1987, where he played under manager Arsene Wenger. The next year he became the first Englishman to be a part of a French championship-winning side.

● IN 1993 Hoddle, in the role of player-manager, led Swindon Town into the top

Glenn Hoddle: just two defeats in his first year as England manager

ROY HODGSON

Born: Croydon 9.8.47

NOW MANAGER at Blackburn Rovers, Roy Hodgson is one of Europe's top coaches. Perhaps the highlight of his career was leading Switzerland to the second round of the World Cup in 1994. Apart from Ireland manager Jack Charlton, Hodgson was the only Englishman involved in the finals!

● AT CLUB LEVEL Hodgson has enjoyed successful stints in four different countries: in Sweden, he won a league title with Halmstads in 1976 and the Double with Malmo ten years later; he finished runners-up in the Swiss league in 1991 with Neuchatel Xamax; he guided Inter Milan to the UEFA Cup Final in 1997; and he helped Blackburn win a UEFA Cup place in his first season at Ewood Park in 1998.

● THE ONLY unsuccessful spell Hodgson has experienced as a manager was with Bristol City in 1982. He only lasted five months with the cash-strapped club, who were relegated to the old Fourth Division at the end of the season.

● His return to Blackburn, however, signalled instant success. The club topped the Premiership early in the season and finished in sixth spot, qualifying for Europe.

● AS A PLAYER Hodgson had an undistinguished career. He had a spell at Crystal Palace without breaking through into the first team, and then tried his luck in South Africa.

HOLLAND

First international: Holland 4 Belgium 1 (friendly, Antwerp, 1905)
First World Cup appearance: Holland 2 Switzerland 3 (Italy, 1934)
Highest capped player: Ruud Krol (83)
Highest goalscorer: Dennis Bergkamp (36)
Best win: 9–0 v Finland, 1912
Worst defeat: 9–1 v England Amateurs, 1909
Colours: Orange shirts, white shorts, orange socks

HOLLAND weren't always a major force in international football. In fact at one time they were among the whipping boys. In one spell in the early 1950s they lost 22 matches out of 26, and in 1963 they were knocked out of the European Championships by minnow neighbours Luxembourg, the most humiliating moment in the country's sporting history.

● IN THE 1970s there was a renaissance in Dutch football. They were considered the best side in Europe and star player Johan Cruyff the best player in the world. The Dutch invented a system of playing that became known as 'total football', which involved every outfield player being comfortable in possession and a good deal of positional switches.

● HOLLAND have never won the World Cup. They reached the Final in '74 and '78, but lost unluckily on each occasion to the host nations West Germany and Argentina.

● AT FRANCE 98 the Dutch were considered by many to be the best team in the competition but they lost a semi-final penalty shoot-out to eventual runners-up Brazil after drawing 1–1.

● THEIR GREATEST TRIUMPH came in 1988 when they won the European Championship, a competition they co-host with Belgium in 2000.

WORLD CUP RECORD

1930	Did not enter
1934	Round 1
1938	Round 1
1950	Did not enter
1954	Did not enter
1958-70	Did not qualify
1974	Runners-up
1978	Runners-up
1982	Did not qualify
1986	Did not qualify
1990	Round 2
1994	Quarter-finals
1998	Semi-finals

HOME AND AWAY

BRENTFORD hold the all-time record for home wins in a season. They won all 21 of their games at Griffin Park in Division Three (South) in 1929/30. However, their away form let them down and they missed out on promotion to champions Plymouth.

● LIVERPOOL are the proud holders of the longest unbeaten home run in all competitions. No team returned victorious from Anfield between January 1978 and January 1981, a period which spanned 85 games (63 League, 9 League Cup, 7 European, 6 FA Cup). Ironically it was bottom-of-the-table Leicester City who ended the run by beating The Reds 2–1.

● DONCASTER have the best away record in the football league. Rovers won an incredible 18 out of 21 times on their travels in Division Three (North) in 1946/47. They also broke the record for total wins in a season (33) and were promoted as champions. For the record they were relegated again a year later.

HUDDERSFIELD TOWN

Year founded: 1908
Ground: Sir Alfred McAlpine Stadium (19,500)
Highest ever crowd: 67,037, 27th February 1932 v Arsenal (FA Cup rd 6)
Nickname: The Terriers
Colours: Blue-and-white-striped shirts, white shorts, white socks

HUDDERSFIELD Town are the proud owners of one of the most modern stadiums in Britain. It may look more like a spaceship, but the Sir Alfred McAlpine stadium is as splendid a football venue as you will find anywhere.

● BETWEEN 1913–32 Huddersfield set the longest unbeaten run at home in the FA Cup. Nineteen years passed between defeats at Leeds Road by non-league Swindon (2–1) and Arsenal (2–0); the run covered a total of 25 matches. Luckily for the other teams their away form wasn't quite so good.

● IN 1924 Huddersfield were the first team to win the league on goal average by pipping Cardiff City to the Championship post. They went on to become the first team to win the league three seasons in a row under the astute management of Herbert Chapman.

● PRIME MINISTER and Terriers fan Harold Wilson always carried a photograph of the great 1920s Huddersfield side in his wallet.

● THE 1970s were desperate years for Huddersfield, who dropped from the top flight into the Fourth Division between 1972–75, becoming the first former Champions to be relegated to the bottom division.

Roll of Honour

Div 1 champions 1924, 1925, 1926
Div 2 champions 1970
Div 4 champions 1980
FA Cup 1922

EMLYN HUGHES

Born: Barrow 28.8.47
Height: 5ft 10ins Position: Defender
Club career:
1964–67 Blackpool 28 (0)
1967–79 Liverpool 474 (35)
1979–81 Wolves 58 (2)
1981 Rotherham 24 (2)
International record:
1970–80 England 62 (1)

FORMER ENGLAND skipper Emlyn Hughes has put more goals past Liverpool keepers than any other man in the history of the game… unfortunately they were all own goals when he was playing for them!

● HUGHES, who also captained a 'Question of Sport' team which once included Princess Anne, was the first man to skipper Liverpool to a European Cup triumph in 1976/77. The Reds beat Borussia Moenchengladbach 3–1 in one of the greatest finals of all time. Hughes was also given the Footballer of the Year Award that year.

● HUGHES signed for Liverpool in 1967 from Blackpool (who were subsequently relegated) and won nearly every honour in the game at the club before moving to Wolves in 1979, including two European Cups, one UEFA Cup, four League Championships, and one FA Cup.

● THE ONLY trophy that eluded Hughes at Liverpool was the League Cup, but he completed his set of medals by leading Wolves to a 1–0 victory over Nottingham Forest in 1980.

● HUGHES became manager of Rotherham when he quit playing. He left the job in 1983 when they were relegated to the Third Division.

THE 10 MOST CAPPED PLAYERS CALLED HUGHES!

(Country, dates) and caps

1. Mark Hughes (Wales, 1984–) 66
2. Emlyn Hughes (England, 1970–80) 62
3. Michael Hughes (N. Ireland, 1992–) 41
4. Edwin Hughes (Wales, 1906–14) 16
5. Edward Hughes (Wales, 1899–1907) 14
6. Billy Hughes (Wales, 1938–47) 10
7. (joint) John Hughes (Scotland, 1965–70) 8
and Ceri Hughes (Wales, 1992–) 8
8. Frederick Hughes (Wales, 1882–84) 6
9. William A. Hughes (Wales, 1949) 5

MARK HUGHES

Born: Wrexham 1.11.63
Height: 5ft 10ins Position: Striker
Club career:
1983–86 Manchester United 89 (37)
1986–87 Barcelona 28 (4)
1987–89 Bayern Munich (loan) 18 (6)
1989–95 Manchester United 256 (82)
1995–98 Chelsea 95 (25)
1998– Southampton
International record: 1984– Wales 65 (16)

MARK HUGHES is the only British player to have twice been voted the PFA Player of the Year. He first received the award in 1989, and won it again in 1991.

● IN 1991 Hughes was part of the Manchester United team which became the first English side to win a European trophy after the Heysel ban. He scored the crucial goals, too, as The Reds beat his old club Barcelona 2–1 to lift the European Cup Winners' Cup in Rotterdam.

● KNOWN throughout the game as 'Sparky', with United he won two league titles (1993 and 1994), the European Cup Winners Cup (1991), three FA Cups (1985, 1990 and 1994) and the League Cup (1991).

● IN 1995 he moved to the club he had supported as a boy, Chelsea, and in the process of helping them win the FA Cup in 1997 he became one of just six players to appear in five finals (the others are Joe Hulme, Johnny Giles, Pat Rice, Frank Stapleton and Ray Clemence) and the first and only player in the history of the game to pick up four winners' medals. With the Blues he also won a League Cup winners medal in 1998 and, despite not playing in the final, a European Cup Winners Cup medal in the same season.

Mark Hughes, the only player to have been voted PFA Player of the Year twice, characteristically making sure he's first to the ball

HULL CITY

Year founded: 1904
Ground: Boothferry Park (12,996)
Highest ever crowd: 55,019, 26th February 1949 v Manchester United (FA rd 6)
Nickname: The Tigers
Colours: Black-and-amber-striped shirts, black shorts, amber socks

WITH A population of 270,000 and a catchment area double the size, Hull is the largest English city never to have hosted top flight football. Hull City enjoyed their golden era in the 1940s and 50s when the club's stars included player-manager Raich Carter and Don Revie.

● THE TIGERS' most capped player is Terry Neill, who played 59 games for Northern Ireland. Neill also took the club close to promotion to Division One before managing Arsenal and Spurs.

● IN THE 1970/71 season Hull had two future international managers on their books, Terry Neill of Northern Ireland and Tommy Docherty of Scotland.

● ON 5th AUGUST 1970 Hull became the first football league side to lose a first-class match on penalties. Manchester United outshot them 4–3 after a 1–1 draw in the semi-final of the Watney Cup.

Roll of Honour

Div 3 (N) champions 1933
Div 3 champions 1966

HUNGARY

First international: Austria 5 Hungary 0 (friendly, Vienna, 1902)
First World Cup appearance: Hungary 4 Egypt 2 (Italy, 1934)
Highest capped player: Jozsef Bozsik (100)
Highest goalscorer: Ferenc Puskas (83)
Best win: 13–1 v France, 1926
Worst defeat: 0–7 (three times, most recently v Germany 1941)
Colours: Red shirts, white shorts, green socks

IN THE 1950s Hungary, influenced by the great Ferenc Puskas, were indisputably the best football team in the world. They became the first foreign side to beat England at Wembley in 1953, when they won 6–3, then they thrashed them 7–1 again in Budapest a year later. This remains England's biggest ever defeat.

● THAT HUNGARY team – known as 'The Magnificent Magyars' – were the best side never to win the World Cup. The closest they came was being beaten 3–2 in the 1954 final by West Germany. They had beaten the Germans 8–3 in an earlier round of the competition, but, with an unfit Puskas on the pitch, were muscled out of the second match. They were also beaten 4–2 in the 1938 final by Italy.

● HUNGARY WERE involved in the first international match played between two non-British European countries. They didn't make a good start, losing 5–0 to Austria on 12th October 1902.

● BETWEEN 14th May 1950 and 4th July 1954, Hungary had a record run of 29 matches undefeated, which has yet to be surpassed in international football.

● HUNGARY's Laszlo Kiss became the first man ever to come on as a substitute and score a hat-trick in a World Cup finals match when he hit three past the hapless El Salvador goalkeeper in Group 3 of the 1982 World Cup in Spain. Hungary won 10–1. This was also the first ever double figures finals win in the history of the World Cup.

WORLD CUP RECORD

1930	Did not enter	1970	Did not qualify
1934	Quarter-finals	1974	Did not qualify
1938	Runners-up	1978	Round 1
1950	Did not enter	1982	Round 1
1954	Runners up	1986	Round 1
1958	Round 1	1990	Did not qualify
1962	Quarter-finals	1994	Did not qualify
1966	Quarter-finals	1998	Did not qualify

SIR GEOFF HURST

Born: Ashton-under-Lyme 8.12.41
Height: 5ft 11ins Position: Forward
Club career:
1959–72 West Ham United 410 (180)
1972–75 Stoke City 108 (30)
1975–76 West Bromwich Albion 10 (2)
International record:
1966–72 England 49 (24)

SIR GEOFF HURST – he was knighted in June 1998 – is the first and only man to have scored a hat-trick in a World Cup final. In 1966 his three goals – header, right-foot shot, left-foot shot – helped England to a legendary 4–2 triumph over West Germany.

● HURST IS THE leading scorer in the history of the League Cup with 46 goals (equal with Ian Rush). He is also the last player to score six goals in a top flight league match, bagging a double hat-trick for West Ham in a First Division game against Sunderland in 1968.

● A BARREL-CHESTED centre-forward with a powerful shot, Hurst won an FA Cup winners' medal with West Ham in 1964 and was a member of the Hammers team which won the European Cup Winners' Cup the following year.

● IRONICALLY, as manager of Chelsea between 1979–81, Hurst presided over the club's longest ever run without scoring a goal. For nine games at the end of season 1980/81 The Blues' shot-shy strikers failed to find the net.

PAUL INCE

Born: Ilford 21.10.67
Height: 5ft 10ins Position: Midfield
Club career:
1986–89 West Ham United 72 (7)
1989–95 Manchester United 206 (24)
1995– Inter Milan 53 (5)
1997– Liverpool 31 (8)
International record:
1992– England 43 (2)

IN JUNE 1993 Paul Ince became the first black player to captain England, taking the armband for matches against the USA and Brazil in the United States Cup. He has never given anything but his all for his country, becoming the symbol of England's tenacious qualification to France '98 in Rome in February 1998 thanks to the bloody bandage wrapped round his head after a first half injury. Tragically his missed penalty in the second round shoot-out against Argentina was crucial in England's defeat although it was later revealed that Ince had played the whole tournament with a broken ankle.

● AT MANCHESTER UNITED Ince was a key player in Alex Ferguson's side which won the Premiership in 1992/93 and The Double the following season. In all he won two league titles, two FA Cups, a League Cup and a European Cup Winners' Cup with United.

● IN JULY 1995 Ince moved from Manchester United to Inter Milan for an incredible £7 million, making him the most expensive player ever to leave Britain for foreign climes.

● AFTER A DIFFICULT start Ince proved a huge success with Inter - they reached the 1997 UEFA Cup Final, although they lost on penalties to Schalke 04 of Germany - but the following summer he returned to England in a £7 million transfer to Liverpool where he was made club captain.

Geoff Hurst, moonlighting as a scarecrow in the mid-1970s

INJURY

BACK IN 1872 Lieutenant Cresswell suffered the first major injury in the FA Cup Final when he retired hurt from the Royal Engineers side with a broken collarbone. There were no substitutes in those days, and the ten Engineers went down 1-0 to Wanderers.

● BETTER-KNOWN Cup Final injuries, meanwhile, include the broken neck suffered by Manchester City goalkeeper Bert Trautmann in the 1956 Final (he played on and City won) and the cruciciate knee ligament injury sustained by Paul Gascoigne in 1991. The story of 'Gazza's knee' dominated the sports pages for months afterwards, as his injury jeopardised his proposed move from Spurs to Lazio.

● IN 1980 legal history was made when a player with non-league Whittle Wanderers sued an opponent after suffering a broken leg in a late tackle. He was awarded £4,900 and costs. A year later Dunfermline's John Brown became the first pro to successfully sue an opponent, when he was awarded £20,000 in an out of court settlement as compensation for a serious knee injury sustained in a dangerous tackle.

● ARGUABLY THE MOST injury prone player of all time was Hull City's goalkeeper Billy Bly. Between 1946 and 1959 he sustained an incredible 13 fractures – an average of one every season!

INTER MILAN

Year founded: 1908
Ground: Giuseppe Meazza [San Siro] (85,847 – shared with AC Milan)
League wins: 13
Colours: Blue-and-black stripes, black shorts and black socks

FOUNDED IN 1908 after a breakaway from AC Milan, Internazionale (as they should be called) have a proud footballing tradition and are the third most successful club in Italy with 13 title wins (Juventus have 25 and AC Milan 15).

● INTER were the first Italian club to win the European Cup twice when they recorded their second victory in two years in 1965 (beating Benfica 1–0 after winning 3–1 against the mighty Real Madrid in the previous final).

● UNDER LEGENDARY manager Helenio Herrera Inter were the first club to play the famous 'catenaccio' form of defence, with four-man markers and a sweeper in the 1960s. During this time their defence was almost impregnable and the most common result was a 1–0 win.

● THESE GLORY days were not repeated until the late 1980s, when German stars Lothar Matthaus and Jürgen Klinsmann drove them to win the league title in 1989 (for the first time in nine years) and then the UEFA Cup in 1991.

● INTER WON the UEFA Cup again in 1998, beating Italian Serie A rivals Lazio 3-0 at the Parc des Princes. The third goal was scored by the Brazilian Ronaldo who had been signed from Barcelona the previous summer for a world record-breaking £18 million.

Roll of Honour

Italian League champions 1910, 1920, 1930, 1938, 1940, 1953, 1954, 1963, 1965, 1966, 1971, 1980, 1989
Italian Cup 1939, 1978, 1982
European Champions Cup 1964, 1994
UEFA Cup 1991, 1994, 1998
World Club Cup 1964, 1965

IPSWICH TOWN

Year founded: 1878
Ground: Portman Road (22,559)
Highest ever crowd: 38,010, 8th March 1975 v Leeds United (FA Cup rd 6)
Colours: Blue shirts, white shorts, blue socks

IPSWICH TOWN's greatest era came courtesy of former England and Barcelona boss Bobby Robson. Under Robson the club enjoyed its longest period in the top flight (1968–86), winning the FA Cup in 1978 and the UEFA Cup in 1981 (beating Dutch club AZ Alkmaar in the final)... their greatest achievement.

● ROGER OSBORNE scored the winner against Arsenal in the 1978 Cup Final – Ipswich Town's only FA Cup victory – and then had to be substituted after the achievement had made him feel faint.

● THE FOUNDATIONS for this success had been laid by another future England manager. Under the guidance of Sir Alf Ramsey the club rose from the Third Division (South) in 1957, then won the Second and First Division Championships in successive seasons by 1962.

● IPSWICH's record win was a 10–0 drubbing of Maltese champions Floriana in the European Cup in 1962. A year later the club suffered its worst defeat: 1–10 at Fulham.

● TOWN's record appearance maker is Mick Mills, who turned out 591 times for the club between 1966–82. Another player from the same era, Allan Hunter, is Ipswich's record international appearance maker. He won 47 of his 53 caps for Northern Ireland while at Portman Road.

Roll of Honour

Div 1 champions 1962
Div 2 champions 1961, 1968, 1992
Div 3 (South) champions 1954, 1957
FA Cup 1978
UEFA Cup 1981

Liverpool and England's Paul Ince uses his highly sensitive mouth to maintain balance at all times

Roy Keane fights off Giuseppe Signori during the Republic of Ireland's only World Cup finals victory (apart from on penalties), 1–0 over Italy at USA 94

IRAN

First World Cup appearance:
Holland 3 Iran 0 (Argentina, 1978)
Best win: 17–0 v Maldives, 1996
Colours: Green shirts, white shorts, red socks.

Iran set a World Cup record when they hammered The Maldives 17-0 away in a France '98 qualifier. It was the biggest win ever in the history of the competition and striker Karim Bagheri's personal tally of seven goals equalled the individual goalscoring record for a World Cup match.

● The country's greatest World Cup moment came during France '98.They faced the United States in a match which, for political rather than sporting reasons, was eagerly awaited round the world. They won a thrilling game 2–1 and although they were subsequently eliminated from the tournament after defeat by Germany the whole country was still rejoicing the victory over 'the Great Satan'.

● In 1978 the Middle-Eastern country held much-fancied Scotland to a shock 1-1 draw in Argentina.

● Iran are the only side to have won the Asian Cup – the equivalent of the European Championships – three times in a row. Their hat-trick of wins came in 1968, 1972 and 1976.

WORLD CUP RECORD

1930-70 Did not enter	1986 Did not enter
1974 Did not qualify	1990 Did not qualify
1978 First round	1994 Did not qualify
1982 Did not enter	1998 First round

REPUBLIC OF IRELAND

First international: Republic of Ireland 1 Bulgaria 0 (Olympic Games, Paris, 1924)
First World Cup appearance: Republic of Ireland 1 England 1 (Italy, 1990)
Highest capped player: Paul McGrath (83)
Highest goalscorer: Frank Stapleton (20)
Best win: 8–0 v Malta, 1983
Worst defeat: 0–7 v Brazil, 1982
Colours: Green shirts, white shorts and green socks

ENGLISHMAN Jack Charlton is the most successful manager in the history of Republic of Ireland football. Big Jack attained legendary status in the Emerald Isle by guiding the team to the World Cup finals' for the first time ever in 1990... and then reaching the quarter finals (where they were beaten 1–0 by hosts Italy).

● UNDER CHARLTON Ireland never lost to arch-rivals England. Against the team with which he won a World Cup winners'

medal, under him the Republic won one (1–0 in the 1988 European Championship finals) and drew three (all 1–1). This prompted the gleeful chant whenever the two teams met of 'You'll never beat the Irish'.

● THE REPUBLIC were, in fact, the first foreign team to beat England on English soil when they won 2–0 at Goodison Park in 1949.

● PRIOR TO Jack Charlton's arrival, the Republic's greatest moment was reaching the quarter-finals of the European Championships in 1964 where they were beaten by Spain.

● AFTER THE Republic failed to qualify for Euro 96 Charlton retired and was succeeded by former Millwall boss Mick McCarthy who had himself made 57 appearances for the national side.

WORLD CUP RECORD

1930	Did not enter
1934-86	Did not qualify
1990	Quarter-finals
1994	Round 2
1998	Did not qualify

ITALY

First international: Italy 6 France 2 (friendly, Milan, 1910)
First World Cup appearance: Italy 7 USA 1 (Italy, 1934)
Highest capped player: Dino Zoff (112)
Highest goalscorer: Luigi Riva (35)
Best win: 11–3 v Egypt, 1928
Worst defeat: 1–7 v Hungary, 1924
Colours: Blue shirts, white shorts and blue socks

Italy have won the World Cup on three occasions (1934, 1938 and 1982), making them the most successful European team in the competition alongside Germany. They were also losing finalists in 1970 and 1994.

● THEIR TOTAL of five finals is equal with Brazil (the 1950 tournament, in which the Brazilians finished runners-up, was decided on points so there was no final) and has been bettered only by Germany's six. Only Brazil and West Germany have netted more than Italy's 105 World Cup goals.

● The Azzurri (the Blues) as they are known to their passionate though fickle fans, have reached the World Cup finals stage 14 times, equal second with Germany. Only Brazil have reached all 16. Having been eliminated on penalties in 1990, 1994 and 1998 they have only lost one match in normal play in the World Cup finals since 1978, against France in 1986.

WORLD CUP RECORD

1930	Did not enter	1970	Runners-up
1934	Winners	1974	Round 1
1938	Winners	1978	Fourth place
1950	Round 1	1982	Winners
1954	Round 1	1986	Round 2
1958	Did not qualify	1990	Third place
1962	Round 1	1994	Runners-up
1966	Round 1	1998	Quarter-finals

JAIRZINHO

Born: Caxias, Brazil 25.12.44
Height: 5ft 9ins Position: Forward
Club career:
Botofago (Brazil)
Marseille (France)
Cruzeiro (Brazil)
Portuguesa (Venezuela)
International record:
1964–74 Brazil 87 (38)

JAIRZINHO – full name Jair Ventura Filho – is the only player to have scored in every round of a World Cup finals tournament. In 1970 he scored a total of seven goals against Czechoslovakia, Romania, England, Peru, Uruguay and Italy to help Brazil lift the Jules Rimet trophy for a record third time.

● JAIRZINHO is Brazil's third top leading goalscorer, behind Pele and Zico, and eighth in the list of international appearance makers. He was in the Brazil World Cup squads of 1966, 1970, and 1974.

● AFTER RETIRING from football he kept up links with his last Brazilian club, Cruzerio, and in the late 1980s he was kind enough to recommend to them a particularly promising 13 year old he had spotted... the player's name was Ronaldo.

JAMAICA

First World Cup appearance:
Jamaica 1 Croatia 3 (France, 1998)
Colours: Yellow shirts, black shorts, yellow socks

THE SMALLEST country ever to play at the World Cup, Jamaica reached their first-ever finals by finishing third in their qualifying group behind Mexico and the USA. Prime Minister PJ Patterson declared a national holiday the morning after the Reggae Boyz secured their place, and the party went on all day.... and all night.

● PREMIERSHIP STARS Deon Burton (Derby County), Robbie Earle (Wimbledon) and Frank Sinclair (Chelsea) are just some of the English-based players in the Jamaican squad. Top scorers in the qualifiers though, with five goals each were the Caribbean-based pair Theodore Whitmore and Walter 'Blaka' Boyd.

● Jamaica's best ever result was achieved in a pre-France '98 friendly when they drew 0-0 with world champions Brazil, much to the satisfaction of their Brazilian coach Rene Simoes. The Jamaican boss uses a laptop computer during matches, and in one game against Costa Rica it calculated that the Reggae Boyz hit 544 passes!

● Wimbledon midfielder Robbie Earle scored Jamaica's first ever World Cup goal although it was only a consolation in the 3-1 defeat against Croatia at France '98. The Jamaican's lost their next match 5-0 to Argentina but their 2-1 victory over Japan gave them a historic first ever World Cup win to make up for going out in the first round.

● The Jamaican team's World Cup was disrupted by the screening of a documentary on the eve of the finals which highlighted the difference in earnings and standard of living between the Jamaican and European based players.

WORLD CUP RECORD

1930-62 Did not enter	1982 Did not enter
1966 Did not qualify	1986 Did not enter
1970 Did not qualify	1990 Did not qualify
1974 Did not enter	1994 Did not qualify
1978 Did not qualify	1998 Round 1

ALEX JAMES

Born: Mossend, Lanarkshire 14.9.01
Height: 5ft 6ins Position: Midfielder
Club career:
1922–25 Raith Rovers
1925–29 Preston North End
1929–37 Arsenal 231 (26)
International record:
1929–32 Scotland 8 (3)

WHEN ALEX JAMES moved from Preston to Arsenal for £9,000 in 1929 he became Britain's most expensive player. He immediately justified his fee at Highbury, scoring in The Gunners' FA Cup Final victory over Huddersfield Town in 1930.

● DURING THE 1930s James was a key member of the Arsenal side that dominated English football, winning four league championships and another FA Cup in 1936.

● JAMES was part of arguably the best-ever Scotland team which thrashed England 5–1 at Wembley in 1928. His haul of eight caps was a meagre total for such a talented player, but it seems James's decision to play south of the border did not endear him to the Scottish selectors.

● DIMINUTIVE James, nicknamed 'the Wee Wizard', wore possibly the longest shorts ever seen on a football pitch. He favoured them, he said, because they kept his knees warm.

● AFTER HANGING up his boots, James became a journalist with the News of the World, served in the Army in World War II and then returned to Arsenal to coach the juniors in 1949.

JAPAN

First World Cup appearance:
Japan 0 Argentina 1 (France,1998)
Colours: Blue shirts, white shorts, blue socks

JAPAN qualified for France 1998, their first ever appearance at the finals, by beating Iran 3-2 in a play-off. Masayuki Okano's extra-time 'golden goal' meant Japan avoided another play-off against Australia, and set off wild celebrations in Tokyo.

● CURRENT INTERNATIONAL Kazuyoshi Miura, formerly of Santos and Genoa, is Japan's greatest ever player, having scored an amazing 54 goals in 85 appearances for his country. Fifteen of his strikes came in the qualifiers for France '98.

● MIURA, however, was dropped from the squad for Japan's first ever World Cup finals tournament. Maybe the side could have done with hime, however, since despite some brave performances they lost every match (to Argentina, Croatia and Jamaica). The one consolation came against Jamaica when Nakayama scored his country's first ever World Cup finals goal in the 2-1 defeat.

● THEY will not need to qualify for the World Cup in 2002. Along with South Korea they're hosting it.

WORLD CUP RECORD

1930-50	Did not enter
1954	Did not qualify
1958	Did not enter
1962	Did not qualify
1966	Did not enter
1970-94	Did not qualify
1998	First round

PAT JENNINGS

Born: Newry, N. Ireland 12.6.45
Height: 6ft 0ins Position: Goalkeeper
Club career:
Newry (N. Ireland) 7
1962–64 Watford 48
1964–77 Tottenham Hotspur 472
1977–85 Arsenal 237
International record:
1964–86 Northern Ireland 119

WITH 119 appearances for Northern Ireland, Pat Jennings is easily his country's most-capped player. He made his international debut in 1964, and won his last cap against Brazil on his 41st birthday during the 1986 World Cup.

● FOR FOUR YEARS Jennings held the world record for the most international caps, until Peter Shilton surpassed it in the 1990 World Cup finals (going on to earn 125).

● JENNINGS IS the only goalkeeper in the modern era to have played for both Tottenham and Arsenal. With Spurs he helped the club win the FA Cup in 1967, two League Cups, and the UEFA Cup in 1972.

● IN 1973 he was voted Footballer of the Year. Jennings moved to Arsenal in 1977 for a mere £45,000 and won a Cup winners' medal with the club in 1979.

● JENNINGS IS one of a small band of goalkeepers to have scored a goal with a kick from hands. In the 1967 Charity Shield match against Manchester United he launched a huge punt down the pitch, which bounced over the hapless Alex Stepney and into the net.

SIR ELTON JOHN

Born: Pinner 25.3.47

Sir Elton John (real name Reg Dwight) is now in his second spell as Chairman of Watford. Locally born and bred, he took charge of Watford in 1977 and – thanks partly to his massive cash injection into the club – the Hornets rose from the Fourth Division to the First in five years and reached the FA Cup Final in 1984 (losing 2–0 to Everton).

● JOHN HAS now teamed up with Graham Taylor again in the hope of bringing the glory years back to vicarage Road.

● ELTON JOHN'S uncle Roy Dwight played for Nottingham Forest in the 1959 FA Cup Final and scored his side's first goal in a 2–1 win over Luton Town. Unfortunately he also broke his leg in that game.

Elton John, Watford Chairman during their most successful period in the 1970s and 80s, says cheese for the cameraman

VINNIE JONES

Born: Watford 5.1.65
Height: 5ft 11ins Position: Midfielder
Club career:
1986–89 Wimbledon 77 (9)
1989–90 Leeds United 46 (5)
1990–91 Sheffield United 35 (2)
1991–92 Chelsea 42 (4)
1992–98 Wimbledon 173 (12)
1998– Queens Park Rangers 7 (1)
International record:
1994– Wales 9 (0)

BEFORE he moved from Wimbledon to First Division QPR, Vinnie Jones had been sent off more times than any Premiership player. Up until the start of the 1998/99 season he had been dismissed 12 times in a career which has been plagued by controversy on and off the pitch.

● JONES first came to national prominence in 1987 when he was photographed squeezing Paul Gascoigne's private parts during a match against Newcastle. The following year, before he won the FA Cup with Wimbledon, he threatened to tear Kenny Dalglish's ear off and spit in the hole.

● ON 15th February 1992 he received the quickest yellow card in English football history when he was booked for Chelsea in an FA Cup match against Sheffield United for a foul after just three seconds.

● DESPITE his disciplinary record and reputation, however, Jones has matured and improved as a player over the years. In 1994, at the age of 29, he was called up to play for Wales and he made his debut in a Euro 96 qualifying match against Bulgaria in Cardiff although the following year he was sent off for the first time at international level against Georgia and was suspended for five matches.

● WALES KEPT faith in him, however, and in 1996 Bobby Gould controversially made him captain of the team for the World Cup qualifying match against Holland after getting the rest of their squad to vote for who should be skipper. Unfortunately the Welsh lost the match 7–1.

JUNINHO

Born: São Paulo 22.2.73
Height: 5ft 5ins Position: Midfielder
Club career:
Ituano (Brazil)
1992–95 São Paulo 101 (15)
1995–97 Middlesbrough 55 (14)
1997– Atletico Madrid
International record:
1995– Brazil 20 (2)

WHEN JUNINHO arrived in Britain he was given possibly the biggest reception ever for an overseas player. Five thousand excited schoolchildren turned up at Middlesbrough's Riverside Stadium to welcome the Brazilian in October 1995.

● JUNINHO's signing created the biggest increase in season ticket sales seen on Teeside. Virtually overnight, sales soared from 20,000 to 27,000. Juninho mania also engulfed the Middlesbrough club shop, with 2,000 Brazil shirts being sold in only days.

● JUNINHO was voted Brazilian Footballer of the Year in his last season with São Paulo. He won a number of honours with the club, including the World Club Championship in 1994.

● DURING HIS two seasons at Middlesbrough the Brazilian star – whose real name is Oswaldo Giroldo Junior (Juninho simply means 'little man' in Portuguese) – had the smallest boots in the Premiership. 'They look like something you'd hang up in your car,' said Boro chairman Steve Gibson of the star's size five boots.

● IN APRIL 1997 Juninho, alongside teammate Emerson, became the first Brazilian to play in an English domestic final at Wembley. Boro eventually lost 1–0 to Leicester in the Coca-Cola Cup Final replay. Both also appeared in the 2–0 FA Cup Final defeat by Chelsea in the same year.

Take Zat! Juve's French midfielder Zinedine Zidane thumps a shot at River Plate's goal during the Italian's 1–0 World Club Championship victory in 1997

JUVENTUS

Year founded: 1897
Ground: Stadio Delle Alpi (69,041)
League wins: 25
Colours: Black-and-white-striped shirts, white shorts, white socks

THE MOST FAMOUS and most supported club in Italy, with 25 title wins under their belt Juventus are also by far and away the most successful. Named Juventus ('youth') because the club's early players and supporters were 'youthful', the club adopted their black and white strip from the unlikely source after one of their members returned from a trip to England in 1903 with a set of Notts County shirts.

● KNOWN NOW as The Zebras for obvious reasons, Juventus laid the foundations for their success in the 1930s when they won five league titles in a row. They are now the only Italian club allowed to wear two gold stars on their shirts, signifying 20 title wins.

● 'Juve' have won the European Cup on two occasions (1985 and 1996). However, having appeared in all three finals since 1996, in 1998 they became the first side to lose two finals in a row when they lost 1-0 to Real Madrid, having been beaten 3-1 by Borussia Dortmund the previous year.

● IN 1991 an astonishing run came to an end... it was the first time they had failed to qualify for Europe in 28 years!

Roll of Honour

Italian champions 1905, 1926, 1931, 1932, 1933, 1934, 1935, 1950, 1952, 1958, 1960, 1961, 1967, 1972, 1973, 1975, 1977, 1978, 1981, 1982, 1984, 1986, 1995, 1998
Italian Cup 1938, 1942, 1959, 1960, 1965, 1979, 1983, 1990, 1995
European Champions Cup 1985, 1996
European Cup Winners' Cup 1984
UEFA Cup 1977, 1990, 1993
European Super Cup 1984
World Club Cup 1985

Attack-minded ex-Newcastle boss Kevin Keegan tries an unusual tactic: 'Just one at the back!'

ROY KEANE

Born: Cork 10.8.71
Height: 5ft 10ins Position: Midfielder
Club career:
1990–93 Nottingham Forest 114 (22)
1993– Manchester United 121 (17)
International record:
1991– Republic of Ireland 38 (3)

ROY KEANE (briefly) became Britain's most expensive footballer when he moved from Nottingham Forest to Manchester United in July 1993. Nobody ever shouted 'what a waste of money' at him, though, since he scored two goals for United on his home debut against Sheffield United and went on to help his team win their first ever double. He has been the first name on Ferguson's team-sheet ever since... when he hasn't been suspended that is.

● IN NOVEMBER 1996 Keane signed a four year contract with United making him the highest earner on their payroll (no mean feat at Old Trafford). In doing so he turned down big money offers from AC Milan and Barcelona that could have made him – according to some reports – up to £10 million.

● THE GRITTY midfielder is a key member of the Republic of Ireland team, too, having made his debut at home to Chile in 1991. He starred in the Republic's World Cup campaign in 1994 in the States and first captained the side in a game against Russia in 1996. Keane ended the match in disgrace, though, getting himself sent off in the final minute. It was the fourth time the Irishman's dodgy temperament had led to a red card that season: it is just about the only chink in his armour.

KEVIN KEEGAN

Born: Doncaster 14.2.51
Height: 5ft 8ins Position: Striker
Club career:
1968–71 Scunthorpe United 124 (18)
1971–77 Liverpool 230 (68)
1977–80 Hamburg
1980–82 Southampton 68 (37)
1982–84 Newcastle United 78 (48)
International record:
1973–82 England 63 (21)

KEVIN KEEGAN shocked the football world in January 1997 when he resigned as Newcastle manager, leaving thousands of Geordie fans in mourning. He had wanted to wait till the end of the season, but because the club was about to float on the stock exchange and needed to appear stable he was allegedly forced out immediately. It was a sad end to a five year reign that had seen Keegan take United from the brink of relegation from the Second Division to the brink of the Premiership title (throwing away a 12 point lead in 1995/96).

● KEEGAN HAD been desperate to emulate his success on the pitch as a manager: he was the only British player to be twice voted European Footballer of the Year and only the second player – after Johan Cruyff – to win the award in consecutive seasons (1978 and 1979).

● KEEGAN IS ONE of only two British players to have appeared in the European Cup Final with different clubs. In 1977 he was a winner with Liverpool against Borussia Moenchengladbach, but three years later he had to settle for a runners-up medal in Hamburg. The other player is Frank Gray, who played in 1975 for Leeds (v Bayern Munich) and 1980 for Nottingham Forest (v Hamburg).

● THE FIRST THREE games Keegan played for England were all against Wales. He made his international debut in Cardiff in November 1972, and helped England win 1–0. The first of his 31 appearances as captain was also against Wales, in 1976. His last match was as a substitute against Spain in the 1982 World Cup.

● In the summer of 1997 Keegan was appointed Director of Football at Mohamed Al Fayed's Second Division moneybags Fulham. He appointed Ray Wilkins as team coach but at the end of the season sacked his old friend and took over the reins himself.

GRAHAM KELLY

Born: Blackpool 23.12.45

GRAHAM KELLY has been the Chief Executive/General Secretary of the Football Association since 1989. His first major battle was with Colin Moynihan, Minister for Sport, who wanted to force the introduction of identity cards for football fans. Kelly called the idea 'horrendous'.

● KELLY's reign has been beset with problems and, while he has remained a popular figure at the FA, his lack of TV charisma has made him a much-maligned character with the general public.

● KELLY, whose first job was with Barclay's Bank, was responsible for the FA Cup being sponsored for the first time, by Littlewoods, in 1995, although he insisted that the term 'FA' remained in the cup's title.

● NEVER HAVING played football at a high level, nevertheless Kelly does turn out regularly as a forward for Dinosaur Thursday – the Natural History Museum XI.

Don't Quote Me

'When people meet me for the first time they think I'm a short fat bloke, whereas I'm really a tall fat bloke.'

Graham Kelly

MARIO KEMPES

Born: Cordoba, Argentina 15.7.52
Height: 6ft 0ins Position: Striker
Club career:
Instituto Cordoba (Argentina)
Rosario Central (Argentina)
Valencia (Spain)
River Plate (Argentina)
Hercules (Spain)
Austria Vienna (Austria)
Austria Salzburg (Austria)
International record:
1974–82 Argentina 51 (19)

DASHING ARGENTINIAN striker Mario Kempes was the Golden Boot winner of the 1978 World Cup tournament with six goals. Two of them came in the final in Buenos Aires and helped the hosts to a 3–1 win over Holland

● KEMPES WAS the only foreign-based player in Argentina's World Cup-winning squad, his performances at the 1974 competition in Germany having earned him a transfer to the Spanish club Valencia. In 1980 he was part of the Valencia side which won the European Cup Winners' Cup, beating Arsenal on penalties after a drab 0–0 draw. Kempes was the top scorer in the competition with nine goals but, ironically, was the only Valencia player to miss from the spot.

● HE ALSO PLAYED for Argentina in the 1982 World Cup in Spain, but failed to make much of an impact. However, Kempes remains one of a small group of players to have appeared at three World Cups and is Argentina's seventh highest goalscorer ever, with nineteen.

KICK-OFF

THE QUICKEST a goal has ever been scored in British football is six seconds after the kick off, and it has occurred on three occasions (Albert Mundy for Aldershot against Hartlepool in October 1958, Barrie Jones for Notts County against Torquay in 1962 and Keith Smith for Crystal Palace against Derby in 1964).

● UNTIL THE TURN of the century teams used to change ends before kicking off every time a goal was scored.

● THE KICK-OFF of the FA Cup 3rd round tie between Lincoln and Coventry City in 1963 was postponed 15 times due to one of the worst British winters on record. Coventry eventually won 5–1 on March 7.

● THE TRADITIONAL 3.00 pm kick-off was settled on to give enough time for those who worked Saturday mornings – a pretty standard state of affairs for most people before the 1960s – to get to the match.

● 1997/98 saw a rule change whereby teams were allowed to score directly from the kick off. Perhaps the first man in the country to take advantage of the new rule was Nigel Partridge of Domino Reserves FC, who, after his side had conceded a goal against Parke Davis in September 1997, lofted the restart in off the underside of the bar. It was his side's fifth goal in an eventual 11-1 win. What's more, Partridge repeated the feat in January 1998.

BRIAN KIDD

Born: Manchester 29.5.49
Height: 6ft 0ins   Position: Striker
Club career:
1966–74 Manchester United 203 (53)
1974–76 Arsenal 77 (30)
1976–79 Manchester City 98 (44)
1979–80 Everton 40 (11)
1980–81 Bolton Wanderers 43 (14)
Atlanta Chiefs (USA)
Fort Lauderdale Strikers (USA)
Minnesota Kicks (USA)
International career:
1970 England 2 (1)

BRIAN KIDD, assistant manager to Alex Ferguson at Manchester United, made his name at the club in the late 1960s when he started playing in the great Best-Charlton-Law team whenever he could find a space for himself. In all he made 255 appearances for United, netting 70 goals.

● HIS FINEST moment came in 1968 when, on his 19th birthday, he made the team in Manchester United's first ever European Cup final, at Wembley against Portuguese champions Benfica, in place of the injured Denis Law. Kidd scored Manchester United's third goal, heading the ball onto the bar, then nodding in the rebound. He also set up their second and fourth goals. He remains the youngest Brit to score in a major European final.

● KIDD's playing career never reached such heights again, but as Fergie's assistant he puts the players through their paces at United's Cliff training ground. He has been a vital part of the set-up that led to United winning the country's first ever double Double.

Manchester United wonderkid Brian Kidd, whose powers of levitation were a mighty weapon in his armoury, evades a Dave Webb tackle against Chelsea in 1968

KILMARNOCK

Year founded: 1869
Ground: Rugby Park (18,168)
Highest ever crowd: 35,995, 10th March 1962 v Rangers (Scottish Cup qtr-final)
Nickname: Killie
Colours: Blue-and-white-striped shirts, blue shorts, blue socks

KILMARNOCK, Scotland's oldest club after Queen's Park, featured in the first Scottish Cup tie, losing 3–0 to Renton in 1873. Playing the whole match with only ten men didn't help the team's cause.

● KILLIE's only top-flight league triumph arrived in dramatic fashion in 1965, in the closest finish to a Scottish First Division Championship. A 2–0 victory over championship rivals Hearts resulted in Kilmarnock taking the title on a goal average of 0.04.

● IN THE 1930s the club recorded their best victory, beating Paisley Academical 11–1. Kilmarnock's heaviest defeat, 1–9, came at the hands of Celtic in 1938.

● IN 1945, in a match against Partick, the Killies were ordered to retake a penalty a record seven times before the ref was satisfied. They eventually missed it.

● IN 1995 Kilmarnock paid a club record fee of £300,000 to sign Paul Wright from St. Johnstone. In the same year, the club received an identical fee when Shaun McSkimming was transferred to Motherwell.

Roll of Honour

Div 1 champions 1965
Div 2 champions 1898, 1899
Scottish Cup 1920, 1929

GEORGI KINKLADZE

Born: Tbilisi 6.7.73
Ht: 5ft 11ins   Position: Forward
Club career:
1990–95 Dinamo Tbilisi
1995–98 Manchester City 96 (20)
1998– Ajax Amsterdam
International career:
1994– Georgia 24 (5)

Before his £5.6 million move to Ajax in the summer of 1998, ace midfielder Georgi Kinkladze was the shining star of Manchester City. Nicknamed 'Kinky' when he was brought to Maine Road by former manager Alan Ball, fans were greeted by the alarming headline 'Ball Gets Kinky'.

● Fears of sordid goings on, however, were allayed as soon as the silky skills of the Georgian international went on display - although they weren't enough to stop City sliding disastrously into the Second Division.

● Hero-worshipped by the City faithful during his spell at Maine Road, he was famously serenaded during the height of Britpop with his own version of the Oasis classic 'Wonderwall', which included the line 'and all the runs which Kinky makes are winding'.

DID YOU KNOW?

Kilmarnock's keeper Clemie was the first goalkeeper to save a penalty in a Scottish Cup Final way back in 1929. They went on to beat Rangers 2-0 in a match which also featured the first sending off in a Scottish final (the culprit being Rangers' Jock Buchanan).

German skipper Jürgen Klinsmann, the first player to score in three consecutive European Championship tournaments, lifts the trophy at the end of the Euro 96 Final.

JÜRGEN KLINSMANN

Born: Stuttgart 30.7.64
Height: 6ft 1in   Position: Forward
Club career:

1981–84	Stuttgart Kickers 61 (22)
1984–89	VfB Stuttgart 156 (79)
1989–92	Inter Milan 95 (34)
1992–94	Monaco 65 (29)
1994–95	Tottenham Hotspur 41 (20)
1995–97	Bayern Munich 65 (31)
1997	Sampdoria
1997–98	Tottenham Hotspur 15 (9)

International record:

1987–98	Germany 108 (47)

ONLY LEGENDARY STRIKER Gerd Müller has scored more goals for Germany than Jürgen Klinsmann. His trio of goals during France 98 put him second in the all-time list, alongside former strike-partner Rudi Voller, with 47 goals.

● KLINSMANN'S equaliser against Mexico was his eleventh goal in the World Cup finals. Only Muller (14), Just Fontaine (13) and Pele (12) have scored more.

● KLINSMANN is rather a popular man in some parts of North London. He has played two spells at Tottenham Hotspur finishing as their top scorer both in 1994/95 and 1997/98, when he helped them avoid relegation. In the latter season he almost certainly became the only man ever to have written a 'must-play' clause into a contract with a top English club.

● KLINSMANN finished second equal in ther Euro 96 Golden Boot table, with three goals, and, having netted in the 1988 and 1992 tournaments as well, is the only man to have scored in three seperate European Championships.

● AS WELL AS wining the World Cup with Germany in 1990 and Euro 96, Klinsmann has helped both Inter Milan and Bayern Munich win the UEFA Cup.

BRIAN LAUDRUP

Born: Vienna 22.2.69
Height: 6ft 1in   Position: Forward
Club career:

1986–89	Brondby (Denmark) 49 (13)
1989–90	Bayer Uerdingen (Germany) 34 (6)
1990–92	Bayern Munich 33 (9)
1992–93	Fiorentina 31 (5)
1993–94	AC Milan (loan)
1994–98	Rangers 115 (33)
1998–	Chelsea

International record:

1988–	Denmark 80 (21)

BRIAN AND HIS older brother Michael are sons of the former Danish international Finn Laudrup. In 1967 Finn scored a hat-trick in Denmark's biggest ever win, a 14–2 hammering of Iceland.

● LAUDRUP BEGAN his career at Brondby, where he won two Danish championships. He moved on to the Bundesliga, playing first for Bayer Uerdingen and then Germany's top side, Bayern Munich.

● HE SWITCHED countries again in 1992, joining Fiorentina of Italy. The lowest point of Laudrup's career followed, though, as the club suffered relegation to Serie B.

● IN 1992 Laudrup was a key member of the Danish side which won the European Championships. Six years later he starred alongside brother Michael as Denmark reached the quarter finals of the World Cup, scoring in the memorable though ultimately disappointing 3-2 defeat by Brazil.

● IN JULY 1998 Laudrup moved from Rangers to Chelsea on a free transfer under the Bosman ruling. The deal reportedly made Laudrup the highest paid player in British football with some sources claiming his wages amount to a staggering £75,000 per week.

MICHAEL LAUDRUP

Born: Vienna 15.6.64
Height: 5ft 9ins   Position: Forward
Club career:

1982–83	Brondby (Denmark) 38 (23)
1983–85	Lazio 60 (9)
1985–89	Juventus 102 (16)
1989–94	Barcelona 167 (38)
1994–97	Real Madrid 62 (13)
1997–	Ajax Amsterdam

International record:

1982–	Denmark 102 (37)

OLDER BROTHER of Brian, Michael Laudrup is the second most capped player in the history of Danish football with 102 caps (equal with Morten Olsen and just behind Peter Schmeichel. He is also the fifth top scorer ever for Denmark with 37.

● LAUDRUP, though, missed his country's greatest moment, the 1992 European Championship win, after rowing with coach Richard Moller-Nielsen.

● LAUDRUP is the only player ever to have appeared in a 5–0 victory for Barcelona over Real Madrid, and a 5–0 win for Real over Barça. He is also the only Danish player to have played for both Spanish giants.

● AT THE 1986 World Cup Michael Laudrup was the star of a brilliant but inconsistent Danish side. After thrashing Uruguay 6–1 and beating West Germany the Danes crashed to a 5–1 second round defeat by Spain. He starred at France 98, scoring one goal in the tournament as the Danes reached the quarter-finals.

● AT CLUB LEVEL Laudrup won the World Club Cup with Juventus and the European Cup with Barcelona. In 1996 he left Real Madrid to play in the emerging J-League in Japan.

Brian Laudrup... £75,000 a week and he can't buy clothes that fit

DENIS LAW

Born: Aberdeen 22.2.40
Position: Forward
Club career:
1956–59 Huddersfield Town 81 (16)
1960–61 Manchester City 44 (21)
1961–62 Torino (Italy) 27 (10)
1962–73 Manchester United 309 (171)
1973–74 Manchester City 24 (9)
International record:
1958–74 Scotland 55 (30)

WITH 30 international goals, Denis Law is Scotland's equal leading scorer, along with Kenny Dalglish. Law's goals, though, came in roughly half the number of games Dalglish played in.

● LAW MADE his international debut in 1958, scoring in a 3–0 win over Wales. He is the only Scottish player to have scored four goals for his country on two occasions – against Northern Ireland in 1962 and Norway in 1963.

● AT CLUB LEVEL with Manchester United, Law won a host of honours, including the FA Cup in 1963 and two league championships. In European competitions he scored a record five hat-tricks, but a knee injury ruled him out of United's 1968 European Cup triumph.

● IN 1964 Law was voted European Footballer of the Year to become only the second British player – after Stanley Matthews – to win the award.

● THE LAST GOAL Denis Law scored in first-class football was also the saddest of his career. His cheeky backheel, while playing for Manchester City in 1974, virtually condemned opponents Manchester United to relegation to the Second Division. 'I have seldom felt so depressed as I did that weekend,' he said later.

● DENIS LAW WAS the highest goalscorer in the FA Cup this century with 41 goals until Ian Rush scored his 42nd FA Cup goal against Rochdale in 1995. Law is still in second place.

Denis Law, Scotland's joint record scorer, smiles for the cameras having joined Manchester City from neighbouring United. Little did he know he was soon to doom his old club to relegation

TOMMY LAWTON

Born: Bolton 6.10.19 Died 6.11.96
Height: 6ft 0ins Position: Forward
Club career:
1936–37 Burnley
1937–45 Everton
1945–47 Chelsea 42 (30)
1947–52 Notts County 151 (90)
1952–53 Brentford 50 (17)
1953–56 Arsenal 35 (13)
International record:
1939–49 England 23 (22)

DEMON STRIKER Tommy Lawton is the only English player to have scored in five consecutive internationals twice. His first goal run was in 1939, and he went on another scoring spree in 1946, becoming in the process the first player since 1929 to score four goals in a match for England (v Holland on 27th November).

● LAWTON IS the England striker with the best post-war strike rate, scoring 16 goals in 15 games after 1945. He also scored the quickest ever England goal, notching one past Portugal in 1947 after 17 seconds.

● HE IS ALSO the youngest player to score a football league hat-trick. He was aged just 17 years and four days when he bagged three goals on his debut for Burnley in 1936. He moved to Everton shortly after, and helped The Toffeemen win The League in 1939.

● IN 1947 Lawton became the first £20,000 footballer, when he was transferred from Chelsea to Notts County. Extraordinarily, County were languishing in the Third Division (South) at the time.

● LAWTON MOVED again in 1952, taking over as player-manager at Brentford. The following year he was transferred to Arsenal. In 1957 Lawton was appointed manager of Notts County, but was sacked a year later and retired to run a public house.

LAZIO

Year founded: 1900
Ground: Stadio Olimpico (82,922)
League wins: 1
Colours: Light blue shirts, white shorts and white socks

ARCH-RIVALS of their city adversaries Roma (with whom they share the Stadio Olimpico), Lazio achieved their first and only Italian Championship victory in 1974.

● EVER SINCE THEN they have tried to emulate that achievement. Signing Paul

Gascoigne from Tottenham in 1992 and making him Britain's most expensive player at £5 million, however, did not bring the glory that Lazio had hoped. The deal would have swelled Tottenham's coffers by £8.5 million if Gazza had not snapped his cruciate ligament in the 1991 FA Cup Final.

● Lazio have never won a major European trophy. They came closest in 1998 when they reached the UEFA Cup Final, only to be shot down by Serie A rivals Inter Milan, who beat them 3-0 in the Parc De Princes in Paris.

● A few days earlier, however, the club had recorded only their second ever Italian Cup win (the first was in 1958) when they beat AC Milan 3-2 on aggregate.

Roll of Honour

Italian League champions 1974
Italian Cup 1958, 1998

THE LEAGUE CUP

THE LEAGUE CUP has had more names than any other football trophy. From 1961–81 it was the plain simple League Cup. It has since changed its name to the Milk Cup (1982), The Littlewoods Cup (1987), The Rumbelows League Cup (1991), The Coca-Cola Cup (1993), and now, since 1998/99, the Worthington Cup.

● THE MOST successful League Cup teams are Liverpool and Aston Villa, both of whom have won the cup five times.

● When Ian Rush scored for Newcastle United against Hull City on October 15th 1997 the former Liverpool and Leeds striker equalled Geoff Hurst's record of 46 League Cup goals.

● THE MOST goals ever scored in a League Cup game were scored by Oldham Athletic's Frankie Bunn who netted six times in his side's victory of Scarborough on 25th October 1989.

● THE MOST successful League Cup manager is Brian Clough, whose teams have made more semi-final and final appearances than any other.

● THE YOUNGEST League Cup Final captain was Barry Venison, who led Sunderland out to play Norwich City in 1985 aged just 20 years, seven months and eight days. Unfortunately for poor old Barry they lost 1–0.

● NORMAN WHITESIDE, the youngest man ever to score in an FA Cup Final (for Manchester United v Brighton in 1983), is also the youngest man ever to score in a League Cup Final (for Manchester United v Liverpool also in 1983), aged 17 years and 324 days.

● LIVERPOOL WON the League Cup a record four times in a row between 1981–84, going an unprecedented 25 cup matches undefeated.

● THE FIRST PLAYER to score in every round of the League Cup was West Bromwich Albion's Tony Brown who netted at every stage of the 1965/66 competition, including a goal in the Final in which West Brom beat West Ham 5-3 on aggregate.

● THE FIRST League Cup Final to be played at Wembley was the 1966/67 match between QPR and West Bromwich Albion. QPR at the time were the first Third Division club to reach a major Wembley final and became the first Third Division club to win the League Cup after triumphing 3–2.

LEAGUE CUP FINALS

1961 Aston Villa 3 Rotherham United 2* (2 legs)
1962 Norwich City 4 Rochdale 0 (2 legs)
1963 Birmingham City 3 Aston Villa 1 (2 legs)
1964 Leicester City 4 Stoke City 3 (2 legs)
1965 Chelsea 3 Leicester City 2 (2 legs)
1966 West Bromwich Albion 5 West Ham United 3 (2 legs)
1967 Queen Park Rangers 3 West Bromwich Albion 2
1968 Leeds United 1 Arsenal 0
1969 Swindon Town 3 Arsenal 1*
1970 Manchester City 2 West Bromwich Albion 1*
1971 Tottenham Hotspur 2 Aston Villa 0
1972 Stoke City 2 Chelsea 1
1973 Tottenham Hotspur 1 Norwich City 0
1974 Wolverhampton Wanderers 2 Manchester City 1
1975 Aston Villa 1 Norwich City 0
1976 Manchester City 2 Newcastle United 1
1977 Aston Villa 0 Everton 0
Aston Villa 1 Everton 1* (replay)
Aston Villa 3 Everton 2* (second replay)
1978 Nottingham Forest 0 Liverpool 0*
1979 Nottingham Forest 1 Liverpool 0 (replay)
1980 Wolverhampton Wanderers 1 Nottingham Forest 0
1981 Liverpool 1 West Ham United 1*
Liverpool 2 West Ham United1 (replay)

Milk Cup
1982 Liverpool 3 Tottenham Hotspur 1*
1983 Liverpool 2 Manchester United 1*
1984 Liverpool 0 Everton 0*
Liverpool 1 Everton 0 (replay)
1985 Norwich 1 Sunderland 0
1986 Oxford United 3 Queens Park Rangers 0

Littlewoods Cup
1987 Arsenal 2 Liverpool 1
1988 Luton Town 3 Arsenal 2
1989 Nottingham Forest 3 LutonTown 1
1990 Nottingham Forest 1 Oldham Athletic 0

Rumbelows Cup
1991 Sheffield Wednesday 1 Manchester United 0
1992 Manchester United 1 Nottingham Forest 0

Coca-Cola Cup
1993 Arsenal 2 Sheffield Wednesday 1
1994 Aston Villa 3 Manchester United 1
1995 Liverpool 2 Bolton Wanderers 1
1996 Aston Villa 3 Leeds United 0
1997 Leicester City 1 Middlesbrough 1*
Leicester City 1 Middlesbrough 0* (replay)
1998 Chelsea 2 Middlesbrough 0

* after extra time

ROBERT LEE

Born: West Ham 1.2.66
Height: 5ft 10ins **Position:** Midfielder
Club career:
1984–92 Charlton Athletic 298 (59)
1992– Newcastle United 209 (43)
International record:
1994– England 18 (2)

ONCE DESCRIBED by former manager Kevin Keegan as 'the best midfielder in the country' Robert Lee has been a regular (though by no means surefire) member of the England squad under both Venables and Hoddle since making a scoring debut against Romania at Wembley in October 1994.

● LEE ALSO scored on his debut for Charlton in March 1984. He was a member of the Charlton side which won promotion to the First Division in 1986 despite having to 'borrow' Selhurst Park for home matches.

● LEE's nickname at Newcastle is 'Lurker' because he hangs around the penalty area, unseen by opposing defences. Certainly, Antwerp didn't spot Lee when he scored three goals for Newcastle in a 1994 UEFA Cup match, the only time he has scored a hat-trick for his club.

● WHEN LEE left Charlton in September 1992 he became the most expensive player to leave the club. Newcastle signed him for £750,000, a fee which now looks like a bargain and since overtaken by Lee Bowyer's £2.6 million move from Charlton to Leeds.

● IN HIS FIRST season with The Magpies Lee picked up a First Division championship winner's medal, as Newcastle secured promotion in impressive style.

'Lurker' Lee sizes up his options

LEEDS UNITED

Year founded: 1919
Ground: Elland Road (40,210)
Highest ever crowd: 57, 892, 15th March 1967 v Sunderland (FA Cup rd 5 replay)
Colours: White shirts, white shorts and white socks

LEEDS WERE THE last team to win the old First Division, before it became the Premiership, after catching and overtaking Manchester United in 1991/92.

● LEEDS UNITED were formed in 1919, after Leeds City were disbanded by the FA in an early 'bungs' scandal after being found guilty of making illegal payments to players. The new club joined the Midland League and played their first match in November of that year.

● THE ARRIVAL of Don Revie as manager in 1961 led to a period of unprecedented success for the Yorkshire club, at home and abroad, with the likes of Jack Charlton, Billy Bremner, Peter Lorimer and Eddie Gray in the side. One of the first decisions Revie made was to change the club's strip to all white, in admiring imitation of the mighty Real Madrid.

● IT WAS DURING the Revie era that Leeds enjoyed their record win – a 10–0 hammering of Norwegians Lyn Oslo in the 1969 European Cup (the club's worst ever defeat came in 1934, 1–8 by Stoke City).

● IT WAS ALSO under Revie that Leeds finally ended the longest run in the FA Cup without a victory. Between February 1952 and March 1963 the club went 16 FA Cup matches without a win... an unenviable record which still stands today.

● THEIR FORTUNES were changing, and in 1968/69 Leeds lost just two games out of 42 to win the First Division trophy – a record for a 42-game campaign. They earned 67 points that season, a record until Liverpool earned just one more in the 1978/79 season.

● IN 1973/74 Leeds set the longest unbeaten run at the start of a season, not being defeated for 29 games. This record was equalled (surprise, surprise by Liverpool) in 1987/88 but never beaten.

● ON 15th APRIL 1970 Leeds appeared before the biggest crowd ever to witness a European Cup tie when 135,826 crammed into Hampden Park, Scotland, to watch Celtic beat them 2–1 in the semi-final second leg.

● RIOTING BY LEEDS fans after the European Cup Final of 1975 (which they lost 2–0 to Bayern Munich) led to the club becoming the first from England to be suspended from European competition. The ban lasted three years.

● THEY DID, however, win the European Fairs Cup (which later became the UEFA Cup) in both 1968 and 1971.

● PETER LORIMER is Leeds' leading scorer, notching 168 league goals in two periods at the club: 1965–79 and 1983–86. John Charles holds the record for most goals in a season, hitting 42 in a Division Two campaign in 1953/54.

● JACK CHARLTON holds the record for League appearances for Leeds, playing in 629 games between 1953 and 1973. And fiery skipper Billy Bremner is Leeds' most capped player, winning 54 caps for Scotland in the 1960s and early 70s.

● BETWEEN 1982 and 1994 Leeds shared their ground with Rugby League club Hunslet. And in 1982, Elland Road was the venue for the replay of the Challenge Cup Final – the first football ground to have staged this event. The match produced record receipts for a rugby league game outside Wembley.

● ON 8th JUNE 1995 England played Sweden at Elland Road, in the first home football international to have been played away from Wembley since January 1966.

Since no-score bore draw specialist George Graham took over at Leeds fans have taken up a new song: 'We'll score again, don't know where, don't know when...'

Roll of Honour

Div 1 champions 1969, 1974, 1992
Div 2 champions 1924, 1964, 1990
FA Cup 1972
League Cup 1968
European Fairs Cup 1968, 1971

Leeds Utd's Post-War Record

47 D1 22nd	65 D1 2nd	83 D2 8th
48 D2 18th	66 D1 2nd	84 D2 10th
49 D2 15th	67 D1 4th	85 D2 7th
50 D2 5th	68 D1 4th	86 D2 14th
51 D2 5th	69 D1 1st	87 D2 4th
52 D2 6th	70 D1 2nd	88 D2 7th
53 D2 10th	71 D1 2nd	89 D2 10th
54 D2 10th	72 D1 2nd	90 D2 1st
55 D2 4th	73 D1 3rd	91 D1 4th
56 D2 2nd	74 D1 1st	92 D1 1st
57 D1 8th	75 D1 9th	93 PR 17th
58 D1 17th	76 D1 5th	94 PR 5th
59 D1 15th	77 D1 10th	95 PR 5th
60 D1 21st	78 D1 9th	96 PR 13th
61 D2 14th	79 D1 5th	97 PR 11th
62 D2 19th	80 D1 11th	98 PR 5th
63 D2 5th	81 D1 9th	
64 D2 1st	82 D1 20th	

LEICESTER CITY

Year founded: 1884
Ground: Filbert Street (22,517)
Highest ever crowd: 47, 298, 18th February 1928 v Tottenham Hotspur (FA Cup rd 5)
Previous name: Leicester Fosse
Nickname: The Foxes
Colours: Blue shirts, white shorts and blue socks

LEICESTER CITY'S League Cup Final replay win over Middlesbrough in April 1997 earned them only the second major trophy in their history (they also won the League Cup in 1964 when they beat Stoke City).

● Leicester's Coca Cola Cup victory earned them only their second ever foray into Europe. The first was in 1961 when they were defeated in the second round of the Cup Winners' Cup by Atlético Madrid... and amazingly it was the Spaniards that dumped them out of the UEFA Cup 37 years later.

Leicester's Post-War Record

47 D2 9th	65 D1 18th	83 D2 3rd
48 D2 9th	66 D1 7th	84 D1 15th
49 D2 19th	67 D1 8th	85 D1 15th
50 D2 15th	68 D1 13th	86 D1 19th
51 D2 14th	69 D1 21st	87 D1 20th
52 D2 5th	70 D2 3rd	88 D2 13th
53 D2 5th	71 D2 1st	89 D2 15th
54 D2 1st	72 D1 12th	90 D2 13th
55 D1 21st	73 D1 16th	91 D2 22nd
56 D2 5th	74 D1 9th	92 D2 4th
57 D2 1st	75 D1 18th	93 D1 6th
58 D1 18th	76 D1 7th	94 D1 4th
59 D1 19th	77 D1 11th	95 PR 21st
60 D1 12th	78 D1 22nd	96 D1 5th
61 D1 6th	79 D2 17th	97 PR 9th
62 D1 14th	80 D2 1st	98 PR 10th
63 D1 14th	81 D1 21st	
64 D1 11th	82 D2 8th	

● CITY HAVE appeared in more Wembley play-off finals than any other club, and it was Steve Claridge's goal in the play-off final in May 1996 which secured top flight status again for The Foxes. Since the system was introduced in 1987 they have played at Wembley four times... losing twice (to Blackburn Rovers and Swindon Town) and winning twice (against Derby County and Crystal Palace).

● WHILE PLAYING under the name Leicester Fosse (the club were formed at a meeting house on Roman Fosse Way) they suffered their worst defeat, losing 0–12 to East Midland neighbours Notts Forest in 1909. The score is still a record for a First Division match. Leicester's biggest win was a 10–0 thumping of Portsmouth in 1928.

● ARTHUR CHANDLER holds the club goalscoring record, with 259 strikes between 1923–35. During the 1924/25 season he scored in a record 16 consecutive matches for Leicester City.

● THE RECORD for a single season is held by Arthur Rowley, who grabbed 44 goals for The Foxes in season 1956/7. In all Rowley scored 251 times for Leicester, contributing to his total of 434 in league football (he also played for West Brom, Fulham and Shrewsbury) – more than any other player.

● LEICESTER'S longest-serving player is Adam Black, who made 528 league appearances for the club between 1920–35. John O'Neill, with 39 appearances for Northern Ireland, is the club's most capped player.

● POSSIBLY THE strangest incident in the club's history occurred on 18th December 1954 when two Leicester players, Stan Milburn and Jack Froggatt, were credited with a shared own goal in a match against Chelsea (Chelsea won 3–1). Both men tried to kick the ball at the same time... and it ended up in the back of the net.

● IN 1981 Leicester City, then bottom of the First Division table, ended Liverpool's 86-match unbeaten home record when they recorded a sensational 2–1 victory at Anfield.

● ON 24th SEPTEMBER 1984 striker Alan Smith (who later joined Arsenal) lost three teeth after a collision in the match against Stoke City. They were retrieved from the pitch, however, and later replaced in hospital.

● In the FA Cup Leicester City are one of the unluckiest clubs in the history of the competition. They have reached the final on four occasions (1949, 1961, 1963 and 1969) but have never lifted the famous trophy. In 1969 they suffered the indignity of becoming one of the four teams to be relegated in the same season as reaching the FA Cup Final (the other three are Manchester City in 1926, Brighton in 1983 and Middlesbrough in 1997).

Roll of Honour

Divi 2 champions 1925, 1937, 1954, 1957, 1971, 1980
League Cup 1964, 1997

GRAEME LE SAUX

Born: Jersey 17.10.68
Height: 5ft 9ins Position: Defender
Club career:

1989–93	Chelsea 90 (8)
1993–	Blackburn Rovers 128 (7)
1997–	Chelsea 26 (1)

International record:

1994–	England 29 (1)

Some England fans may take a while to forgive left back Graeme Le Saux for clutching his head instead of tackling team-mate Dan Petrescu, thus letting the Romanian score a last-gasp winner in the France 98 Group G match. England were subsequently thrust into the harder half of the draw and knocked out by Argentina.

● WHEN LE SAUX made his England debut against Denmark back in March 1994 (Terry Venables' first game in charge) he became the first Channel Islander to play for his country, just pipping Matt Le Tissier – a substitute in the same game – to the honour. Le Saux is also the most expensive repurchase in English football. In 1993 he was transferred from Chelsea to Blackburn in a swap deal involving Steve Livingston, a journeyman striker who went on to play just half a match for the Blues. Four years later it cost the west Londoners a cool £5 million to buy him back.

● IN THE MEANTIME Le Saux, an avid Guardian reader, won the Championship at Rovers under Kenny Dalglish. In the subsequent Champions League campaign, however, he showed his more brutal side and achieved international notoriety by thumping team-mate David Batty so hard he damaged three fingers.

MATT LE TISSIER

Born: Guernsey 14.10.68
Height: 6ft 1ins
Position: Midfielder/Forward
Club career:

1986–	Southampton 383 (150)

International record:

1994–	England 7 (0)

MATT LE TISSIER has played more games for Southampton than any other player currently on the club's books. He made his full debut for the club in September 1986 against Spurs, and his boyhood hero Glenn Hoddle.

● WHILE HE WAS still only 18 Le Tissier scored his first hat-trick, in a First Division match against Leicester City.

● IN 1990 Le Tissier was voted PFA Young Player of the Year. Since then he has won a host of personal awards, including Match Of The Day's Goal of the Season in 1995 for a mazy run and audacious 35-yard chip against Blackburn.

● LE TISSIER'S England career has had more downs than ups: he was first picked in Venables' first match against Denmark in 1994 after a concerted media campaign had failed to persuade Graham Taylor to select him. But he never became a regular and was rather unfairly blamed by many journalists for England's 1–0 home defeat against Italy, after Glenn Hoddle had decided to give him a chance.

● OF ALL current league players Le Tissier has the best record from the penalty spot. He has scored 46 times from 12 yards out for the Saints, and only missed once (Nottingham Forest's Mark Crossley becoming the only Premiership goalkeeper ever to save a Matt Le Tissier penalty). Up to the end of the 1997/98 season he had scored 21 penalties on the trot.

● LE TISSIER produced his best form at Southampton under manager Alan Ball. 'To put it in racing terms he's the star horse in a stable full of handicappers,' quipped Ball.

Matthew Le Tissier can't keep a straight face while trying out his famous Frankenstein impersonation

L

LEYTON ORIENT

Year founded: 1881
Ground: Brisbane Road (13,000)
Highest ever crowd: 34,345, 25th January 1964 v West Ham (FA Cup rd 4)
Previous names: Glyn Cricket and Football Club, Eagle FC, Clapton Orient, Orient
Nickname: The O's
Colours: Red and white checked shirts, black shorts, red socks

THE NAME Orient Football club was chosen in 1888 because many of the team's players were working for the Orient Shipping Line.

● ORIENT ARE the only league club to have used Wembley Stadium for league matches. While still named Clapton Orient, during the 1930/31 season the club's Lea Bridge ground did not meet official standards so the two league games against Brentford and Southend were switched to the 'home of football'!

● IN 1994/95 Leyton Orient scored just 30 goals in 46 games on their way to relegation, a Division Two record.

● IN 1995 the club was taken over by boxing promoter Barry Hearn, saving it from financial ruin. It was the third time in Orient's history that they had been rescued from the brink of extinction.

● TOP ENGLAND cap-holder Peter Shilton passed another milestone while playing for the O's in December 1996. He became the first (and very possibly the last) player to play 1,000 Football League games when he kept a clean sheet in the 2–0 victory over Brighton. It was one of ten games 'Shilts' was to play for the London side that season: bizarrely enough he wasn't offered a new contract for the next one, according to manager Pat Holland 'because he couldn't kick the ball far enough'.

● In 1998 a report by the Colman's Football Food Guide voted the food at Leyton Orient the worst of any football club in England.

Roll of Honour

Div 3 (S) champions 1956
Div 3 champions 1970

LINCOLN CITY

Year founded: 1883
Ground: Sincil Bank (11,500)
Highest ever crowd: 23,196, 15th November 1967 v Derby County (League Cup rd 4)
Nickname: The Imps
Colours: Red shirts with white vertical stripe, black shorts, red socks

HAVING SPENT their entire history in the lower reaches of the league, Lincoln City's most stunning achievement was their Houdini-style escape act to avoid relegation to the Third Division in 1958. Needing to win their last six matches to stay up, The Imps did exactly that and missed the drop by a single point.

● LINCOLN are well known as the club which launched Graham Taylor's managerial career. Taylor was just 28 when he was appointed Lincoln manager in 1972, becoming the youngest manager in the history of the football league.

● UNDER TAYLOR's leadership the club was promoted from the Fourth Division in 1975/76 with a record points tally of 74.

● IN JANUARY 1932 Lincoln City scored an amazing seven goals in a 21-minute burst against Halifax Town. Even more incredibly, six of them were scored by Frank Keetley. They won the match 9–1, and at the end of the season they won the Division Three (North) Championship... on goal average!

● IN 1987 The Imps became the first ever team to be automatically relegated from the Football League. The following season, however, they won the Vauxhall Premier League at the first time of asking to become the second team ever to be automatically promoted into the Football League.

● When the club appointed Keith Alexander as manager in 1993 he became the first black manager in the history of British football.

Roll of Honour

Div 3 (N) champions 1932, 1948, 1952
Div 4 champions 1976

GARY LINEKER

Born: Leicester 30.11.60
Height: 5ft 10ins Position: Striker
Club career:
1978–85 Leicester City 194 (95)
1985–86 Everton 41 (30)
1986–89 Barcelona 99 (44)
1989–92 Tottenham Hotspur 105 (67)
1992–94 Nagoya Grampus 8 (Japan)
International record:
1984–92 England 80 (48)

GOALSCORING HERO turned TV presenter, Gary Lineker is England's second highest scorer, with 48 goals, just one behind the great Bobby Charlton. He had a chance to equal the record in a friendly against Brazil in 1992, but his weak penalty was saved.

● HE IS, however, England's leading scorer in World Cup finals tournaments with 10 goals. He scored six in Mexico in 1986 (making him the tournament's top scorer and winning him the Golden Boot) and four in Italia 90.

● LINEKER made his England debut in May 1984 as a substitute against Scotland, and the first of his five hat-tricks for England was in October 1985, in a World Cup qualifier against Turkey.

● HE IS the only player to have twice scored all four England goals in a match, grabbing them in two 4–2 away wins – over Spain in 1987 and Malaysia in 1991.

Gary Lineker, the first footballer since Des Walker to have a packet of crisps named after him, celebrates one of his 48 goals for England

● AT CLUB level Lineker had to wait until he joined Barcelona before winning a major honour. He was a member of the Spanish club's victorious European Cup Winners' Cup team which beat Sampdoria 2–0 in Berne in 1989. With Spurs he won the FA Cup in 1991.

● IN HIS last international, against Sweden in 1992, Lineker was substituted by Graham Taylor in favour of Alan Smith, perhaps the most controversial substitution in England's history. The tactical switch failed as England lost the match and limped out of the European Championships.

● LINEKER WAS not booked once throughout his entire career.

LINFIELD

Year founded: 1886
Ground: Windsor Park (28,500)
League wins: 42
Colours: Blue shirts, white shorts, blue socks

BY FAR and away the most successful club in Northern Ireland, Linfield have won the Irish league an astonishing 42 times and the Irish Cup on 37 occasions.

● THE TEAM shares Windsor Park with the national team, and has strong links with the Protestant community in the province and with Rangers in Scotland.

● DESPITE qualifying for Europe practically every year since 1959, the closest Linfield have come to glory outside Northern Ireland was when they reached the quarter-finals of the Cup Winners' Cup in the 1966/67 season, eventually bowing out to CSKA Sofia of Bulgaria.

● LINFIELD have supplied more Northern Ireland internationals than any other club (63).

Roll of Honour

Irish League champions 1891, 1892, 1893, 1895, 1898, 1902, 1904, 1907, 1908, 1909, 1911, 1914, 1922, 1923, 1930, 1932, 1934, 1935, 1949, 1954, 1956, 1959, 1961, 1962, 1966, 1969, 1971, 1975, 1978, 1979, 1980, 1982, 1983, 1984, 1985, 1986, 1987, 1989, 1993, 1994

Irish Cup 1891, 1892, 1893, 1895, 1898, 1899, 1902, 1904, 1912, 1913, 1915, 1916, 1919, 1922, 1923, 1930, 1931, 1934, 1936, 1939, 1942, 1945, 1946, 1948, 1950, 1953, 1960, 1962, 1963, 1970, 1978, 1980, 1982, 1994, 1995, 1997

LIVERPOOL

Year founded: 1892
Ground: Anfield (45,000)
Highest ever crowd: 61,905, 2nd February 1952 v Wolverhampton Wanderers (FA Cup rd 4)
Nickname: The Reds
Colours: Red shirts, red shorts, red socks

THE MOST successful team in the history of English football, Liverpool have won 18 league titles (more than any other club), five FA Cups, and have appeared in Europe on more occasions than any other English club... winning the European Cup four times (1977, 1978, 1981 and 1984).

● IN WINNING the League Championship in 1978/9, Bob Paisley's Liverpool set two records. The Reds conceded just 16 goals all season, the fewest by any league club in a 42-match programme. Liverpool's total of 68 points was also the highest ever top-flight points tally before the introduction of three points for a win.

● After taking over as Liverpool manager from the legendary Bill Shankly in 1974, Bob Paisley went on to become English football's most successful manager ever. Before retiring in 1983 Paisley had won a total of 13 major trophies, despite never leading Liverpool to success in the FA Cup.

● LIVERPOOL also hold the record for the most points in a season (three points for a win) in the old Division One, Kenny Dalglish's team romping home with 90 in the 1987/88 campaign in which they were beaten just twice. In 1984/85 Everton recorded the same tally but played two extra games over the season. Manchester United hold the top flight record, running up 92 points in the 1993/94 Premiership season.

● IN 1985/86 they also became just the third side this century to 'do the double', winning the league (again!) and beating Everton in 3-1 in the final thanks to two goals from Ian Rush.

● Rush is the top scorer is the FA Cup this century with 43 goals (39 for Liverpool, three for Chester and one for Newcastle) and has scored more goals in FA Cup finals than any other player, netting five in his legendary spell at Liverpool.

● RUSH IS also Liverpool's most capped player, winning 65 caps for Wales whilst on the books at Anfield.

● THE CLUB's European record is the best in the land. In 1977 they became the first English club to win the trophy since Manchester United in 1968 – beating Borussia Moenchengladbach 3–1 in Rome – and in 1984 they became the first team to win the European Cup on penalties, defeating Roma in Rome.

● THE FAMOUS club was formed as a splinter from local rivals Everton in 1892, when the majority of Evertonians decamped to Goodison Park after a dispute with the owners of their original ground, Anfield. The landlord, John Houlding, founded Liverpool FC in the same year, after his attempts to retain the name 'Everton' had failed.

● WHEN LIVERPOOL played their first league game in 1893, all the outfield players were Scottish. The goalkeeper was English, but even he had a Scottish-sounding name – Bill McOwen. The 1986 FA Cup-winning side also included only one English player.

● THE CLUB's best victory was in 1974, when Stromsgodset Drammen (of Norway) were overcome 11–0 in the European Cup Winners' Cup. Nine Liverpool players figured on the scoresheet, with only Brian Hall and goalkeeper Ray Clemence failing to grab goals. The club's worst defeat was inflicted by Birmingham City, who beat The Reds 9–1 in a Second Division fixture in 1954.

● ROGER HUNT holds two Liverpool scoring records. Between 1959–69 he netted 245 league goals for the club, with 41 of his goals arriving in the 1961/62 season (a club record for goals in a season).

● IAN CALLAGHAN holds the record for league appearances with the Merseysiders, playing in 640 games between 1960 and

Liverpool's Robbie Fowler and Jason McAteer congratulate the ref after another dodgy penalty decision goes the Reds' way in front of the Kop

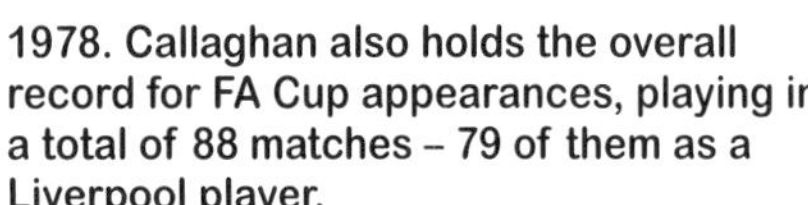

1978. Callaghan also holds the overall record for FA Cup appearances, playing in a total of 88 matches – 79 of them as a Liverpool player.

Roll of Honour

Div 1 champions 1901, 1906, 1922, 1923, 1947, 1964, 1966, 1973, 1976, 1977, 1979, 1980, 1982, 1983, 1984, 1986, 1988, 1990
Div 2 champions 1894, 1896, 1905, 1962
FA Cup 1965, 1974, 1986, 1989, 1992
Double 1986
League Cup 1981, 1982, 1983, 1984, 1995
European Cup 1977, 1978, 1981, 1984
UEFA Cup 1973, 1976

Liverpool's Post-War Record

47 D1 1st	64 D1 1st	81 D1 5th
48 D1 11th	65 D1 7th	82 D1 1st
49 D1 12th	66 D1 1st	83 D1 1st
50 D1 8th	67 D1 5th	84 D1 1st
51 D1 9th	68 D1 3rd	85 D1 2nd
52 D1 11th	69 D1 2nd	86 D1 1st
53 D1 17th	70 D1 5th	87 D1 2nd
54 D1 22nd	71 D1 5th	88 D1 1st
55 D2 11th	72 D1 3rd	89 D1 2nd
56 D2 3rd	73 D1 1st	90 D1 1st
57 D2 3rd	74 D1 2nd	91 D1 2nd
58 D2 4th	75 D1 2nd	92 D1 6th
59 D2 4th	76 D1 1st	93 PR 6th
60 D2 3rd	77 D1 1st	94 PR 8th
61 D2 3rd	78 D1 2nd	95 PR 4th
62 D2 1st	79 D1 1st	96 PR 3rd
63 D1 8th	80 D1 1st	97 PR 4th
		98 PR 3rd

LIVINGSTON

Year founded: 1995
Ground: Almondvale Stadium (6,400)
Highest ever crowd: 4,148, 11th November 1995 v East Stirling (Div 2)
Previous name: Meadowbank Thistle
Nickname: The Wee Jags
Colours: Amber shirts, amber shorts, black socks

FORMERLY Meadowbank Thistle, the club took on the name of the town it moved to after (reluctantly in many quarters) uprooting from Meadowbank and relocating to a purpose-built stadium 15 miles away in Livingston.

● IN FACT the club's first season as Livingston was an unqualified success, the team winning the Third Division title and earning promotion in spectacular style.

● FOR THE club's first ever home game it recorded a capacity crowd of more than 4,000 for the visit of East Stirling. Meadowbank Thistle's last game against Stenhousemuir in May 1995 attracted just 463.

Nat Lofthouse helped Bolton win the FA Cup Final against Manchester United in 1958 by scoring two goals. The second was one of the most controversial in the history of the game: he charged both goalkeeper and ball into the net

NAT LOFTHOUSE

Born: Bolton 27.8.25
Height: 5ft 10ins Position: Striker
Club career:
1946–60 Bolton Wanderers 452 (255)
International record:
1951–59 England 33 (30)

NAT LOFTHOUSE is the leading scorer in the history of Bolton Wanderers. In 505 matches in all competitions for the club he knocked in a phenomenal 285 goals.

● OF THOSE 285, however, the two most important goals came in Bolton's 2–0 FA Cup Final win over Manchester United in 1958.

● LOFTHOUSE made his England debut in 1951, scoring twice in a 2–2 draw with Yugoslavia at Highbury. During his international career Lofthouse scored two goals in a game on 12 occasions, but never went on to score a hat-trick. His total of 30 goals makes him England's joint fourth top scorer with Tom Finney, behind Bobby Charlton, Gary Lineker and Jimmy Greaves.

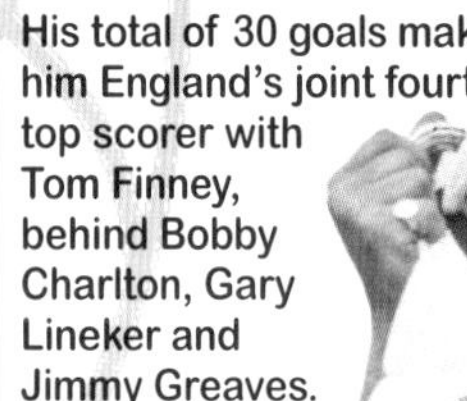

● AFTER PUTTING in a barnstorming performance against Austria in 1952 – a match in which he scored his customary two goals – Lofthouse was dubbed 'The Lion of Vienna' by the press. The nickname stayed with him for the rest of his career.

● LOFTHOUSE is one of only four players to score in every round of the FA Cup, including the final, but end up on the losing side at Wembley. His goals helped Bolton reach the final in 1953 against Blackpool and Stanley Matthews, but The Trotters lost 4–3.

ATTILIO LOMBARDO

Born: Milan 6.1.66
Height: 1.75m
Position: Midfielder
Club career:
1983-85 Pergacrama 38 (9)
1985-89 Cremonese 141 (17)
1989-95 Sampdoria 201 (35)
1995-97 Juventus 35 (2)
1997- Crystal Palace 24 (5)
International record:
Italy 17 (3)

In March 1998 Attilio Lombardo became the second bald Italian to manage a London Premiership club when he took over as Crystal Palace boss. Unlike his compatriot and former Juventus team-mate Gianluca Vialli, however, Lombardo did not take easily to management and resigned after only six weeks when Palace were relegated to Division One.

● Lombardo's appointment was a shock because he can barely speak a

word of English. In his brief spell as Palace player-manager the Bald Eagle relied on a local Italian restaurant owner, Dario Magri, to act as an interpreter.

● Lombardo became Palace's highest-paid player when he joined them for £1.6 million from Juventus in June 1997. The deal nearly fell through, however, when the Italian reportedly demanded that a mansion complete with maid and butler be included in his financial package.

● The Italian international's most successful spell was at Sampdoria, with whom he won the league in 1991. Lombardo was less fortunate at Juventus, breaking a leg almost as soon as he joined the Turin giants in 1995. The following season his opportunities were limited and he sat out Juve's 1997 European Cup Final defeat against Borussia Dortmund.

LUTON TOWN

Year founded: 1885
Ground: Kenilworth Road (9, 975)
Highest ever crowd: 30, 069, 4th March 1959 v Blackpool (FA Cup 6th rd replay)
Nickname: The Hatters
Colours: White shirts with blue sleeves, blue shorts, blue socks

AN AMALGAMATION of two local sides – the famous Wanderers (who won the first ever FA Cup Final) and Excelsior – in 1885 Luton Town became the first professional club south of Birmingham.

● LUTON have had their moments – winning the League Cup in 1988 and reaching the FA Cup Final in 1959, as well as enjoying an extended run in the top flight in the 1980s – but have never quite relived those Wanderers glory days.

● THE CLUB'S record win was a 12-0 victory over Bristol Rovers in a Third Division (South) fixture in 1936. The match is best remembered as the one in which Joe Payne scored 10 goals, a record for English league football. Remarkably it was only Payne's fourth game for Luton and his first as centre forward.

● LUTON were the first and only club ever to ban away supporters from their ground in 1986 after a riot by Millwall 'supporters' at Kenilworth Road. This led to Luton being excluded from the League Cup in 1986.

● LUTON's most famous supporter for many years was the comedian Eric Morecombe. He was a director of the club from 1976 until his death in 1983.

Roll of Honour

Div 2 champions 1982
Div 3 (S) champions 1937
Div 4 champions 1968
League Cup 1988

Luton Town's greatest moment: a 3–2 League Cup Final triumph over Arsenal in 1988

DES LYNAM

Born: Co. Clare, Ireland 17.9.42

DES LYNAM, the Beeb's very own Mr Smoothie, first began broadcasting on football at the 1972 European Championships, when he was a presenter for BBC Radio. At the 1980 championships he worked as a commentator, before moving in front of the camera to become the unflappable host of 'Grandstand' and 'Match of the Day'.

● IT'S PROBABLY fair to say that Lynam is not top of Graham Taylor's Christmas card list. At the 1992 European Championship the pair clashed on air after the sleek-tongued presenter had asked Gary Lineker about the mood of the England manager. 'I wasn't trying to undermine him,' says Lynam, 'I was merely saying, look, shouldn't this guy lighten up a bit?'

● LYNAM WAS once reported to have proposed marriage to sex-change Bond girl Caroline Cossey, who was called Barry until the age of 17. She turned him down. 'We didn't get on over certain issues,' she says.

MICK McCARTHY

Born: Barnsley 7.2.59.

MICK MCCARTHY had a hard act to follow when he replaced Jack Charlton as Ireland manager in February 1996. Under Big Jack the Irish had qualified for two World Cups and a European Championship. McCarthy, though, only just failed to match the successes of his predecessor when Ireland lost a France '98 play-off to Belgium.

● MCCARTHY BEGAN his managerial career in 1992 as player-manager of Millwall. The Lions had good cause to regret his departure across the Irish Sea, as three months later they were relegated to Division Two under new manager Jimmy Nicholl.

● AN UNCOMPROMISING centre-half in his playing days, McCarthy won 57 caps for Ireland and captained the side to the quarter-finals at Italia '90. At club level he played for Barnsley, Manchester City, Celtic (with whom he won a Scottish league winners' medal in 1988) and Millwall.

ALLY McCOIST

Born: Bellshill 24.9.62
Height: 5ft 10ins Position: Striker
Club career:
1978–81 St. Johnstone 57 (22)
1981–83 Sunderland 56 (8)
1983– Rangers 410 (251)
International record:
1986– Scotland 58 (19)

ALLY McCOIST lies fifth in the all-time list of top scorers for Scotland and is Rangers' record scorer in all competitions.

● ON JANUARY 18th 1996 he became Rangers' all time record league scorer when he scored against Raith Rovers. In total he has scored more than 350 goals for the Glasgow giants (his 350th coming against Dundee in the Scottish Cup in March 1998), his total tally now standing at 355.

● AFTER AN UNHAPPY spell at Sunderland he quickly settled in at Ibrox and in 1984 scored a hat-trick in the Scottish League Cup Final against old firm rivals Celtic.

● IN 1992 McCoist scored a personal best 34 goals and won the European Golden Boot. In the same year he was voted Scottish Player of The Year.

● McCOIST has won more honours than any other current Scottish player. With Rangers he has picked up no fewer than ten championship medals, and in 1992 he gained his first Scottish Cup medal as The Gers won The Double.

● THE LOWEST point in McCoist's career came in 1993 when he broke his leg playing in a World Cup qualifier against Portugal. Typically, he marked his comeback game against Hibs in the Scottish League Cup Final with a goal in a 2–1 Rangers victory.

● In August 1997 McCoist broke yet another record when he became the highest Scottish scorer in European football. His two strikes against the champions of the Faroe Islands, GI Gotu, took him to 20 goals in Europe, two more than former Celtic hero Willie Wallace.

1992 European Golden Boot winner and Rangers' top scorer Ally McCoist

1 England 9 Scotland 3 (1961)
2 England 7 Scotland 2 (1955)
3 Scotland 0 England 5 (1973)
4 Scotland 0 England 5 (1888)
5 England 5 Scotland 1 (1975)
6 England 5 Scotland 2 (1893)
7 England 5 Scotland 2 (1930)
8 Scotland 0 England 4 (1958)
9 England 4 Scotland 1 (1969)
10 Scotland 1 England 4 (1892)

DANNY McGRAIN

Born: Finnieston 1.5.50
Height: 5ft 9ins Position: Defender
Club career:
1967–87 Celtic 657 (8)
International record:
1973–82 Scotland 62 (0)

DANNY McGRAIN first played for Scotland in 1973, and the following year starred in the Scottish side which came back undefeated from the World Cup in West Germany... but still didn't qualify for the 2nd round.

● IN A 20-year career with Celtic, during which he played more than 600 games, McGrain won seven championship medals and five Scottish Cup winners' medals. In 1978 Jock Stein appointed him club captain, and two years later he captained his country in the first of 10 matches.

● SCOTLAND's sixth most capped player (62), McGrain would have played many more games but for illness and injury. In 1972 he fractured his skull in a clash of heads with Falkirk's Doug Somner. Two years later he was diagnosed as having diabetes, and in 1977 he suffered a serious ankle injury which kept him out of football for over a year.

● A VERSATILE player who liked to get forward down the wing, McGrain was voted Scottish Player of the Year in 1977.

● McGRAIN is Celtic's second most capped player after Paul McStay.

DAVE MACKAY

Born: Edinburgh 14.11.34
Position: Defender
Club career:
Hearts
1958–68 Tottenham Hotspur 268 (42)
1968–71 Derby County 122 (5)
1971 Swindon Town 26 (1)
International record:
1957–66 Scotland 22 (4)

DAVE MACKAY first caught the eye as the tireless midfield dynamo who pushed Hearts to their first Scottish Championship this century back in 1958.

● MACKAY SOON moved south and became the driving force behind the Tottenham team that won the Double in 1961. It was the first time a team had triumphed in both the League and FA Cup this century.

● MACKAY, whose 22 caps for Scotland spanned a 10-year period, broke his left leg twice in a year, which seriously threatened his career, but he was back in the Spurs' driving seat for the 1967 FA Cup Final against Chelsea, which Tottenham won 2–1.

● HE MOVED to Second Division Derby in 1968, and won the Footballer of the Year Award in 1969 for helping The Rams win promotion to the top flight. In 1974 he replaced Brian Clough as manager at the club and, remarkably, within a year had won his first championship, the most inexperienced post-war manager to do so.

STEVE McMANAMAN

Born: Bootle 11.2.72
Height: 5ft 11ins Position: Forward
Club record:
1990– Liverpool 233 (43)
International record:
1994– England 22 (0)

STEVE McMANAMAN leapt to instant national prominence in the 1992 Liverpool v Sunderland FA Cup Final. Having made the team at the last minute in place of the injured John Barnes, he switched flanks at half-time and a star was born. He tore at the Sunderland defence and created the Michael Thomas goal that broke the deadlock.

● McMANAMAN obviously likes Wembley – three years later he was back for the League Cup Final against Bolton, and again he was the difference between the two sides. He scored two stunning goals and won the Man of the Match Award after wandering through the Wanderers' defence. Before the game, Sir Stanley Matthews, 'the Wizard of Dribble', had praised his skills when introduced to him in the line-ups.

● HE MADE his England debut as substitute against Nigeria in November 1994 and, while he took some time to settle in at international level, has now become a key member of the squad... although he only made one appearance in the France 98 World Cup.

LAWRIE McMENEMY

Born: Gateshead 9.2.38.

In 1998 Lawrie McMenemy was appointed manager of Northern Ireland, the first Englishman to do the job. He got off to a winning start, too, when Northern Ireland beat Slovakia 1–0 in Belfast.

● This is not McMenemy's first taste of international management – between 1990 and 1993 he was number two to then England manager Graham 'Turnip' Taylor.

● McMenemy began his club management career with Doncaster Rovers in 1968, leading them to the Fourth Division title in his first season in charge. He repeated this trick at Grimsby Town in 1972, before moving on to Southampton. In 1976 he guided the south coast side to an improbable FA Cup triumph over Manchester United while they were still in the Second Division. In 1985 he took over at Sunderland and was hailed as a 'messiah' on Wearside. In 1987 he succeeded in taking the Rokerites into the Third Division for the first time in their history.

● McMenemy never played professional football. The closest he got was playing part-time as a central defender for his home team, Gateshead.

Lanky winger Steve McManaman takes on grizzly veteran Dave Mackay

MACCLESFIELD TOWN

Year founded: 1874
Ground: Moss Rose (6,500)
Highest ever crowd: 9,008, 4th February 1948 v Winsford University (Cheshire Senior Cup rd 2)
Nickname: The Silkmen
Colours: Royal blue shirts, white shorts, blue socks

IN MAY 1998 Macclesfield became only the second side to be promoted from the Vauxhall Conference to the Third Division and then to the Second Division in successive seasons. The club's meteoric rise has coincided with neighbours Manchester City's meteoric fall to the same division and 1998/99 sees a new Manchester derby.

● Macclesfield should have joined the league when they first won the Vauxhall Conference in 1995. Unfortunately, their Moss Rose ground was deemed unsuitable for League football and they were refused entry – a bizarre decision considering that Moss Rose was used by Chester City for league matches for two years from 1990!

● With 88 caps, Macclesfield manager Jimmy McIlroy is the third most-capped Northern Ireland player ever. His international career spanned 15 years from 1972 to 1987.

● Macclesfield recorded their best ever win back in 1886, thumping Chester St Marys 15-0 in the Cheshire Senior Cup. Their worst defeat was a 1-13 trouncing at the hands of Tranmere reserves in 1929.

Roll of Honour

Vauxhall Conference Champions 1995, 1997

PAOLO MALDINI

Born: Milan, 26.6.68
Height: 6ft 0ins Position: Defender
Club career:
1985– AC Milan 400 (20)
International record:
1988– Italy 93 (6)

PAOLO MALDINI is thought by the female half of Italy to be the best-looking player in the world, and by the male half to be the best attacking full back in the world. There is little doubt that the latter is true.

● MALDINI made his debut for Milan at age 17 in '85, and has been the Italian club's left-back since, winning five Scudetti and three European Cups with The Rossoneri.

● A REGULAR for the national team ever since, he made his debut as a substitute in a friendly against Yugoslavia in 1988. In 1994 he was part of the team which finished runners-up to Brazil in the USA World Cup and at France 98 he captained the side to the quarter-finals.

● WHEN Franco Baresi retired from international football in 1995 Maldini became the most-capped player in the Italian squad. Now on 93 caps he is third in his country's appearances list and looks destined to become Italy's most capped player ever (he has Dino Zoff's record of 112 caps in his sights).

MANCHESTER CITY

Year founded: 1887
Ground: Maine Road (31,458)
Highest ever crowd: 84,569, 3rd March 1934 v Stoke City (FA Cup rd 6)
Previous name: Ardwick
Nickname: The Citizens
Colours: Sky blue shirts, white shorts, white socks

MANCHESTER CITY have never in their entire 111 year history dropped as far down the football league as they did when they were relegated to the Second Division in May 1998.

● BUT IT all started so well. In 1892 the club, then playing as Ardwick, began their league career with a bang... thrashing Bootle 7–0. City's most impressive league victory was in 1987 when Huddersfield Town were beaten 10–1 in a Division Two match. The club's worst defeat was in 1906, 1–9 against Everton.

● BEFORE settling at Maine Road in 1923, City played at five previous grounds, including the evocatively named Pink Bank Lane. The Maine Road pitch is the biggest in the English League, measuring a stonking 9,440 square yards.

● IN 1924 legendary Billy Meredith played for City in an FA Cup semi-final at the ripe old age of 49. City lost, and Meredith never played for the club again. City's youngest ever player is Glyn Pardoe, who turned out for the first team aged 15 and 314 days, in 1961.

● IN 1926 City became the first team to reach the FA Cup Final and be relegated in the same season, a dubious feat only achieved three times since (including Middlesbrough in 1997).

● HAVING WON the league title in 1937, the following season they became the first and only club to be relegated from the top flight as champions. During that troubled 1937/38 season they were relegated despite the fact that they scored 50 goals, three more than champions Arsenal.

● CITY's travelling supporters suffered a miserable time during the 20 months from February 1986 to October 1987. The club played 34 consecutive away league matches without a win.

● IN 1993 Peter Reid only lasted 12 days of the new season before being sacked as manager, equalling the league record for the earliest sacking in a season.

● TOMMY JOHNSON holds two of the club's scoring records. He scored the most goals in a season (38 in 1928/29) and has scored more goals in total than

I'm too sexy for this team! Paolo Maldini fights off an ugly challenge from the Czech Republic's Karel Poborsky during Euro 96

THE EIGHT PLAYERS TO HAVE SCORED IN EVERY ROUND OF THE FA CUP

With club and goals

1 Sandy Brown (Spurs, 1901) 15
2 Frank O'Donnell (Preston, 1937) 11
3 Jeff Astle (West Bromwich Albion, 1968) 9
4 Eric Rimmer (Sheffield Wednesday, 1935) 8
5 Jackie Milburn (Newcatle United, 1951) 8
6 Nat Lofthouse (Bolton Wanderers, 1953) 8
7 Peter Osgood (Chelsea, 1970) 8
8 Charlie Wayman (Preston, 1954) 7

Even the brilliant Georgi Kinkladze couldn't stop Manchester City from sliding down the league

any other City player (158 between 1919–30).

● OASIS ARE currently the club's best known fans (along with 'comedian' Bernard Manning). The group played a sell-out gig at Maine Road in 1996, and at one time were rumoured to be negotiating a sponsorship deal to put their logo on the team's shirts.

Roll of Honour

Div 1 champions 1937, 1968
Div 2 champions 1899, 1903, 1910, 1928, 1947, 1966
FA Cup 1904, 1934, 1956, 1969
League Cup 1970, 1976
European Cup Winners' Cup 1970

MANCHESTER UNITED

Year founded: 1878
Ground: Old Trafford (55,500)
Highest ever crowd: 76,962, 25th March 1939 Wolves v Grimsby (FA Cup semi-final)
Previous name: Newton Heath
Nickname: The Red Devils
Colours: Red shirts, white shorts and black socks

MANCHESTER UNITED – the biggest club in Britain and winners of 11 league titles and a record nine FA cups – were originally known as Newton Heath, a team formed by employees of the Lancashire and Yorkshire Railway in 1878. But Newton Heath (who played in yellow and green halved shirts) were declared bankrupt in 1902, and the club was reformed under its present name.

● NOW A HUGE multinational business as well as a football team, United are the richest club in Britain, having reported a turnover of £88 million and a pre-tax profit of £27.5 million in 1997.

● IT HASN'T BEEN plain sailing all the way, however. On 5th May 1934 United discarded their by now famous red shirts - the inspiration for the club nickname, The Red Devils - for a crucial relegation clash, in the hope that a change of luck would follow. The team turned out in cherry and white hoops for the first and only time, and beat Millwall 2-0 to stay in the Second Division.

● OLD TRAFFORD was badly damaged by the Luftwaffe's bombs during World War II, and in the immediate post-war period United were forced into exile at Maine Road (the cause of a recent craze at City of 'Uwe Rosler's dad bombed Old Trafford!' T-shirts).

● UNITED's biggest win came in the European Cup. In 1956 RSC Anderlecht were overwhelmed 10–0. Blackburn Rovers (1926), Aston Villa (1930) and Wolves (1931) have all recorded 7–0 wins over United – the club's worst defeats.

● UNITED hold the record for the biggest win in the history of the Premiership. On 4th March 1995 Ipswich were crushed 9–0 at Old Trafford, with Andy Cole scoring five goals – another Premiership record.

● UNITED have won the FA Cup on a record nine occasions, moving ahead of Spurs with the 1996 Wembley triumph over Liverpool. That victory also meant that United became the first English club to win The Double on two occasions (the 'double Double' as it became known). United have also played in 14 FA Cup finals – more than any other club.

● SIR MATT BUSBY managed Manchester United for a record 24 years between 1945–69. During that period Sir Matt won seven domestic trophies, narrowly survived the 1958 Munich air crash which, among the 23 who died, claimed the lives of eight of his players, and saw United become the first English team to lift the European Cup in 1968 (beating Benfica 4–1 at Wembley).

● BOBBY CHARLTON, now Sir Bobby, is United's leading appearance maker. From 1956 until his emotional farewell game at Stamford Bridge in 1973, Charlton played in 606 league matches. He is also the club's highest scorer, with a total of 199 league

goals for United. The record for most goals in a season, though, is held by Dennis Viollet with 32 in 1959/60.

● UNITED's most capped player is Bobby Charlton, who played 106 times for England, scoring a record 49 goals, many of them pile-drivers from outside the penalty area.

● THE BEST-SUPPORTED team in the country (in 1997/98 just over a million fans passed through the Old Trafford turnstiles), United's fortunes are followed by a host of celebrity fans including Simply Red's Mick Hucknall, former England cricket captain Mike Atherton, actor/presenter Angus Deayton and radio and TV babe Zoe Ball.

Roll of Honour

Div 1/Prem League champions 1908, 1911, 1952, 1956, 1957, 1965, 1967, 1993, 1994, 1996, 1997
Div 2 champions 1936, 1975.
FA Cup 1909, 1948, 1963, 1977, 1983, 1985, 1990, 1994, 1996
Double 1994, 1996
League Cup 1992
European Cup 1968
European Cup Winners' Cup 1991
Super Cup 1991

Manchester United's Post-War Record

47 D1 2nd	64 D1 2nd	81 D1 8th
48 D1 2nd	65 D1 1st	82 D1 3rd
49 D1 2nd	66 D1 4th	83 D1 3rd
50 D1 4th	67 D1 1st	84 D2 4th
51 D1 2nd	68 D1 2nd	85 D2 4th
52 D1 1st	69 D1 11th	86 D1 4th
53 D1 8th	70 D1 8th	87 D1 11th
54 D1 4th	71 D1 8th	88 D1 2nd
55 D1 5th	72 D1 8th	89 D1 11th
56 D1 1st	73 D1 18th	90 D1 13th
57 D1 1st	74 D1 21st	91 D1 6th
58 D1 9th	75 D2 1st	92 D1 2nd
59 D1 2nd	76 D1 3rd	93 PR 1st
60 D1 7th	77 D1 6th	94 PR 1st
61 D1 7th	78 D1 10th	95 PR 2nd
62 D1 15th	79 D1 9th	96 PR 1st
63 D1 19th	80 D1 2nd	97 PR 1st
		98 PR 2nd

WILF MANNION

Born: Teesside 16.5.18
Height: 5ft 5in Position: Forward
Club career:
1936–54 Middlesbrough 368 (110)
1954–55 Hull City 16 (1)
International record:
1947–56 England 26 (11)

IN 1947 Middlesbrough striker Wilf Mannion had a dream start to his international career, scoring a hat-trick on his England debut against Northern Ireland.

● A DIMINUTIVE inside-forward, Mannion played all of his career (apart from his last season) in the town of his birth, Middlesbrough. He remains the Teessiders' most capped player, with 26 England appearances, during which he scored 11 times.

● HE WAS one of the members of the team that lost 1–0 to the USA in the 1950 World Cup, still considered the most embarrassing result in the country's history. 'Bloody ridiculous,' he said after the match. 'Can't we play them again?'

● MANNION was always a controversial figure who refused to play for 'Boro for six months after a wage dispute in 1948, and retired in 1955 after a few months at Hull after making allegations about illegal payments.

MANSFIELD TOWN

Year founded: 1910
Ground: Mill Field (5,289)
Highest ever crowd: 24,467, 10th January 1953 v Nottingham Forest (FA Cup rd 3)
Nickname: The Stags
Colours: Amber-and-blue-striped shirts, blue shorts, blue socks

IN 1977 Mansfield were promoted to the old Second Division for the first time in their history... only to be relegated the following year.

● THE STAGS recorded their best win in 1932, with a 9–2 victory over Rotherham. The club's worst defeat came a year later, 8–1 against Walsall.

● MANSFIELD players have made little impact at international level, although John McClelland did win six of his 53 Northern Ireland caps while with the club.

● ROD ARNOLD is Mansfield's record appearance maker, turning out in 440 league games between 1970–83.

● MANSFIELD's record goalscorer is Harry Johnson, with 104 goals between 1931–36.

● TED HARSTON holds the club record for goals in a season, netting 55 in the 1936/37 campaign.

● IN 1972 Mansfield made their worst start to a season, failing to score in their first nine matches.

● THE CLUB's biggest splash into the transfer market came in September 1989, when the club paid Leicester £80,000 for Steve Wilkinson. In the same month The Stags received a record £600,000 when Simon Coleman moved to Middlesborough.

Roll of Honour

Div 3 champions 1977
Div 4 champions 1975
Freight Rover Trophy 1987

DIEGO MARADONA

Born: Buenos Aires 30.10.60
Position: Forward
Club career:
1976–80 Argentinos Juniors 116 (28)
1980–82 Boca Juniors (Argentina) 40 (28)
1982–84 Barcelona 36 (22)
1984–91 Napoli 186 (81)
1992–93 Seville 26 (5)
1993–94 Newell Old Boys (Argentina)
1995–97 Boca Juniors
International record:
1978–94 Argentina 90 (33)

Even David May managed to get on the scoresheet as Manchester United stormed to a 4–0 victory over Portuguese giants Porto in the 1996/97 Champions League

DIEGO ARMANDO MARADONA is considered by some to be the best player ever, and by most to be the best player of his generation.

● MARADONA has smashed three transfer records. First, his £1 million move from Argentinos Juniors to Boca Juniors in 1980 was a record for a teenager. Then he broke the world transfer record when he moved from Boca Juniors to Barcelona for £4.2 million in 1982, and again when he signed for Napoli for £6.9 million in 1984.

● HE BECAME a demigod at the Naples club, leading the club to the league and cup double in 1986/87, which included the Southern Italian club's first ever Scudetto. He then inspired Napoli to their first ever European trophy, winning the UEFA Cup in 1989.

● MARADONA HAS appeared in 21 World Cup finals matches, a record he shared with three other players (Lothar Matthaus, Uwe Seeler and Wladislaw Zmuda) until Matthaus played for Germany at France '98. It was a record he too would have broken if he had not failed a drugs test in USA 94 and been thrown out of the competition and banned from playing in the rest of the tournament. This wasn't his first problem with drugs - in 1991 he was given a worldwide 15 month ban after being charged with cocaine abuse in Argentina.

● LEADING his country to victory in the 1986 World Cup Final was Maradona's greatest triumph, after scoring two unforgettable goals to put England out in the quarter-finals (the 'Hand of God' first was probably the most controversial World Cup goal ever). He also captained his countrymen to the 1990 final.

● WITH 33 goals, he is Argentina's second highest scorer ever (behind Gabriel Batistuta) and second highest appearance maker (behind Oscar Ruggeri) with 90 caps.

MARSEILLE

Year founded: 1898
Ground: Stade Vélodrome (60,000)
League wins: 8
Colours: White shirts, white shorts and white socks

OLMPIQUE MARSEILLE became the first French club to win a European trophy when they beat Milan 1–0 in 1993 with a header by tough centre-back Basile Boli to lift the European Champions Cup.

● ALMOST immediately afterwards they were relegated from the French First Division after it was discovered they had 'fixed' a vital league match against Valenciennes to ensure they were fresh for the European Cup Final a few days later against Milan. As a result of the scandal Marseille became the first holders not allowed to defend the European Cup.

● IN 1988 Marseille paid £4.5 million for the services of winger Chris Waddle, then a record British fee. In 1990 they also signed Trevor Steven from Rangers for £5 million, then a record Scottish fee.

● THE SOUTH of France team enjoyed the best spell in their history after French millionaire Bernard Tapie injected millions into the club, allowing them to buy the best players around and helping them win five consecutive French titles and the European Cup.

Roll of Honour

French champions 1937, 1948, 1971, 1972, 1989, 1990, 1991, 1992, 1993 (withdrawn)
French Cup 1924, 1926, 1927, 1935, 1938, 1943, 1969, 1972, 1976, 1989
European Cup 1993 (later stripped of title)

'Didn't I pay you enough?' Diego asks for a divine 'Hand' in the 1990 World Cup finals

RODNEY MARSH

Born: Hatfield 11.10.44
Position: Midfielder
Club career:

1962–66	Fulham 63 (22)
1966–72	Queens Park Rangers 211 (106)
1972–76	Manchester City 118 (36)
1976	Fulham 16 (5)

International record:
1972–73 England 9 (1)

FOR RODNEY MARSH heading the winning goal for Fulham against Leicester City in 1963 was a mixed blessing... it left him with permanent deafness in one ear!

● IN 1967 Marsh caught the public eye after a brilliant solo goal helped Third Division QPR beat top flight West Bromwich to lift the League Cup. When Marsh was made QPR captain in 1970 he shaved off his beard in a bid to appear more dignified.

● THE FLAMBOYANT forward moved to Manchester City for the huge sum of £200,000 (making him the second most expensive player in British football) in 1972, and helped City to the League Cup Final in 1974. However when Wolves won 2–1 with a late goal, Marsh refused to applaud the opposing team or collect his losers' medal.

● IN 1977 he joined George Best at Fulham, and for a while enjoyed a lucrative business partnership with the Irishman.

MATCH-FIXING

THE EARLIEST recorded episode of match-fixing took place in 1898 when Stoke City played Burnley as part of a play-off round robin tournament. Both teams needed a draw to stay in the First Division. Neither side made an attempt at goal and the 4,000 crowd was enraged. The following year the FA introduced automatic relegation and promotion.

● IN FEBRUARY 1997 Bruce Grobbelaar, John Fashanu and Hans Segers were charged with match fixing in the Premier league but, after two trials, they were eventually acquitted of all charges.

● IN 1978 Argentina, hosting the World Cup, had to beat Peru by four clear goals to progress to the final of the World Cup. It has been alleged (though never proved) that they offered the Peruvian government

35,000 tons of free grain and the unfreezing of $50 million in credits for their team to take it easy. Argentina won 6–0 and went on to win the competition.

● IN 1993 MARSEILLE became the first holders not allowed to defend the European Cup after it was revealed they had 'fixed' a crucial encounter against Valenciennes to give them a chance to be completely fresh for the Final itself. Police found 250,000 francs buried in Valenciennes star Christophe Robert's mother-in-law's garden! When the scandal broke Marseille were immediately relegated from the French First Division.

Funny Old Game

'We knew something was up when we couldn't even get a throw-in.'

Ian St John on Liverpool's 1968 European Cup semi-final second leg match against Inter Milan.

Liverpool had won the first leg 3-1 but lost the return 3-0. It was later proved that referee Ortiz De Mendibi had been 'fixed', as Bill Shankly had always claimed.

LOTHAR MATTHÄUS

Born: Erlangen 21.3.61
Position: Midfielder/sweeper
Club career:

1978–79	Herzogenaurach
1979–84	Bor. Moenchengladbach 162 (37)
1984–88	Bayern Munich 117 (57)
1988–92	Inter Milan 102 (39)
1992–	Bayern Munich 110 (22)

International record:

1980–94	Germany 125 (22)

MIDFIELD GENERAL Lothar Mätthaus – Germany's most capped player ever – holds the record for the most games played in World Cup finals tournaments (25). Having first played in the 1982 tournament on Spain, France '98 was his fifth tournament which is also a record (shared with Mexican goalkeeper Antonio Carbajal, 1950-66).

● MATTHÄUS was West Germany's most expensive player when he moved in 1984 from Borussia Moenchengladbach to Bayern Munich for £650,000. Four years later Bayern sold him on to Inter Milan at quite a profit, for £2.4 million. In between times Bayern won three championships and two German cups under Matthäus's captaincy. That's what you call a sound investment.

● IN 1989 Inter won the Italian Scudetto with a record number of points (58) under the guidance of the free-scoring midfielder. This record was only beaten when Serie A adopted the three points for a win system in 1994/95.

● CAPTAIN MATTHÄUS inspired Germany to World Cup victory in 1990 (after a semi-final victory over England) and was voted the Player of the Tournament by the year's media. He was also made European Footballer of the Year that season.

Stanley Matthews, first and only footballer to be knighted while still playing, shows his CBE off in March 1957

SIR STANLEY MATTHEWS

Born: Stoke 1.2.15
Height: 5ft 10ins Position: Forward
Club career:

1932–47	Stoke City 259 (51)
1947–61	Blackpool 379 (17)
1961–65	Stoke City 59 (3)

International record:

1935–57	England 54 (11)

ON 6th FEBRUARY 1965 Stanley Matthews became the only man over 50 years old to make an appearance in the First Division, when he played his last game for Stoke City against Fulham. He had celebrated his birthday five days earlier.

● MATTHEWS – nicknamed 'the Wizard of Dribble' – was a brilliant winger and one of the greatest English footballers ever, if not the greatest, who played his club football at Stoke City and Blackpool. He also made 54 international appearances in a career that was interrupted by the war.

● HE IS PERHAPS most famous for his appearance in the 1953 FA Cup Final, in which he inspired Blackpool to a 4–3 win over Bolton Wanderers after being 3–1 down. Despite a hat-trick by his teammate Stan Mortensen, the match has gone down in history as 'the Matthews Final'. He had never won an FA Cup winners' medal and the whole country (apart from Bolton) was willing him on to victory.

● IN 1956 Matthews had the honour of becoming the first ever European Footballer of the Year.

BERTIE MEE

Born: 18.12.18

BERTIE MEE was the inspiration behind Arsenal's only League and FA Cup Double win in 1971, a feat which finally stopped the Spurs cockerels crowing (Spurs did The Double in 1961).

● 'IT WAS A SURPRISE, but a pleasant one,' said Mee of his appointment as Gunners' gaffer in 1966 after the sacking of Billy Wright. 'I hadn't planned to become a football manager.' Amazingly, Mee was physiotherapist at the club when he was asked if he wanted to take over the hot seat.

● HE IMMEDIATELY brought stars like George Graham and Bob McNab into the team and The Gunners reached the League Cup Final in 1968 and 1969, then went one better to win the European Fairs Cup in 1970 and, of course, The Double in 1971. Mee was voted Manager of the Year, naturally.

● MEE LATER became assistant manager to Graham Taylor at Watford and helped the club launch itself from the Fourth Division doldrums in 1978 to second place in the top flight in 1983.

JOE MERCER

Born: Ellesmere Port 9.8.14
Died: 9.8.90

MERCER IS ONE of that rare breed who had what it takes to be a top-class player and a top-class manager, winning major honours for his clubs in both roles.

● HE WAS A youngster finding his feet as a wing-half at Everton when they won the League Championship in 1932, and an established international when they repeated the feat in 1939.

● THE WAR INTERRUPTED his career, and when it was over he changed club and position, playing in the Arsenal defence. He was equally successful, however, captaining the Gunners to the League title in 1948 and 1953, making him the only man to win titles with different clubs either side of the war. He also lifted the FA Cup in 1950.

● AS A MANAGER he won the League Cup with Aston Villa in 1960 before presiding over the most successful period in Manchester City's history.

● CITY WON the League in 1968, the FA Cup in 1969 and a League Cup and European Cup Winners' Cup double in 1970.

MEXICO

First international: Guatemala 2 Mexico 3, Guatemala City 1923
First World Cup appearance: Mexico 1 France 4 (Uruguay, 1930)
Highest goalscorer: Hugo Sanchez (46)
Best win: 11-0 v St Vincent, 1992
Worst defeat: 0-8 v England, 1961
Colours: Green shirts, white shorts and red socks

With 11 appearances in the finals, Mexico have appeared at more World Cups than any country except Brazil, Argentina, Italy and Germany. However, the central American country's playing record in the finals is a poor one. Mexico have never been past the quarter-final stage and didn't achieve their first win in the finals until their 14th attempt – a 3-1 victory over Czechoslovakia in 1962.

● Mexico have twice hosted the World Cup – in 1970 and 1986 – and on both occasions reached the quarter-finals. The 1986 side was desperately unlucky, only losing in a shoot-out to penalty kings West Germany.

● Football's most eccentric goalkeeper, Jorge Campos, plays for Mexico. Not only does Campos design his own multi-coloured kit (he claims it distracts opposition strikers), he is also officially described by the Mexican federation as 'a goalkeeper and forward'. In 1989 he played more than half his games for Mexican club side UNAM up front and finished the season as top goalscorer with 14 goals!

● Campos sported a less garish strip at France '98 where the Mexicans became known as the comeback kings after recovering from 2-0 down against both Belgium and Holland and 1-0 down to South Korea to make it to the second round. Unfortunately they made the mistake of going ahead against Germany in the knockout stages and were promptly defeated 2-1.

● Apart from Campos, Mexico's star player at France 98 was Luis Hernandez. The blond bombshell striker scored four goals in total but, had he taken an easy chance when his side were already 1–0 up against the Germans, he could have made an even bigger name for himself.

WORLD CUP RECORD

1930 First round	1970 Quarter-finals
1934 Did not qualify	1974 Did not qualify
1938 Did not enter	1978 First round
1950 First round	1982 Did not qualify
1954 First round	1986 Quarter-finals
1958 First round	1990 Did not enter
1962 First round	1994 Second round
1966 First round	1998 Second round

MIDDLESBROUGH

Year founded: 1876
Ground: Cellnet Riverside Stadium (30,000)
Highest ever crowd: 53,596, 27th December 1949 v Newcastle (Div One)
Nickname: 'Boro
Colours: Red shirts, white shorts, white socks

Middlesbrough are the only club in football history to reach three major Wembley finals in two years... and they lost them all. In 1997 they lost the Coca Cola Cup Final to Leicester City after a replay and the FA Cup Final to Chelsea. The following year they reached the Coca Cola Cup Final again, only to come up against Chelsea again and another 2-0 defeat.

● It had been an amazing couple of seasons for Boro. Before the 1996/97 season they had never even been in an FA Cup semi-final before. Then on top of their cup exploits, there was the small matter of relegation from the Premiership and then – following the signing of star names like Paul Merson and Paul Gascoigne – promotion at the first attempt.

● MIDDLESBROUGH FC were formed in 1876 by members of the Middlesbrough Cricket Club, at a meeting held in the gymnasium of a local hotel. For many years the club's status alternated between professional and amateur, before Middlesbrough finally joined the Football League in 1899.

● THE YEAR previously, Middlesbrough had won the Amateur Cup for a second time in 1898 in strange circumstances. The semi-final against Thornaby had had to be switched from Darlington following a smallpox scare, and was eventually played in the isolated Cleveland hill village of Brotton.

● THE CLUB's longest-serving player is Tim Williamson, who appeared in 563 league matches from 1902 until 1923.

● IN THE MID-1900s Middlesbrough went four and a half years without an away league victory. The dismal run finally ended after 33 games in 1907.

● MIDDLESBROUGH were the first club to sign a player for a four-figure transfer fee. In 1905 England international Alf Common joined the club for £1,000 from local rivals Sunderland.

● THE CLUB – known as 'Boro or The Ironsides, in reference to the region's heavy industries – enjoyed their record win as far back as 1890, when Scarborough were hammered 11–0 in a qualifying round of the FA Cup. Middlesbrough's worst defeat, a 9–0 humiliation at Blackburn, was in a Second Division match in 1954.

● GEORGE CAMSELL holds two goalscoring records for the club. During his 14-year Middlesbrough career between 1925–39 he hit 326 league goals, with an astonishing 59 of them arriving in season 1926/27. This was a league record at the time and is still a record for the old Second Division. It included eight hat-tricks, a Football League record.

● MIDDLESBROUGH's most capped player is Wilf Mannion, who played 26 times for England as an inside-forward.

● BRIAN CLOUGH is one of the three Middlesbrough players to have scored five goals in a match. Cloughie achieved his feat in a 9-0 thrashing of Brighton in 1958. In his nine-

Craig Hignett is pictured in the days when he was Boro's most exotic player... ie, some time ago

M

year 'Boro career Clough scored 197 goals in 217 matches, before joining Sunderland.

● Middlesbrough's record signing was the fiery silver-haired Italian Fabrizio Ravanelli who cost £7 million from Juventus in July 1996. Just over a year later, however, Ravanelli was on his way to Olympique Marseille in France for £5.5 million. He is not the club's record sale, however. That honour falls to Juninho who was sold to Atletico Madrid for a whacking £12 million in the summer of 1997.

Roll of Honour

First Division champions 1995
Div 2 champions 1927, 1929, 1974
Amateur Cup 1895, 1898
Anglo-Scottish Cup 1976

Middlesbrough's Post-War Record

47 D1 11th	65 D2 17th	83 D2 16th
48 D1 16th	66 D2 21st	84 D2 17th
49 D1 19th	67 D3 2nd	85 D2 19th
50 D1 9th	68 D2 6tt	86 D2 21st
51 D1 6th	69 D2 4th	87 D3 2nd
52 D1 18th	70 D2 4th	88 D2 3rd
53 D1 13th	71 D2 7th	89 D1 18th
54 D1 21st	72 D2 9th	90 D2 21st
55 D2 12th	73 D2 4th	91 D2 7th
56 D2 14th	74 D2 1st	92 D2 2nd
57 D2 6th	75 D1 7th	93 PR 21st
58 D2 7th	76 D1 13th	94 D1 9th
59 D2 13th	77 D1 12th	95 D1 1st
60 D2 5th	78 D1 14th	96 PR 12th
61 D2 5th	79 D1 12th	97 PR 19th
62 D2 12th	80 D1 9th	98 D1 2nd
63 D2 4th	81 D1 14th	
64 D2 10th	82 D1 22nd	

Jackie Milburn, Newcastle's greatest ever centre-forward despite never being able to head the ball, in training at Gallowgate in the 1950s

JACKIE MILBURN

Born: Ashington 11.3.24 Died: 8.10.88
Height: 5ft 11ins Position: Striker
Club career:
1946–57 Newcastle United 354 (178)
International record:
1949–56 England 13 (10)

'WOR' JACKIE MILBURN is the biggest footballing hero ever to have pulled on the black-and-white-striped shirt of Newcastle United, and he is commemorated by a bronze statue in the city centre.

● HE WAS a swashbuckling centre forward in the great Magpies side that collected FA Cup wins in 1951, 1952 and 1955. In 1951 he scored in every round of the Cup (including two in the Final) and in 1955 he scored what was then the fastest ever goal in a Cup Final, after just 45 seconds, to help Newcastle to a 3-1 win over Manchester City (a record beaten by Chelsea's Roberto Di Matteo in 1997).

● SCORING MORE goals for United than any player before or since, Milburn got a total of 178 between 1946–57. He also pulled on the three lions of England a total of 13 times, scoring 10 goals.

● MILBURN's initials (J.E.T.) were appropriate for such a speedy forward!

● MILBURN WAS more like his younger nephew Bobby Charlton in temperament than Jackie and, although he took over from Alf Ramsey at Ipswich in 1963, he never made it as a manager, instead becoming a journalist back in his beloved Newcastle. When he died in 1988 the whole of the city came on to the streets to mourn him.

ROGER MILLA

Born: Cameroon 20.5.52
Position: Striker
Club career:
Leopard Douala (Cameroon)
Tonnerre Yaounde (Cameroon)
Valenciennes (France)
Monaco (France)
Bastia (France)
St. Etienne (France)
St. Denis (France)
Montpellier (France)
International record:
1972–94 Cameroon

WHEN ROGER MILLA played for Cameroon in the 1994 World Cup finals in the USA he became, at 42, the oldest man ever to appear in the tournament.

● NOT CONTENT with that statistic, in Cameroon's final match against Russia he scored the African side's consolation goal in a 6–1 defeat to become the oldest player ever to score in the tournament. Remarkably the record he broke was his own, set at the age of 38 during Italia 90.

● MILLA WAS FONDLY remembered from the Italia 90 tournament, in which he celebrated his four goals with extravagant 'wiggles' round the corner flag that started off a fashion the world over. He also appeared for his country during the 1982 finals in Spain.

● IT WAS IN 1990 that Milla became the first player to be made African Player of the Year for a second time – he was first given the award back in 1976.

● HE PLAYED MOST of his club football in France, winning a French Cup winners' medal with Monaco in 1980 and another with Bastia in 1981.

MILLWALL

Year founded: 1885
Ground: The New Den (19,000)
Highest ever crowd: 20,093, 10th January 1994 v Arsenal (FA Cup rd 3)
Previous name: Millwall Rovers
Nickname: The Lions
Colours: Blue shirts, white shorts, blue socks

MILLWALL WERE founded in 1895 as Millwall Rovers by employees of a local jam and marmalade factory, Morton and Co. Since then they have become one of London's most passionately supported clubs... enjoying their first spell in the top flight in the late 1980s.

● MILLWALL HAVE recorded two 9–1 victories, over Torquay and Coventry, and strangely both these impressive scores came in the same season, 1927/28, which ended with Millwall winning the Third Division (South) Championship. The club's record defeat, 9–1, came in an FA Cup tie at Aston Villa in 1946.

● TEDDY SHERINGHAM is the leading scorer in the club's history. From 1984 until his transfer to Nottingham Forest in 1991, Sheringham scored 93 league goals. Richard Parker holds the record for a single season, with 37 goals for The Lions in 1926/27.

● MILLWALL'S MOST capped player is Eamonn Dunphy, who won all but one of his 23 Republic of Ireland caps while at The Den. Dunphy is now a football journalist, and became the most hated man in Ireland when he criticised Jack Charlton's tactics at the 1990 World Cup.

● ROCK-LIKE DEFENDER Barry Kitchener has made more appearances for Millwall

Did You Know?

In October 1949 Jackie Milburn became England's first ever hat-trick scorer in the World Cup, hitting three of his country's goals in their 4–1 defeat of Wales in the Home Championships, which doubled up as the World Cup qualifiers that year.

than any other player. Between 1967–82 he played in 523 league matches for the East Londoners.

● MILLWALL ARE the only football league club to have been undefeated at home over a season in four different divisions: Division Three (S) 1927/28, Division Four 1964/65, Division Three 1965/66 and 1984/85, Division Two 1971/72.

● MILLWALL REMAINED undefeated at their old ground 'The Den' for almost three years from April 1964 to January 1967, a run which lasted 59 league matches.

Roll of Honour

Div 2 champions 1988
Div 3 (S) champions 1928, 1938
Div 4 champions 1962

Monaco

Year founded: 1924
Ground: Louis II (18,500)
League wins: 6
Colours: Red and white diagonal halved shirts, red shorts, white socks

With six French championship titles and five French Cups, Monaco are France's third most successful club ever, behind Marseille and Saint Etienne. Considering that they sometimes attract crowds of less than 5,000 to their matches - the casino is a bigger attraction in this rich man's paradise - the men from Monaco haven't done at all badly.

● Monaco's ground, the Louis II, is unique in Europe in that it is built on top of an underground car park. Just eight inches of soil separate the playing surface from the car park's concrete roof, making the pitch bone hard.

● Arsenal manager Arsene Wenger used to be manager of Monaco. During his reign on the French Riviera the club won the championship in 1987, the French Cup in 1991 and reached the final of the European Cup Winners' Cup in 1992.

● Highbury star Emmanuel Petit played under Wenger at Monaco, as did England boss Glenn Hoddle. More recently Scotland's John Collins has turned out for them.

Roll of Honour

French champions 1961, 1963, 1978, 1982, 1988, 1997
French Cup 1960, 1963, 1980, 1985, 1991

Did You Know?

Bobby Moore holds a record 18 caps for the England Youth Team.

MONTROSE

Year founded: 1879
Ground: Links Park (4,350)
Highest ever crowd: 8,983, 17th March 1973 v Dundee (Scottish Cup rd 3)
Nickname: The Gable Endies
Colours: Blue shirts, white shorts, red socks

WHEN MONTROSE were formed back in 1887, they were so poor that they had to borrow goalnets, their pitch was rented out for circuses and grazing livestock and their first stand was a leftover from the Highland Games (costing £120).

● MONTROSE's most memorable season was probably in 1975, when the club reached the semi-final of the League Cup and the quarter-final of the Scottish Cup.

● IN THAT SEASON The Gable Endies – as they are known – recorded their best victory, thrashing Vale of Leithen 12–0 in the Scottish Cup. Impressive stuff, but not quite up to the mark set by the club's heaviest defeat – a 0–13 trouncing at Aberdeen in 1951.

● MONTROSE PLAYERS have only rarely been called up for international duty, but the club can point to Alexander Keillor who won two of his six Scottish caps while at Links Park.

● DAVID LARTER holds the club appearance record, playing 408 league games from 1987-1997.

Roll of Honour

Second Division champions 1985

BOBBY MOORE

Born: Barking 12.4.41 Died: 24.2.93
Height: 6ft 0ins Position: Defender
Club career:
1985–74 West Ham United 544 (22)
1974–77 Fulham 124 (1)
1976 San Antonio Thunder
1978 Seattle Sounders
International record:
1962–74 England 108 (2)

BOBBY MOORE was the greatest captain England ever had (he captained his country more often than any other player), and very possibly their greatest defender too. And he was, of course, the first and only Englishman ever to lift the World Cup back in 1966.

● MOORE WAS the first captain to lift three trophies at Wembley Stadium in three consecutive years. He lifted the FA Cup in 1964 and the European Cup Winners' Cup in 1965, both with West Ham, both beneath the Twin Towers, before making it a hat-trick with the big one in 1966.

● MOORE'S RECORD of 108 caps for his country was a record until it was surpassed by Peter Shilton in 1989. He is still England's second most capped player in history.

● IN 1970 Bobby Moore thwacked an attempted clearance which unfortunately hit the referee on the head and knocked him unconscious. Ever quick to take control of the situation, Moore immediately picked up the ref's whistle and blew it to stop play.

● THE WHOLE country mourned when Bobby Moore died of cancer in 1993.

Bobby Moore displays the Player of the Year Award, the second most important trophy he won in 1966

BRIAN MOORE

Born: Weald of Kent 28.2.32

Before his retirement after the 1998 World Cup, Brian Moore was the longest serving commentator on ITV's books, having been the football voice of the channel since 1968. He has covered World Cups, European competition and even the Endsleigh League, but will be best remembered for fronting ITV's Sunday afternoon show The Big Match in the 1970s and 80s.

● MOORE HAS been a Gillingham supporter since his schooldays in the 1940s, watching the club gain league status in 1948. In the 1970s he became Vice-President of the supporters' club, a position he still holds, and in 1974 he became a director of the club, a position he held until 1985. He is the Gills' most famous fan by a mile.

● THE GILLINGHAM fanzine, 'Brian Moore's Head Looks Uncannily Like London Planetarium', was named after a song by quirky 1980s band Half Man Half Biscuit.

Motty, the youngest man ever to do the TV commentary for an FA Cup Final, smiles on realising he already knew every fact in this book

MOROCCO

First World Cup appearance: Morocco 1 West Germany 2 (Mexico, 1970)
Colours: Green shirts, green shorts, green socks

In 1970 Morocco became the first ever African country to play in the World Cup finals. The Atlas Lions, as they are known, finished bottom of their group, but gave West Germany a real fright by taking a half-time lead before eventually losing 2–1.

● Morocco did much better the second time they qualified in 1986, finishing top of a group which included England. In the second round it took an 89th-minute goal by West Germany's Lothar Matthaus to knock the plucky North Africans out.

WORLD CUP RECORD

1930-58	Did not enter
1962	Did not qualify
1966	Did not enter
1970	Round 1
1974	Did not qualify
1978	Did not qualify
1982	Did not qualify
1986	Round 2
1990	Did not qualify
1994	Round 1
1998	Round 1

MOTHERWELL

Year founded: 1886
Ground: Fir Park (13,741)
Highest ever crowd: 35, 632, 1st March 1952 v Rangers (Scottish Cup rd 4 replay)
Nickname: The Well
Colours: Amber shirts with claret trim, claret shorts, amber socks

SET IN AN industrial heartland and a footballing hotbed, Motherwell FC have a fine footballing tradition – although their one and only Scottish Championship victory came way back in 1932.

● THE 1930s saw the club's most successful spell, although in the seasons either side of that famous title win they lost two Scottish Cup finals.

● MOTHERWELL enjoyed their best victory in 1954, when they beat Dundee United 12–1 on their way to the Second Division title. The club's worst defeat came in 1979 – an 8–0 debacle against Aberdeen.

● THE WELL's most capped player is George Stevenson, who played 12 times for Scotland.

● WILLIE McFADYEN scored a remarkable 52 league goals for Motherwell in 1931/32, a First Division record which still stands. The overall club scoring record is held by Hugh Ferguson, who notched 283 goals between 1916–25.

Roll of Honour

Div 1 champions 1932
First Division champions 1982, 1985
Div 2 champions 1954, 1969
Scottish Cup 1952, 1991
League Cup 1951

JOHN MOTSON

Born: Salford 7.10.45

IN 1977 John Motson became, at the age of 33, the youngest man ever to commentate on an FA Cup final. When Manchester United's Martin Buchan walked up to collect the Cup he said: 'How apt that a man named Buchan should climb the 39 steps,' a comment he later admitted he had rehearsed.

● 'MOTTY' MADE his TV debut commentating on a 0–0 draw between Liverpool and Chelsea, and has been giving us his particular blend of moral outrage and well-researched facts and figures ever since.

● MOTSON, who has witnessed many an exciting sporting moment, says the most memorable was when Hereford beat Newcastle United 2–1 in the 1972 FA Cup. If you look back at the clips (as the BBC do every January) you can hear the excitement clearly in his voice.

● MOTTY QUOTE: 'I try very hard to think of something clever or witty to say when the ball goes into the net but I usually end up saying, "Oh, what a goal!"'

● MOTTY CLASSIC: 'And Stuart Pearce has got the taste of Wembley in his nostrils.'

GERD MÜLLER

Born: Germany 3.11.45
Position: Striker
Club career:
TSV Nordlingen
1965–79 Bayern Munich 427 (365)
International record:
1966–74 Germany 62 (68)

'DER BOMBER' is the greatest striker ever to play for Germany: he had an incredible strike rate of 68 goals in the 62 internationals he played for his country, easily making him the country's leading goalscorer ever.

Gerd Müller, the best striker ever to come out of Germany, celebrates one of the 68 goals he scored for his country in only 62 appearances

● MÜLLER HAS scored more World Cup finals goals – 14 – than any other player.

● IN 1970, after a typical Müller close-range volley had put England out of the World Cup finals in Mexico, he became the first German ever to win the European Player of the Year Award. He finished top scorer in the tournament (in which Germany were knocked out in the semi-final by Italy) with 10 goals.

● MÜLLER WON everything there was to win in a glittering career, including the European Championship in 1972, the World Cup in 1974 (when he scored the winner), and an incredible hat-trick of European Cup victories with Bayern Munich between 1974–76. He scored in four out of those five finals.

● MÜLLER ALSO had a brilliant strike rate in domestic football, scoring 365 goals in the Bundesliga – more than any player before or since.

JOHAN NEESKENS

Born: Holland 15.9.51
Position: Midfielder
Club career:
Haarlem
Ajax
Barcelona
New York Cosmos
International record:
1970–81 Holland 49 (17)

IN 1974 Johan Neeskens scored the fastest ever goal in a World Cup Final, a penalty for Holland against hosts West Germany after just a minute.

● JOHAN CRUYFF dribbled through the German defence straight from kick off and was brought down in the box. It was the first penalty in a World Cup Final, given by English referee Jack Taylor, but that didn't deter Neeskens, who put the ball past Sepp Maier, and the Dutch were ahead. The Germans, as is their wont, pulled it back to win 2–1. Neeskens finished third top scorer in the tournament on four goals.

● NEESKENS was the steely heart of the flamboyant 'total football' Holland and Ajax sides in the 1970s. He won a hat-trick of European Cups with the Dutch club before moving, alongside teammate Cruyff, to Barcelona, where he won the Spanish Cup and the Cup Winners' Cup.

● ALL THIS, plus numerous domestic Dutch honours and a second World Cup Final appearance in 1978, make Neeskens one of the most successful players in the history of the game.

Did You Know?

Gerd Müller is the only man to have scored in two European Championship finals. He scored two of West Germany's goals in their 3–0 win over the USSR in 1972 and one in their 2–2 draw with Czechoslovakia in 1976.

'Three lions on his scarf' – Gary Neville celebrates his England call-up in 1995

GARY NEVILLE

Born: Bury 18.2.75
Height: 5ft 11ins Position: Defender
Club career:
1994– Manchester United 108 (1)
International Record:
1995– England 30 (1)

GARY NEVILLE had played fewer games for his club (19) than any England debutant since the War when he first played for England (against Japan in June 1995).

● WHEN Manchester United won the Double it made Gary and younger brother Phil Neville the first brothers to appear in a Double-winning team this century.

● THE NEVILLES are not, however, the first brothers to appear in a Cup Final team together for Manchester United. Brian and Jimmy Greenhoff were both in their 1977 Cup-winning team.

● THE NEVILLES are the first brothers to play together for England since the Charltons.

PHILIP NEVILLE

Born: Bury 21.1.77
Height: 5ft 11ins Position: Defender
Club career:
1994– Manchester United: 84 (1)
International record:
1996– England 8 (0)

WHEN PHIL NEVILLE played for England against China in May 1996, he became the youngest England player since his former Manchester United colleague Lee Sharpe to play for his country. He was 19 years four months old.

● SAYING THE NEVILLES are a sporting family is an understatement to say the least... Phil's twin sister Tracey is an England netball international.

● PHILIP NEVILLE made Glenn Hoddle's final 28 for France 98, but not the final squad. Gary, who fought his way into Hoddle's first team during the tournament, was reported as being 'gutted' at the news.

● PHIL AND GARY Neville's father is called Neville Neville.

N

NEWCASTLE UNITED

Year founded: 1881
Ground: St. James' Park (38,800)
Highest ever crowd: 68,386,
3rd September 1930 v Chelsea (Div 1)
Previous names: Stanley,
Newcastle West End
Nickname: The Magpies
Colours: Black-and-white-striped shirts,
black shorts, black socks

NEWCASTLE UNITED began life as Stanley in 1881, before becoming Newcastle West End a year later. After a poor run West End went out of existence, and the club became Newcastle United in 1892.

● IN THEIR EARLY years as a league club Newcastle suffered their record defeat, losing 9–0 against Burton Wanderers in a Second Division match in 1895. The Magpies recorded their most impressive win in 1946, when Newport County were humbled 13–0 at St. James' Park. Len Shackleton scored six of the goals (on his debut) – a club record.

● NEWCASTLE MANAGER Frank Watt is the most successful manager in the history of the FA Cup, taking the side to a record total of six finals between 1905–24. The club holds the record for the biggest ever FA Cup semi-final win, 6–0 over Fulham in 1908.

● THE OLDEST PLAYER to represent Newcastle was William Hampson, who was nearly 45 when he played against Birmingham City in 1927. Hampson is the oldest player to have played in a Cup Final. He represented United at the age of 41 years 257 days in the 1924 final against Aston Villa.

● THE YOUNGEST PLAYER to have donned the black-and-white stripes is Steve Watson, who was aged 16 years and 223 days when he made his Newcastle debut against Wolves in 1990.

● NEWCASTLE SIDES have often been led from the front by charismatic centre-forwards. One such figure was Jackie Milburn, the club's overall top scorer with 178 league goals between 1946–57. Milburn's goal after 45 seconds in the 1955 FA Cup Final against Manchester City was the fastest Wembley Cup Final goal ever until Roberto di Matteo scored after 43 for Chelsea in 1997 and Milburn also notched a goal in every round in 1951. Another great forward was Hughie Gallagher, who set a club scoring record with 36 league goals in 1926/27.

● NEWCASTLE's most capped player is Alf McMichael, who made 40 appearances for Northern Ireland.

● IN 1969 Newcastle qualified for the Fairs Cup after coming a lowly 10th in the First Division. To everyone's surprise they went on to win the competition, beating Ujpest Dozsa in the final 6–2 on aggregate.

● NEWCASTLE GOT to the FA Cup Final in 1974, but were easily beaten by Liverpool, managed that day by future Toon Army manager Kevin Keegan. Malcolm MacDonald, who was hoping to emulate Jackie Milburn by scoring in every round of the cup, hardly got a look in. MacDonald was the swashbuckling goalscoring hero of the Geordie fans at the time, who in 1972 scored a goal in a friendly against St. Johnstone in just five seconds.

● WHEN Newcastle stormed to promotion in 1993, Kevin Keegan's side accumulated 96 points... then a record for the new First Division.

Footballer and long distance walker David Batty

● IN THE 1995/96 season Newcastle let the Premiership title slip away despite holding a 12-point lead over Manchester United in January. Previously, no other side had led the Premiership by such a margin and failed to become champions.

● After the shock resignation of Kevin Keegan, Kenny Dalglish took over the reins of the club and was entrusted with the task of trying to win Newcastle their first major trophy for 29 years. He came close in 1998, reaching the FA Cup Final but losing it 2-0 to Arsenal.

● ONE OF Newcastle United's most famous fans is Prime Minister Tony Blair, others include Cardinal Basil Hulme, the head of The Catholic Church in Britain, and oddball racing pundit John McCririck.

'Moi, je ne regrette rien' – David Ginola finds the heart to make a kid's day after seeing United lose the 1995/96 Premiership race on the last day of the season

Did You Know?

Newcastle's 13–0 win over Newport County on 5th October 1946 is the biggest ever score in the Football League, equal with Stockport County's victory by the same margin over Halifax in 1934.

Roll of Honour

Div 1 champions 1905, 1907, 1909, 1927
First Division champions 1993
Div 2 champions 1965
FA Cup 1910, 1924, 1932, 1951, 1952, 1955
Fairs Cup 1969

Newcastle United's Post-War Record

47 D2 5th	64 D2 8th	81 D2 11th
48 D2 2nd	65 D2 1st	82 D2 9th
49 D1 4th	66 D1 15th	83 D2 5th
50 D1 5th	67 D1 20th	84 D2 3rd
51 D1 4th	68 D1 10th	85 D1 14th
52 D1 8th	69 D1 9th	86 D1 11th
53 D1 16th	70 D1 7th	87 D1 17th
54 D1 15th	71 D1 12th	88 D1 8th
55 D1 8th	72 D1 11th	89 D1 20th
56 D1 11th	73 D1 9th	90 D2 3rd
57 D1 17th	74 D1 15th	91 D2 11th
58 D1 19th	75 D1 15th	92 D2 20th
59 D1 11th	76 D1 15th	93 D1 1st
60 D1 8th	77 D1 5th	94 PR 3rd
61 D1 21st	78 D1 21st	95 PR 6th
62 D2 11th	79 D2 8th	96 PR 2nd
63 D2 7th	80 D2 9th	97 PR 2nd
		98 PR 13th

BILL NICHOLSON

Born: Scarborough 26.1.19

BILL NICHOLSON became the first manager to win The Double this century when he steered Spurs to their League Championship and FA Cup triumph in 1961.

● NICHOLSON had already won the title with Tottenham ten years before, in 1951, as a player. He was the team's right-half and inspiration.

● 1951 WAS THE YEAR Nicholson earned his one and only England cap. He made quite a start, scoring with his first touch after 19 seconds, making him the fastest-scoring England debutant ever. It was the second fastest goal ever scored for England.

● NICHOLSON came very close to winning every club trophy in the book while Tottenham manager: he won the Championship in 1961, the FA Cup in 1961, 1962 and 1967, the League Cup in 1971 and 1973, the UEFA Cup in 1972 and the European Cup Winners' Cup in 1963. Only elimination from the European Cup at the semi-final stage in 1962 prevented the full house.

NIGERIA

First World Cup appearance: Nigeria 3 Bulgaria 0 (USA, 1994)
Colours: Green shirts, green shorts and green socks

NIGERIA became the first nation to qualify for the France '98 World Cup when they beat group rivals Kenya in June 1997. The Super Eagles, as they are nicknamed, were expected to pose a strong challenge just as they had at their first World Cup in 1994 – when they lost narrowly to Italy in the second round – but were soundly thrashed 4-1 by Denmark at the same stage.

● AT ATLANTA in August 1996, Nigeria won the Olympic title, beating Argentina 3–2, to become the first African team to win a major international tournament.

● IN 1985 the Nigerian youth team became the first African team to win an international FIFA competition when they beat West Germany 2–0 in the final of the first ever World Under 17 Championship. They got to the finals in 1989, and beat Ghana in the final in 1993 to make them the most successful nation in the competition's short history.

● NIGERIA have a relatively poor record, however, in the African Nations Cup. They have only won the competition twice, in 1980 and 1994. They refused to enter the 1995 edition of the tournament in South Africa for political reasons, and were subsequently banned from the competition for five years.

WORLD CUP RECORD

1930–58	Did not enter
1962	Did not qualify
1966	Did not enter
1970–90	Did not qualify
1994	Round 2
1998	Round 2

NORTHAMPTON TOWN

Year founded: 1897
Ground: Sixfields Stadium (7,700)
Highest ever crowd: 24,523, 23rd April 1966 v Fulham (Div 1)
Nickname: The Cobblers
Colours: Claret shirts with white shoulders, white shorts, claret socks

NORTHAMPTON TOWN have twice recorded 10–0 victories. The first came in a preliminary round FA Cup tie against Sutton in 1907, the second in a Division Three (South) fixture against Walsall in 1927. The club's heaviest defeat, 11–0, was against Southampton in 1901.

● NO OTHER English club can match the tumultuous decade Northampton experienced in the 1960s. After gaining promotion from Division Four in 1961, The Cobblers continued their rise, reaching the First Division in 1965 (becoming the first team to reach the top flight via all three lower divisions).

● THE CLUB's descent, however, was just as rapid, and by 1969 Northampton were back in the basement division.

● IN 1970 Northampton Town lost 8–2 to Manchester United in the 4th round of the FA Cup... with George Best scoring six!

● TOMMY FOWLER has made most league appearances for the club, turning out on 521 occasions between 1946 and 1961.

● IN MAY 1997 the club were promoted to the Second Division via the play-offs.

Roll of Honour

Div 3 champions 1963
Div 4 champions 1987

NORTHERN IRELAND

First international: Northern Ireland 2 England 1 (Belfast, 1923)
First World Cup appearance: Northern Ireland 1 Czechoslovakia 0 (Sweden, 1958)
Highest capped player: Pat Jennings (119)
Highest goalscorer: Colin Clarke (13)
Best win: 7–0 v Wales, 1930
Worst defeat: 2–9 v England, 1949
Colours: Green shirts, white shorts, green socks

NORTHERN IRELAND's Norman Whiteside is the youngest player ever to appear in a World Cup tournament. At 17 years 42 days, he beat Pele's record by a clear 195 days during Spain 82.

● THE 1982 tournament saw the Irish beat hosts Spain 1–0 in Valencia to record their greatest moment in recent memory. Gerry Armstrong scored for the Irish to put them into the second round of the competition.

● THEY WENT one better, however, in the 1958 edition of the World Cup in Sweden. Then, inspired by their captain Danny Blanchflower, they got to the quarter-finals of the competition after beating Czechoslovakia and drawing with West Germany.

● THE IRISH FA is the fourth oldest international football association in the world. However, they played nothing but Home Championship internationals until 1951 when France visited Belfast.

● JOE BAMBRICK scored six of Northern Ireland's seven goals v Wales on 1st February 1930 to make him the highest goalscorer in a Home International match.

WORLD CUP RECORD

1930–38	Did not enter
1950–54	Did not qualify
1958	Quarter-finalists
1962–78	Did not qualify
1982	Round 2
1986	Round 1
1990–98	Did not qualify

Northern Ireland players celebrate the 0–0 Wembley draw which booked their passage to the Mexico 86 World Cup, only the third time they had made it to the finals

Even a joker with a tube of superglue couldn't halt Norwich's progress in their first season in Europe, in 1993/94

NORWAY

First international: Norway 3 Sweden 11 (Gothenburg, 1908)
First World Cup appearance: Norway 1 Italy 2 (France, 1938)
Highest capped player: Thorbjørn Svenssen (104)
Highest goalscorer: Jørgen Juve (33)
Best win: 12–0 v Finland, 1946
Worst defeat: 9–0 v Sweden, 1913
Colours: Red shirts, white shorts, red socks

NORWAY's best moment came in the 1936 Olympic Games in Berlin, when they beat hosts Germany 2–0 to reach the semi-finals of the competition... causing Hitler to storm out of the stadium in a huff (and, who knows, invade the country four years later). They lost 2–1 in the next round to Italy's professionals, but only after extra time.

● VIRTUALLY the same Norwegian team also qualified for the World Cup in 1938 after an exciting qualifying preliminary with the Republic of Ireland. Again they lost to Italy, and again the score was 2–1.

● NORWAY WENT into a period of decline after that until the 1990s, with the notable exception of a 2–1 victory over England in 1981, when Norwegian commentator Burge Lillelien declared: 'Lord Nelson, Lord Beaverbrook, Anthony Eden, Henry Cooper, Lady Diana, we have beaten them all. Maggie Thatcher, your boys took a helluva beating'.

● Norway qualified for both the 1994 and 1998 World Cups with a nucleus of players plying their trade in the English Premiership. However, on both occasions they failed to live up to their superb qualifying form, failing at the group stage in the USA and in the second round against Italy in 1998. In 1998, however, they did beat Brazil twice... 4-2 in a friendly and then 2-1 in the World Cup.

WORLD CUP RECORD

1930–34	Did not enter
1938	Round 1
1950	Did not enter
1954–90	Did not qualify
1994	Round 1
1998	Round 2

NORWICH CITY

Year founded: 1902
Ground: Carrow Road (20,500)
Highest ever crowd: 43,984, 30th March 1963 v Leicester City (FA Cup rd 6)
Nickname: The Canaries
Colours: Yellow shirts, green shorts, yellow socks

FORMED IN 1902 by two schoolteachers, Norwich City were soon in trouble with the FA and were expelled from the FA Amateur Cup in 1904 for being 'professional'.

● NORWICH achieved their best result against Coventry in 1930 when they routed the Midlanders 10–2. The club's worst defeat was by the same scoreline, back in 1908 against Swindon.

● IN THEIR 1950/51 season in Division Three (South) Norwich fielded an unchanged side for a record 21 matches.

● JOHN GAVIN is Norwich's leading overall scorer, with 122 league goals between 1949–58. Ralph Hunt, though, hit most goals in a season (31 in 1955/56).

● BETWEEN 1977–79 the Norwich team set an unenviable club record, going 41 away league matches without a win. During the 1978/79 season they set a football league record for drawn games, coming away with a single point on no fewer than 23 out of 42 occasions.

● NORWICH's most capped player is Mark Bowen. The former Tottenham defender made 30 appearances for Wales during his Carrow Road career.

● NORWICH were denied their first European campaign in 1985 when – after they'd earned a place in the UEFA Cup draw by winning the League Cup – British clubs were banned from all competitions after the Heysel disaster. When they finally did make it into the competition in 1993/94 they had a fine run, beating Vitesse Arnhem and Bayern Munich before going out to Inter Milan.

● High profile TV cook Delia Smith is a director of the Norfolk club.

Roll of Honour

Div 2 champions 1972, 1986
Div 3 (S) champions 1934
League Cup 1962, 1985

Did You Know?

Norwich City's Carrow Road ground was previously owned by the Colman mustard company – now, incidentally, the club's shirt sponsors – who used the land to graze horses.

NOTTINGHAM FOREST

Year founded: 1865

Ground: The City Ground (30,539)

Highest ever crowd: 49,946, 28th October 1967 v Manchester United (Div 1)

Nickname: The Reds

Colours: Red shirts, white shorts, red socks

NOTTINGHAM FOREST are one of the oldest football clubs in the world. The club was formed at a meeting in a local pub, the Clinton Arms, in 1865 by players of a game called 'shinny' (a type of hockey). They decided to switch to football and the club was born.

● NOTTINGHAM FOREST players heard the first ever referee's whistle, which was tried out at their ground during a match with Sheffield Norfolk in 1878.

● BEFORE SETTLING at the City Ground in 1898, Forest played at six other venues, including a two-year spell at Trent Bridge Cricket Ground between 1880–82.

● FOREST's record score is an amazing 14–0 triumph away to Clapton in the FA Cup, way back in 1891. The club's worst defeat, 9–1, came in a Division Two match at Blackburn in 1937.

● BRIAN CLOUGH, of course, is Forest's most successful manager. After taking the club out of the Second Division in 1977, Cloughie led Forest to the league title the following season, a feat which has not been achieved by any promoted side since.
In 1979 Forest became only the third English side to win the European Cup, beating Malmo in the final, and regained the trophy the following season with a 1–0 win over Hamburg.

● FORMER FOREST hero Stuart Pearce is the club's leading international appearance maker, with 76 England caps. The inspirational left back – known to fans as 'Psycho' – was England's most capped player in Terry Venables' Euro 96 squad.

● FORMER FOREST hero Stuart Pearce is the club's leading international appearance maker, with 76 England caps. The inspirational left back – known to fans as 'Pyscho' – was England's most capped player in Terry Venables' Euro 96 squad.

● NOTTINGHAM Forest's ground is only 330 yards from that of rivals Notts County, making the two clubs the nearest neighbours in English football.

● GRENVILLE MORRIS has scored more goals for Forest than any other player. He spent 15 years with the club until 1913, and ended his career one goal short of a double century haul. Wally Ardron holds the club record for goals in a single season, whacking in 36 in 1950/51 to help Forest win the Third Division (South) championship.

● CENTRE-HALF Bobby McKinlay is The Reds' longest-serving player. He made his Forest debut in 1951 and over the next 19 seasons he turned out in 614 league games. Astonishingly, McKinlay only missed one Forest league match between 1959–68.

● SAM WIDDOWSON, the man who came up with the idea of shinguards, in 1874, was a Nottm Forest player.

Roll of Honour

Div 1 champions 1978
Div 2 champions 1907, 1922
Div 3 (S) champions 1951
FA Cup 1898, 1959
League Cup 1978, 1979, 1989, 1990
European Cup 1979, 1980
Div 1 (post Premiership) champions: 1998

Nottingham Forest's Post-War Record

47 D2 11th	64 D1 13th	81 D1 7th
48 D2 19th	65 D1 5th	82 D1 12th
49 D2 21st	66 D1 18th	83 D1 5th
50 D3 4th	67 D1 2nd	84 D1 3rd
51 D3 1st	68 D1 11th	85 D1 9th
52 D2 4th	69 D1 18th	86 D1 8th
53 D2 7th	70 D1 15th	87 D1 8th
54 D2 4th	71 D1 16th	88 D1 3rd
55 D2 15th	72 D1 21st	89 D1 3rd
56 D2 7th	73 D2 14th	90 D1 9th
57 D2 2nd	74 D2 7th	91 D1 8th
58 D1 10th	75 D2 16th	92 D1 8th
59 D1 13th	76 D2 8th	93 PR 22nd
60 D1 20th	77 D2 3rd	94 D1 2nd
61 D1 14th	78 D1 1st	95 PR 3rd
62 D1 19th	79 D1 2nd	96 PR 9th
63 D1 9th	80 D1 5th	97 PR 20th
		98 D1 1st

28th May 1980. Brian Clough's Nottingham Forest celebrate the club's incredible rise from Division Two to double European Champions in little over two years

N

NOTTS COUNTY

Year founded: 1862
Ground: Meadow Lane (21,000)
Highest ever crowd: 47,310, 12th March 1955 v York City (FA Cup rd 6)
Nickname: The Magpies
Colours: Black-and-white-striped shirts, white shorts, black socks

NOTTS COUNTY are the world's oldest surviving football club. Formed in 1862, the club became a founder member of the League in 1888.

● COUNTY ARE also the most relegated club in the football league, suffering the dreaded drop on 14 miserable occasions.

● HENRY CURSHAM scored a record 48 goals in the FA Cup for Notts County between 1880 and 1887 (Ian Rush's tally of 43 goals is the post war record). Henry played alongside his two brothers in the same Notts County team.

● DURING THE 1997/98 season in which they ran away with the Division 3 title, County became the first side since the War to be promoted before the end of March.

● GIANT GOALKEEPER Albert Iremonger is The Magpies' record appearance maker. Between 1904–26 he turned out 564 times for the club, the last occasion when aged nearly 42... also making him the club's oldest player ever.

● IN 1974 three different Notts County players took the same penalty against Portsmouth... and they all failed to score. The first kick had to be retaken because the referee said the goalkeeper had moved, the second went in but the referee hadn't signalled, and the third was saved.

Roll of Honour

Div 2 champions 1897, 1914, 1923
Div 3 (S) champions 1931, 1950
Div 3 champions 1998
Div 4 champions 1971
FA Cup 1894
Anglo-Italian Cup 1995

O

OLDHAM ATHLETIC

Year founded: 1895
Ground: Boundary Park (13,544)
Highest ever crowd: 47,671, 25th January 1930 v Sheffield Wednesday (FA Cup rd 4)
Previous name: Pine Villa
Nickname: The Latics
Colours: Royal blue shirts, blue shorts, and blue socks

OLDHAM ATHLETIC enjoyed the best period of their recent history in the early 1990s, reaching a League Cup Final (1990), two FA Cup semi-finals (1990 and 1994) and earning promotion to the top flight (1991).

● IT WAS during the oh so nearly glorious season of 1989/90 (they lost the League Cup Final to Forest, the FA Cup semi to Manchester United and just missed out on promotion) that Oldham's Frankie Bunn set a competition record for the League Cup, when he smashed in six goals in the 7–0 Third Round win over Scarborough.

● BUNN's striking colleague Roger Palmer is Oldham's leading all-time scorer. Between 1980–94 he scored 141 goals. The record for an individual season is held by Tom Davis, who grabbed 33 goals in 1936/7.

● HAVING LOST many of their best players and suffered relegation in 1994, Oldham were unable to maintain their incredible momentum. They only just escaped the drop to Division Two in 1996, but finally succumbed to further relegation in 1997.

● DURING Oldham's other golden era, in 1910, the club achieved a remarkable turnaround in fortunes to gain promotion to the First Division. On Boxing Day 1909 they lost 6–2 to Glossop and had earned only 17 points out of 34. After that, however, they lost only one game (earning 36 points from 21 games) and were duly promoted on the last day of the season.

● IN 1924 Sammy Wynne, Oldham's left back, scored four goals in one match against Manchester United in the Second Division... unfortunately two of them were own goals (fortunately Oldham still won 3–2).

● IN 1962 Oldham produced their most convincing win ever, thrashing Southport 11-0 in a Division Four fixture, a record for that division. During the game, centre-forward Bert Lister scored six goals, one less than Eric Gemmill's club record. The Latics' most humiliating defeat was a 4-13 stuffing at the hands of Tranmere Rovers in 1935. The 17-goal total is a record aggregate score for the Football League.

● NO OLDHAM player has turned out more often for The Latics than Ian Wood. He made 525 league appearances for the club between 1966–80, incredibly missing just one match in a four-year spell in the early 1970s.

Roll of Honour

Div 2 champions 1991
Div 3 (N) champions 1953
Div 3 champions 1974

MICHAEL OWEN

Born: Chester 21.10. 71.
Height: 5ft 8in
Position: Striker
Club career:
1997– Liverpool 37 (19)
International record:
1998– England 8 (3)

Record-breaker extraordinaire Michael Owen is the youngest player to play for England and the youngest player ever to score in his country's famous white shirt.

● When the lightning-quick striker made his international debut at Wembley against Chile on February 11th 1998 he was aged just 18 years and 59 days, beating the previous record held by Duncan Edwards by 124 days! And when he scored in his third England game, against Morocco, he was just 18 and 166 days old, beating Tommy Lawton's record (he was 19 years and 17 days when he scored on his debut against Wales on October 22nd 1938) which had stood for 60 years.

● After scoring on his Liverpool debut against Wimbledon in May 1997, the following season Owen was joint Premiership top scorer with 18 goals (equal with Blackburn's Chris Sutton and Coventry's Dion Dublin). And at the end of the 1997/98 season in which he had terrorised defences with his pace and finishing skills Owen was voted Young Player of the Year by both the PFA and the Football Writer's Association.

● Selected in Glenn Hoddle's England squad for the World Cup, Owen came off the bench to score in his second game of the tournament against Romania and then scored arguably the goal of the tournament against Argentina. And after France '98 Sir Bobby Charlton tipped him to break his record of 49 goals for England.

OWN GOALS

THE FIRST EVER own goal occurred on the very first day of the first football season in 1888, the unfortunate scorer being George Cox of Aston Villa, who put through his own net against Wolverhampton Wanderers.

● THE FASTEST own goal was scored by Torquay player Pat Kruse who managed to head past his own keeper after just six seconds of a match against Cambridge Utd on 3rd January 1977.

Did You Know?

1st April 1995 turned out to be no joke for Blackburn Rovers. That was the day on which Nottingham Forest beat them 7-1 at Ewood Park to record the highest ever away win in the Premier League.

● EVEN ENGLAND great Alan Mullery has had a go... he scored an own goal for Fulham after 30 seconds in 1961, before a single opposition player had touched the ball. And at international level even England greats Bobby Moore and Tony Adams have put through their own net.

● THREE PLAYERS have scored at both ends during the same FA Cup Final. The first was Charlton's Bert Turner against Derby in 1946 (Derby won 4–1), Manchester City's Tommy Hutchison against Tottenham in 1981 (the match finished 1–1 but Spurs won the replay 3–2) and Tottenham stalwart Gary Mabbutt in the 3–2 defeat by Coventry City in 1987.

● MIDDLESBROUGH's Robert Stewart was not the most popular man at Ayresome Park after breaking the record for own goals in a season... notching five strikes against his own team in 1934/35.

● THE ONLY own goal ever credited to two players was scored at Stamford Bridge on 18th December 1954. It was scored by Leicester City players Stan Milburn and Jack Froggatt who both tried to kick the ball at the same time against Chelsea... it ended up in the back of the net.

● THE MOST infamous own goal ever was scored by the unfortunate Colombian Andreas Escobar against the USA in the first round of the 1994 World Cup. It condemned much-fancied Colombia to a 2–1 defeat... and condemned Escobar to death. A few days later, back home in Medellin, Colombia, he was shot dead.

OXFORD UNITED

Year founded: 1893
Ground: The Manor Ground (9,572)
Highest ever crowd: 22,750, 29th February 1964 v Preston North End (FA Cup rd 6)
Previous names: Headington, Headington United
Nickname: The U's
Colours: Yellow shirts, blue shorts, blue socks

OXFORD UNITED did not turn professional until 1949, and didn't join the Football League until 1962. The club was, however, the first in Britain to install floodlights, in 1951 (while still known as Headington).

● THE CLUB's most successful era was in the late 1980s, when they were promoted from the Second Division (a year after achieving promotion from the Third) and spent three years in the top flight. In 1986 they also won the League Cup, beating QPR 3–0 in the final to the delight of celebrity fans Jim Rosenthal and famous anthropologist Desmond Morris.

● IN 1964 OXFORD UNITED became the first Fourth Division team ever to reach the quarter finals of the FA Cup when they beat Blackburn 3–1 in the fifth round. Unfortunately they lost the next match 2–1 to Preston.

● OXFORD were involved in the longest FA Cup tie on record. Their tie against Alvechurch in the fourth qualifying round in the 1970/71 season took six matches and 11 hours to complete. Alvechurch eventually won the last game 1–0.

● In 1997 work began on a new 15,000 capacity all-seater stadium at Minchery Farm, Littlemore. The team was due to kick off the 1997/98 season there but the club ran into financial and logistical problems (including the fact that the site was adjacent to a sewage works) and building work was halted.

Roll of Honour

Div 2 champions 1985
Div 3 champions 1968, 1984
League Cup 1986

BOB PAISLEY

Born: County Durham 23.1.19
Died: 14.2.96

LIVERPOOL LEGEND Bob Paisley was the most successful manager in the history of English football. In his managerial reign (1974-83) he won no fewer than 13 major trophies: six League championships, three European Cups, three League Cups and one UEFA Cup. Incredibly, however, Paisley never won the FA Cup with Liverpool.

● HE WAS the first manager to win the European Cup with Liverpool when, in 1977, his team beat Borussia Moenchengladbach 3–1 in Rome. On arriving in the Italian city, referring to his war service, Paisley had said: 'The last time I was here I was in a tank.'

● BOB PAISLEY's first season in charge at Anfield (1974/75) was unique: it was the only one in which he didn't win a trophy.

● HE WAS ONE of only nine players to both play in and manage championship-winning teams, taking the title with Liverpool as a player in 1947.

● DURING HIS career Paisley won 22 managerial awards (Manager of the Month, Manager of the Year etc.)... only Brian Clough has won more.

● IT WAS a sad day for Liverpool and for football in general when, in February 1996, Bob Paisley passed away after a long illness. Kenny Dalglish said: 'He was the greatest of them all. There will never be another like him.'

● PAISLEY started his playing career with Bishop Auckland with whom he won the FA Amateur Cup. He signed for Liverpool in 1939 and played wartime games for the club while serving in the army.

Liverpool's Bob Paisley, who won more trophies than any other manager in English football

PARAGUAY

First international: Paraguay 1 Argentina 5 (Asuncion, 1919)
First World Cup appearance: Paraguay 0 USA 3 (Uruguay, 1930)
Highest capped player: Roberto Fernandez (78)
Highest goalscorer: Saturnino Arrua and Julio Cesar Romero (13)
Best win: 7-0 v Bolivia, 1949
Worst defeat: 0-8 v Argentina, 1926
Colours: Red and white striped shirts, blue shorts, blue socks

Despite winning the South American Championship on two occasions, in 1953 and 1979, Paraguay have always been overshadowed by their giant South American neighbours Argentina and Brazil.

● The most flamboyant player in the current Paraguay team is goalkeeper Jose Luis Chilavert. A controversial character with a fearsome temper, he was once banned from the game for 18 months after punching a stadium assistant. He also loves to take free-kicks and penalties, and boasts five goals for his country.

● Chilavert was in tears in France 98 after Paraguay became the first country ever to be knocked out of the World Cup by a 'golden goal'. With just minutes left of extra time in their second round match against France, the hosts' Laurent Blanc prevented a penalty shoot out by scoring a dramatic late winner.

● Paraguay also reached the last 16 in 1986 when they had the misfortune of meeting an in-form England for the first and only time. Bobby Robson's men beat them 3–0 with two goals from Gary Lineker.

WORLD CUP RECORD

1930 Round 1
1934 Did not enter
1938 Did not enter
1950 Round 1
1954 Did not enter
1958 Round 1
1962-1982 Did not qualify
1986 Round 2
1990 Did not qualify
1994 Did not qualify
1998 Round 2

PARIS ST. GERMAIN

Year founded: 1970
Ground: Parc des Princes (48,590)
League wins: 2
Colours: Blue shirts with broad red stripe, blue shorts and blue socks

PARIS ST. GERMAIN are currently one of France's top clubs, but this recent success is something of a new thing. The club was only formed in 1970 and only won its first of only two league titles in 1986 (the other was in 1995).

● IN RECENT years, however, PSG have been the major force in French football and in 1996 they became only the second club in the history of the French game to win a European trophy... beating Rapid Vienna 1–0 in the European Cup Winners' Cup Final. They lost the 1997 final 1–0 to Barcelona (no side has ever retained the trophy).

● THE CLUB has provided a berth for some of Europe's greatest talent in recent years, including the likes of AC Milan superstar and 1996 European Footballer of the Year George Weah and David Ginola.

Roll of Honour

French League champions 1986, 1994
French Cup 1982, 1983, 1993, 1995
European Cup Winners' Cup 1996

PARTICK THISTLE

Year founded: 1876
Ground : Firhill Park (20,676)
Highest ever crowd: 49,838, 18th February 1922 v Rangers (Scottish Div 1)
Nickname: The Jags
Colours: Yellow and red hooped shirts, black shorts, red and yellow socks

LIVING IN THE shadow of Glasgow neighbours Rangers and Celtic, Partick Thistle have tasted real glory on just two occasions, winning the Scottish Cup in 1921 and the Scottish League Cup in 1972.

● THE CLUB has the worst record in the Scottish Cup of any club over the past 13 years, winning just three games in that time and none in the past ten years. In 1993 they had the chance to improve their record, after being drawn at home to Cowdenbeath, who had won just three league games all season and had conceded 100 goals. Thistle lost 1–0.

● IT HASN'T BEEN all bad though. Partick's record victory was a more than emphatic 16-0 win over Royal Albert in the first round of The Scottish Cup in 1931. The club's heaviest defeat came in the same competition – a 0-10 hammering at Queen's Park, way back in 1881.

● FAMOUS Thistle fan Billy Connolly once revealed in his stand-up routine that for years he believed that the name of his beloved club was in fact 'Partick Thistle-nil'.

● NOBODY has played more often for The Jags than goalkeeper Alan Rough. Between 1969–82 he played in 410 league matches, and set another club record by winning 51 Scottish caps while at Firhill Park.

● IN 1926/27 Alec Hair set a club scoring record, notching 41 goals in a single Division One campaign.

Roll of Honour

First Division champions 1976
Div 2 champions 1897, 1900, 1971
Scottish Cup 1921
League Cup 1972

DANIEL PASSARELLA

Born: Argentina 25.5.53
Height: 5ft 9ins Position: Defender
Club career:
Sarmiento
River Plate
Fiorentina
Internazionale
International record:
1976–85 Argentina 69 (20)

Daniel Passarella was the first Argentinian to lift aloft the World Cup when he led his country to triumph on home soil in the 1978 World Cup.

● AN UNCOMPROMISING defender who often slipped powerfully into midfield, Passarella scored an impressive 20 goals for his country. He is Argentina's fifth most capped player ever with 69 caps.

● AFTER SPELLS with Fiorentina and Inter in Italy he returned to coach Argentinian giants River Plate and, following the World Cup of 1994 was given the task of coaching the national team. He immediately stepped into controversy, however, and insisted he would not pick players with long hair who refused to get it cut. Claudio Cannigia and Real Madrid's Fernando Redondo have not played for their country since. He retired from the post after Argentina's quarter final defeat by Holland at France '98.

STUART PEARCE

Born: Hammersmith 24.4.62
Height: 5ft 10ins Position: Defender
Club career:
1983–85 Coventry City 52 (4)
1985–97 Nottingham Forest 401 (62)
1997– Newcastle 25 (0)
International record:
1987–96 England 76 (5)

OVER THE LAST ten years Stuart Pearce has been one of England's finest and most dedicated players. Nicknamed 'Psycho', he has also been just about the toughest and most uncompromising defender a forward could hope not to meet.

● LEFT BACK Pearce was the most capped and most experienced member of the England squad under both Terry Venables and Glenn Hoddle (who brought him out of international retirement for the World Cup qualifying campaign), and altogether has earned 76 caps for his country.

● NOTTINGHAM FOREST'S most capped player ever, Pearce was able to put the nightmare of missing in the 1990 World Cup semi-final shoot-out against Germany behind him in Euro '96 by scoring in the quarter final shoot-out against Spain and then the semi-final one against Germany.

● BEFORE joining Newcastle United, Pearce won the League Cup twice in 1989 and 1990 with Forest. he also suffered relegation from the Premiership twice (1993 and 1997).

● PEARCE was famous for winding himself and the other Forest players up by playing punk music in the dressing room. His favourite track is Anarchy in the UK by the Sex Pistols and he once appeared on the cover of an album by The Lurkers (pictured in the crowd).

● A FORMER electrician, Pearce began his career at non-league Wealdstone. They certainly breed them tough down in that part of the world... it's where Vinnie Jones came from too.

Stuart Pearce, one of the hardest tacklers in the game, gets a taste of his own medicine against Spain in Euro 96

PELE

Born: Tres Coracoes, Brazil 21.10.40
Height: 5ft 10ins Position: Forward
Club career:
1956–74 Santos
1975–77 New York Cosmos
International record:
1957–71 Brazil 92 (77)

BORN Edson Arantes do Nascimento, he soon became known the world over simply as Pele – the greatest footballer ever to play the game

● PELE BECAME the youngest ever World Cup winner in 1958 when, at the age of just 17, he scored two goals to help Brazil beat hosts Sweden in the Final.

● FAST, STRONG and outrageously skilful, Pele was nothing short of a footballing genius. After missing most of the 1962 World Cup triumph through injury and being kicked out of the 1966 competition, in 1970 he inspired probably the best football team the world has ever seen to victory in the World Cup in Mexico... beating Italy 4–1 in the final (Pele scoring the first goal).

● ON 19th NOVEMBER 1969 Pele scored his 1,000th senior goal when he struck a penalty for Santos against Vasco da Gama.

● THOUGH HE scored an astonishing 1,282 times in his career, Pele is not the highest goalscorer in football history. That honour falls to fellow Brazilian Artur Freidenreich who notched 1,329 between 1909 and 1935.

● HE IS Brazil's top scorer of all time with his astonishing 77 goals in just 92 games (making him the fourth highest capped Brazilian). He is also the third highest scorer in World Cup finals tournaments, with 12 goals.

● MANY PLAYERS have been labelled 'the new Pele' but none has ever matched him. In 1993, when Partick Thistle manager John Lambie was told his striker Colin McGlashen had been injured in a clash of heads and didn't know who he was, Lambie said 'Brilliant. Tell him he's Pele.'

The world's greatest ever player, Pele, who once said: 'Football, it's the beautiful game'.

PENALTIES

The first penalty kick to be taken anywhere in the world was converted by Andrew Mitchess of Royal Albert against Airdrieonians in March 1891, three days after the new rule had been adopted. The first penalty in the English League was scored by J Heath of Wolverhampton Wanderers against Accrington Stanley in September of the same year.

● THE MOST penalties ever awarded in a British match – between Crystal Palace and Brighton at Selhurst Park in 1989 – was five. All came in a 27-minute spell either side of half-time. Palace were awarded four of the kicks (one scored, three missed) by referee Kelvin Morton, and Brighton got one (scored). The match finished 2–1 to Palace.

● THE WORLD record for the number of penalties awarded in one game, six, was set in a Cypriot First Division match between Omonia Nicosia and Olympiakos. Each team was awarded three penalties each, they were all converted and Omonia won 6–4.

● FRANCIS LEE holds the record for the most penalties scored in an English League season, netting 13 times from the spot for Manchester City in 1972.

● IPSWICH GOALKEEPER Paul Cooper holds the English League record from the goalkeepers' point of view, saving an incredible eight of the 10 he faced during 1979/80. His technique was to leave a slightly bigger gap at one side of the goal, tempting the striker to shoot there.

● COOPER's record is remarkable when you consider that a recent scientific study of the last four World Cups revealed goalkeepers only have a 14 per cent chance of saving a penalty!

● PENALTIES were first used to decide drawn World Cup matches in 1982. That year West Germany became the first country to win a shoot-out when they beat France 5–4 on penalties after their semi-final was drawn 3–3.

● The British record for the longest shoot-out is the 28-penalty marathon between Aldershot and Fulham in the 1987 Freight Rover Trophy, while the world record is held by Argentine teams Juniors and Racing Club, who fought out a 20-19 thriller in 1988. However, these marathons were eclipsed by the shoot-out between under-10 teams Mickleover Lightning Blue Sox and Chellaston Boys B in the Derby Community Cup in January 1998. In a shoot-out lasting as long as the match itself (which had finished 1-1) the first 62 penalties were missed and Mickleover eventually won it 2-1 after 66 kicks.

PETERBOROUGH UNITED

Year founded: 1934
Ground: London Road (15,500)
Highest ever crowd: 30,096, 20th February 1965 v Swansea (FA Cup rd 5)
Nickname: The Posh
Colours: Royal blue shirts, white shorts, white socks

PETERBOROUGH were finally elected to the football league on 26th May 1960 – at the 21st attempt! No doubt their cup exploits helped their cause: in the previous seven seasons they had reached the 3rd round twice and the 4th round on two other occasions.

● IN THEIR first season they stormed to the Fourth Division title, scoring a record 134 goals. In that campaign Terry Bly set an amazing club record by notching up 52 league goals.

● IT IS THOUGHT Peterborough acquired the nickname of The Posh back in 1934, when a smart new team kit was unveiled for a match against Gainsborough Trinity.

● PETERBOROUGH's record win and defeat are both by the same score. In 1969 they hammered Oldham Athletic 8–1 in a Division Four match for their best ever win. The club, though, went down by the same margin in a cup-tie against Northampton in 1946.

● IN 1968 the club had 19 points deducted after being found guilty of making illegal payments to players and were duly relegated to Division Four.

● AND IN 1992 the club were forced to replay their FA Cup tie against Kingstonian because with the score at 3–0 the Kingstonian goalkeeper had been hit by a missile. The original match ended 9–1 to Peterborough – they only won the closed door replay 1–0.

Roll of Honour

Div 4 champions 1961, 1974

EMMANUEL PETIT

Born: Dieppe (France) 22.10.70
Position: Midfielder
Monaco: 1988-97 222 (4)
Arsenal: 1997 32 (3)
International career: France 26 (2)

EMMANUEL PETIT is the first English-based foreign player ever to score in a World Cup Final. The Arsenal midfielder coolly slotted France's third goal at the Stade de France against Brazil at the climax of France 98 to put paid to any fears of a South American comeback and spark off the biggest party in Paris since Liberation Day 1944.

● It was quite a season for the blond pony-tailed Arsenal midfielder. He joined the French squad fresh from winning the Double after his first season at Highbury, helping the Gunners to be only the second ever team to win 'the Double Double'. Arsenal signed 'Manu' from Monaco for £3.5 million after he had helped the money-bags Monte Carlo team to their first French Championship for nearly a decade. He also won the French Cup at the club back in 1991 – under current Arsenal manager Arsene Wenger.

● As a youngster Petit (who was voted the French Young Player of the Year in 1990) was traumatised by the death of his older brother while playing amateur football, and dedicates his every success to his memory.

MARTIN PETERS

Born: Plaistow 8.11.43
Height: 6ft 0ins Position: Midfielder
Club career:
1961–70 West Ham United 302 (81)
1970–75 Tottenham Hotspur 189 (46)
1975–80 Norwich 207 (44)
1980– Sheffield United 24 (4)
International record:
1966–74 England 67 (20)

THE 'OTHER' England scorer in the World Cup Final of 1966, if German defender Weber hadn't equalised in the last minute of normal time in that match, Martin Peters would have been immortalised as the scorer of England's World Cup winning goal.

● HIS ROLE in that team, as in all the teams he played for, was vital. England manager Alf Ramsey described him as 'ten years ahead of his time' in terms of tactics and footballing intelligence, and Peters' ability to play anywhere on the pitch was testimony to this.

● PART OF the trio of West Ham players that formed the backbone of the 1966 team – Peters, Hurst and Moore – he won the European Cup Winners' Cup with The Hammers in 1965 before moving to Tottenham in March 1970, where he won the UEFA Cup in 1972 and the League Cup in 1971 and 1973.

● IN 1978 Peters was awarded the MBE in the New Year Honours List.

● AFTER AN unsuccessful spell as player-coach at Sheffield United in 1980, Peters left the game to work in the insurance business.

1 **Bastard, Segal Richard (1880)**
2 **Daft, Harry Butler (1889-92)**
3 **Strange, Alfred Henry (1930-34)**
4 **Von Donop, Pelham George (1873-75)**
5 **Ruddlesdin, Herod (1904-5)**
6 **Sandilands, Rupert Renorden (1892-96)**
7 **Tweedy, George Jacob (1937)**
8 **Blenkinsop, Ernest (1928-33)**
9 **Scattergood, Ernald Oak (1913)**
10 **Batty, David (1991-)**

Martin Peters, not just a World Cup winner but the sort of clean-cut lad you could bring round to your mum's for tea too

PITCHES

ACCORDING TO FIFA rules, a football pitch must be between a maximum of 100 yards by 130 yards and a minimum of 50 yards by 100 yards… in other words, sizes vary dramatically from one pitch to another.

● MANCHESTER CITY have the largest pitch in the football league, providing plenty of room for wingers on their 117 x 78 yard pitch. Unfortunately it is opposition attackers that have put it to the best use in recent years.

● THE LARGEST Scottish pitch is at Clyde (9,204 sq yds) and the smallest is at Brechin City (7,370 sq yds).

● THE SMALLEST pitch in the football league – at just 6,686 square yards - is that of Bristol Rovers. This is not that surprising since the Memorial Ground pitch, which Rovers share with Bristol RFU, was designed for rugby union.

● THE FIRST portable natural grass was used in the Detroit Silverdome in the 1993 America Cup match between England and Germany, and then a year later in the World Cup. The grass was grown in hexagonal segments in the stadium car park and then reassembled inside the covered stadium.

● THE PITCH at Wembley is renowned for being the most tiring in the world. This is because the turf is made mainly from strong, spongy rye grass and not – as is often wrongly believed – because of its size. At 8,567.5 square yards it is not even among the 25 biggest pitches in the country!

MICHEL PLATINI

Born: Joeuf, France 21.6.55
Position: Midfielder
Club career:
Nancy-Lorraine
St. Etienne
Juventus
International record:
1976–87 France 72 (41)

THREE TIMES European Footballer of the Year (1983, 1984 and 1985 – the only man to win it three times in a row) and captain of the finest French team ever, Michel Platini was, and is, a legendary figure in world football. Michel Platini was the organising co-president of the France 98 World Cup and was present at every match in the tournament (bar eight group games).

● AFTER APPEARING for France at the 1976 Olympics, the graceful attacking midfielder starred alongside Alain Giresse and Joel Tigana in the 1982 World Cup, when France lost controversially and unfortunately to Germany in the semi-final (on penalties after leading 3–1 in extra time).

● AFTER THAT tournament he signed for Italian giants Juventus for £1.2 million where he was the Italian league's top scorer on three occasions. He scored the winning goal (a penalty) in Juventus's first ever European Cup win in 1985, albeit rightly overshadowed by the Heysel tragedy.

● IN 1984 he captained France to their first ever trophy when, as host nation, they won the European Championships, beating Spain 2–0 in the final (Platini scoring the first goal from a free kick). In all he scored nine goals in the tournament... a European Championships record.

● PLATINI is France's record goalscorer with 41 in his 11 year career (1976–87) and has the third highest number of appearances for his country (72).

DAVID PLATT

Born: Oldham 10.6.66
Height: 5ft 10ins Position: Midfielder
Club career:
1984–88 Crewe Alexandra 134 (56)
1988–91 Aston Villa 121 (50)
1991–92 Bari 29 (11)
1992–93 Juventus 16 (3)
1993–95 Sampdoria 55 (17)
1995–98 Arsenal 86 (13)
International record:
1989–96 England 62 (27)

ENGLAND's top scoring midfielder of all time with 27 goals in just 62 games, David Platt's international record is impressive to say the least. In all he is England's eighth highest scorer of all time, one goal ahead of Bryan Robson who played 28 more games.

● HIS MOST famous goal came when he volleyed home spectacularly in the last minute of extra time against Belgium to put England through to the quarter-finals of the 1990 World Cup.

● PLATT HAS been the subject of four multi-million pound transfers in his illustrious career. His moves from Crewe to Aston Villa (£200,000), Aston Villa to Bari (£5.5 million), Bari to Juventus (£6.5 million), Juventus to Sampdoria (£4.5 million) and Sampdoria to Arsenal (£4.8 million) have cost a total of £21.5 million.

● DESPITE HIS TRAVELS Platt has won surprisingly little in the way of silverware although he did pick up Premiership and FA Cup winners medals with Arsenal in 1998. And in 1990 he was voted the PFA Player of the Year.

● AT THE END of the 1997/98 season Platt hung up his boots. Despite being still under contract at Arsenal he decided to take time off to learn about management and vowed to travel the world learning about different coaching methods and tactics.

David Platt, England's top-scoring midfielder of all time, chases a runaway ball in England's build-up to Euro 96

PLYMOUTH ARGYLE

Year founded: 1886
Ground: Home Park (19,600)
Highest ever crowd: 43,596, 10th October 1936 v Aston Villa (Div 2)
Previous name: Argyle Athletic Club
Nickname: The Pilgrims
Colours: Green and white shirts, black shorts, green, white and black socks

THE MOST southerly home of an English league club, Plymouth is the second largest city in England never to have been blessed by a team in the top flight (Hull is the largest).

● IN 1984 Plymouth Argyle became only the sixth Third Division club to reach the FA Cup semi-finals. They met Watford at Villa Park but, despite the presence of 20,000 Argyle fans, lost 1–0 to a George Reilly goal.

● 'The Pilgrims' as they are known to their supporters have twice recorded 8-1 victories: against Millwall in 1932, and more recently away to Hartlepool in a Division Two match in 1994. The club's most embarrassing defeat, a 9-0 loss to Stoke City, came in a Second Division match in 1960.

● Peter Shilton is the oldest player to appear for Argyle, turning out as player/manager against Burnley in 1993 aged 44 years and 21 days. Funnily enough his son, Sam, was the club's youngest ever player, making his debut at the age of 16 years and four months in 1994, until his record was broken by Lee Philips who was 16 years and 43 days old when he played against Gillingham in October 1996.

● IN 1968 Plymouth were victims of the only recorded league goal to be scored by the referee. The goal in the 1–0 Division Three defeat by Barrow was a deflection off the inside of referee Ivan Robinson's foot from 15 yards... and it proved to be the winner.

● FORMER Labour leader Michael Foot is Plymouth's most famous fan, having supported the club since he was a child.

Roll of Honour

Div 3 (S) champions 1930, 1952

KAREL POBORSKY

Born: Trebon, Czech Republic 30.3.72
Height: 5ft 7ins Position: Midfielder
Club career:
1991–94 Budejovice 82 (15)
1994–95 Viktoria Zizkov 27 (8)
1995–96 Slavia Prague 26 (11)
1996–98 Manchester United 22 (4)
1998– Benfica
International record:
1994– Czech Republic 26 (1)

KAREL POBORSKY was the star player in the Czech team which surprised everybody, even their own supporters, by reaching the final of Euro 96. His goal in the quarter-final – an outrageous chip over Portuguese keeper Baia – was one of the best strikes of the tournament.

● MANCHESTER UNITED were so impressed by Poborsky they immediately snapped him up for £3.5 million. With his long matted hair the tricky Czech, nicknamed 'The Express Train', immediately joined Premiership's Wierd Haircut XI although he failed to find his Euro 96 form. In 1998 he was sold to Benfica (although the Portuguese club's cheque to United for £2 million bounced).

● IN 1994 POBORSKY won a Czech Cup winners' medal with Viktoria Zizkov, who beat Sparta Prague on penalties. Later that year he played in England for the first time, as part of the Zizkov side beaten 4–2 by Chelsea in the Cup Winners' Cup.

POLAND

First international: Hungary 1 Poland 0 (Budapest, 1921)
First World Cup appearance: Poland 5 Brazil 6 (France, 1938)
Highest capped player: Grzegorz Lato (104)
Highest goalscorer: Wlodzimierz Lubanski (50)
Best win: 9–0 v Norway, 1963
Worst defeat: 8–0 v Denmark, 1948
Colours: White shirts, red shorts, white socks

FOR A COUNTRY whose borders have been chopped and changed more than any other in history (in the first days of football it didn't even exist), Poland have a fine footballing tradition... finishing third in the World Cup twice (1974 and 1982).

● POLAND's most famous player is certainly Zbigniew Boniek, a powerful and skilful forward who played for Juventus in Italy and scored 24 goals for his country in the late 1970s and 80s.

● Incredibly, England have been drawn against Poland in every World Cup and European Championship qualifying group they have taken part in since 1988 (qualifying for the 1990, 1994 and 1998 World Cups and for the 1992 and 2000 European Championships).

● POLISH GOALKEEPER Jan Tomaszewski is responsible for one of England's darkest days. To qualify for the 1973 World Cup England knew they had to beat the Poles on 17th October at Wembley but Tomaszewski – dubbed 'the clown' before the game – made save after save to deny them. He was finally beaten by an Alan Clarke penalty, but Poland had scored at the other end and England missed the boat to Germany.

WORLD CUP RECORD

1930	Did not enter	1970	Did not qualify
1934	Did not qualify	1974	Third place
1938	Round 1	1978	Round 2
1950	Did not qualify	1982	Third place
1954	Did not qualify	1986	Round 2
1958	Did not qualify	1990	Did not qualify
1962	Did not qualify	1994	Did not qualify
1966	Did not qualify	1998	Did not qualify

FC PORTO

Year founded: 1893
Ground: Dos Antas (76,000)
League wins: 17
Colours: Blue-and-white-striped shirts, blue shorts and white socks

CURRENTLY PORTUGAL's most successful side, in recent years Porto have overshadowed their main rivals Benfica and Sporting Lisbon.

● SO DOMINANT has the club been that it has won the Portuguese championship seven times in the 1990s... including in 1996 under the management of ex-England boss Bobby Robson before he was head-hunted by Spanish giants Barcelona.

● PORTO are the only Portuguese club other than Benfica to have won the European Cup, beating the mighty Bayern Munich 2–1 in 1987 with a 79th-minute goal by Juary.

● IN THE same year as that triumph the club won the World Club Cup (beating Penarol of Uruguay 2–1) and the European Super Cup. They are the only Portuguese club to win either trophy.

Roll of Honour

Portuguese champions 1935, 1939, 1940, 1956, 1958, 1959, 1978, 1979, 1985, 1986, 1988, 1990, 1992, 1993, 1995, 1996, 1997, 1998
Portuguese Cup 1922, 1925, 1932, 1937, 1956, 1958, 1968, 1977, 1984, 1988, 1991, 1994
European Champions Cup 1987
European Super Cup 1987
World Club Cup 1987

PORTSMOUTH

Year founded: 1898
Ground: Fratton Park (29,500)
Highest ever crowd: 51,385, 26th February 1949 v Derby County (FA Cup rd 6)
Nickname: Pompey
Colours: Blue shirts, white shorts, red socks

PORTSMOUTH's heyday came after World War II when they won the League Championship twice in a row in 1949 and 1950... no doubt sparking mass renditions of the Pompey Chimes ('play up Pompey, Pompey play up!') all over the city.

● WHEN THE club won its first title in 1948/49, it became the first ever team to win the championship after rising from the lowly depths of Division Three. When Pompey won it again the following year they became the first team to win consecutive titles in the post-war era.

● POMPEY's success was based upon the influential midfield of Jimmy Scoular, Reg Flewin and the legendary Jimmy Dickinson. Dickinson is the club's record appearances holder with 764 outings for Pompey (between 1946–65), the second highest number of football league appearances with any one club. Dickinson is also Portsmouth's most capped player ever, winning 48 caps for England.

● PORTSMOUTH's biggest win was back in 1927 when Notts County were crushed 9–1 in a Second Division match. The following year, the club suffered their worst defeat, crashing 10–0 at Leicester.

● PORTSMOUTH manager Jack Tinn wore a pair of 'lucky' white spats throughout his team's 1939 Cup run. It worked, because Pompey surprisingly beat Wolves 4–1 in the final (their only FA Cup win) and remained holders for a record seven years,

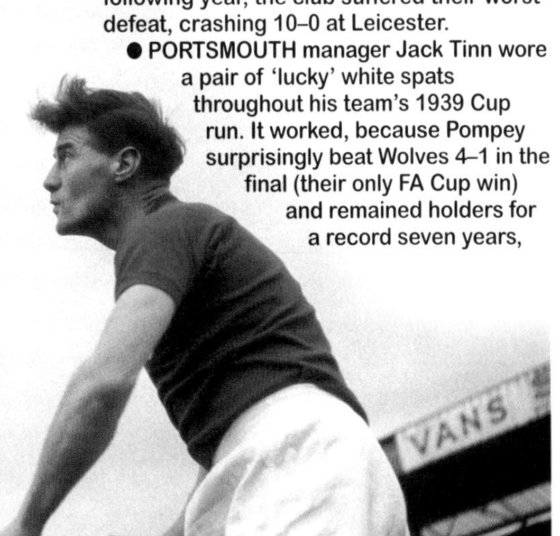

Portsmouth's record appearance maker Jimmy Dickinson displaying how a spot of Brylcreem on your quiff can add power to your heading

thanks to the disruption caused to the sporting programme by World War II. Britain's most famous strategist during that conflict, Field Marshal Montgomery, is a past President of Portsmouth.

● ON 22nd FEBRUARY 1956 Portsmouth staged the first ever Football League game under floodlights at Fratton Park when Newcastle United were the visitors.

● IN 1996 former England boss Terry Venables briefly became Chairman of the club making his two jobs (the other as coach of Australia) almost literally worlds apart.

Roll of Honour

Div 1 champions 1949, 1950
Div 3 (S) champions 1924
Div 3 champions 1962, 1983
FA Cup 1939

Portugal's João Pinto hurdles a Swiss Roll during his country's vain World Cup 94 qualifying campaign

PORTUGAL

First international: Spain 3 Portugal 1 (Madrid, 1921)
First World Cup appearance: Portugal 3 Hungary 1 (England, 1966)
Highest capped player: João Pinto (80)
Highest international goalscorer: Eusebio (41)
Best win: 8–0 v Leichtenstein, 1994
Worst defeat: 9–0 v Spain, 1934
Colours: Red shirts, green shorts, red socks

PORTUGAL'S BEST international performance was in reaching the World Cup semi-finals in their first ever finals tournament, in 1966... losing 2–1 to eventual winners England at Wembley.

● THE STAR of that team was the great Eusebio (the 'Black Panther'), Portugal's record goalscorer, who scored 41 goals in all for his country and was top scorer with nine goals in the 1966 World Cup tournament.

● PORTUGAL'S best showing in the European Championships was not in reaching the quarter-finals of Euro 96 (where they lost 1–0 to the Czech Republic) but in 1984, when they lost in the semi-final to host nation France in a thrilling game in Marseille. By far and away the best and most dramatic game of the tournament, it ended France 3 Portugal 2 (although the Portuguese were leading 2–1 with six minutes of extra time left).

● Portugal narrowly failed to qualify for France '98 (they had the best record of any team that didn't make it). Millions thought they had earned a reprieve on 1st April 1998, however, when a Lisbon radio station announced that Iran had pulled out of the tournament for political reasons and that Portugal had been nominated in their place. There were celebrations in the streets... until someone noticed the date.

WORLD CUP RECORD

1930	Did not enter
1934–62	Did not qualify
1966	Third place
1970–82	Did not qualify
1986	Round 1
1990-98	Did not qualify

PORT VALE

Year founded: 1876
Ground: Vale Park, Burslem (19,000)
Highest ever crowd: 50,000, 20th February 1960 v Aston Villa (FA Cup rd 5)
Previous name: Burslem Port Vale
Nickname: The Valiants
Colours: White shirts, black shorts, white socks

PORT VALE's name derives from the house where the founding members of the club met to establish the team. At first the club was known as Burslem Port Vale – Burslem being the name of the Stoke-on-Trent town where the club is based – but that was changed to plain Port Vale in 1911.

● THE VALIANTS, as they are known to their supporters (including former Take That star Robbie Williams), produced their best win in 1932, when they hammered Chesterfield 9–1 in a Second Division encounter. In that game Stewart Littlewood grabbed six of the goals to set another club record.

● THE VALIANTS' worst defeat is 10–0, suffered against Sheffield United in 1892 and again against Notts County three years later.

● IN THE 1953/54 season Port Vale produced a run of 30 consecutive league matches without conceding a single goal... a Football League record.

● THE TEAM's rock solid defence only let in 21 goals during the whole season – a record for the old Third Division (North). Not surprisingly, Vale won the title that year and also reached the FA Cup semi-final, losing to West Bromwich Albion but becoming the first Third Division side since the war to get that far.

● WILF KIRKHAM holds two scoring records for Port Vale. In 1926/27 he grabbed an unsurpassed 38 goals in a Second Division season, and in two spells at the club he collected a club record total of 154 goals.

● THE LOYAL Roy Sproson is Vale's longest-serving player of all time. Between 1950–72 the defender was a Vale stalwart, appearing in no less than 761 league matches – the third highest number of football league games played by one man for one club.

● PORT VALE were the only English team ever managed by the legendary Sir Stanley Matthews. He took over at Vale Park in 1965, and stayed until 1968, the year when Vale were briefly expelled from the league for making illegal payments to players.

● IN 1979, manager Dennis Butler was sacked after just 12 days of the new season... the quickest early season sacking ever (equal with the dismissals of Peter Reid of Manchester City in 1993, Mick Jones of Peterborough in 1989 and Len Richley of Darlington in 1971).

Roll of Honour

Div 3 (N) champions 1930, 1954
Div 4 champions 1959
Autoglass Trophy 1993

PRESTON NORTH END

Year founded: 1881
Ground: Deepdale (21,500)
Highest ever crowd: 42,684, 23rd April 1938 v Arsenal (Div 1)
Nickname: The Lilywhites
Colours: White and navy shirts, navy shorts, white socks

PRESTON NORTH END are the holders of the record win in any English competition. In 1887 they demolished Hyde 26–0 in the FA Cup. Legend has it that the referee lost his watch during the game and the match lasted two hours, although even if this is true it's hardly an excuse for poor Hyde.

● THE FAMOUS club was also the first English team to win The Double, winning both the league and cup in the Football League's inaugural season of 1888/89. The club took the title without losing a single one of their 22 matches, the only time this feat has been achieved in the top division.

● THE LEGENDARY Tom Finney is Preston's most capped player, appearing on the wing for England in 76 internationals. Finney also holds the club scoring record, with 187 strikes between 1946 and 1960.

● PRESTON HAVE been at Deepdale since 1881, the second longest spell at the same ground in the football league.

● JIM ROSS set a record when he hit seven First Division goals in one game for Preston against Stoke in 1888.

Roll of Honour

Div 1 champions 1889, 1890
Div 2 champions 1904, 1913, 1951
Div 3 champions 1971
Third Division champions 1996
FA Cup 1889, 1938

PSV EINDHOVEN

Year founded: 1913
Ground: Philips Stadium (30,000)
League wins: 14
Colours: Red and white shirts, white shorts and white socks

OWNED BY electronics giant Philips (Philips SV Eindhoven), PSV became the third Dutch club (after Ajax and Feyenoord) to win the European Cup when they beat Benfica on penalties in 1988.

● THAT EUROPEAN CUP victory also meant that they joined those other two famous clubs in doing a treble of league title, domestic cup and European Cup all in the same season.

● PSV had also won the UEFA Cup 10 years earlier in 1978.

● THE CLUB won its first of 14 league titles back in 1929 (the last in 1997) and recent stars who have played at the Philips Stadium include Ruud Gullit, Ronald Koeman and Brazilian aces Romario and Ronaldo.

● EX-ENGLAND boss Bobby Robson was manager of the club for three years from 1990 but, despite winning the league title, was sacked after a lack of success in Europe.

Roll of Honour

Dutch League champions 1929, 1935, 1951, 1963, 1975, 1976, 1978, 1986, 1987, 1988, 1989, 1991, 1992, 1997
Dutch Cup 1950, 1974, 1976, 1988, 1989, 1990
European Cup 1988
UEFA Cup 1978

FERENC PUSKAS

Born: Budapest 2.4.27
Height: 5ft 7ins Position: Forward
Club career:
Kispest (Hungary)
Honved (Hungary)
Real Madrid
International record:
1945–56 Hungary 84 (83)
1962 Spain 4 (0)

THE GREATEST Hungarian player of all time, and one of the best footballers ever, Ferenc Puskas and his lethal left foot are legendary.

● HUNGARY'S top scorer ever with a world record 83 goals, Puskas captained his country to Olympic victory in 1952 and to the World Cup Final of 1962 (when he was injured but played on against Germany and his team surrendered a 2-0 lead to lose 3-2).

● PUSKAS led Hungary to their most famous victory in 1953, his side becoming the first foreign team to beat England at Wembley. It was more of a thrashing really, Hungary winning 6–3 with Puskas scoring twice. Before the game one English player is said to have commented: 'Look at that little fat chap there, we'll murder this lot.' He was referring to Puskas.

● IN 1956 Puskas fled his country after the Hungarian revolution and sought sanctuary in Spain with the mighty Real Madrid. Here he truly starred alongside the great Alfredo Di Stefano, four times becoming top scorer in the Spanish league. He also played for his adopted country, turning out for Spain in the 1962 World Cup.

● WITH REAL MADRID he won the European Cup in what many believe is the greatest game of all time when, in front of 120,000 at Hampden Park, they beat Eintracht Frankfurt 7–3 in 1960. Puskas scored four times, the only man ever to do so in a European Cup Final. He also scored a hat-trick in the 1962 final but Real still lost 5–3 to Benfica.

Ferenc Puskas showing off his famous double-jointed ankle trick

QUEEN OF THE SOUTH

Year founded: 1919
Ground: Palmerston Park, Dumfries (8,352)
Highest ever crowd: 24,500, 23rd February 1952 v Hearts (Scottish Cup rd 3)
Nickname: The Doonhamers
Colours: Royal blue shirts, white shorts, blue and white socks

QUEEN OF THE SOUTH – so-called after the nickname of their hometown Dumfries – enjoyed their best win in 1932, when Stranraer were overwhelmed 11–1. The club's worst defeat, 10–2, came at Dundee in 1962.

● ALLAN BALL – no relation to he of the flat cap and squeaky voice – is the club's record appearance maker, turning out in 619 league games for The Doonhammers between 1962–83.

● IN THE 1988/89 campaign the club set a record for the fewest wins in a season ever in the new format Division One (i.e. after the Premier League was set up)... in their 39 games they recorded just two wins! That same season they set another unenviable record for the division, this time for the most defeats in a season... a miserable 29 out of 39 matches. You could say it was a poor season.

● FEW QUEEN OF THE SOUTH players have ever been called up for international duty, although Billy Houliston won a club record three caps for Scotland while at Palmerston Park in the 1940s.

● JIMMY GRAY hit a club record 33 goals for Queen of the South in a Second Division campaign in 1927/28.

Roll of Honour

Div 2 champions 1951

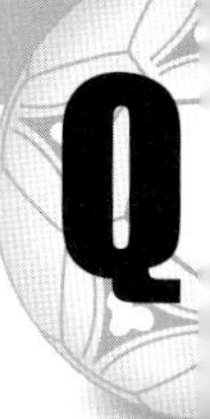

Pint-sized John Spencer, QPR's record signing, has got even shorter since his move from Chelsea

QUEEN'S PARK

Year founded: 1867
Ground: Hampden Park, Glasgow (9,222)
Highest ever crowd: 95,772, 18th January 1930 v Rangers (Scottish Cup rd 1)
Nickname: The Spiders
Colours: White-and-black-hooped shirts, white shorts, white with black-hooped socks

QUEEN'S PARK, known to their fans as The Spiders, are Scotland's oldest football club. Founded in 1867, they have always maintained a strict amateur status.

● THE CLUB dominated the Scottish Cup in the last two decades of the nineteenth century, winning the trophy in its first three years. Apart from Kilmarnock, Queen's Park are the only surviving club out of the original 16 entrants of the Scottish Cup.

● IT WAS NOT until Park's third season in the cup – 1875/76 – that they conceded their first goal in the competition. In all they have won it 10 times, the last being in 1893.

● QUEENS PARK are the only Scottish team to have appeared in the English FA Cup Final. They lost to Blackburn Rovers in 1884 and 1885.

● DESPITE their currrently lowly position in the league, Queen's Park still play at the home of Scottish football, Hampden Park, where the record attendance was a whopping 149,547 for the Scotland v England match in 1937.

Roll of Honour

Div 2 champions 1923, 1956
Second Division champions 1981
Scottish Cup 1874, 1875 , 1876, 1880, 1881, 1882, 1884, 1886, 1890, 1893

QUEENS PARK RANGERS

Year founded: 1885
Ground: Rangers Stadium, Loftus Road (18,919)
Highest ever crowd: 35,353, 27th April 1974 v Leeds Utd (Div 1)
Nickname: The R's
Colours: Blue-and-white-hooped shirts, white shorts, white socks

QPR HAVE had 12 home grounds, and in all have used 18 different venues to stage their matches... more than any other English league club. Not content with this record, they have also changed their strip on four occasions... settling in recent years for their famous blue and white hoops.

● QPR came closest to winning the League Championship in 1975/76, when they were pipped by Liverpool in the very last game of the season and finished runners-up.

● IN 1967 QPR pulled off a unique double, winning the Third Division Championship and the League Cup. It was the first time the final had been played at Wembley, and The R's put on a memorable display in coming back from two goals down to beat West Bromwich Albion.

● CULT HERO Rodney Marsh struck a club record 44 goals that year, with an astonishing 11 of those goals coming just in the League Cup. George Goddard, though, holds the QPR record for league goals in a season with 37 in 1929/30. Goddard is also the leading scorer in the history of the club, with 172 goals in league matches between 1926–34.

● QPR recorded an unprecedented six consecutive 1-1 draws during the 1957/58 season.

● IN 1961/62 QPR hit 111 goals in Division Three, a divisional record which still stands.

● QPR's biggest win was a 9–2 hammering of Tranmere in a Third Division match in 1960. Two clubs with very different pedigrees have crushed Rangers 8–1: Mansfield in 1965 and Manchester United four years later.

Vinnie Jones gets to grips with his new role at QPR... and anything else that gets in his way

Roll of Honour

Div 2 champions 1983
Div 3 (S) champions 1948
Div 3 champions 1967
League Cup 1967

RAITH ROVERS

Year founded: 1883
Ground: Stark's Park (10,271)
Highest ever crowd: 31,306, 7th February 1953 v Hearts (Scottish Cup rd 2)
Colours: Navy blue shirts, white shorts, white socks

RAITH ROVERS hold the unfortunate record of being the only British League club ever to fail to win a single home league match in a season. Of their games at Stark's Park in the 1962/63 season they lost 15 and drew two.

● THE CLUB – whose home is Kirkcaldy in Fife – does hold one more impressive British record, however, that of the most goals ever scored in a single season. During the 1937/38 campaign the club notched an incredible 142 goals (Peterborough's 134 in the 1960/61 season is the highest total south of the border).

● RAITH's biggest victory was in 1954, when Coldstream were blitzed 10–1 in a Scottish Cup match. Rovers suffered their worst defeat in 1936, going down 2–11 at Morton.

● IN SEASON 1994/95 the club pulled off a unique double, winning both the First Division title and the Scottish League Cup. The following season Rovers entered Europe for the first time, and put up a gallant showing in the Cup Winners' Cup before going out to German giants Bayern Munich... their first and only foray into Europe.

Roll of Honour

Div 2 champions 1908, 1910 (shared with Leith), 1938, 1949
Div 1 champions 1993, 1995
Scottish League Cup 1995

SIR ALF RAMSEY

Born: Dagenham 21.1.20

SIR ALF RAMSEY is the first and only man ever to guide England to victory in a World Cup Final.

● ENGLAND were hosts of the tournament in 1966 and had the advantage of playing all their matches at Wembley. Due to a lack of quality wingers Ramsey (a full-back for Spurs during his career) developed a 4-4-2 formation which gave the team the nickname 'the Wingless Wonders'.

● HIS MOST telling contribution came in the interval before extra time after Germany had just equalised. `You've beaten them once,' he told his dispirited players, 'now go and do it again. Look at them, they're knackered.' England scored two further goals to win 4–2.

● AS A CLUB manager Ramsey had taken over Third Division Ipswich Town in 1955. By 1962 he had made them League Champions, a remarkable feat. It remains Ipswich's only championship win. Ramsey then left the East Anglian club to replace Walter Winterbottom at England.

● RAMSEY was sacked from the England post after he failed to guide the team to the Germany 1974 World Cup Tournament. Under his management, England played 113 matches, winning 69 and losing 17.

● AS A PLAYER Ramsey played at right-back for Southampton and Spurs, turning out 32 times for England and scoring three times (including a goal in the infamous 6–3 Wembley drubbing by Hungary in 1953).

Will Rangers players be celebrating a world record 10 titles in a row at the end of the 1997/98 season?

RANGERS

Year founded: 1873

Ground: Ibrox Stadium (44,500)

Highest ever crowd: 118,567, 2nd January 1939 v Celtic (Div 1)

Nickname: The Gers

Colours: Royal blue shirts, white shorts, black and red socks

DESPITE BEING by far and away the most successful Scottish club by a mile in recent years, having equalled arch rivals Celtic's record of nine league wins on the trot in 1996/97, they went the following season without picking up a single trophy, the first time that had happened since 1986.

● IN ALL the club have won The Scottish League championship a record 47 times... this figure includes a shared title with Dumbarton in the very first year of the competition, 1890/91.

● RANGERS' championship-winning seasons have produced a host of Scottish records. In 1920/21 the club won a record number of points (76) and games (35) to lift the old First Division title.

● THE CLUB also holds the records for most points in the Premier Division, with 73 points from 44 matches in 1992/93 and 33 wins from 44 matches in 1991/92 and 1992/93.

● 1991/92 was a bumper year for The Gers' attack, as McCoist and co. whacked in a Premier League record of 101 goals. The defence was at its tightest, though, in 1989/90 creating another Premier record by conceding just 19 goals.

● IT WAS way back in 1898/99, however, that Rangers had their most successful league season – winning all 18 of their fixtures – a feat considered to be a world record.

● RANGERS also hold two Scottish League Cup records, with more wins (20) and more appearances in the final (26) than any other club. The Gers got off to a good start in the competition, beating Aberdeen 4–0 in the first final in 1947.

● STATISTICALLY, Rangers' performance in the Scottish Cup has been less impressive, partly because the club had to wait 20 years until 1894 before celebrating their first victory. Nevertheless, The Gers have won three consecutive finals on a record three occasions.

● WHILE KEEPING goal for Rangers Chris Woods set a British record, going 1,196 minutes without conceding a goal from 26th November 1986 to 31st January 1987.

● ALLY McCOIST is the club's record scorer, notching 251 league goals (355 in all competitions) for Rangers. Sam English holds the record for a single season with 44 goals in the 1931/32 campaign.

● NO PLAYER has turned out more often for the club than John Greig. The Rangers' favourite and former manager pulled on the navy blue shirt for 496 league matches between 1962–78.

● ALLY McCOIST has represented Scotland more often than the dozens of other international players the club has produced. He has played a total of 59 games for Scotland.

● RANGERS' record victory was in a

Scottish Cup match in 1934. Blairgowrie were overwhelmed 14–2. The club's worst ever defeat was back in 1886, when The Gers were humbled 2–10 by Airdrieonians.

Roll of Honour

Div 1 champions 1891 (shared), 1899, 1900, 1901, 1902, 1911, 1912, 1913, 1918, 1920, 1921, 1923, 1924, 1925, 1927, 1928, 1929, 1930, 1931, 1933, 1934, 1935, 1937, 1939, 1947, 1949, 1950, 1953, 1956, 1957, 1959, 1961, 1963, 1964, 1975
Premier League champions 1976, 1978, 1987, 1989, 1990, 1991, 1992, 1993, 1994, 1995, 1996, 1997
Scottish Cup 1894, 1897, 1898, 1903, 1928, 1930, 1932, 1934, 1935, 1936, 1948, 1949, 1950, 1953, 1960, 1962, 1963, 1964, 1966, 1973, 1976, 1978, 1979, 1981, 1992, 1993, 1996
Scottish League Cup 1947, 1949, 1961, 1962, 1964, 1965, 1971, 1976, 1978, 1979, 1982, 1984, 1985, 1987, 1988, 1989, 1991, 1993, 1994, 1997
European Cup Winners' Cup 1972

Rangers' Post-War Record

47 D1 1st	64 D1 1st	81 PR 3rd
48 D1 2nd	65 D1 5th	82 PR 3rd
49 D1 1st	66 D1 2nd	83 PR 4th
50 D1 1st	67 D1 2nd	84 PR 4th
51 D1 2nd	68 D1 2nd	85 PR 4th
52 D1 2nd	69 D1 2nd	86 PR 5th
53 D1 1st	70 D1 2nd	87 PR 1st
54 D1 4th	71 D1 4th	88 PR 3rd
55 D1 3rd	72 D1 3rd	89 PR 1st
56 D1 1st	73 D1 2nd	90 PR 1st
57 D1 1st	74 D1 3rd	91 PR 1st
58 D1 2nd	75 D1 1st	92 PR 1st
59 D1 1st	76 PR 1st	93 PR 1st
60 D1 3rd	77 PR 2nd	94 PR 1st
61 D1 1st	78 PR 1st	95 PR 1st
62 D1 2nd	79 PR 2nd	96 PR 1st
63 D1 1st	80 PR 5th	97 PR 1st
		98 PR 2nd

FABRIZIO RAVANELLI

Born: Perugia, Italy 11.12.68
Height: 6ft 2ins Position: Forward
Club career:

1986–89	Perugia 90 (41)
1989	Avellino 7 (0)
1989–90	Casertana 27 (12)
1990–92	Reggiana 66 (24)
1992–96	Juventus 115 (44)
1996–97	Middlesbrough 35 (16)
1997–	Marseille

International record:
1994– Italy 21 (9)

FABRIZIO RAVANELLI was believed to be the highest paid player in Britain when he signed for Middlesbrough in 1996 (from Juventus for £7 million) for a reputed £42,000 a week in 1996. The club was relegated and lost two cup finals before, just over a year later, Ravanelli was sold to French club Marseille for £5.5 million.

● RAVANELLI – nicknamed 'The White Feather' or 'The Silver Fox' after going prematurely grey at the age of 20 – scored his last goal for Juventus in the 1996 European Cup Final against Ajax. In his four-year spell at Juve he scored 44 goals in 115 Serie A games, picking up a championship medal in 1995. In 1994 he scored all five goals in Juventus' 5–1 win against CSKA Sofia in the UEFA Cup.

● NOW AGED 30, Ravanelli burst onto the international scene during the qualifiers for Euro 96. He scored on his debut for Italy in a 4–1 win over Estonia in Salerno in March 1995. He is a regular squad player under current coach Cesare Maldini although his appearances in the starting line-up are rare.

READING

Year founded: 1871
Ground: Madejski Stadium (25,000)
Highest ever crowd: 33,042, 19th February 1927 v Brentford (FA Cup rd 5)
Nickname: The Royals
Colours: Navy-and-white-hooped shirts, white shorts, white socks

READING's record victory was against Crystal Palace in a Division Three (South) fixture in 1946 when The Royals strolled to a 10–2 win. That, though, was a tight encounter compared to the club's heaviest defeat – an 18–0 pounding handed out by Preston in the FA Cup back in the 1893/94 season.

● READING's most capped international is former manager Jimmy Quinn. The gangly centre-forward played 15 times for Northern Ireland while based at Elm Park. The aristocratic-sounding Beaumont Ratcliffe is the oldest player to play for Reading, appearing against Northampton in 1947/48 when aged nearly 40.

● IN THE 1985/86 season Reading set a football league record by winning their opening 13 matches. Perhaps unsurprisingly after such an outstanding start, Reading went on to lift the Third Division title.

● READING FANS particularly enjoyed their visits to Elm Park between 1933–36. The team went 55 home matches without defeat to set a club record.

● OVER THE YEARS a number of well known names have been associated with Reading. In 1983 Robert Maxwell unveiled plans to merge the club with Oxford United, but had to back down when Reading's new chairman opposed the scheme. Cricket commentator John Arlott was a fan of The Royals, and the world's most famous spoon-bender, Uri Geller, developed a passion for the club during the 1990s. Rumours that he tried to teach the players to bend free kicks are unfounded.

● In August 1998 the club moved into its brand-new, state-of-the-art stadium. Modestly named the Madejski Stadium after millionaire chairman John Madejski, unfortunately the move was soured by relegation to the Second Division at the end of the 1997/98 campaign.

Roll of Honour

Div 2 champions 1994
Div 3 (S) champions 1926
Div 3 champions 1986
Div 4 champions 1979
Simod Cup 1988

REAL MADRID

Year founded: 1902
Ground: Bernabeu Stadium (95,000)
League wins: 27
Colours: White shirts, white shorts and white socks

REAL MADRID's European Cup win over Juventus in 1998 made them not only the most successful team in the history of the world's most prestigious club competition, but also the most successful team ever in European football. The famous Spanish club have won the European Cup a record seven times, giving them a grand total of nine major European trophies, one more than nearest rivals and fellow Spaniards Barcelona.

● REAL WON the first ever European Cup in 1956, the first of a record five consecutive victories in the competition. During those great years the team featured such greats as Alfredo di Stefano, Ferenc Puskas and Didi.

● REAL's mid-1980s side, which included Argentine international Jorge Valdano, lifted the UEFA Cup in 1985 and 1986 to become the first side to win it twice in succession after the Fairs Cup was renamed the UEFA Cup.

● REAL HAVE dominated Spanish football, winning the Spanish championship 27 times, 12 times more than nearest rivals Barcelona.

Roll of Honour

European Cup 1956, 1957, 1958, 1959, 1960, 1966, 1998
UEFA Cup 1985, 1986
World Club Cup 1960
Spanish League 1932, 1933, 1954, 1955, 1957, 1958, 1961, 1962, 1963, 1964, 1965, 1967, 1968, 1969, 1972, 1975, 1976, 1978, 1979, 1980, 1986, 1987, 1988, 1989, 1990, 1995, 1997
Spanish Cup 1905, 1906, 1907, 1908, 1917, 1934, 1936, 1946, 1947, 1962, 1970, 1974, 1975, 1980, 1982, 1989, 1993

Hugo Sanchez's mum must be very proud that her son's picture adorns thousands of toilet seats

RED STAR BELGRADE

Year founded: 1945
Ground: Crvena Svezda (97,422)
League wins: 20
Colours: Red-and-white striped shirts, red shorts, red socks

THE HIGH POINT of Red Star Belgrade's history came in 1991 when they became the first Yugoslav, and only the second eastern European team, ever to lift the European Cup. They beat Chris Waddle's Marseille 5–3 on penalties after a 0–0 draw, with stars such as Robert Prosinecki, Dejan Savicevic and Darko Pancev.

● THE FACT that all these stars moved on to foreign clubs is indicative of the problems Red Star have faced over the years in their attempt to compete with other European clubs. They have sold over 40 players to foreign clubs in their history, more than any other club.

● RED STAR have dominated domestic football over the years, however, winning the Yugoslav league 20 times, and the cup 14 times, far more than their main rivals Partizan Belgrade and, before the civil war, Hajduk Split (who now play in the newly formed Croatian league).

● RED STAR were the last team to play the Manchester United 'Busby Babes' before the tragic air crash – as the United team returned from the match – in Munich in 1958.

● RED STAR became the first Eastern European club to win the World Club Cup when they beat Colo Colo 3–0 in Tokyo in 1991.

Roll of Honour

League champions 1951, 1953, 1956, 1957,1959, 1960, 1964, 1968, 1969, 1970, 1973, 1977, 1980, 1981, 1984, 1988, 1990, 1991, 1992, 1995
Cup winners 1948, 1949, 1950, 1958, 1959, 1964, 1968, 1970, 1971, 1982, 1985, 1990, 1993, 1995, 1997
European Cup 1991 **World Club Cup** 1991

HARRY REDKNAPP

Born: Poplar 2.3.47

ONLY THE EIGHTH West Ham manager in the history of the club, Harry Redknapp has been in the Upton Park hotseat since August 1994 when he replaced Billy Bonds. He is yet to win his first trophy for the Hammers, but he came close to guiding his side to a UEFA Cup place in 1997/98.

● REDKNAPP, though, admits he 'made a ricket' in the transfer market the previous season when a West Ham side full of foreign players only narrowly avoided relegation to Division One. 'Raducioiu was more interested in whether he could get his dog into the country than playing for West Ham,' he claimed.

● 'ARRY, as he is universally known, had to break the West Ham bank to keep his beloved Irons up. He splashed out a club record £3.2 million on John Hartson and another £2.3 million on Paul Kitson in the spring of 1997. The pair immediately formed a deadly strikeforce and their combined tally of 13 goals saved the Hammers.

● AS A PLAYER Redknapp made over 250 appearances for West Ham and Bournemouth (where he began his managerial career). His son, Jamie, plays for Liverpool.

Jamie 'Snozzle' Redknapp, Liverpool's baby-faced England midfielder, tries out a prototype nose-strip breathing enhancer

JAMIE REDKNAPP

Born: Barton 25.6.73
Height: 5ft 11ins Position: Midfielder
Club career:
1990–91 Bournemouth: 13 (0)
1991– Liverpool 179 (19)
International record:
1995– England 8 (0)

JAMIE REDKNAPP – son of West Ham manager Harry – must be one of the unluckiest players ever. Whenever he seems to be on the verge of great things for England he gets injured. During Euro '96 he suffered a serious ankle injury after coming on as a substitute against Scotland, then he had to pull out of the initial squad for France '98 with a knee injury.

● REDKNAPP MADE his England debut against Colombia on 6th September 1995, and forced one of the most bizarre saves of all time, when Rene Higuita 'scorpion kicked' his shot back into play.

● REDKNAPP WAS Bournemouth's most lucrative sale when he transferred to Liverpool for £350,000 in 1990, despite having started only six matches for the south coast club.

● THE BABY-FACED midfielder – reputedly the best-looking player at Liverpool – is sent a huge amount of fan mail (sometimes including pairs of knickers), mainly by female supporters, despite his marriage to pop singer Louise.

REFEREES AND LINESMEN

THE ONLY REFEREE ever to score a goal in a first class game in Britain was the unfortunate Ivan Robinson. Refereeing a match between Barrow and Plymouth Argyle in 1968, he inadvertently deflected a Plymouth cross past Barrow keeper Pat Dunne from 15 yards… leaving him with no option but to signal a goal. It turned out to be the winner!

● REFEREES HAVE to put up with plenty of abuse, but in 1912 William Ernest Williams was attacked and killed in the dressing rooms after a match between Wattstown and Aberaman Athletic in South Wales. His attacker was later jailed for manslaughter.

● THE FIRST referee to send a player off in an FA Cup Final was Peter Willis, who gave Manchester United's Kevin Moran his marching orders in 1985 for a tackle on Everton's Peter Reid. Video replays showed it was a harsh decision.

● IN PERU there is often violence on the pitch, but a referee and a linesman came to blows in an amazing incident in 1974. It happened in a league match in Chimbote when referee Alipio Montejo awarded a goal which the linesman Gonzalo Morote had flagged offside. The linesman ran on the pitch, a heated argument started, and punches ensued. For once the players had to separate referee and linesman instead of it being the other way around.

DON REVIE

Born: Middlesbrough 10.7.27
Died: 26.5.89

THE LATE Don Revie made Leeds United the best team in England, and one of the most feared in Europe, in the late 1960s and early 70s, although the team finished runners-up far more than winners.

● REVIE INHERITED a side that was threatened with relegation to the Third Division in 1961, and made them League Champions in 1969, repeating the feat in 1974. The hallmark of his side was team spirit, epitomised by the backbone of his side – defender Jack Charlton, Billy Bremner, Norman Hunter and Johnny Giles.

● REVIE IS the only Leeds manager to have guided the team to European success, taking the club to Fairs Cup wins in 1968 and 1971. His only stab at the European Cup ended in heartbreak, however, as Leeds fell to Celtic in the semi-final in 1970, in front of 133,000 fans, the biggest crowd ever to watch a European Cup tie.

● REVIE BECAME England manager in 1974, but early success turned to failure as his team failed to qualify for the 1978 World Cup. He resigned from the England job after pulling out of a team tour to negotiate a secret deal to manage the United Arab Emirates... making him just about the most unpopular man in Britain for a while.

● AS A PLAYER, Revie was a fine deep-lying centre-forward who helped Manchester City win the FA Cup in 1956. He was voted Footballer of the Year in 1955, and Manager of the Year on three separate occasions.

LUIGI RIVA

Born: Leggiuno 7.11.44
Club career:
1960–63 Legnano
1963–74 Cagliari
International record:
1965–74 Italy 42 (35)

'GIGI' RIVA scored 35 international goals for Italy, more than any other player before or since. His strike rate was phenomenal – he hit his goals in only 42 games – but tragically two broken legs shortened his illustrious career.

● LEFT-FOOTED Riva was signed by Cagliari in 1963 from Third Division Legnano. The club came from nowhere to eventually win the Scudetto in 1969/70, one of three seasons that 'the Rumble of Thunder' (as he became known) finished top scorer in Serie A. It remains the only major trophy the Sardinian side has ever won.

● RIVA PLAYED a big part in plotting Italy's course to the 1970 World Cup Final, scoring twice against Mexico and once against West Germany. He couldn't do anything, however, about the Brazilians, who whomped The Azzurri 4–1 in the final.

ROBERTO RIVELINO

Born: Brazil 1.1.46
Position: Midfielder
Club career:
Corinthians
Fluminense
International record:
1965–78 Brazil 94 (26)

FAMOUS FOR his shooting ability, Roberto Rivelino scored what was then the quickest recorded goal in world football. After three seconds of a Brazilian league match in the 1970s he hit the ball over the head of the opposition keeper straight from the kick-off... the goalkeeper was still praying when he struck his shot!

● RIVELINO'S international career for Brazil spanned 13 years, in which time he competed in three World Cup tournaments: 1970, 1974 and 1978. He has represented his country more times than any other player bar two, scoring a total of 26 goals.

● ONE OF RIVELINO's greatest strengths lay in his dead-ball kicking. He could bend the ball amazingly, making an art form of what became known as 'the banana shot'. One of the best examples was the goal he scored from a free-kick in the 1974 World Cup against East Germany, which curled over a ducking teammate who'd ingratiated himself into the wall.

RIVER PLATE

Year founded: 1901
Ground: Monumental, Buenos Aires (76,000)
League wins: 18
Colours: White shirts with red diagonal sash, black shorts, white socks

RIVER PLATE are the most successful ever Argentinian club side, having won a total of 26 major trophies in their long and illustrious history. The highlight of that history came as recently as 1986 when they won the World Club Cup, the South American Copa Libertadores, the Inter-American Cup and the Argentine League Championship in the same year, a unique and unprecedented quadruple.

● RIVER PLATE won the World Club Cup by beating Romanian European Cup holders Steaua Bucharest 1–0 in Tokyo on 14th December 1986. The side that won the tournament included the likes of internationals Pumpido, Ruggeri and Gallego.

● BACK IN ARGENTINA, however, the most respected River Plate side was that of the 1940s, whose forward line – which starred Muñoz, Moreno, Pedernera, Labruna and Loustau – was nicknamed La Maquina or 'the Machine'.

Roll of Honour

Argentinian League champions 1932, 1936, 1937, 1941, 1942, 1945, 1947, 1952, 1953, 1955, 1956, 1957, 1975, 1979, 1980, 1986, 1990, 1992, 1995
Argentinian National champions 1975, 1979, 1981
Copa Libertadores 1986, 1996, 1998
World Club Cup 1986
Inter-American Cup 1986

Did You Know?

On October 9th 1982 Bournemouth manager Harry Redknapp, who hadn't played League football for six years, played himself at number 7 during an injury crisis. Bournemouth won the game 3-1. West Ham fans take note.

Dead-ball specialist Roberto Rivelino is granted another banana shot free-kick opportunity in the 1970 World Cup Final

GIANNI RIVERA

Born: Alessandria 18.8.43
Club career:
Alessandria
AC Milan
International record:
Italy 60 (14)

GIANNI RIVERA, nicknamed 'the Golden Boy' of Italian soccer, was one of the youngest players ever to play Serie A football when he made his debut for Alessandria in 1958 at the tender age of 15. AC Milan almost immediately paid an incredible £65,000 for a half share in the gifted teenager, before snapping him up completely.

● RIVERA PROVED something of a bargain. The graceful attacking midfielder, who scored 14 goals for his country in 60 appearances, won two European Cups with Milan as well as two European Cup Winners' Cups and a host of domestic trophies for the Rossoneri.

● RIVERA BECAME only the second Italian-based player to win the European Player of the Year Award in 1969. A year later he appeared in the World Cup Final – but only, controversially, as substitute for the last six minutes during Italy's 4–1 mauling by Brazil.

BOBBY ROBSON

Born: Sacriston, Co. Durham 18.2.33

WITH BOBBY ROBSON England won more World Cup matches than under any other manager since the legendary Sir Walter Winterbottom.

● HE GUIDED the country to the World Cup finals in Mexico 86, where they reached the quarter-finals, and to Italia 90, where they got to the semis. He was quite easily the most successful England manager since Alf Ramsey, yet he was much maligned by the tabloid press.

● THE PINNACLE of Robson's internat-ional career was also, in many ways, the low point: England's semi-final exit to Germany in Italia 90. As in Euro 96, the Germans needed a penalty shoot-out to get to the final instead of England.

● ROBSON WAS best known for his astute management of Ipswich Town before he took the England post. He guided the modest East Anglian club to FA Cup victory in 1978 and UEFA Cup victory in 1981, making them one of the best sides in the land.

● AFTER RESIGNING as England manager Robson took over at PSV Eindhoven, who he guided to two consecutive championships, before moving on to Sporting Lisbon, Porto, where he also won two, and Barcelona, where he won the Spanish Cup and the European Cup Winners Cup in 1997. Then after spending a year as Barca's Director of Football, Robson returned to PSV in the summer of 1998.

● ROBSON MADE his league debut with Fulham in 1951, moving to West Bromwich Albion five years later, before returning to Craven Cottage in 1962. He had a great start to his England career, scoring twice in a 4–0 Wembley win over France in 1957. The following year he played three games in the World Cup in Sweden, when England failed to qualify for the 2nd Round.

BRYAN ROBSON

Born: Chester-Le-Street 11.1.57
Height: 5ft 10ins Position: Midfielder
Club career:
1971–81 West Bromwich Albion 198 (39)
1981–94 Manchester United 345 (74)
1994– Middlesbrough 24 (1)
International record:
1980–92 England 90 (26)

BRYAN ROBSON, current Middlesbrough manager, is still best known for his inspirational midfield performances for Manchester United and England... for which he earned the nickname 'Captain Marvel'.

● ROBSON, though, may have to wait a while before he becomes known as 'Manager Marvel'. His up-and-down spell in the Boro hotseat has seen promotion to the Premiership (twice), relegation from the top flight (once) and three Wembley Cup finals (Coca Cola Cup finals in 1997 and 1998, and one FA Cup Final, in 1997) which were all lost.

● ROBSON's move from West Bromwich Albion to Manchester United on 1st October 1981 broke the British transfer record. He set United back a cool £1.5 million, but turned out to be worth every ha'penny.

● ROBSON IS the fifth most capped Englishman of all time: in his 90 matches he scored 26 goals, which puts him eighth in the top 10 goalscorers for his country.

● DURING THE 1982 World Cup match against France, Robson scored what was then thought to be the quickest ever goal in the World Cup finals, after just 27 seconds. However, FIFA recently discovered that in fact Czech player Vaclav Masek had scored v Mexico in 1962 after just 15 seconds.

● IN 1993 Robson finally won his first championship medal at Manchester United, to add to the League Cup, three FA Cup and European Cup Winners' Cup medals he'd already got on his mantelpiece. A year later he became player-manager of Middlesbrough, where he won the First Division Championship in his first season in charge.

ROCHDALE

Year founded: 1907
Ground: Spotland (9,223)
Highest ever crowd: 24,231, 10th December 1949 v Notts County (FA Cup rd 2)
Nickname: The Dale
Colours: Blue shirts, blue shorts, blue socks

ROCHDALE's finest moment came in 1962 when the club reached the final of the League Cup. The Dale lost to Norwich 4–0 on aggregate, but remain the only side to reach the final of a major competition while languishing in the basement division. This was also the first major cup final not to feature a top flight club (Norwich were in Division Two).

● ROCHDALE hold the record for the longest spell without a victory in the FA Cup. Between November 1927 and November 1945 (a run spanning 13 matches), the club failed to win a single match in the famous competition... that's a staggering 18 years of cup misery!

● AT ONE POINT during this period – in 1931 – Rochdale recorded 13 consecutive home defeats. They finished the season with only four wins, although in 1973/74 they won just two matches all season... a Division Three record.

● ROCHDALE are one of just seven English League clubs who have never supplied a full international.

Partly because of his fearless tackling, Bryan Robson's playing career was plagued by injury. He is pictured here dropping out of the 1986 World Cup in Mexico with a dislocated shoulder

R

ROMANIA

First international: Romania 2 Yugoslavia 1 (Belgrade, 1922)
First World Cup appearance: Romania 3 Peru 1 (Uruguay, 1930)
Highest capped player: Georghe Hagi (108)
Highest goalscorer: Georghe Hagi (32)
Best win: 9-0 v Finland, 1973
Worst defeat: 0-9 v Hungary, 1948
Colours: Yellow shirts, yellow shorts, yellow socks

Romania are the only country – apart from Italy – to have been knocked out of consecutive World Cups on penalties. In 1990 the Balkan side lost to the Republic of Ireland on spot-kicks and four years later they suffered more sudden death misery at the hands of Sweden in the quarter-finals.

● In 1930 Romania played in front of the smallest crowd ever to watch a match at the World Cup finals. Only 300 people turned up to watch their match against Peru in the Uruguayan capital, Montevideo. The lack of atmosphere didn't seem to bother the Romanians, however, as they won the game 3-1.

● Having beaten England at France '98 the entire Romanian team bleached their hair in celebration at qualifying for the next round. It seemed to sap their powers, however, for the blond bombshells could only draw with Tunisia in their final group game and then lost 1-0 to Croatia in the second round.

WORLD CUP RECORD

1930 Round 1	1970 Round 1
1934 Round 1	1974 Did not qualify
1938 Round 1	1978 Did not qualify
1950 Did not enter	1982 Did not qualify
1954 Did not qualify	1986 Did not qualify
1958 Did not qualify	1990 Round 2
1962 Did not enter	1994 Quarter-finals
1966 Did not qualify	1998 Round 2

ROMARIO

Born: Rio de Janeiro, Brazil 29.1.66
Club career:
1985–89 Vasco da Gama (Brazil)
1989–93 PSV Eindhoven
1993–95 Barcelona
1995– Flamengo (Brazil)
International record:
1988– Brazil 62 (43)

THE HIGHLIGHT of headstrong Brazilian striker Romario's career so far has been the World Cup 1994 when he was, alongside Italy's Roberto Baggio, the player of the tournament, scoring five crucial goals to take Brazil to the final against Italy. Having been recalled to the squad for the 1998 tournament in France, however, the star striker was forced to tearfully pull out on the eve of the tournament through injury.

● ROMARIO – real name Romario da Souza Faria – first caught the world's eye when he starred in the 1988 Seoul Olympics. Again his goals helped Brazil to a final, but despite putting his country ahead against Russia, they lost in extra time.

● ROMARIO WENT on to play at PSV Eindhoven, where he won three championships in five seasons, scoring a total of 98 goals before moving onto Barcelona in 1993. He helped Barça win the league title in 1994, but could do nothing to stop Italian giants Milan mauling the Catalans 4–0 in the European Cup that year. After USA 94 he moved back to Brazil to play for Flamengo.

RONALDO

Born: Rio De Janeiro 22.9.76
Ht: 6ft Position: Striker
Club career:
1991–93 Sao Cristovao 54 (36)
1993–94 Cruzerio (Brazil) 60 (58)
1994–96 PSV Eindhoven (Holland) 56 (55)
1996–97 Barcelona (Spain) 36 (34)
1997–98 Inter Milan 32 (25)
International record:
1993– Brazil 42 (30)

BRAZILIAN SENSATION RONALDO is the world's most famous footballer. Blessed with incredible speed, balance and skill he is the most devastating striker in the game... which is why Inter Milan paid a then world record £18 million to sign him in 1997.

● Fame has its price, however, and the pressures of superstardom became too much for the Brazil number 9 at France 98. Having fired his team to the World Cup final with four goals, he was rushed to hospital on the day of the match suffering what some have claimed was a stress-related fit. The rest is history.

● Ronaldo has been voted FIFA World Player of the Year for 1997 and 1998 (the only man to win the award two years in a row) and 1997 European Player of the Year in recognition of his supreme talent which has also earned him a multi-million pund tie-up with sportswear giants Nike.

● He moved from Brazil to PSV Eindhoven in Holland in 1994 (after being picked for the USA 94 World Cup squad aged 18) for a club record £ 5 million, and in 1996 Barcelona splashed out a then world record £13 million to take him to the Nou Camp. There he scored an amazing 34 goals in 36 league games and won the Spanish Cup and European Cup Winners Cup. In 1998 he won the UEFA Cup with Inter, scoring in the final against Lazio.

ROSS COUNTY

Year founded: 1929
Ground: Victoria Park, Dingwall (5,400)
Highest ever crowd: 10,600, 28th February 1966 v Rangers (Scottish Cup rd 2)
Nickname: The County
Colours: Navy blue shirts, white shorts, red socks

SCOTLAND's northenmost club, set in the scenic Highland town of Dingwall in the shadow of Ben Wyvis, Ross County were elected to the Scottish League in 1994 after 65 years in the Highland League.

● THE CLUB was formed in 1929 and its scenic Victoria Park ground was built in Jubilee Park between the local jail (of which only the watchtowers now remain), Dingwall Station and a caravan park.

● THE CLUB's record crowd is the 10,600 one which crammed its way into the ground in September 1966 for the Scottish Cup 2nd round match against Rangers (which Rangers won 2–0), the proceeds of which were spent on the 319-seater main stand, which still stands today.

● ROSS COUNTY's record win was an 11–0 thrashing of St. Cuthbert Wanderers in the Scottish Cup in December 1993, and their record defeat came in the Highland League when they were beaten 10–1 by Inverness Thistle.

Ronaldo, here shown in Brazil kit, is the world's most famous (and stressed out?) player

PAOLO ROSSI

Born: Prato, Italy 23.9.56
Position: Forward
Club career:
Prato
Juventus
Como
Lanerossi
Vicenza
Perugia
Juventus
AC Milan
International record:
1977–86 Italy 46 (20)

PAOLO ROSSI burst onto the world stage when he became the highest scorer in the Spain 82 World Cup Tournament, with six crucial goals as Italy stormed to their third World Cup triumph.

● PROVINCIAL PERUGIA shocked football when they paid a then world record £3.5 million to buy Rossi from Vicenza in 1979. A player with one of the most up and down histories of any footballer, however, it wasn't long before Rossi was banned from football for his part in the biggest match-fixing scandal ever to rock Italy (and there have been a few!).

● ROSSI HAD only played three post-ban matches when he exploded back onto the World Cup scene (he had played in Argentina in 1978) in Spain. His comeback was truly complete when he was made European Footballer of the Year to complete an annus mirabilis in 1982.

● HE RETIRED from football at the tender age of 29, and moved to his beloved Spain where, strangely, he became a scout for the national team. With 20 goals he is Italy's ninth highest scorer ever.

ROTHERHAM UNITED

Year founded: 1884
Ground: Millmoor (11,533)
Highest ever crowd: 25,000,
13th December 1952 v Sheffield United (Div 2)
Colours: Red shirts with white sleeves, white shorts and white socks

ROTHERHAM have never appeared in the top flight, but they only missed out on promotion to the First Division in 1955 on goal difference. It was the best period in the club's history, and six years later (in 1961) they reached the first ever final of the League Cup, losing 3–2 on aggregate to Aston Villa after extra time in the second leg.

● THE CLUB holds the record for the biggest away win ever in the Fourth Division, set on 8th September 1973 when they thrashed Crewe Alexandra 8–1 at Gresty Road.

● THIS ISN'T Rotherham's best victory, however. That record was set by the 8–0 thrashing of Oldham in 1947 in the Third Division (North). The club's worst defeat came in the same division in 1928, an 11–1 humiliation inflicted by Bradford City.

● ROTHERHAM's most capped player is striker Shaun Goater, with 18 appearances for Bermuda!

Paulo Rossi on his way to becoming top scorer in the 1982 World Cup

Roll of Honour

Div 3 (N) champions 1951
Div 3 champions 1981
Div 4 champions 1989
Auto Windscreens Shield 1996

SIR STANLEY ROUS

Born: Watford 25.4 1895   Died: 18.2.86

STANLEY ROUS – who in 1934 was elected Secretary of the FA and in 1961 became the most powerful man in football as President of FIFA – was also a well respected referee who took charge of the 1934 FA Cup Final and no fewer than 36 international matches. Before that he had played in goal for Lowestoft!

● THE VISIONARY Rous made many improvements to the game, changing the way referees and linesmen controlled matches, introducing yellow and red cards and altering the look of the pitch by adding arcs on the penalty area and in the corners.

● HE ALSO designed the simplified set of 17 rules that dictate how modern football is played. He did much to encourage international tournaments, modern methods of coaching and the growth of the world game.

● ROUS – who was knighted for his services to football in 1949 – became honorary Life President of FIFA when he retired as President in 1974, and in 1975 he became the first person to receive the Sports Writers annual award for services to sport.

Did You Know?

In 1990 Dino Zoff was sacked as Juventus manager – after winning the UEFA Cup and Italian Cup for the club!

IAN RUSH

Born: St. Asaph 20.10.61
Height: 6ft 0ins   Position: Striker
Club career:
1978–80 Chester 34 (14)
1980–87 Liverpool 182 (109)
1987–88 Juventus 29 (7)
1988–96 Liverpool 287 (124)
1996–97 Leeds United 36 (3)
1997– Newcastle United 10 (0)
International record:
1980– Wales 73 (28)

IAN RUSH has scored more goals in FA Cup Finals – a total of five, all for Liverpool – than any other man. He scored two in 1986 against Everton, two as substitute against Everton in 1989 and one in 1992 against Sunderland... ending up on the winning side on each occasion.

● RUSH is also the top scorer (post war) in the FA Cup with 43 goals and equal top scorer (with Geoff Hurst) in the League Cup with 46.

● HE IS LIVERPOOL's second highest scorer, coming just 12 short of Roger Hunt's record of 245 with 233 league goals. He does hold the Liverpool record for the most goals in a single season, however, after he netted 47 in all competitions in 1983/84.

● RUSH TOPS the all-time goalscoring charts for his native Wales, having notched 28 goals for his country in 73 appearances. He is also the fourth most capped Welshman in history.

● THE ONE LOWPOINT in his career came in 1987 after he moved, for a club record £2.9 million fee, from Liverpool to Juventus, where he was expected to replace Michel Platini. He only managed to **score seven goals all season and came back home after a year. 'It was like being in a foreign country out there,' he complained.**

RUSSIA (formerly SOVIET UNION)

First international: Russia 1 Finland 2 (Stockholm, 1908)
First World Cup appearance: USSR 2 England 2 (Sweden, 1958)
Highest capped player: Oleg Blokhin (Soviet Union 109)
Highest goalscorer: Oleg Blokhin (Soviet Union 39)
Best win: 11–1 v India, 1952 (Soviet Union)
Worst defeat: 0–16 v Germany, 1912 (Russia)
Colours: White shirts, blue shorts, red socks

RUSSIA MADE an appalling hash of their first international fixtures back in 1912/13, losing their first five on the trot, scoring just two goals and conceding 43.

● HOWEVER, playing as the USSR they were the first team to win the European Championship (in 1960). With the legendary Lev Yashin in goal they beat Hungary, Czechoslovakia and then Yugoslavia 2–1 in the final, to take the title.

● YASHIN WAS also in the 1956 Soviet side that won Olympic gold, again beating Yugoslavia in the final. The Soviets repeated their Olympic triumph in 1988, this time beating Brazil 2–1 in the final. Only Hungary, with three victories, have won the Olympic title more times than Russia.

● RUSSIA (and the Soviet Union) have always flattered to deceive in the World Cup, however, and have never reached the final. The closest they came was getting to the semis in 1966, before being knocked out by eventual runners-up West Germany.

● IN 1958 Eduard Strelitsov was withdrawn from the USSR World Cup team to serve a 12-year prison sentence. He was later freed and became Russian Player of the Year in 1967.

WORLD CUP RECORD

1930–54	Did not enter	1990	Round 1
1958	Quarter-finals	1994	Round 1
1962	Quarter-finals	1998	Did not qualify
1966	Fourth place		
1970	Quarter-finals		
1974	Withdrew		
1978	Did not qualify		
1982	Round 2		
1986	Round 2		

Ian Rush models Liverpool's worst ever kit

SACKINGS

IN 1959 Bill Lambton was sacked as manager of Scunthorpe United after just three days in charge, an English league record. His reign in the Old Showground hot seat took in just one match – a 3–0 defeat at Liverpool in a Second Division encounter.

● TOMMY DOCHERTY has been sacked more times than any other manager, and is one of the few gaffers to have been dismissed from the same job twice. In 1968 The Doc was ordered to clear his desk at QPR after just 29 days, and his second spell at Loftus Road in 1979 ended equally unhappily after a year.

● STOCKPORT COUNTY have sacked more managers since the war than any other club. The Second Division outfit have made 27 different managerial appointments since 1945, an average of one every two years. Their longest-serving manager in that period – Danny Bergara, appointed in 1989 – was shown the door in 1995 after exchanging punches with the Stockport chairman at a club dinner.

● FORMER WEST BROM manager Johnny Giles once said 'the only certainty about management is the sack'.

● GILES may well be right, but managers at West Ham certainly get a good run for their money before they receive their P45 form. The Hammers have only had seven managers since the second world war, fewer than any other league club. He may not realise it, but lucky Harry Redknapp has probably got the safest job in football!

IAN ST. JOHN

Born: Motherwell 7.6.38
Height: 5ft 7ins Position: Forward
Club career:
1957–61 Motherwell (80)
1961–71 Liverpool 336 (95)
1971–72 Coventry City 18 (3)
1972 Tranmere Rovers 9 (1)
International record:
1959–65 Scotland 21 (9)

IAN ST. JOHN began his career at Motherwell, where he once scored a hat-trick in just two and half minutes – the fastest ever in Scottish football.

● WHEN ST. JOHN signed for Liverpool from Motherwell in 1961 for £35,000 he became the Anfield club's most expensive player. In his first season 'the Saint' contributed 18 goals as Liverpool won the Second Division.

● IN 1965 St. John scored the winning goal in the FA Cup final, as Liverpool beat Leeds 2–1 to lift the trophy for the first ever time. In all, St. John played 419 games for The Reds, scoring 118 goals.

● SINCE RETIRING from the game, St. John has built a successful career as a television sports presenter and football pundit, usually as the serious half of a double act with the wisecracking Jimmy Greaves.

ST. JOHNSTONE

Year founded: 1884
Ground: McDiarmid Park, Perth (10,721)
Highest ever crowd: 10,504, 20th October 1990 v Rangers (Premier Div)
Nickname: The Saints
Colours: Royal blue shirts, white shorts, royal blue socks

ST. JOHNSTONE enjoyed their record victory in 1946, crushing Albion Rovers 9–0 in a Scottish League Cup match. Saints' worst defeat was back in 1903, when they were beaten 10–1 by Third Lanark in the Scottish Cup.

● NOBODY HAS scored more goals for St. Johnstone than John Brogan. Between 1977–83 he found the back of the net 114 times. The club's record appearance maker is Drew Rutherford, who turned out for The Saints in 298 matches.

● BACK IN 1982 a young Ally McCoist left McDiarmond Park for Sunderland for £400,000 – a record fee for a player leaving the club until Scott Booth's £750,000 transfer to Aberdeen in 1994.

Roll of Honour

First Division champions 1983, 1990, 1997
Second Division champions 1988
Div 2 champions 1924, 1960, 1963

ST. MIRREN

Year founded: 1877
Ground: Love Street, Paisley (12,000)
Highest ever crowd: 47,438 20th August 1949 v Celtic (Scottish League Cup)
Nickname: The Buddies
Colours: Black-and-white-halved shirts, white shorts, white socks

ST. MIRREN gave Glasgow University a football lesson in 1960, drubbing the students 15–0 in the Scottish Cup. The score remains a record for The Buddies. Their worst defeat was inflicted by Rangers – a 0–9 thrashing back in 1897.

● FORMER MANAGER Tony Fitzpatrick is St. Mirren's longest-serving player, appearing in 351 matches between 1973–88. David McCrae, a striker from the pre-war era, is the club's leading scorer with 221 goals.

● IN 1986 St. Mirren player Billy Abercromby was shown the red card a record three times in one game – the first time for a playing offence and twice more for dissent. He was banned, fined, and put on the transfer list, but he was stubborn to say the least and a year later led the club to a famous Scottish Cup triumph.

Roll of Honour

First Division champions 1977
Div 2 champions 1968
Scottish Cup 1926, 1959, 1987
Anglo-Scottish Cup 1980

MARCELO SALAS

Born: 24.12.74
Height: 1.73 metres
Position: Striker
Club career:
1994–96 Universidad de Chile 63 (50)
1996–98 River Plate 25 (17)
1998– Lazio
International record:
Chile 40 (25)

MARCELO SALAS' £13 million transfer from River Plate to Lazio in the summer of 1998 was the second biggest deal between a South American and a European club - only beaten by the world record £21.5 million Real Betis paid Sao Paulo for Denilson.

● SALAS' VALUE soared after he scored one of the greatest goals ever seen at Wembley in February 1998. Playing in a friendly away to England the Chilean controlled a long pass from Jose Luis Sierra on his thigh before swivelling to smash a left-foot volley past Nigel Martyn.

● FOR GOOD MEASURE he also fired home from the penalty spot to become the first player to score twice against England at Wembley since West Germany's Karl-Heinz Rummenigge in 1982.

● SALAS MADE a blistering start to France '98 with a brace of goals against Italy in Chile's opening match, and added to that with a score against Austria to head, for a short while, the Golden Boot table.

MATTHIAS SAMMER

Born Dresden 5.9.67
Ht: 5ft 9ins Position: Defender
Club career:
1985–90 Dynamo Dresden 102 (39)
1990–92 VFB Stuttgart 63 (20)
1992–93 Inter Milan 11 (4)
1993– Borussia Dortmund 125 (22)
International career
1988–90 East Germany 23 (6)
1990– Germany 51 (8)

IN 1997 Matthias Sammer became the fifth German, but the first from the former East Germany, to be voted European Footballer of the Year. It capped a fine 18 months for the man rated the world's best sweeper after he helped Germany to win Euro 96 and then captained his club, Borussia Dortmund, to their first ever European Cup victory when they beat Juventus 3-1 in Munich. However, having missed most of the following season with an ankle injury, Sammer was unable to appear at the World Cup in France.

● DURING THE previous two seasons the elegant yet ruthless defender with an eye for attack had skippered Dortmund to two successive Bundesliga titles (1995 and 1996) and had been voted Germany's Footballer of the Year at the end of both campaigns.

● SAMMER began his career with Dynamo Dresden in his native East Germany, where he won two league titles (1989 and 1990) before moving to VFB Stuttgart, where he won the Bundesliga for the first time (1992). After playing just 11 games for Inter Milan he returned to Germany in 1993 for the start of a highly succesful spell at Dortmund.

● IN 1990 he became the first East German to play for the new united Germany national team.

SAN MARINO

First international: San Marino 0 Switzerland 4 (San Marino, 1990)
Colours: Sky blue shirts, sky blue shorts, sky blue socks

WITH A POPULATION of just 22,000, San Marino is the smallest member of UEFA. The tiny country became a member in 1988 and entered the 1992 European Championships.

● IN 1993 San Marino scored the fastest ever goal in the history of the World Cup when Davide Gualtieri pounced on a weak Stuart Pearce back pass to shock England with a goal after just nine seconds in a qualifier for USA 94.

SAUDI ARABIA

First World Cup appearance:
Saudi Arabia 1 Holland 2 (USA, 1994)
Highest capped player: Majed Abdullah (147)
Colours: Green shirts, white shorts, green socks

SAUDI ARABIA made a great start to their World Cup career at USA '94 beating both Belgium and Morocco, before narrowly losing to eventual semi-finalists Sweden in the second round.

● ONE OF THE STARS of the 1994 side was Sayeed al-Owairan, the 'Desert Maradona', who scored the winner against Belgium following a mazy 60-yard dribble. The following year, though, al-Owairan was caught at an illicit drinks party and under Saudi Arabia's strict Islamic law he was jailed for six months.

● SAUDI ARABIA'S Majed Abdullah is the most capped footballer in world football. He made an incredible 147 appearances for his country in an international career that lasted from 1978 to 1994.

● DESPITE going through seven coaches in four years, Saudi Arabia qualified for France '98 where they were led by Carlos Alberto Parreira,

Brazil's World Cup-winning coach from 1994. Parreira, however, was sacked after first round defeats by Denmark and France and the Saudi's went home with a solitary point under their belts after a lucky 2–2 draw with South Africa.

WORLD CUP RECORD

1930-74	Did not enter	1994	Round 2
1978-90	Did not qualify	1998	Round 1

SANTOS

Year founded: 1912
Ground: Vila Belmiro (20,000)
League wins: 5
Colours: White shirts, white shorts, white socks

SANTOS were the first team to retain the World Club Championship. In 1962 they beat Benfica 8–4 on aggregate, thanks in part to an oustanding Pele hat-trick in a 5–2 win in Lisbon. The following year the Brazilians beat Milan 1–0 in a Rio play-off, watched by 125,000 spectators.

● IN 1933 Santos became only the second Brazilian club to go professional, 17 years after joining the São Paulo state championship. The club's heyday, though, was in the late 1950s and early 60s, when a side built around the legendary Pele beat Penarol of Uruguay and Boca Juniors of Argentina to win the Copa Libertadores final in successive years.

● SANTOS were one of the first clubs to realise the earning power of world tours. Trading on the name of Pele, the club often played two or three exhibition matches a week in the 1960s.

● SANTOS is the only Brazilian club that Pele ever played for (the great man only playing for New York Cosmos in the latter stages of his career).

SCARBOROUGH

Year founded: 1879
Ground: McCain Stadium (7,500)
Highest ever crowd: 11,130, 8th January 1938 v Luton Town (FA Cup rd 3)
Colours: White shirts with red and green band, white shorts, white socks

SCARBOROUGH were the first club to be promoted automatically from the Vauxhall Conference to the Football League. In 1987 Boro' replaced Lincoln City in the old Fourth Division.

● THE OLDEST PLAYER to turn out for Scarborough is evergreen goalkeeper John Burridge, who was less than a month short of his 42nd birthday when he played against Doncaster Rovers in 1993.

● SCARBOROUGH's record win was a 6–0 hammering of Rhyl in 1930 in the FA Cup. The club's worst defeat was against Northern League outfit Southbank who stuffed them 16–1 in 1919.

● AMAZINGLY THE CLUB recorded their record league win in their first month as a Football League club, a 4-0 hammering of Bolton on August 29th 1987.

● IAN IRONSIDE is Boro's record appearance-maker, playing in 183 league games between 1988 and 1997.

Roll of Honour

Vauxhall Conference champions 1987

PETER SCHMEICHEL

Born: Gladsaxe, Denmark 18.11.63
Height: 6ft 4ins Position: Goalkeeper
Club career:
1983–91 Brondby (Denmark)
1991– Manchester United 266
International record:
1987– Denmark 93

PETER SCHMEICHEL is now Denmark's most capped player of all time. During the France 98 World Cup the giant goalkeeper – regarded by many as being the best in the world – earned his 105th cap for his country.

● THE HIGHLIGHT of Schmeichel's international career undoubtedly came in 1992 when, having tasted disappointment in the European Championship qualifiers, Denmark sneaked in through the back door after the withdrawal of Yugoslavia, and won the tournament – beating Germany in the final.

● WITH MANCHESTER UNITED he has picked up plenty of honours at domestic level too: in all he has won four league titles and two FA Cups with United since he joined the club from Brondby in 1991 for £550,000 (including the league and cup double twice (1993/94 and 1995/96).

● AS WELL as earning much silverware in his time at United, Schmeichel has gained an authentic-sounding Manc accent, which he uses to yell at his defenders in times of crisis.

● IN THE 1995/96 UEFA Cup he became the first goalkeeper to head a goal for an English club in European competition when he came up for a corner, rose above the opposition defence (and his own attack!) to score against Russian side Rotor Volgograd. Unfortunately for United, though, they were still knocked out.

PAUL SCHOLES

Born: Salford 16.11.74.
Height: 5ft 7in
Position: Midfielder/Striker
Club career:
1994– Manchester United 98 (26)
International career:
1997– England 11 (4)

JACK-IN-THE-BOX goal poacher Paul Scholes made one of the most impressive full England debuts of recent times when he played against Italy in Le Tournoi in June 1997. The carrot-topped youngster, who can play in midfield or attack, scored one and laid on another for Ian Wright as England won 2-0.

● HE CONTINUED his 'duck-to-water' start to international football by scoring the vital opener in the 4-0 Wembley defeat of Moldova in a France '98 qualifier in September 1997. He immediately made an impression on the World Cup '98 tournament with a match-clinching goal against Tunisia, an edge-of-the-box shot-on-the-turn which had the world sitting up and taking notice. Scholes was impressive throughout England's French campaign, so much so that the tabloid papers practically stopped mentioning Paul Gascoigne, who he replaced in the team, once the tournament had begun.

● IN A RELATIVELY brief club career Scholes has enjoyed phenomenal success. In 1996 he was a part of Manchester United's 'double Double' winning side and he picked up another Premiership winners' medal in 1997.

SCOTLAND

First international: Scotland 0 England 0 (Glasgow, 1872)
First World Cup appearance: Scotland 0 Austria 1 (Switzerland, 1954)
Highest capped player: Kenny Dalglish (102)
Highest goalscorers: Denis Law, Kenny Dalglish (30)
Best win: 9–0 v Wales, 1878
Worst defeat: 7–0 v Uruguay, 1954
Colours: Blue shirts, white shorts and red socks

SCOTLAND hold the unenviable record of being the country who have qualified for the most World Cup Finals tournament (a total of nine) without ever having made it through to the second round.

● THE SCOTS first qualified in 1950, but were withdrawn from the competition by the Scottish FA. They also qualified in 1954, 1959, 1974, 1978, 1982, 1986, 1990 and 1998 but despite several close calls never managed to

WORLD CUP RECORD

1930–38	Did not ente	974	Round 1
1950	Withdrew	78	Round 1
1954	Round 1	82	Round 1
1958	Round 1	[illegible]	Round 1
1962	Did not qualify	0	Round 1
		94	Did not qualify

John Collins demonstrates his newly learnt Gallic shrug while controlling the ball

beat their postcards home. In their latest attempt, at France 1998, they finished bottom of their group with a single point after losing to Brazil (2-1) and Morocco (3-0) and drawing with Norway.

● SCOTLAND have fared even worse in the European Championships, only managing to qualify for the first time in 1992, and repeating the feat in 1996. Again, however, they have never got past the first stage, coming closest in Euro 96 when a late Patrick Kluivert goal in Holland's match against England put them out on the 'goals scored' rule.

● SCOTLAND ARE, along with England, the oldest international team in the world. The two played the first official international fixture back in 1872, which they drew 0–0. Since then honours have been pretty even between the 'Auld Enemies', with England winning 44 matches, Scotland winning 40 and 20 ending in a draw.

● SCOTLAND's most humiliating match took place at Wembley in 1961, when England knocked nine goals past their debutant goalkeeper Frank Haffey, with the Scots only managing three in reply. 'What's the time?' went the popular joke at the time... 'Nearly ten past Haffey!' was the reply. The unfortunate Haffey never played a game for Scotland again, and Scottish goalkeeper humour was born.

● SCOTLAND, however, have produced some memorable teams and players over the years. In 1928 the Scots delivered England their worst ever home defeat, 'the Wembley Wizards' beating their Sassenach rivals 5–1.

● TWO MEN share the top-scoring record for Scotland, Denis Law and Kenny Dalglish, both of whom notched 30 goals in the dark blue shirt. Dalglish also holds the record for most caps, having appeared for his country no fewer than 102 times between 1972–87.

SCOTTISH CUP

THE SCOTTISH CUP was initiated in 1874, shortly after the formation of the Scottish FA. Queen's Park, who the previous year had participated in the English FA Cup, won the first final, beating Clydesdale 2–0. Queen's Park were to win 10 of the first 20 finals before the likes of Rangers and Celtic started taking over.

● SINCE THEN the Old Firm giants have ruled the roost. Celtic have the edge over their Protestant rivals having won 30 finals to Rangers' 27. Remarkably Queens Park, who haven't won the Cup for over 100 years and are unlikely to do so again, are still third in the roll of honour with 10 wins.

● CELTIC also share the biggest Scottish Cup Final win, 6–1 over Hibernian in 1972, equalling the 1888 score when Renton beat Cambuslang by the same score.

● TALKING OF big wins, the biggest two in the history of British football took place on the same day in the Scottish Cup. On 12th September 1885 Dundee Harp beat Aberdeen Rovers 35–0 to take their place in the record books. Or so they thought. When they found out the other results in the competition they discovered that Arbroath had beaten Bon Accord 36–0!

SCOTTISH FA

THE SCOTTISH FA is the second oldest football association in the world, formed in 1873, just 10 years after the English version. Queen's Park's exploits in the FA Cup led to Scottish clubs deciding to form an Association of their own.

● IN 1950 the Scottish FA made their most controversial decision to date. Scotland had qualified for the World Cup in Brazil having finished second in the home championships, but they were stopped from going by the suits in the association who stubbornly deemed second place was not good enough.

● Renowned for their tough disciplinary line, in 1979 the SFA sensationally banned five top Scottish internationals from playing for their country. Billy Bremner, Joe Harper, Pat McCluskey, Willie Young and Arthur Graham were all banned for life after a boozy night on the town after Scotland's 1-0 win over Denmark on 9th September 1975. It included a run-in with Danish police and allegedly ended with Bremner throwing a glass of rum and coke over a barmaid.

SCUNTHORPE UNITED

Year founded: 1899
Ground: Glanford Park (9,183)
Highest ever crowd: Glanford Park 8,775, 1st May 1989 v Rotherham (Div 4): Old Showground 23,935, 30th January 1954 v Portsmouth (FA Cup rd 4)
Nickname: The Iron
Colours: White shirts, sky blue shorts, sky blue socks

SCUNTHORPE are one of just eight English league clubs who have never supplied a full international. Not in football anyway, although former England cricket captain Ian Botham made seven appearances for the club as a defender in the early 1980s.

● OTHER WELL-KNOWN names to have played for Scunthorpe – and later for England – include Kevin Keegan and Ray Clemence.

● SCUNTHORPE's biggest win was against Boston United in the FA Cup in 1953, a match which they won 9–0. The club's worst defeat was an 8–0 drubbing by Carlisle in 1952.

● STEVE CAMMACK is Scunthorpe's leading scorer. In two spells with the club between 1979–86 he notched a total of 110 league goals.

● FULL-BACK Jack Brownsword has played more games for Scunthorpe than any other player. Between 1950–65 he lined up in 595 league games for the club. Brownsword is also Scunthorpe's oldest ever player, playing his last match at the age of 41.

Roll of Honour

Div 3 (N) champions 1958

Did You Know?

Falkirk have only reached two post-war Scottish Cup Finals, and on both occasions their opponents were Kilmarnock. In 1957 Falkirk won 2–1 after a replay, while in 1997 The Killies triumphed 1–0.

DAVID SEAMAN

Born: Rotherham 19.9.63
Height: 6ft 4ins Position: Goalkeeper
Club career:
1981–82 Leeds United 0
1982–84 Peterborough 91
1984–86 Birmingham 75
1986–90 Queens Park Rangers 141
1990– Arsenal 280
International record:
1989– England 44

DAVID SEAMAN has been England's undisputed first choice goalkeeper since the run-up to Euro 96, keeping his place during France '98.

● A GREAT SHOT-STOPPER with immaculate handling, Seaman has a reputation for saving penalties. According to his coach Bob Wilson he has worked out a system which determines which way he will dive based on studying the run-up of his opponent. He did save one penalty in the heartbreaking World Cup shoot-out against Argentina but unfortunately his opposite number, Carlos Roa, saved two.

● SEAMAN PLAYED for Peterborough, Birmingham and QPR in the 1980s, but really made his name with Arsenal after his £1.3 million move across London... which at the time made him the most expensive keeper in England.

● Seaman was an integral part of Arsenal's parsimonious defence which let in only 18 goals in the 1990/91 season to win the League Championship - the fewest for a First Division team in over a decade. The England keeper won his second championship medal when Arsenal won the Premiership again in 1998, the season in which the Gunners also won the FA Cup to complete the double.

● Seaman also won thc FA and League Cup with Arsenal in 1993, and the European Cup Winners Cup in 1994, although it was a misjudgement of a lob by Nayim 'from the halfway line' that lost them the 1995 final in that competition.

UWE SEELER

Born: West Germany 5.11.36
Position: Midfielder
Club career:
1952–72 Hamburg 239 (137)
International record:
1954–70 West Germany 72 (43)

WEST GERMANY striker Uwe Seeler is one of only two men to score in four different World Cup tournaments... the other one is Pele.

● UNTIL compatriot Lotthar Mattheus made his international comeback for Germany during France '98, Seeler held the joint record for World Cup appearances with Matthaus, Diego Maradona and Wladislaw Zmuda with a total of 21 appearances.

● SEELER BECAME one of the youngest players ever to play for Germany when he made his debut aged 18 in 1954 at Wembley v England, a match which England won 3–1. He was to return 12 years later, this time captain of his team, in a rather more famous match which the Germans lost 4–2.

● SEELER GOT his revenge four years later, however, when his bizarre equalising backheader slipped past Peter Bonetti in Mexico 70, enabling the Germans to push for a winner in extra time.

● THREE TIMES German Player of the Year, Seeler was a loyal one-club man who helped Hamburg to European Cup Winners' Cup victory in 1968.

LEN SHACKLETON

Born: Bradford 3.5.22
Height: 5ft 7ins Position: Forward
Club career:
1940–46 Bradford Park Avenue
1946–47 Newcastle United 57 (26)
1947–58 Sunderland 320 (98)
International record:
1949–55 England 5 (1)

LEN SHACKLETON was nicknamed 'the Clown Prince of Soccer' for his tomfoolery and love of quipping, but opposing defences weren't often laughing: especially Newport County's after Newcastle United debutant Shackleton had knocked six goals past them in a 13–0 defeat in 1946. 'And they were lucky to get nil,' he said afterwards. It remains the best debut any player has made for Newcastle.

● SHACKLETON HAD just been transferred to Newcastle from Bradford Park Avenue for the then-huge fee of £13,000 (at the time making him the third most expensive player ever). They soon sold him on, in 1947, to neighbours Sunderland, for a record £22,500.

● SHACKLETON STAYED put with Sunderland for a further 10 years, before being forced to quit in 1958, after making 320 appearances with the club. He became a journalist, wrote an autobiography and tipped Derby County off that they were onto a good thing if they signed Brian Clough as manager.

SHAMROCK ROVERS

Year founded: 1899
Stadium: Royal Dublin Society Showgrounds (22,000)
League wins: 15
Colours: White shirts with green hoops, white shorts, white socks

SHAMROCK ROVERS are by far the most successful club in the Republic of Ireland, having won the League 15 times and the Cup 24 times, a total of 39 trophies. Dundalk, the second most successful team, have only won a total of 17.

● ROVERS, based in Dublin, have always been a dominant force in Irish football. They won the inaugural Republic of Ireland Cup Final in 1922 (beating St. James Gate 1–0 in a replay) and the second ever Championship in 1923 (finishing above local rivals Shelbourne).

● ROVERS' best period came in the mid 1980s, when they won an unprecedented four consecutive league championships between 1984–87. In the last three years of this run, they also won the cup to take home The Double.

● THE MANCHESTER UNITED Busby Babes travelled to Dublin to play Rovers in the preliminary round of the European Cup in 1957. They won 6–0.

Roll of Honour

Republic of Ireland League champions 1923, 1925, 1927, 1932, 1938, 1939, 1954, 1957, 1959, 1964, 1984, 1985, 1986, 1987, 1994
Republic of Ireland Cup 1922, 1925, 1929, 1930, 1931, 1932, 1933, 1936, 1940, 1944, 1945, 1948, 1955, 1956, 1962, 1964, 1965, 1966, 1967, 1968, 1969, 1978, 1985, 1986, 1987

BILL SHANKLY

Born: Glenbuck 2.9.13 Died: 29.9.81

THE LATE, great Bill Shankly turned Liverpool from an also-ran Second Division outfit into the most feared team in England, and laid the foundations for Bob Paisley to build The Reds into the most formidable team in Europe.

● SHANKLY took up the reins at Anfield in 1959, bought Ian St. John and Ron Yeats, and led The Reds to the Second Division Championship in 1962. Two rollercoaster years later the First Division Championship was in the bag (1964), and in 1965 the club lifted the FA Cup for the first time in its history.

● BY 1974, when he surprised the football world by retiring, the bluff, quotable Scotsman had added two more League Championships, another FA Cup, and Liverpool's first success in Europe, the UEFA Cup, to the Anfield trophy cabinet.

● SHANKLY DIED in 1981, after a heart attack. His legacy will never be forgotten, and neither will some of his quotes, especially one which has become a football cliché: 'Football isn't a matter of life and death; it's more important than that.'

Bill Shankly wasn't too fond of Everton. 'If they were playing at the end of my garden I'd close the curtains,' he once said

ALAN SHEARER

Born: Newcastle 13.8.70
Height: 6ft 0ins Position: Striker
Club career:

1987–92	Southampton 118 (23)
1992–96	Blackburn Rovers 138 (122)
1996–	Newcastle United 48 (27)

International record:

1992–	England 43 (20)

IN JULY 1996 Alan Shearer became the world's most expensive footballer when he moved from Blackburn Rovers to Newcastle United for a phenomenal £15 million. This fee almost doubled the British record set when Stan Collymore moved to Liverpool from Nottingham Forest for £8.5 million in 1995.

● SHEARER repaid Newcastle by netting 25 league goals and ending as the Premiership's top scorer in 1996/97, despite missing much of the season with a groin injury.

● PRIOR TO moving to Newcastle Shearer had been awarded the Euro 96 Golden Boot award after finishing the tournament with five goals to his name, two more than any other player. His total included a brace in England's 4–1 humiliation of Holland, and the quickest goal in the tournament in the semi final against Germany after just two minutes. Alas, it wasn't enough.

● WHAT MAKES Shearer's record even more astounding is that he hadn't scored an international goal for nearly two years (12 matches) before Euro 96 started, the worst goal drought an England striker has ever suffered without being dropped.

● SHEARER, however, couldn't emulate the feat during France '98, partially because England were prematurely ousted from the competition by Argentia. Unfortunately it was a Shearer foul on the goalkeeper that led to a late England goal being disallowed. His brace of goals did, however, make him joint top England scorer in the competition alongside Michael Owen.

● IN SEPTEMBER 1996 Glenn Hoddle made Shearer England captain.

Alan Shearer: could he score the 34 goals necessary to become England's top scorer of all time?

SHEFFIELD UNITED

Year founded: 1889
Ground: Bramall Lane (30,370)
Highest ever crowd: 68,287, 15th February 1936 v Leeds Utd (FA Cup rd 5)
Nickname: The Blades
Colours: Red-and-white-striped shirts, black shorts, black socks

SHEFFIELD UNITED enjoyed their best win in 1892, trouncing Burslem Port Vale 10–0 to become the first club in the English league to hit double figures in an away match.

● TWO YEARS earlier The Blades suffered their heaviest defeat, going down 13–0 to Bolton Wanderers in the FA Cup.

● SHEFFIELD UNITED were the last club to win the FA Cup before the competition was interrupted by the small matter of World War I.

● UNITED BEAT Chelsea 3–0 in a match which was dubbed 'the Khaki Final', a reference to the large numbers of soldiers present.

● SHEFFIELD UNITED share the record for the highest number of drawn games in the Premier League (with Manchester City and Southampton). They drew 18 of their matches during the season in which they were relegated (1993/94).

● BRAMALL LANE saw the world's first ever floodlit match when, on 14th October 1878, lamps were erected on 30ft wooden towers in each corner of the ground for a match between two representative teams from Sheffield.

● AT THE START of the 1990/91 season Sheffield United went a record 16 games on the trot without a win. Amazingly, however, Dave Bassett's team survived the drop from the top flight after producing championship-winning form in the second half of the season.

● ACTOR SEAN BEAN is Sheffield United's most famous supporter. In the 1996 film 'When Saturday Comes' he fulfilled a lifetime's ambition by playing at Bramall Lane when he starred as a park footballer who is signed up by Sheffield United (and got to snog a stripper with a United tattoo!).

Roll of Honour

Div 1 champions 1898
Div 2 champions 1953
Div 4 champions 1982
FA Cup 1899, 1902, 1915, 1925

SHEFFIELD WEDNESDAY

Year founded: 1867
Ground: Hillsborough (36,020)
Highest ever crowd: 72,841, 17th February 1934 v Manchester City (FA Cup rd 5)
Previous name: The Wednesday
Nickname: The Owls
Colours: Blue-and-white-striped shirts, blue shorts, white socks

KNOWN SIMPLY as 'The Wednesday' until 1929, Sheffield Wednesday are the only league team to take their name from a day of the week. The club was formed by members of the Sheffield Wednesday Cricket Club, who originally met on Wednesday afternoons as many workers had a half day.

● IN 1904 Wednesday became the first club this century to win consecutive league championships. The Owls achieved another title double in 1928/29 and 1929/30, but have never won the league since.

● WEDNESDAY's biggest victory was back in 1891 in the FA Cup against Halliwell. The Owls strolled into the second round with a 12–0 win. The club's heaviest defeat, 10–0, was against Aston Villa in 1912.

● ANDREW WILSON holds two important records for the club. Between 1900–20 he played in 502 league matches, scoring 199 goals. No Wednesday player, before or since, can match these figures.

● DEREK DOOLEY, though, holds the scoring record for a single season, contributing 46 goals to Wednesday's 1952 Second Division championship-winning campaign. The following season Dooley was seriously injured and had to have a leg amputated. He did go on to manage the club for a three-year spell in the early 1970s, however.

● NIGEL WORTHINGTON is Wednesday's most capped player. The hard-running left-back played 61 times for Northern Ireland while at Hillsborough.

● THE LAST TIME Wednesday won the FA Cup, in 1935, striker Ellis Rimmer became only the second player in English football history to score in every round of the competition. The Owls beat West Bromwich Albion 4–2 in the final, Rimmer scoring twice.

● WEDNESDAY's Jim McCalliog, aged 19 years and 234 days, became the third youngest player to score in an FA Cup Final in 1966. He has since slumped to fifth in that particular table.

● LABOUR politicians Roy Hattersley and Joe Ashton are two of the most famous fans of Sheffield Wednesday.

Despite trying to make himself look as silly as possible with his white boots and sideburns, Paolo Di Canio is a Hillsborough hero

Above: The Sheffield Wednesday kit designer ensured in 1996/97 that Reggie Blinker had plenty of room for all those tricks up his sleeve

Sheffield Wednesday's Post-War Record

47 D2 20th	65 D1 8th	83 D2 6th
48 D2 4th	66 D1 17th	84 D2 2nd
49 D2 8th	67 D1 11th	85 D1 8th
50 D2 2nd	68 D1 19th	86 D1 5th
51 D1 21st	69 D1 15th	87 D1 13th
52 D2 1st	70 D1 22nd	88 D1 11th
53 D1 18th	71 D2 15th	89 D1 15th
54 D1 19th	72 D2 14th	90 D1 18th
55 D1 22nd	73 D2 10th	91 D2 3rd
56 D2 1st	74 D2 19th	92 D1 3rd
57 D1 14th	75 D2 22nd	93 PR 7th
58 D1 22nd	76 D3 20th	94 PR 7th
59 D2 1st	77 D3 8th	95 PR 13th
60 D1 5th	78 D3 14th	96 PR 15th
61 D1 2nd	79 D3 14th	97 PR 7th
62 D1 6th	80 D3 3rd	98 PR 18th
63 D1 6th	81 D2 10th	
64 D1 6th	82 D2 4th	

Roll of Honour

Div 1 champions 1903, 1904, 1929, 1930
Div 2 champions 1900, 1926, 1952, 1956, 1959
FA Cup 1896, 1907, 1935
League Cup 1991

Funny Old Game

Ron and Peter Springett were the first brothers to be exchanged between clubs in 1967. Ron went back to QPR from where he had come in 1957, and his younger brother Peter left QPR to join Wednesday (costing his brother plus £22,000).

TEDDY SHERINGHAM

Born: Higham Park 2.4.66
Height: 6ft 0ins Position: Forward
Club career:
1984–91 Millwall 220 (93)
1984– Aldershot (loan) 5 (0)
1991–92 Nottingham Forest 42 (14)
1993–97 Tottenham Hotspur 166 (76)
1997– Manchester United 31 (9)
International record:
1993– England 35 (9)

TEDDY SHERINGHAM established himself under Terry Venables as England's first choice strike partner for Alan Shearer... until a certain Michael Owen turned up on the scene halfway through England's France '98 campaign. He had served his country well, particularly during Euro '96, when he repaid Venables' loyalty with a brace of goals during England's 4-1 mauling of Holland. But his standing in the England camp was threatened just days before World Cup '98 started when he was caught drinking away the wee hours in a Portuguese nightclub, for which he was made to issue a humiliating public apology.

● HE HAS scored more League goals for Millwall than any other player in their history (93), an amazing record considering that when he was playing for them he'd hardly started his career.

● SHERINGHAM moved from Millwall to Nottingham Forest in 1991 for £2 million – a record transfer fee for the East Londoners – then moved on to Tottenham Hotspur a year later for £2.1 million in a controversial transfer that became the subject of a number of dodgy transfer deal allegations (of the cash-in-brown-paper-bag-at-service-station variety).

Teddy Sheringham and his famous lunatic fringe

PETER SHILTON

Born: Leicester 18.10.49
Height 6ft 1in Position: Goalkeeper
Club career:
1965–75 Leicester City 286 (1)
1975–78 Stoke City 110
1978–82 Nottingham Forest 202
1982–87 Southampton 188
1987–92 Derby County 175
1992–95 Plymouth Argyle 34
1995–96 Bolton Wanderers 1
1996–97 West Ham United
1997 Orient 6
International record:
1971–90 England 125

ON 22nd December 1996 Peter Shilton became the first player in the history of English football to make 1,000 league appearances when he played for Leyton Orient against Brighton, keeping a clean sheet in the Os' 2–0 win.

● PETER SHILTON has won more England caps than any other player, a total of 125 between 1970 and 1990, keeping a record 65 clean sheets for his country. He has also made more appearances in World Cup finals matches – a total of 17 – than any other Englishman.

● AT THE AGE of 19 he made his only ever appearance in the FA Cup Final, for Leicester City in 1969 (losing 1–0 to Manchester City), and had to wait just under 10 years before his first honours, with Brian Clough at Nottingham Forest. Forest won the League Championship in their first year back in the First Division in 1977/78, and then went on to win two European Cups.

● SHILTON became player manager at Plymouth in 1992 (as well as their oldest ever player), but wasn't as good a manager as he'd been a goalkeeper, and was sacked three years later.

SHREWSBURY TOWN

Year founded: 1886
Ground: Gay Meadow (7,500)
Highest ever crowd: 18,917, 26th April 1961 v Walsall (Div 3)
Nickname: The Shrews
Colours: Blue shirts, blue shorts, blue socks

SHREWSBURY's record victory was an 11-2 drubbing of Marine in the 1995 FA Cup. 'The Shrews' have twice suffered 8-1 defeats – against Norwich in 1952 and Coventry in 1963.

● THE PROLIFIC Arthur Rowley is the club's record scorer, grabbing 152 goals between 1958–65 to complete his all-time league record of 434 goals (he also played for West Bromwich Albion, Fulham, Leicester City and Shrewsbury Town). In season 1958/59 Rowley hit a club best 38 goals.

● NO PLAYER has appeared more often for Shrewsbury than Colin Griffin. He played in a total of 406 league games during his 14-year career at Gay Meadow between 1975 and 1989.

● SHREWSBURY have won the Welsh Cup on six occasions – a record for an English club.

● ON 12th FEBRUARY 1994 Shrewsbury established a club record of 14 league games without defeat. In the same month Fred Davies became the longest-serving caretaker-manager in league football, having been appointed as such in May 1993.

Roll of Honour

Div 3 champions 1979, 1994
Welsh Cup 1891, 1938, 1977, 1979, 1984, 1985

TREVOR SINCLAIR

Born: Dulwich 2.3.73
Height: 5ft 10ins Position: Forward
Club career:
1990–93 Blackpool 112 (15)
1993–97 Queens Park Rangers 167 (13)
1997– West Ham United 14(7)

TREVOR SINCLAIR, who moved from QPR to West Ham in December 1997, has always made career decisions for footballing rather than financial resons. He once turned down Manchester United to play for Blackpool, and in 1993 rejected moneybags Blackburn in favour of QPR.

● SINCLAIR, one of the first Lilleshall graduates to play in the Football League, played a total of 13 games for the Under 21 side, and got called up to the England squad pre-Euro 96 by Terry Venables although he didn't make the final 22.

● THE FLEET-FOOTED forward can either play as a winger or as a centre-forward, and is pretty devastating as both. His spectacular overhead kick against Barnsley in the fourth round of the 1996/97 FA Cup was one of the greatest goals ever captured on camera.

SIZE

THE HEAVIEST player in the history of the professional game was William 'Fatty' Foulkes, who kept goal for Sheffield United, Chelsea and Bradford City. By the end of his career the keeper, who gained a single cap for England, weighed in at 23 stone.

● AT JUST five feet tall, Thames, Clapton Orient and Watford's Fred Le May is the smallest player ever to have made an appearance in the Football League. He played between 1930–33. He was not a centre-half!

● CHELSEA's JOHN CRAWFORD is the shortest and lightest player ever to have appeared for England. The 5ft 2ins winger weighed just 8st 6lb when he won his single international cap against Scotland in 1931.

● OXFORD UNITED's Kevin Francis is the tallest professional footballer playing in England. The former Derby and Stockport striker stands at a towering 6ft 7ins, a good couple of inches taller than his nearest rivals.

● THE TALLEST football league player of all time was Bournemouth's goalkeeper in the mid-1920s, Bill Carr, who was one quarter of an inch short of 6ft 9ins.

● IN 1958/59 Lincoln City boasted a 6ft 3ins centre half called Ray Long and a 5ft 2ins outside left called Joe Short.

WALTER SMITH

Born: Lanark 24.2.48

WALTER SMITH – who retired after ten seasons in charge of Scottish giants Rangers in May 1998 to take over as Everton boss – won his first Scottish Championship at Rangers in 1991 after only four games in charge! It was a perfect start for the former Dundee United player after the resignation of previous manager Graeme Souness.

● From there Smith guided Rangers to nine league titles in a row - equalling Celtic's famous record - but when he left the club they had won nothing all season for the first time since 1986. During his time at the club, he also won three Scottish Cups (1992, 1993 and 1996) and five Scottish League Cups (1989, 1991, 1993, 1994 and 1997).

● HIS SIDE has been singularly unsuccessful, however, in European football (apart from one campaign in the 1992/93 season when they just missed out on a place in the European Cup Final to Olympique Marseille, having reached the quarter-final group stage). In 1995 Tony Blair quipped 'Walter Smith has done more than the Tory backbenchers to keep Britain out of Europe.'

SOCRATES

Position: Midfielder
Club career:
Corinthians (Brazil)
International record:
1979–86 Brazil

Graeme Souness brings the ball away from a crunching tackle for Scotland in the 1986 World Cup

SOCRATES was the Brazilian captain at the 1982 and 1986 World Cups. In both tournaments he scored his country's opening goal, in a 2–1 win over the Soviet Union in 1982 and a 1–0 win over Spain four years later.

● A CLASSY MIDFIELDER with excellent ball skills, Socrates burst onto the international scene in the late 1970s. He scored his first goals for Brazil with a brace in a 5–1 hammering of South American neighbours Uruguay in Rio in 1979.

● LIKE HIS famous compatriot Gerson, Socrates was a heavy smoker, rumoured to get through three packets of cigarettes a day. His habit did not, however, prevent him from being one of the finest players Brazil has produced. Considering that he was a qualified doctor, however, he should have known better!

GRAEME SOUNESS

Born: Edinburgh 6.5.53
Height: 5ft 9ins Position: Midfielder
Club career:
1970–73 Tottenham Hotspur 0 (0)
1973–78 Middlesbrough 176 (22)
1978–84 Liverpool 247 (38)
1984–86 Sampdoria
1986–91 Rangers 73 (5)
International record:
1975–86 Scotland 54 (3)

GRAEME SOUNESS had a highly successful playing career at Liverpool after moving to Anfield in 1978 from Middlesbrough for £352,000... then a record fee between two English clubs.

● A TENACIOUS, hard-tackling midfielder, he won five League Championships, three European Cups and four League Cups with the club before moving to Sampdoria in 1984, where he won the Italian Cup.

● IN 1986 Souness became Glasgow Rangers' first ever player-manager. Entrusted with vast sums of money, he spent most of it persuading English players like Chris Woods, Terry Butcher, Gary Stevens and Trevor Stevens to move north of the border, creating the multi-national, multi-cultural base on which the club's phenomenal recent success is built.

● SOUNESS won four league titles as manager of Rangers, but in 1991 he was lured back to his beloved Liverpool after Kenny Dalglish's surprise resignation. He dismantled a highly successful side, however, and only had the FA Cup and a serious heart attack in 1992 to show for his four years at the club.

● In 1995 he moved to Turkish side Galatasaray, where he won the cup, before moving briefly to Torino in Italy and Southampton in England and then on to manage Benfica in Portugal.

Don't Quote Me

'You cannot guarantee a thing in this game. All you can guarantee is disappointment.'

Graeme Souness gets a wee bit confused in 1990, but we think we know what he means.

SOUTH AFRICA

First international (post-apartheid):
v Cameroons (friendly, 1992)
Colours: Gold, black and white shirts, green shorts and white socks

SOUTH AFRICA qualified for their first ever World Cup finals in 1998, although the team didn't make it past the first round. It was a disappointing showing from the South Africans, none more so than defender Pierre Issa who had the misfortune to score two own goals in the tournament.

● In February 1996 South Africa (nicknamed 'Bufana, Bufana' which means 'the boys, the boys') won the African Nations Cup for the first time, beating Tunisia in the final at the Soccer City stadium in Soweto. It was only the second time that South Africa had entered the competition, and at the following tournament, in 1998, they lost the final 2-0 to Burkina Faso.

● UNDER THE old apartheid regime football was one of the few racially-integrated activities in South Africa. In 1978 the white National Football League and non-white National Professional Soccer League merged to form the National Soccer League.

WORLD CUP RECORD

1930–90 Did not enter 1994 Did not qualify

● NEVERTHELESS South Africa experienced almost 30 years of international exile before rejoining the African Football Confederation, the CAF, and FIFA in 1992. In June of that year South Africa celebrated their return by playing three matches against Cameroon.

SOUTH AMERICAN CHAMPIONSHIPS

THE SOUTH AMERICAN CHAMPIONSHIP (or the Copa America) has been officially running since 1917, making it the oldest official international football competition in the world (apart from the Olympics). The period between tournaments has been haphazard but has settled to one every two years.

● THE FIRST OFFICIAL winners of the competition were Uruguay, who headed a four-nation round robin tournament including Brazil, Argentina and Chile.

● Argentina have won the tournament a total of 15 times, one ahead of Uruguay. Surprisingly Brazil lie in third place, having only won the competition five times.

● The Brazilians did win the 1997 tournament, however, which was held in Bolivia. They beat the host nation 3-1 in a hugely entertaining final.

● ARGENTINA's Norbert Mendez and Brazil's Zizinho are the all-time top scorers in the competition, with 17 goals apiece.

South Africa battle their way to their first ever international trophy, winning the African Nations Cup by beating Tunisia 2–0 on home soil in 1996

NEVILLE SOUTHALL

Born: Llandudno 16.9.58
Height: 6ft 1in Position: Goalkeeper
Club career:
1980–81 Bury 39
1981–98 Everton 578
1982–83 Port Vale (loan) 9
1998– Stoke City 12
International record:
1982–97 Wales 92

GIANT GOALKEEPER Neville Southall has played for Wales more than any other man, making 92 appearances up until the start of the 1997/98 season. He made his debut way back in 1982.

● SOUTHALL made more League appearances for Everton than any other player in the history of the club, totting up 578 games before moving to Stoke City in March 1998.

● AT HIS PEAK often described as the best goalkeeper in the world, Southall was between the sticks during Everton's most successful period ever – in the mid-1980s – when they won two league championships, the FA Cup, and the European Cup Winners' Cup.

● A QUIET, family man, Southall (who was a dustman before becoming a footballer) refused to join the celebrations after Everton's 1995 FA Cup win over Man United, preferring to drive straight home to Wales, despite having been made Man of the Match.

SOUTHAMPTON

Year founded: 1885
Ground: The Dell (15,352)
Highest ever crowd: 31,044, 8th October 1969 v Manchester United (Div 1)
Previous name: Southampton St. Mary's
Nickname: The Saints
Colours: Red-and-white-striped shirts, black shorts, white socks

IN 1976 Southampton, then a Second Division side, won the FA Cup for the only time in their history, beating Manchester United 1–0 at Wembley. The late Bobby Stokes scored the winning goal, and was rewarded with the prize of a new car, even though he couldn't drive.

● THE LEGENDARY TERRY PAINE – a member of England's 1966 World Cup winning squad – is Southampton's longest-serving player. Between 1956–74 he played a staggering 713 games for the club. After establishing himself in the Saints side in 1957, Paine was a model of consistency. He never played fewer than 36 league games in a season, was an ever-present in seven campaigns, and missed just one match in another five seasons.

● PAINE's loyal service at Southampton means he has the fourth highest number of appearances by any player in one spell at the same club.

● MICK CHANNON is Southampton's leading all-time scorer, his goals coming in two periods at the club between 1966–82. Channon, now a successful racehorse trainer, grabbed a total of 185 goals, and celebrated the majority of them with a hallmark windmilling of his right arm.

● SOUTHAMPTON enjoyed their best win in 1965, thrashing Wolves 9–3, with Martin Chivers scoring four of the goals. The Saints have twice been humbled 8–0: at Tottenham in 1936, and at Everton in 1971.

● DEREK REEVES holds the club record for most goals in a season. His tally of 39 in 1959/60 helped Southampton to the Division Three championship.

● IN 1900 Southampton, then playing in the Southern League, became the first southern team since The Old Etonians in 1883 to reach the FA Cup Final. Unfortunately, The Saints could not entirely break the northern monopoly, going down to Bury 0–4.

● THE SAINTS were also losing finalists in the FA Cup in 1902, and lost the 1979 League Cup Final to Brian Clough's Nottingham Forest (3–2).

● PETER SHILTON is Southampton's most capped player. Of his 125 caps, 49 were earned while he was a player at the Dell.

● SOUTHAMPTON have been a fixture in the top division since 1978, an unbroken spell only five Premiership clubs can better. During this period The Saints enjoyed their best league season, finishing second in 1984 with a club record haul of 77 points.

● FORMER GAFFER Graeme Souness was only the eleventh manager Southampton had had since the war, a record beaten by just four league teams (West Ham United, Manchester United, Nottingham Forest and Liverpool). The longest-serving of these managers was Ted Bates, who led the club from Third Division obscurity into the First Division during his 18-year reign at The Dell... the second longest managerial reign in English football since the war.

● THE DELL has the smallest capacity of any Premiership ground although the club have plans to move to a brand new 30,000 capacity stadium on the outskirts of the city in the near future.

● SOUTHAMPTON'S RECORD of 18 draws in the 1994/95 season is a Premiership record (shared with Manchester City and Sheffield United – both in 1993/94)

'Ere Glenn, chuck us another England cap mate!' suggests Matt Le Tissier

Roll of Honour

Div 3 (S) champions 1922
Div 3 champions 1960
FA Cup 1976

Southampton's Post-War Record

47 D2 14th	64 D2 5th	81 D1 6th
48 D2 3rd	65 D2 4th	82 D1 7th
49 D2 3rd	66 D2 2nd	83 D1 12th
50 D2 4th	67 D1 19th	84 D1 2nd
51 D2 12th	68 D1 16th	85 D1 5th
52 D2 13th	69 D1 7th	86 D1 14th
53 D2 21st	70 D1 19th	87 D1 12th
54 D3 6th	71 D1 7th	88 D1 12th
55 D3 3rd	72 D1 19th	89 D1 13th
56 D3 14th	73 D1 13th	90 D1 7th
57 D3 4th	74 D1 20th	91 D1 14th
58 D3 6th	75 D2 13th	92 D1 16th
59 D3 14th	76 D2 6th	93 PR 18th
60 D3 1st	77 D2 9th	94 PR 18th
61 D2 8th	78 D2 2nd	95 PR 10th
62 D2 6th	79 D1 14th	96 PR 17th
63 D2 11th	80 D1 8th	97 PR 16th
		98 PR 12th

SOUTHEND UNITED

Year founded: 1906
Ground: Roots Hall (12,306)
Highest ever crowd: 31,090, 10th January 1979 v Liverpool (FA Cup rd 3)
Nickname: The Shrimpers
Colours: Blue shirts, white shorts, white socks

The only title ever held by Southend United is that of Fourth Division Champions in 1981. The club did enjoy an extended run in Division One in the 1990s, but that ended with relegation to the Second Division in 1997 and again to the Third in 1998.

● THE SHRIMPERS have twice enjoyed club record 10–1 victories in the FA Cup, against Golders Green in 1934 and Brentwood in 1968. Their worst defeat was a 9–1 drubbing by fellow seasiders Brighton in 1965.

● AFTER JOINING the league in 1920, Southend remained in Divisions Three and Division Three (South) for a record 46 seasons, before sliding into Division Four in 1966.

● SOUTHEND's nickname should really be The Saints. Between joining the League in 1920 and 1952 not a single player was sent off in 1,027 Third Division (South) matches.

● SANDY ANDERSON is the club's leading appearance maker, turning out in 451 league games between 1950–63. Southend's leading scorer is Roy Hollis, who hit the target 122 times in a seven-year stay at the club between 1953–60.

● THE RECORD for goals in a single season is shared by two players. In 1928/29 Jim Shankly netted on 31 occasions, a feat matched by Sammy McCory in 1957/58.

● SOUTHEND have only rarely given their supporters something to cheer in the FA Cup. The club has never reached the 6th round, and has only played in the 5th round on a meagre four occasions.

● SINGER ALISON MOYET is one of Southend's most famous fans. The former Yazoo star is a regular at Roots Hall.

Roll of Honour

Div 4 champions 1981

Spain's Alberto Belsue hoofs the ball right out of this book

SOUTH KOREA

First World Cup appearance: South Korea 0 Hungary 9 (Switzerland, 1954)
Colours: Red shirts, blue shorts, red socks

SOUTH KOREA have qualified for more World Cups, five, than any other Asian country. Their finals record is poor, however, and they have yet to win a match in 14 attempts.

● Their first finals match – a 9-0 thrashing by Hungary – was the heaviest World Cup defeat until The Magyars trumped that score with a 10-1 walloping of El Salvador in 1982.

● South Korea qualified for France '98 in style, winning their group with a six-point margin over Japan. Attacking midfielder Yong-Soo Choi was the star of the campaign, contributing ten of South Korea's 28 goals. They started the tournament well, with a goal by Ha Seok-Ju against Mexico, but they eventually succumbed 3-1 in that match after the scorer became the first man in the tournament to be sent off and their 1-1 draw with Belgium in their final group game did little to make up for the humiliation of an earlier 5-0 drubbing by Holland.

● In 1956 South Korea won the first ever Asian Cup, and retained their title four years later. They have since been runners-up on three occasions.

● South Korea will co-host the 2002 World Cup with Japan – as long as the country's faltering economy can bear the strain.

● It will be the first World Cup to be held in Asia and the first tournament ever to be shared between two nations. The fact that the two nations in question are traditional arch enemies should make things very interesting indeed.

WORLD CUP RECORD

1930-50	Did not enter	1970 -82	Did not qualify
1954	Round 1	1986	Round 1
1958	Did not enter	1990	Round 1
1962	Did not qualify	1994	Round 1
1966	Did not enter	1998	Round 1

SPAIN

First international: Spain 1 Denmark 0 (Olympic Games, Brussels, 1920)
First World Cup appearance: Spain 3 Brazil 1 (Italy, 1934)
Highest capped player: Andoni Zubizaretta (112)
Highest goalscorer: Emilio Butragueño (26)
Best win: 13–0 v Bulgaria, 1933
Worst defeat: 7–1 v Italy, 1928
Colours: Red shirts, blue shorts, blue socks

TSpain's performance in France '98 was symbolic of their international history as a football team – they never live up to expectations in the big competitions. Tipped by many as possible winners, the Spaniards lost their opening match against Nigeria, could only draw against Paraguay. Then, as if to frustrate their fans even more, the team showed what they were capable of by thrashing Bulgaria 6-1 (the highest score in the whole tournament) only to find that Paraguay had beaten Nigeria and they were out. In the past, despite the huge success of their club teams Real Madrid and Barcelona, they have never managed to reach the semi finals of the World Cup. Their one and only international success was a European Championship win, back in 1964.

● ON THAT OCCASION thay had the advantage of playing their semi-final and final on home ground, at the Bernabeu stadium in Madrid. They beat the holders the Soviet Union 2–1 in front of 105,000 spectators, the biggest crowd to witness a European Championship match.

● MORE RECENTLY the Spanish U23 side won the 1992 Olympic Games, again on home ground, at the Nou Camp in Barcelona, beating Poland 3–2 in a thrilling match in front of 95,000 fans.

● IN 1952 and 1954 Spain won the International Youth Championships, both times on the toss of a coin after drawing.

WORLD CUP RECORD

1930	Did not enter	1970	Did not qualify
1934	Quarter-finals	1974	Did not qualify
1938	Did not enter	1978	Round 1
1950	Round 2	1982	Round 2
1954	Did not qualify	1986	Quarter-finals
1958	Did not qualify	1990	Round 2
1962	Round 1	1994	Quarter-finals
1966	Round 1	1998	Round 1

Football Records Quiz

What major car company sponsors AC Milan, Bayern Munich, Paris St. Germain and the Republic of Ireland?

Answer at bottom of page 137

SPONSORSHIP

THE FIRST COMPETITION in England to be sponsored was the Watney Cup in 1971, a competition between the highest scorers of the Football League.

● THE FIRST FA-affiliated club to wear shirt sponsorship was Kettering Town in 1976 (Kettering Tyres). Manchester United (Sharp electronics) and Arsenal (JVC) are the only English clubs who have only ever had one sponsor.

● SPANISH GIANTS Barcelona are the only major club in the world who have never worn shirt sponsorship, claiming it would devalue the famous blue and red stripes.

● THE LEAGUE CUP has been sponsored since 1982, also being known as the Milk Cup, the Littlewoods Cup, the Rumbelows Cup, the Coca-Cola Cup and the Worthington Cup. The Football League has been sponsored by Canon, Today Newspapers, Barclays and, since Premiership days, Endsleigh Insurance and the Nationwide Building Society (the Premiership itself is sponsored by Carling).

● THE FA CUP, the oldest competition in the world, held out till 1996, when it became, in the spirit of compromise, the FA Cup sponsored by Littlewoods.

● THE ENGLAND TEAM is sponsored by Mercury One 2 One mobile telephones although sponsors' names are not allowed on shirts in international football.

STADIUMS

The largest stadium in the world is the Maracana in Rio de Janeiro, Brazil. The biggest crowd in football history (199,589) attended the Maracana to watch Brazil play Uruguay in the final game of the World Cup in 1950, the year the stadium was constructed.

● Britain's largest stadium is Wembley with a capacity of 80,000. Before it became all-seater, Wembley used to have a capacity of 100,000, although an estimated crowd of around 170,000 (many of whom had entered the ground illegally) crammed into the ground for the 1923 FA Cup Final between Bolton and West Ham – the first ever game played at 'The Venue of Legends'.

● In 1998 plans were unveiled to demolish the old Wembley (retaining only the famous twin towers) and build a brand new, state-of-the-art 80,000 all-seater stadium. If it goes ahead the project will cost £340 million and work will begin in 2002.

● The world's oldest football ground is The Drill Field, home to Vauxhall Conference side Northwich Victoria. Built in 1874, the ground was saved from demolition in 1995 when fans raised £80,000 to pay off property developers.

● Pittodrie, home of Aberdeen, became Britain's first all-seater stadium in 1978. The first all-seater in England was Coventry City's Highfield Road in 1981. The new-style ground wasn't very popular with fans of the Sky Blues, however, and the club reopened a small standing area in 1983.

STEAUA BUCHAREST

Year founded: 1947
Ground: Steaua Stadium (30,000)
League wins: 19
Colours: Red shirts, blue shorts, blue socks

STEAUA BUCHAREST became the first Eastern Bloc country to lift the European Cup in 1986. Pitted against hot favourites Barcelona, managed by Terry Venables, in the final, the Romanians managed to scrape a 0–0 draw and win on penalties.

● THEIR 2–0 win is the lowest penalty shoot-out score to have won a major tournament... Barcelona missed all four they took!

● STEAUA went on to become the first Eastern European team to compete in the World Club Cup, but were beaten 1–0 by River Plate in Tokyo.

● VIRTUALLY the same side achieved the remarkable task of winning a unique consecutive treble league and cup double between 1987–89. The team was trounced 4–0 by Ruud Gullit's AC Milan, however, in the 1989 European Cup Final.

● STEAUA are easily the most successful side in Romania. They should be, though, because until the Iron Curtain came down they had the legal right to sign players from any other club in the country.

Roll of Honour

Romanian champions 1951, 1952, 1953, 1956, 1960, 1961, 1968, 1976, 1978, 1985, 1986, 1987, 1988, 1989, 1993, 1994, 1995, 1997, 1998
Romanian Cup 1949, 1950, 1951, 1952, 1955, 1962, 1966, 1967, 1969, 1970, 1971, 1976, 1979, 1985, 1987, 1988, 1989, 1992, 1997
European Cup 1986
European Super Cup 1986

JOCK STEIN

Born: Burnbank 5.10.23 Died: 10.11.85

LEGENDARY MANAGER Jock Stein was the first British manager to win the European Cup or, as the Scots always insist, the first Scottish manager to win the European Cup. He guided his Celtic team, who became known as the 'Lisbon Lions', to victory over Inter Milan in 1967.

● STEIN MADE Celtic the most dominant side in the history of Scottish football, helping them to win an amazing nine consecutive titles between 1966 and 1974 (a feat equalled by Rangers between 1989 and 1997). He added a tenth in 1977 before leaving the club in 1978.

● AS A PLAYER he had helped the Glasgow club to The Double in 1954. Celtic had bought him, bizarrely enough, from the Welsh League team Llanelli.

● BEFORE ARRIVING at Parkhead, he turned things round at Dunfermline, winning the Scottish Cup there in 1961. After leaving Celtic he managed Leeds for a short time before taking the Scottish side to the World Cup finals in 1982.

● STILL MANAGER of Scotland, it was after guiding his team to qualification for the 1986 World Cup finals at Ninian Park in November 1985 that he died of a heart attack after collapsing in the players' tunnel. He was mourned by the whole of Scotland.

STENHOUSEMUIR

Year founded: 1884
Ground: Ochilview Park (3,480)
Highest ever crowd: 12,500, 11th March 1950 v East Fife (Scottish Cup rd 4)
Nickname: The Warriors
Colours: Maroon shirts, white shorts, white socks

STENHOUSEMUIR's biggest win was against Dundee United in 1937. The Warriors, as the club are known, romped to a 9–2 victory. In 1930 Stenhousemuir suffered their worst defeat, 11–2, against Dunfermline Athletic.

● ARCHIE ROSE is the club's longest-serving player, appearing in 360 league matches.

● STENHOUSEMUIR were the first Scottish club to install floodlights. On 7th November 1951 the club entertained Hibs at Ochilview Park in the first senior match in Scotland played under modern floodlights.

● OCHILVIEW PARK boasts the third largest pitch in the Scottish league, covering 8,814 square yards. Only the pitches at Clyde and Stirling Albion are longer.

● HOWEVER, ONLY TWO Scottish clubs – Albion Rovers and East Stirlingshire – have grounds with lower capacities than Ochilview Park.

● The Warriors' most recent flirtation with glory came in 1995, when they were just 90 minutes away from a place in the semi-finals of the Scottish Cup, having beaten Roy Aitken's Aberdeen 2-0 in the Fourth Round. Alas, on the day class won through and opponents Hibernian reached the last four after a 4-0 win at Ochilview Park.

Did You Know?

The longest game in the history of English league football was the Wartime Cup first round replay between Stockport County and Doncaster Rovers on 23rd March 1946. It had been decided that, to avoid fixture congestion, if no team had won after extra-time they'd carry on until someone scored. But after 500 minutes and with the scores level at 2–2, the match was eventually abandoned because of bad light. Legend has it that supporters went home, had their tea, came back and carried on watching.

STIRLING ALBION

Year founded: 1945
Ground: Forthbank Stadium (3,808)
Highest ever crowd: 26,400, 14th March 1959 v Celtic (Scottish Cup rd 4)
Nickname: The Binos
Colours: Red shirts with white sleeves, white shirts and white socks

IN 1987 STIRLING became the first Scottish club to play on artificial turf, but they were ordered to return to grass in 1992.

● THE CLUB achieved its biggest win this century in the 1984 Scottish Cup, when they thrashed amateur side Selkirk 20–0. Manager Alex Smith was surprised by the final result. He'd lost track of the score and thought his team had only scraped through 19–0. The club's worst defeat, a 0–9 loss, was at Dundee United, in 1967.

● Stirling Albion hold the British record for the fewest goals scored in a season, having hit the back of the net just 18 times in their 1980/81 Scottish First Division campaign. The club also holds the British record for the fewest points earned in a season, having scored a pitiful six points from 30 games in the Scottish First Division, 1954/55.

Roll of Honour

Div 2 champions 1953, 1958, 1961, 1965
Second Division champions 1977, 1991

STOCKPORT COUNTY

Year founded: 1883
Ground: Edgeley Park (12,500)
Highest ever crowd: 27,833, 11th February 1950 v Liverpool (FA Cup rd 5)
Nickname: The Hatters
Colours: White shirts, white shorts and white socks

STOCKPORT'S greatest ever season came as recently as 1996/97 when they reached the Coca Cola Cup semi-final. They lost narrowly to Middlesbrough having beating Premiership sides Everton, West Ham and Southamton along the way.

● STOCKPORT enjoyed their biggest win in 1934, demolishing Halifax 13–0 in a Third Division (North) fixture...
a league record victory shared with Newcastle United (who beat Newport County by the same score in 1946). No team has ever scored more than 13 goals in an English league game.

● THE CLUB's worst defeat, an 8–1 humiliation, was against Chesterfield back in 1902.

● NO PLAYER has appeared more often for The Hatters than Andy Thorpe. In two spells at the club between 1978–92 he played in a total of 489 league games.

● JACK CONNOR is County's leading scorer, notching 132 goals between 1951–56.

● THE FIRST FATHER and son to play in the same team in an English league game were Alec and David Herd, who played for Stockport County in a Division Three (North) game in 1951.

● GOALKEEPER Henry Hardy is the only Stockport County player to have played for England, winning a single cap in 1925. After retiring from football he became a professional musician!

Roll of Honour

Div 3 (N) champions 1922, 1937
Div 4 champions 1967

'Look, it's come out whiter than white!' Hristo Stoichkov puts in some extra PR work for Daz while playing for Parma

HRISTO STOICHKOV

Born: Bulgaria 2.8.66
Position: Forward
Club career:
1984–90 CSKA Sofia 119 (81)
1990–95 Barcelona 151 (76)
1995–96 Parma 24 (5)
1996–97 Barcelona 20 (6)
1997– CSKA Sofia
International record:
1987– Bulgaria 74 (35)

HRISTO STOICHKOV is one of the most volatile – and talented – players in the game. When Barcelona paid £2 million to buy him from CSKA Sofia in 1990 it was a Bulgarian record.

● IN HIS first spell at Barcelona, between 1990–95, he won four Spanish Championships, one European Cup and scored 104 goals: he also totted up a total of 11 red cards. He returned to Barca in 1996 after a year at Parma in Italy and came on

as a sub in the club's 1–0 European Cup Winners Cup Final win over Paris St. Germain in May 1997.

● STOICHKOV has been the inspiration behind the most successful Bulgarian team of all time. Before 1994 the team had never won a match in the World Cup finals. In the States they got to the semis, disposing of Germany on the way, and Stoichkov finished joint top scorer (with Oleg Salenko) on six goals.

● STOICHKOV was banned from Bulgarian football for life for his part in a violent brawl in the 1985 Cup final while playing for CSKA Sofia. But he was such an important player for the country that he was re-instated within six months.

Purists say Stoke City's tactic of lying on the ball and creeping towards goal is unfair

STOKE CITY

Year founded: 1863
Ground: The Britannia Stadium (28,000)
Highest ever crowd: 51,380, 29th March 1937 v Arsenal (Div 1)
Nickname: The Potters
Colours: Red-and-white-striped shirts, white shorts, red socks

STOKE ARE the second oldest league club and founder members of the Football League. The club finished bottom of the first league table in 1889, failed to improve their position in the following season, and dropped out of the League in 1890 after failing to be re-elected.

● THE LEGENDARY Gordon Banks is Stoke's most capped player. The World Cup winning goalkeeper gained 36 of his 73 England caps while at The Victoria Ground.

● WHILE PLAYING for Stoke, the great Stanley Matthews became the oldest player to appear in the top flight. Five days after celebrating his 50th birthday in February 1965, Matthews played his last game for the club against Fulham.

● STOKE's record win was a 10–3 pummelling of West Brom in 1937. The Potters suffered their worst defeat back in 1889, crashing 10–0 at Preston.

● FREDDIE STEELE is Stoke's leading scorer, hitting 142 goals between 1934 and 1939, including a club record 33 goals in season 1936/37.

● STOKE HAVE been involved in a number of bizarre matches in their long history. In 1894 City played one of the shortest matches on record, when the Victoria Ground was hit by a blinding snowstorm and the game with Wolves was abandoned after just four minutes.

● FOUR YEARS later, in 1898, Stoke took part in arguably the most boring game ever played. City and Burnley both needed a point to stay in the First Division, and played out a mind-numbing goalless draw which didn't feature a single shot on goal.

● ON AT LEAST two occasions Stoke players have made an impression on a game in record time. In 1979, Brendan O'Callaghan scored on his debut for the club within 10 seconds of coming on as a substitute. In 1972, John Ritchie was sent off in a European tie without touching the ball after coming off the bench.

● STOKE's most famous fan is Nick Hancock, the presenter of the popular sports comedy show 'They Think It's All Over'... it is now!

Roll of Honour

Div 2 champions 1933, 1963
Div 3 (N) champions 1927
Second Division champions 1993
League Cup 1972

STRANRAER

Year founded: 1870
Ground: Stair Park (6,100)
Highest ever crowd: 6,500, 24th January 1948 v Rangers (Scottish Cup rd 1)
Nickname: The Blues
Colours: Royal blue shirts, white shorts, royal blue socks

STRANRAER are the third oldest club in the Scottish League, although they didn't become members until 1949. For the first 108 years of their existence The Blues didn't have a manager. Instead, the team was picked by a committee of 12 directors.

● THE COMMITTEE got it right on the day Stranraer enjoyed their record win in 1965, beating Brechin City 7–0, although what were they thinking of when they sent the team out to face Queen of the South in the Scottish Cup in 1932? (The Blues recorded their worst defeat, an 11–1 humiliation.)

● IN 1987/88 STRANRAER won just 16 points and four games all season to set two unenviable Division Two records.

● STRANRAER were the last league club in either England or Scotland to install floodlights. It was not until 1981 that the lights finally went on at Stair Park.

Roll of Honour

Second Division champions 1994

GORDON STRACHAN

Born: Edinburgh 9.2.57.

Coventry City manager Gordon Strachan is, quite possibly, the Premiership's most excitable boss. He spends most games standing on the touchline screaming at his players, waving his arms around and generally working himself into a lather.

● During his touchline tantrums he has been known to use the occasional swear word and in February 1998 Southampton fans reported Strachan to the police for turning the air blue at The Dell. The Coventry boss was unimpressed: 'The only reason they claimed my language was out of order is because they can't stomach the thought that Coventry beat their beloved Saints,' he said.

● In 1997/98 Strachan, who took over the Highfield Road hotseat from Ron Atkinson in November 1996, guided the Sky Blues to 11th position in the Premiership - their best league placing since 1989. It made a nice change for City fans, who are more accustomed to watching their side battle against relegation.

● In a hugely successful playing career with Dundee, Aberdeen, Manchester United,

Answer to quiz on page 134: Opel

The greatest moment in Sunderland's recent history... Ian Porterfield celebrates scoring the 1973 FA Cup Final winner

Leeds and Coventry, Strachan played over 600 league games. His son, Gavin, has followed in his father's footsteps and made his debut for Coventry in 1997/98.

STREAKS

EVERTON HOLD the all-time record for winning streaks in the top flight of the football league. They won 12 successive games in 1894. There was, however, a close season splitting up the wins.

● TOTTENHAM HOTSPUR hold the record for most consecutive wins in one season in the First Division. They went 11 matches without dropping a point during their double-winning season of 1960/61.

● MANCHESTER UNITED, Bristol City and Preston North End share the English record for wins on the trot, managing 14 apiece in 1904/05, 1905/06 and 1950/51.

● NONE OF those sides were a patch on Morton's 1963/64 side, who won an incredible 23 games in sequence. They were promoted to the Scottish First Division as proud champions that year.

● THE LONGEST unbeaten start to a season is shared by Leeds United (1973/74) and Liverpool (1987/99), both of whom went 29 matches before coming a cropper.

ALAN SUGAR

Born: 24.3.47

ALAN SUGAR, the Tottenham chairman since 1991, is one of the most most controversial figures in soccer. He once famously dismissed foreign players as 'Carlos Kick-a-Balls' and followed that with a scathing public attack on some of his own players in an address to the Cambridge University Union in 1997.

● Sugar is best known for his bitter falling-out with former Spurs boss Terry Venables. The feud between the two ended up in court, with Sugar suing Venables for libel. The case dragged on for almost two years, but was finally settled in 1996 with Venables being ordered to pay his arch enemy £100,001.

● Sugar made the millions that enabled him to buy into Tottenham through his company Amstrad, which made cheap personal computers and satellite dishes in the late 1980s and early 1990s.

SUNDAY FOOTBALL

FOR RELIGIOUS REASONS the FA didn't allow affiliated teams to play football on Sunday until 1955.

● OF THE 42,000 teams affiliated with the FA now, about half play their football on a Sunday. Sunday league football is famous for the enthusiasm, if not for the technical ability, of the players concerned. In all there are 2,250,000 players registered with the English FA.

● THE FIRST FOOTBALL League match to be played on a Sunday didn't take place until 20th January 1974, when Millwall beat Fulham 1–0 at The Den.

CHRIS SUTTON

Born: Nottingham 10.3.73.
Height: 6ft 3in
Position: Striker
Club career:
1991-94 Norwich City 102 (35)
1994- Blackburn Rovers 113 (44)
International record:
1997- England 1 (0)

CHRIS SUTTON scored the most spectacular own goal of last season when he refused to play for England B against Chile B in February 1998. Glenn Hoddle was less than impressed with the Blackburn striker's attitude, and consequently refused to consider him for the England World Cup squad.

● IT WAS A great shame for Sutton, who had just enjoyed his most prolific season with Blackburn – his 18 Premiership goals making him the league's joint top scorer with Michael Owen and Dion Dublin. His most successful campaign, though, was in 1994/95 when he picked up a Premiership winners' medal with the Ewood Park club.

● A versatile player who has played many games at centre-half, Sutton began his career at Norwich. He came to national prominence in the 1993/94 season when he notched up a career-best 25 goals.

● For a while Sutton was Britain's most expensive footballer. When he joined Rovers in July 1994 he became this country's first ever £5 million player.

SUNDERLAND

Year founded: 1879
Ground: Stadium of Light (42,000)
Highest ever crowd: 75,118, 8th March 1933 v Derby County (FA Cup rd 6 replay)
Previous name: Sunderland and District Teacher's AFC
Nickname: The Rokermen
Colours: Red-and-white-striped shirts, black shorts, red socks

SUNDERLAND WERE the first club to win the League Championship three times, lifting the title in 1892, 1893 and 1895. Their points total of 48 in 1893 is a record for the nineteenth century.

● SUNDERLAND were the first Second Division team to win the FA Cup in the post-war period. Their 1–0 triumph over then-mighty Leeds in 1973 is arguably the biggest Cup Final upset of all time, and was achieved by a Sunderland team without a single international player.

● THEN IN 1992 Sunderland became the first Second Division side in the post-war era to reach two FA Cup finals. The Rokermen, though, were unable to repeat their 1973 heroics and lost rather tamely 2–0 to Liverpool.

● IN 1958 Sunderland were relegated after a then record 68 years in the First Division. Arsenal have since overtaken The Wearsiders with an unbroken run of 79 years in the top flight. They would have been hoping for a similar run after promotion to the Premiership in 1996, but they were relegated again a year later.

● SUNDERLAND's biggest ever victory, 11–1, was against Fairfield in the FA Cup in 1895. However, The Rokermen probably enjoyed their record league win more. In 1908 they thrashed local rivals, and eventual champions, Newcastle 9–1 at St. James' Park – a record victory unsurpassed by any away team in the top division before or since.

● SUNDERLAND have twice been on the wrong end of 8–0 scorelines – against West Ham in 1968 and Watford in 1982.

● IN 1893 Sunderland became the first club to score 100 football league goals. Inside-forward Charlie Buchan is Sunderland's record scorer, with an amazing haul of 209 league goals for the club between 1911–25. Dave Halliday holds the record for a single season, striking 43 times in 1928/29.

● NOBODY HAS played more games for Sunderland than goalkeeper Jim Montgomery. A star of that 1973 Cup final victory, Montgomery played in goal for The Rokermen in 537 league matches between 1962–77.

● IN 1994/95 Sunderland drew 18 Division One matches to equal a club record established in 1954/55.

● WHEN THEY won the league title in 1935/36 Sunderland conceded 74 goals, a record by any First Division champions.

● SUNDERLAND's most capped player is Martin Harvey, who played in 34 matches for Northern Ireland while at Roker Park.

● SUNDERLAND's oldest ever player is former Newcastle favourite, Bryan 'Pop' Robson. In 1984 he played against Leicester aged 38 and 128 days. At the other end of the age scale, Derek Foster played for Sunderland aged 15 and 184 days in 1964...

the club's youngest ever player.

● SUNDERLAND have played Preston North End seven times in the FA Cup and never lost. Their most memorable victory in this fixture was a 3–1 final win in 1937.

● IN 1890 Sunderland became the first club to have points deducted for fielding an illegal player.

● SUNDERLAND's most famous fan is middle-distance runner Steve Cram.

● During the 1997/98 season Kevin Phillips scored in seven consecutive games and in nine consecutive home games, both club records. And when the hot-shot striker, signed from Watford in the close season, scored against Charlton in the play-off final in May 1998 he broke Brian Clough's post-war record for goals-in-a-season for Sunderland taking his tally to 35.

Roll of Honour

Div 1 champions 1892, 1893, 1895, 1902, 1913, 1936
First Division champions 1996
Div 2 champions 1976
Div 3 champions 1988
FA Cup 1937, 1973

Sunderland's Post-War Record

47 D1 9th	64 D2 2nd	81 D1 17th
48 D1 20th	65 D1 15th	82 D1 19th
49 D1 8th	66 D1 19th	83 D1 16th
50 D1 3rd	67 D1 17th	84 D1 13th
51 D1 12th	68 D1 15th	85 D1 21st
52 D1 12th	69 D1 17th	86 D2 18th
53 D1 9th	70 D1 21st	87 D2 20th
54 D1 18th	71 D2 13th	88 D3 1st
55 D1 4th	72 D2 5th	89 D2 11th
56 D1 9th	73 D2 6th	90 D2 6th
57 D1 20th	74 D2 6th	91 D1 19th
58 D1 21st	75 D2 4th	92 D2 18th
59 D2 15th	76 D2 1st	93 D1 21st
60 D2 16th	77 D1 20th	94 D1 12th
61 D2 6th	78 D2 6th	95 D1 20th
62 D2 3rd	79 D2 4th	96 D1 1st
63 D2 3rd	80 D2 2nd	97 PR 18th
		98 D1 3rd

SUPERSTITIONS

Many players adhere to superstitions before and during matches: Paul Ince, for example, never puts his shirt on until he reaches the pitch.

● TEAMS, TOO, have their superstitions. The Newcastle side in the early part of the century, for instance, felt they would win if they saw a wedding on the way to the match. If they saw a funeral, on the other hand, they would lose... if they needed a point all they had to do was avoid churches.

● MANAGERS ALSO have their foibles. Brian Clough never watched Nottingham Forest play without wearing his trusty green sweatshirt. George Graham used to wear a red scarf to Arsenal matches. Brighton manager Jimmy Melia wore white dancing shoes to his team's FA Cup matches on their run to the final in 1983, and Malcolm Allison wore his 'lucky' Fedora hat until Third Division Crystal Palace got to the semi-final of the 1976 FA Cup against Southampton... where the luck ran out.

● SOME SUPERSTITIONS are based on experience: Arsenal always make sure their goalkeepers' new shirts are washed before matches after their 1927 FA Cup Final keeper, Dan Lewis, blamed Cardiff's winning goal on the sheen of his brand spanking new jumper causing the ball to slip into the net.

● IN AFRICA SUPERSTITION is very much part of the game, with many teams employing witch doctors to bring them good fortune. In 1983 a second round African Cup Winners' Cup match between Stationery Stores and Asecs was abandoned after a series of fights. The problem started at the start of the second half when the Asec goalkeeper was seen to bury an object behind his goal. Enraged Stationery players were convinced there was black magic going on and tempers led to fights on and off the pitch, and the referee taking both teams off the pitch.

SWANSEA CITY

Year founded: 1912
Ground: Vetch Field (11,477)
Highest ever crowd: 32,796, 17th February 1968 v Arsenal (FA Cup rd 4)
Nickname: The Swans
Colours: White shirts, white shorts, white socks

THE MOST GLORIOUS period in Swansea's history was in the late 1970s and early 80s when - under the guidance of manager John Toshack - the club rose from Division Four to Division One in just four seasons. The champagne bubbles soon turned flat, however, and by 1986 The Swans were back in the basement division.

● IN 1982, during the Toshack era, the club enjoyed a record 12-0 victory over Sliema Wanderers of Malta in the European Cup Winners' Cup. No fewer than eight Swansea players got their names on the scoresheet, to set another club record.

● THE CLUB's most famous wins, though, have been in the FA Cup. In 1926 Swansea knocked out mighty Arsenal before losing to Bolton in the semi-finals. It was a similar story in 1964 - Swansea beat Liverpool at Anfield, only to go out to fellow Second Division side Preston one step from Wembley.

● IVOR ALLCHURCH holds the goalscoring record for Swansea, notching 166 goals in two spells at the club between 1948–67.

Roll of Honour

Div 3 (S) champions 1925, 1949
Welsh Cup 9 times
Autoglass Trophy 1994

SWEDEN

First international: Sweden 11 Norway 3 (Gothenburg, 1908)
First World Cup appearance: Sweden 3 Argentina 2 (Italy, 1934)
Highest capped player: Thomas Ravelli (143)
Highest goalscorer: Sven Rydell (49)
Biggest victory: 12–0 v Latvia, 1927
Biggest defeat: 1–12 v England Amateur, 1908
Colours: Yellow shirts, blue shorts, yellow socks

SWEDEN MADE one of the best international debuts ever when they beat neighbours Norway 11–3 on 7th December 1908.

● SWEDEN's only major trophy was won in 1948, when they were awarded Olympic Gold after beating Yugoslavia 3–1 in London. Milan scouts were so impressed with their forward line of Gren, Nordhal and Liedholm that they signed all three and they soon became the most feared attacking force in Europe.

● THE 1948 SIDE was managed by Englishman George Raynor, who also took Sweden to the semis of the 1950 World Cup, and the final of the 1958 edition... played at home in Sweden. The Swedes were destroyed 5–2 that day by a Brazil side featuring a 17–year–old by the name of Pele, becoming the only team to concede five goals in a World Cup Final.

● SWEDEN MANAGED to get to the semis again in USA 94, where again Brazil were their vanquishers, this time by a more modest 1–0. But at least the Scadinavians trounced Bulgaria 4–0 to claim third place.

● WITH 143 international appearances under his belt Sweden's flamboyant keeper Thomas Ravelli is Europe's most capped player, and second only to Saudi Arabia's Majed Abdullah (147) in the world.

WORLD CUP RECORD

1930	Did not enter	1970	Round 1
1934	Quarter-finals	1974	Round 2
1938	Fourth place	1978	Round 1
1950	Third place	1982	Did not qualify
1954	Did not qualify	1986	Did not qualify
1958	Runners-up	1990	Round 1
1962	Did not qualify	1994	Semi-finals
1966	Did not qualify	1998	Did not qualify

Thomas Ravelli points out to his defence that he is Europe's most capped footballer of all time

FRANK SWIFT

Born: Blackpool 26.12.13 Died: 6.2.58
Height: 6ft 0ins Position: Goalkeeper
Club career:
1932–49 Manchester City 338
International record:
1947–49 England 19

FRANK SWIFT was an extremely popular Manchester City goalkeeper in the 1930s and 40s who became the first man to captain England from between the sticks.

● SWIFT WAS AN integral part of Manchester City's FA Cup run in 1934 which eventually saw them lift the trophy. It was all too much for nervous 20-year-old 'Big Swifty' who fainted on his goal-line just after the final whistle.

● ANOTHER HIGHLIGHT of his long career was Manchester City's League Championship triumph of 1937.

● WHEN SWIFT retired in 1950 he became a coach and a journalist. He died tragically in the 1958 Munich air disaster, having travelled with the Manchester United team to report on their match against Red Star Belgrade.

SWINDON TOWN

Year founded: 1881
Ground: County Ground (15,341)
Highest ever crowd: 32,000, 15th January 1972 v Arsenal (FA Cup rd 3)
Nickname: The Robins
Colours: Red shirts, red shorts, red socks

SWINDON WERE founder members of the Third Division in 1920 and got off to a magnificent start, crushing Luton 9–1 in their first ever match. The score remains a club record. The Robins suffered their worst defeat, 10–1, in an FA Cup tie against Manchester City in 1930.

● DEAD-EYED marksman Harry Morris holds a number of Swindon goalscoring records. He is the club's leading scorer with 216 league goals, the highest scorer in a season with 47 goals in 1926/27, and the only Swindon player to have twice scored five goals in a match (v QPR in 1927 and v Norwich in 1930).

● IN 1969 Swindon became only the second Third Division club to win the League Cup at Wembley, flying winger Don Rogers inspiring the team to a shock 3–1 win over Arsenal on a mud-clogged pitch.

● THE FOLLOWING YEAR Swindon became the first winners of the Anglo Italian Cup with a resounding 3-0 win over Napoli.

● JOHN TROLLOPE is Swindon's longest-serving player. Between 1960–80 he played in an astounding 770 matches for The Robins. This is a record number of appearances for one club, beating Roy Sproson's 761 for Port Vale between 1950–72.

● Swindon's whopping tally of 102 points in division four in the 1985/86 season is an English league record.

'Do I not like this miserable picture of me going in this book!' – Graham Taylor in his England heyday

● IN 1990 Swindon became the first and only team to win a Wembley play-off and not gain promotion. The club was forced to stay down as a punishment for financial irregularities committed during the stewardship of former manager Lou Macari.

● IN 1993/94 Swindon set two unwanted Premiership records during their relegation campaign. First, The Robins' leaky defence conceded exactly 100 goals, the only time that figure has been reached in the new top division. Second, Swindon only won five games in the entire season, fewer than any Premiership club before or since.

Roll of Honour

Div 4 champions 1986
League Cup 1969

SWITZERLAND

First international: France 1 Switzerland 0 (Paris, 1905)
First World Cup appearance: Switzerland 3 Holland 2 (Italy, 1934)
Highest capped player: Heinz Hermann (117)
Highest goalscorer: Max Abegglen (32)
Best win: 9-0 v Lithuania, 1924
Worst defeat: 0-9 v Hungary, 1911
Colours: Red shirts, white shorts, red socks

IN 1954 SWITZERLAND played in the highest-scoring match at the World Cup finals, losing in the quarter-finals 5–7 to Austria in Lausanne. After 23 minutes the Swiss were 3–0 up and strolling to victory. Then their defence developed more holes than emmenthal, and they conceded an incredible five goals in ten minutes.

● BETWEEN May 1928 and March 1932 Switzerland only managed one win in 27 internationals. The dismal run included a sequence of eleven consecutive defeats.

● THE 1990s have been the most successful period in Switzerland's history. In 1994, under Englishman Roy Hodgson, the Swiss reached the second round of the World Cup for the first time in 40 years, and two years later they qualified for Euro 96, holding England to a draw in the first match of the tournament.

● NO SWISS CLUB team has ever reached the final of a European competition. FC Zurich, though, have made two appearances in the European Cup semi-finals.

WORLD CUP RECORD

1930	Did not enter	1950	Round 1
1958	Did not qualify	1970–90	
1934	Quarter-finals		Did not qualify
1962	Round 1	1954	Quarter-finals
1938	Quarter-finals	1994	Round 2
1966	Round 1	1998	Did not qualify

GRAHAM TAYLOR

Born: Worksop 15.9.44

IN GRAHAM TAYLOR's three years as England manager England only lost seven times: but did he not choose the right matches to lose! Against Sweden in the European Championship finals, against Holland and Norway in the World Cup qualifiers for USA 94 and, perhaps most embarrassingly of all, against the United States in a summer friendly in 1993.

● TAYLOR BECAME the most pilloried England manager in the history of the game. The Sun, in particular, was extremely vitriolic, superimposing a picture of a turnip on his head after defeat by the Swedes (Swedes 2 Turnips 1!).

● TAYLOR is, however, an extremely successful club manager. He took Watford from the Fourth Division to runners-up in the old First between 1977 and 1981, achieved another runners-up spot with Aston Villa in 1990 and, returning to his roots, guided Watford back to the new First Division in 1998.

● Taylor's strength has traditionally been getting the most out of slim pickings by using a long ball game designed to unsettle better opponents. A modest player with Grimsby and Lincoln, he wasn't the ideal choice, with the benefit of hindsight, for the England job.

THROW- INS

BARNSLEY's Frank Bokas became the first man in British football ever to score straight from a throw-in in 1938. The Manchester United goalkeeper touched the ball into the net thus legitimising a score that would otherwise have been disallowed.

● THROW-INS were done away with in the Diadora League in season 1994/5 as an experiment, replaced with kick-ins from the touch-line. It was not popular. 'If the rule continues everyone will have a team of giraffes and no midfield,' commented one disgruntled manager.

● THE LONG throw-in has become a common tactic amongst British clubs – Gary Neville of Manchester United and England is particularly good at hurling the ball into the penalty area, making a throw-in as good as a corner.

● NEWCASTLE DEFENDER Steve Watson certainly impressed Newcastle fans during his debut for the club in 1992. Instead of doing a traditional throw-in he somersaulted in the air before landing on his feet and launching the ball goalwards.

TORQUAY UNITED

Year founded: 1898
Ground: Plainmoor (6,500)
Highest ever crowd: 21,908, 29th January 1955 v Huddersfield Town (FA Cup rd 4)
Nickname: The Gulls
Colours: Yellow-and-navy-striped shirts, navy shorts, yellow socks

TORQUAY'S ROLL of honour is not exactly a lengthy one, their only real sniff of glory coming in 1989 when they reached the Sherpa Van Trophy Final at Wembley – unfortunately they lost 4–1 to Bolton!

● TORQUAY ENJOYED their biggest victory in 1952, trouncing Swindon Town 9–0, but The Gulls have twice been on the wrong end of 10–2 scorelines – at Fulham in 1931, and at Luton two years later.

● LEE SHARPE is the most famous player to have been on Torquay's books. He only played 14 games for the Plainmoor club, though, before he was snapped up by Manchester United in 1988 for £180,000, the biggest transfer fee Torquay have ever received.

● TORQUAY HAVE the equal worst FA Cup record in the whole of the Football League... apart from Hartlepool United. They have never appeared in the last 16 and have only made five appearances (to Hartlepool's four) in the last 32.

● TORQUAY DEFENDER Pat Kruse has the unfortunate honour of having scored the fastest own goal in the history of English football... netting against his own goalkeeper on 3rd January 1977 for Cambridge United after just six seconds.

Scottish international David Hopkin demonstrates his long throw technique in his Chelsea days

JOHN TOSHACK

Born: Cardiff 22.3.49
Position: Forward
Club career:
1966–70 Cardiff City 162 (75)
1970–78 Liverpool 172 (74)
1978–84 Swansea City 63 (24)
International record:
1969–80 Wales 40 (13)

JOHN TOSHACK first caught the eye as a teenage forward in the Cardiff City side that became the most successful Welsh club in European competition. This was in 1967/68 and they reached the semi-final of the Cup Winners' Cup where they lost to Hamburger SV.

● TOSHACK formed one of the deadliest strike partnerships of all time, nicknamed 'the Old Firm', with Kevin Keegan at Liverpool in the mid-1970s, helping The Reds to win the FA Cup, the UEFA Cup and several championships.

● IN 1978 he returned to Wales to become Swansea City's most successful manager of all time. He took The Swans from the Fourth Division to sixth in the First in four years at the club between 1978–82. Unfortunately three years later he escorted them back down to the Third again.

● TOSHACK went to try his luck abroad, and thrived in Spain where he managed Real Madrid (winning the title in 1990), Real Sociedad and Deportivo la Coruña. In 1997 he moved on to Turkish side Besiktas.

Did You Know?

The first foreign player ever to play professional football in England was Max Seeburg, a German who played for Tottenham before the First World War. He made his debut for Spurs in season 1908/09 and later played for Leyton, Burnley, Grimsby and Reading.

Spurs celebrate their 1991 FA Cup win. But where's Gazza?

TOTTENHAM HOTSPUR

Year Founded: 1882
Ground: White Hart Lane (32,786)
Highest ever crowd: 75,038, 5th March 1938 v Sunderland (FA Cup rd 6)
Nickname: Spurs
Colours: White shirts, navy blue shorts, white socks

IN 1961 TOTTENHAM HOTSPUR became the first club this century to win the League and Cup Double. Their triumph was founded on an explosive start to the season, the side notching up 11 straight wins from the opening day to set a record for the top flight which has never been beaten.

● GUIDED BY manager Bill Nicholson, the team created another record by winning 31 of their 42 games, and finished a comfortable eight points clear of runners-up Sheffield Wednesday.

● SPURS ENJOYED their best ever win against Crewe Alexandra in the FA Cup in 1960. The minnows were humbled 13–2 in a fourth round replay at White Hart Lane, with Les Allen equalling the club record by netting five times for Spurs. Tottenham's worst ever defeat, 7–0, was at Anfield against a rampant Liverpool in 1978, one of Ossie Ardiles' and Ricky Villa's first games in the First Division.

● TOTTENHAM, as Arsenal fans like to point out, have not won the League since those 'Glory, Glory' days, but it has been a different story in the FA Cup. In 1982 Spurs became the last team to retain the Cup, beating QPR in a replay the year after a dramatic 3–2 Wembley win over Manchester City, again in a replay.

● SPURS HAVE made a habit of winning the FA Cup over two games. The club's first success, in 1901 against Sheffield United, also required a second match. More importantly, that early triumph is the only time this century that a non-league side has lifted the Cup – Spurs being a Southern League club at the time.

● THE CLUB also has a habit of winning the cup when there is a '1' at the end of the year, having lifted it in 1901, 1921, 1961, 1981 and 1991. In all Spurs have won the FA Cup eight times; only Manchester United have won it more times (nine).

● IN THE 1901 cup run, Tottenham striker Sandy Brown scored 15 goals, at least one in every round.

● IN 1963 SPURS became the first British club to win a major European trophy. Atletico Madrid were hammered 5–1 in Rotterdam – Jimmy Greaves scoring twice – as Tottenham won the European Cup Winners' Cup in style.

● IN 1972 SPURS recorded a second European victory, beating Wolves 3–2 on aggregate in the final of the UEFA Cup. It was the first and only time two English clubs have met in a European final.

● THE LEGENDARY Jimmy Greaves holds two goalscoring records for Tottenham. His total of 220 league goals between 1961–70 is a club best, as is his tally of 37 league goals in 1962/63. Clive Allen, though, struck a magnificent 49 goals in all competitions in 1986/87.

● NOBODY HAS pulled on Tottenham's famous white shirt more often than Steve Perryman. Between 1969–86 he played in 655 league games.

● TOTTENHAM ARE the only club to have won and lost the FA Cup thanks to own goals. In the 1987 final Gary Mabbutt put through his own net to give Coventry the trophy, but four years later Spurs were the beneficiaries when Nottingham Forest's Des Walker beat his own goalkeeper with a powerful header.

● THE MOST EXPENSIVE player to leave the club is former favourite Paul Gascoigne, who moved to Lazio for £5.5 million after a long-running transfer saga in 1991.

● FAMOUS TOTTENHAM supporters include the singing duo Chas 'n' Dave, veteran gameshow host Bruce Forsyth, actor Warren Mitchell and smoothie TV host and DJ Russ Williams.

Roll of Honour

Div 1 champions 1951, 1961
FA Cup 1901, 1921, 1961, 1962, 1967, 1981, 1982, 1991
League Cup 1971, 1973
European Cup Winners' Cup 1963
UEFA Cup 1972, 1984

Spurs' Post-War Record

47 D2 6th	64 D1 4th	81 D1 10th
48 D2 8th	65 D1 6th	82 D1 4th
49 D2 5th	66 D1 8th	83 D1 4th
50 D2 1st	67 D1 3rd	84 D1 8th
51 D1 1st	68 D1 7th	85 D1 3rd
52 D1 2nd	69 D1 6th	86 D1 10th
53 D1 10th	70 D1 11th	87 D1 3rd
54 D1 16th	71 D1 3rd	88 D1 13th
55 D1 16th	72 D1 6th	89 D1 6th
56 D1 18th	73 D1 8th	90 D1 3rd
57 D1 2nd	74 D1 11th	91 D1 10th
58 D1 3rd	75 D1 19th	92 D1 5th
59 D1 18th	76 D1 9th	93 PR 8th
60 D1 3rd	77 D1 22nd	94 PR 15th
61 D1 1st	78 D2 3rd	95 PR 7th
62 D1 3rd	79 D1 11th	96 PR 8th
63 D1 2nd	80 D1 14th	97 PR 10th
		98 PR 14th

Pretty butch for a bloke called Lesley, huh?

T

TRANMERE ROVERS

Year founded: 1884
Ground: Prenton Park (17,000)
Highest ever crowd: 24,424, 5th February 1972 v Stoke City (FA Cup rd 4)
Previous name: Belmont AFC
Colours: White shirts, white shorts, white socks

ROVERS' PLAYER/MANAGER John Aldridge is Tranmere's most capped player, winning 30 of his 69 caps for the Republic of Ireland while at Prenton Park. Of Aldridge's English record haul of 475 goals, 179 of them were scored with Rovers.

● TRANMERE's record win was a 13–0 battering of Oswestry in the FA Cup in 1914. The club's worst defeat, a 9–1 demolition job, came at Tottenham in 1953 in the same competition.

● THE CLUB's best ever league win – 13–4 against Oldham in 1935 – holds the record for the highest number of goals ever scored in a football league match. Robert 'Bunny' Bell's nine goals in the match stands as a record for the old Third Division (North).

● HAROLD BELL is Tranmere's record appearance maker, playing in 595 league games for Rovers between 1946–64. Bell appeared in 401 consecutive league games for the club, to set a record that has never been matched by any other player in the English League.

● TRANMERE ROVERS were the first club of the legendary 'Dixie' Dean. The prolific goalscorer made his debut for the Birkenhead club aged 16 and 355 days in 1924, and remains the youngest player ever to have appeared for Rovers.

● TRAVELLING Tranmere fans had to endure a miserable time between 1977–79 as their team failed to win an away match in 35 attempts. Manager John King was clearly satisfied with his side's efforts, though: in the 1977/78 season he left the Tranmere line-up unchanged for all but five games of a 46-match programme.

Roll of Honour

Div 3 (N) champions 1938
Welsh Cup 1935
Leyland Daf Cup 1990

Tranmere Rovers player-boss John Aldridge shows his colours

TRANSFERS

THE BIGGEST ever transfer deal took place in the summer of 1998 when Spanish club Real Betis signed Brazilian international Denilson from his hometown club Sao Paolo for a staggering £21.5 million, a figure which overtook the £18 million Inter Milan had paid Barcelona for his team-mate Ronaldo.

● THE HIGHEST sum to pass between English club coffers was the £15 million that Newcastle United paid Blackburn Rovers to procure the services of striker Alan Shearer, who they had rejected as a youngster after giving him a trial – in goal.

● Other players in the exclusive eight-figure-fee club include Gianluigi Lentini (Torino to Milan, £12 million, 1992) Gianluca Vialli (Sampdoria to Juventus, £12 million, 1992) Enrico Chiesa (Sampdoria to Parma, £11 million, 1995) Jaap Stam (PSV to Manchester United, £10.5 million, 1998) Roberto Baggio (Juventus to AC Milan, £10 million, 1992) and Jean-Pierre Papin (£10 million, Marseille to AC Milan, 1992).

● AT £3 MILLION, sparkling midfielder Lee Bowyer became the most expensive ever teenager in Britain when he was transferred from Charlton to Leeds on 3rd July 1996.

● THE FIRST man to be transferred for a four-figure fee in England was Alf Common, who went from Sunderland to Middlesbrough for a cool £1,000 on 19th February 1905.

● THE FIRST SIX-FIGURE fee transfer saw Alan Ball move from Blackpool to Everton for £110,000 in 1966. Trevor Francis became the first million pound man when he signed for Nottingham Forest from Birmingham for £1,150,000 in 1979.

TUNISIA

First World Cup appearance: Tunisia 3 Mexico 1 (Argentina, 1978)
Colours: White shirts, white shorts, white socks

TUNISIA performed heroically at their first World Cup finals in 1978, only missing out on a second round place by a point. A 3–1 win against Mexico made qualification a distinct possibility, but defeat against Poland made a victory against World Champions West Germany a necessity – and the Africans could only draw, 0–0.

● In 1997 the North Africans qualified for their second ever World Cup by heading a tough group which included African champions Egypt and George Weah's Liberia... in the end the Tunisian defence only conceded one goal in six qualifying matches. Drawn in the same group as England, Columbia and Romania in the tournament proper the Tunisians battled bravely, but only managed a single point and a single goal, which for a time looked like being enough to beat Romania and allow England to top their group, but ultimately wasn't.

● Tunisia have never won the African Nations Cup but have twice reached the final, on home ground in 1965 (losing 3–2 to Ghana) and in South Africa in 1996, where they lost 2–0 to the hosts.

WORLD CUP RECORD

1930-58 Did not enter	1974 Did not qualify
1962 Did not qualify	1978 Round 1
1966 Did not enter	1982-94 Did not qualify
1970 Did not qualify	1998 Round 1

TV AND RADIO

ON 22nd JANUARY 1927 the public were able to tune in to live football on the radio for the first time, when the BBC broadcast the clash at Highbury between Arsenal and Sheffield United. The Radio Times printed a pitch marked into numbered squares, and the commentators used the numbers to describe where play had reached (hence the phrase 'back to square one').

● THE 1937 FA CUP FINAL between Sunderland and Preston was the first to be televised. It is estimated that ten times more people watched it at the stadium than on the box because hardly anyone had a television. Sunderland won 3–1.

● THE FIRST SCOTTISH match to be shown live on television, with commentary by Ken Wolstenholme, was the 1955 Scottish Cup final between Clyde and Celtic, which finished in a 1–1 draw.

● THE BIGGEST AUDIENCE for an FA Cup Final was the 14.9 million people who watched the 1991 match between Tottenham Hotspur and Nottingham Forest in 1991. The biggest ever TV audience for a football match in Britain, however, was the staggering 26 million who tuned in for the titanic England v Argentina clash in the France 98 World Cup (beating the 25.1 million who watched England lose on penalties two years previously, this time to Germany at Euro 96). Indeed, France 98 was watched in a record total of over 200 countries with an estimated average audience of 500 million. A cumulative audience of 38 billion viewers is thought to have watched the tournament, more than any other sporting event in history.

● THE BIGGEST ever television deal in the history of the game was when BSkyB paid £670 million to the Premier League for four years' rights to Premiership football in 1996.

● WHEN CHARLTON won at West Brom on 5th February 1995 it was their first victory on live television for 48 years, since their FA Cup triumph in 1947.

Funny Old Game

Tony Cascarino was once transferred from Crockenhill to Gillingham for 13 sets of tracksuits.

UEFA

UEFA, the Union of European Football Associations, is the second most important footballing organisation in the world. It holds power over all the national FAs in Europe, and is itself under the jurisdiction of FIFA.

● UEFA WAS formed in 1954 at a meeting during the Swiss World Cup, and within two years had organised the first edition of the European Cup, won by Real Madrid in 1956.

● THE FIRST competition it organised was the Inter City Fairs Cup, the first edition of which started in 1955 and ended with Barcelona beating London in 1958.

● CONTROVERSIAL UEFA decisions include the use of penalty kicks (rather than the toss of a coin) to decide drawn European ties (from 1970) and the banning of English clubs from Europe in 1985 after the Heysel tragedy.

UEFA CUP

THE UEFA CUP started life as the Fairs Cup in 1955: it was set up as a competition between cities, rather than clubs, and the first winners were Barcelona who beat London 6–2 on aggregate. It was the first official international club competition in Europe.

● THE FIRST team to win the newly-named UEFA Cup was Tottenham Hotspur in 1972, who beat Wolves 3–2 on aggregate in the only all-English final of a European competition.

● IN 1969 NEWCASTLE won the Fairs Cup after finishing a lowly 10th in the First Division the season before, the lowest placed team ever to win the competition. In 1996 Bordeaux got to the final having qualified for the competition through the Inter Toto Cup... the first team to do so.

● ENGLISH AND ITALIAN clubs have both won the trophy nine times, with Spanish teams hot on their heels with eight wins.

● ONLY THREE SIDES have ever retained the trophy, all Spanish. They are Barcelona, who won the first two editions of the Fairs Cup; Valencia, who won the Fairs Cup in 1962 and 1963; and Real Madrid, who won the UEFA Cup in 1985 and 1986.

Funny Old Game

Football, they say, is a 'game of two halves'... but in 1894 a 'game of three halves' was played. The match was between Sunderland and Derby, and kicked off with a reserve referee in charge as Mr Kirkham, the official ref, was late. When he turned up at half-time Derby were 3–0 down, so when Mr Kirkham asked them if they wanted to re-start they jumped at the chance and two more halves were played. (Sunderland still won 8–0).

URUGUAY

First international: Uruguay 2 Argentina 3 (Montevideo, 1902)
First World Cup appearance: Uruguay 1 Peru 0 (Uruguay, 1930)
Highest capped player: Rodolfo Rodriguez (78)
Highest goalscorer: Hector Scarone (29)
Best win: 9–0 v Bolivia, 1927
Worst defeat: 1–6 v Argentina, 1919 and 1955; v Brazil, 1944; and v Denmark, 1986
Colours: Sky blue shirts, black shorts, black socks

IN 1930 URUGUAY became the first winners of the World Cup. Playing on home soil, the team – inspired by captain Nasazzi and striker Cea – beat neighbours and bitter rivals Argentina 4–2 to lift the trophy.

● IT WAS NO FLUKE: Uruguay had won the last two editions of the Olympic Games football tournament, in 1924 and 1928 (again against Argentina), the first non-European side to achieve such an honour.

● URUGUAY and Argentina have played more international matches against each other than any other pair of international teams, a total of 184 since 1901.

● THE BIGGEST crowd in the history of football went to see Uruguay play Brazil in the final game of the World Cup in 1950. In front of 199,589 screaming fans Uruguay won 2–1 to become the first South American side to win two World Cups.

● Uruguay are the only former winners of the World Cup who failed to qualify for France '98.

WORLD CUP RECORD

1930	Winners	1970	Fourth place
1934	Did not enter	1974	Round 1
1938	Did not enter	1978	Did not qualify
1950	Winners	1982	Did not qualify
1954	Fourth place	1986	Round 2
1958	Did not qualify	1990	Round 2
1962	Round 1	1994	Did not qualify
1966	Quarter-finals	1998	Did not qualify

USA

First international: USA 0 Canada 1 (Newark, 1885)
First World Cup appearance: USA 3 Belgium 0 (Uruguay, 1930)
Best win: 8–1 v Cayman Islands, 1993
Worst defeat: 10–0 v England, 1964 and v Italy, 1975
Colours: Blue and white shirts, white shorts, white socks

THE USA CREATED probably the biggest shock in international football history on 29th June 1950 at Belo Horizonte in Chile in the World Cup. They beat an England side which included the likes of Finney, Mannion, Mortenson and Wright 1–0 in the World Cup, with a flukey goal by Larry Gaetjens. England hit the woodwork a total of 11 times in the match. Sour grapes? You bet.

● ON JUNE 9, 1993 the USA beat England again to scrawl another chapter in England's book of humiliating moments. Defenders Tom Dooley and Alexi Lalas scored to create the memorable Sun headline 'Yanks 2 Planks 0'.

● THE USA's finest moment, however, came in the 1994 World Cup, which they hosted. The States beat much-vaunted Colombia 2–1 to get to the 2nd round of the competition before going out, honour intact, to Brazil. Their performances started a soccer craze in the country.

● THEIR GREATEST ever World Cup performance, however, came in the first tournament in 1930 when (with a team of ex-pat Englishman and Scotsmen) they reached the semi-finals, losing 6–1 to Argentina.

● THE STATES' performance at France 98 dampened the enthusiasm somewhat, however. They lost every game in their first round group including a humiliating defeat at the hands of traditional political enemies Iran.

WORLD CUP RECORD

1930	Semi-finals	1990	Round 1
1934	Round 1	1994	Round 2
1938	Did not qualify	1998	Round 1
1950	Round 1		
1954–86	Did not qualify		

Marco Van Basten celebrates one of his 24 goals for Holland with a certain dreadlocked teammate

CARLOS VALDERRAMA

Born: Colombia 2.9.61
Position: Midfield
Club career:
Santa Marta (Colombia)
Millionarios (Colombia)
Atletico Nacional (Colombia)
Montpellier (France)
Valladolid (Spain)
Medellin (Colombia)
Atletico Junior Baranquilla (Colombia)
International record:
1983– Colombia 110 (10)

CARLOS VALDERRAMA, muppet-haired midfield genius, masterminded Colombia's qualification to the 1990, 1994 and 1998 World Cups.

● TWICE VOTED South American Player of the Year (1987 and 1994), Valderrama became known as the 'South American Ruud Gullit' for his sublime skills and all-round vision.

● HE TRIED HIS luck on European fields, signing for Montpellier (of France) in 1988 and Valladolid (of Spain) in 1991, but could never recreate the sort of form that made him such a hero in his country.

● WHILE PLAYING for Valladolid against Real Madrid, Valderrama was involved in a Vinny/Gazza-type incident – Spanish star Michel was caught on camera squeezing (it seemed more a tickle than Vinny's squeeze) the South American's private parts. Michel was henceforth ridiculed from the terraces every match he played.

● Valderrama captained Colombia at their third successive World Cup finals at France 98, but for the second successive tournament they went out at the first hurdle... a 2–0 defeat by England proving the last appearance of the World Cup's most striking haircut ever.

MARCO VAN BASTEN

Born: Utrecht 31.10.64
Height: 6ft 2ins Position: Forward
Club career:
1982–87 Ajax 133 (128)
1987–94 AC Milan
International record:
1983–92 Holland 58 (24)

MARCO VAN BASTEN was the greatest goalscorer of his generation, one of only three men to have won the European Player of the Year Award three times (alongside Johan Cruyff and Michel Platini).

● HE WON a European Cup Winners' Cup medal at Ajax in 1987, and the European Golden Boot Award in 1986, after scoring 36 league goals in the season (in all he scored 128 goals for Ajax). He then moved to Milan – a snip at £1.5 million – to form part of the Dutch triumvirate of Gullit, Rijkaard and Van Basten. He won three Italian titles and two European Cups at the Italian club.

● VAN BASTEN scored five goals to finish top scorer of the 1988 European Championships (which Holland won), one of them a stunning volley from a tight angle in the final against Russia. His tally also included a hat-trick against England – the last player to achieve that.

● HE WAS the first man to score five goals in an international for Holland in the match against Malta in 1990. Bosman had achieved the feat against Cyprus three years earlier, but the match was declared void.

● AN ANKLE injury ended Van Basten's career early – too many bad tackles had put paid to a major world talent.

LOUIS VAN GAAL

Born: Holland 8.8.51

Barcelona manager Louis van Gaal enjoyed a glorious start to his managerial career in the Catalan capital last season as Barca won the Spanish title by the huge margin of 9 points. His side were much less successful in Europe, however, finishing bottom of their Champions League group – behind even Newcastle!

● After a spell in charge of AZ Alkmaar, Van Gaal made his name at Ajax where he was manager for six years from 1991. His greatest triumph at the Amsterdam club was winning the European Cup in 1995, with a young side including future stars Patrick Kluivert, Edgar Davids, Marc Overmaars and Finidi George.

● Van Gaal began his playing career with RKSV De Meer, before signing for Ajax. However, as a centre-forward his first-team opportunities were limited by a certain Johan Cruyff, and he moved on to FC Antwerp in Belgium in 1973.

TERRY VENABLES

Born: Bethnal Green 6.1.43

CRYSTAL PALACE boss Terry Venables is one of England's most successful managers. He took England as far in the European Championships as they had ever gone (losing on penalties to Germany in the Euro 96 semi-final). Under Sir Alf Ramsey they reached the same stage in 1968.

● APART FROM caretaker manager Joe Mercer's seven-game spell, England lost less under Venables than under any other gaffer. They were defeated just once in 23 matches, and that to World Champions Brazil (won 11, drew 11 and lost 1).

● VENABLES had previously been manager of Crystal Palace (where he created the much-vaunted then much-ridiculed 'team of the eighties' and has since returned), QPR (where he installed Britain's first artificial pitch), Barcelona (where he won the championship for the first time in over ten years) and Tottenham (where he won the FA Cup). At Barcelona he became the first Briton to win the World Manager of the Year Award.

● VENABLES was a good but not great player, turning out for London clubs Chelsea, Spurs, QPR and Crystal Palace. He was the first man to play for England at all five levels – schoolboy, youth, amateur, Under 23 and full. In all he won two full caps for his country.

Terry Venables laughs for the first time since England lost on penalties to Germany

GIANLUCA VIALLI

Born: Cremona 9.7.64
Height: 5ft 11ins Position: Forward
Club career:
1981–84 Cremonese 105 (23)
1984–92 Sampdoria 333 (140)
1992–96 Juventus 137 (25)
1996– Chelsea 49 (20)
International record:
1985–93 Italy 59 (16)

GIANLUCA VIALLI had an astonishingly successful start to his managerial career. After taking over from the deposed Ruud Gullit as player-manager at Chelsea in February 1998, by the end of the season he had won two trophies (the Coca Cola Cup and the European Cup Winners' Cup) for the Blues.

● HIS RECORD as a player is equally impressive – only two Italians have scored more than his 34 in European competitions. He one of only three Italians to have won all three European trophies – and the only Italian to have won them whilst at three different clubs (Sampdoria, Juventus and Chelsea).

● IN 1992 Vialli moved from Sampdoria to Juventus for a then world record £12 million fee. He had won three Italian Cups, the European Cup Winners' Cup and the league title with Sampdoria. He went on to inspire Juventus to a League and Cup

double and the European Cup, before signing for Chelsea.

● VIALLI HAS scored more goals at Under 21 level (11) than any other Italian. At full international level he has notched 16 goals in 59 appearances.

CHRIS WADDLE

Born Hepworth 14.12.60
Height: 6ft 2ins Position: Midfield/winger
Club career:
1980–85 Newcastle United 170 (46)
1985–89 Tottenham Hotspur 138 (33)
1989–92 Marseille 107 (22)
1992–96 Sheffield Wednesday 100 (10)
1996–97 Bradford 25 (6)
1997 Sunderland 7 (1)
1997–98 Burnley 31 (1)
International record:
1985–92 England 62 (6)

SADLY, CHRIS WADDLE will always be remembered for his penalty shoot-out miss for England in the 1990 World Cup semi-final against Germany in Turin. Sadly, because Waddle was one of the best players of his generation.

● WADDLE BECAME Britain's then most expensive player in 1989, when he moved from Tottenham to Marseille for £4.5 million. In 1991 he helped Marseille to their first European Cup Final, which they lost on penalties to Red Star Belgrade. The Geordie, for the record, didn't take one.

● WADDLE MADE his debut for Newcastle in 1980, and moved to Tottenham in 1985 for £590,000. After leaving Marseille he joined Sheffield Wednesday in 1992 for £1 million. In 1993 Wednesday became the first side to lose both domestic Cup Finals, each time to Arsenal, each time 2–1. Nevertheless Waddle was honoured with the Player of the Year Award that season.

● WADDLE WILL ALSO be remembered for the short-top-and-sides-but-long-at-the-back Chris Waddle haircut. He didn't become a truly great player until he got himself a more conventional barnet.

● Waddle began his managerial career at the start of the 1997/98 season at Burnley, but after they narrowly avoided relegation to Division Three he parted ways with the club by mutual consent at the end of the season.

Did You Know?

The first Fourth Division player ever to appear in a full international was Vic Rouse of Crystal Palace, who played for Wales against Northern Ireland on 22nd April 1959... Wales lost 4-1 and Rouse never played for his country again.

WALES

First international: Scotland 4 Wales 0 (friendly, Glasgow, 1876)
First World Cup appearance: Wales 1 Hungary 1 (Sweden, 1958)
Highest capped player: Neville Southall (86)
Highest goalscorer: Ian Rush (28)
Best win: 11–0 v Ireland, 1888
Worst defeat: 9–0 v Scotland, 1878
Colours: Red shirts, red shorts and red socks

WALES ARE the least successful of the British national sides, having qualified for only two major tournaments in their history.

● THEIR GREATEST hour came in 1958, when they qualified for the World Cup finals in Sweden. With such greats as Ivor Allchurch and John Charles in the team, they drew all their group matches before beating Hungary in a play-off, then went out honourably, 1–0 to eventual winners Brazil, in the quarter-finals.

● IN 1976 THEY got to the two-legged quarter-final of the European Championship against Yugoslavia. After losing 0–2 in Zagreb they could only draw 1–1 at Ninian Park, having missed a penalty and had two goals disallowed.

● WELSH INTERNATIONAL winger Billy Meredith won his 48th and final cap in 1920 at the ripe old age of 45 years and 229 days, 25 years after making his debut. He is the oldest player ever to play at international level.

● RYAN GIGGS' record as the youngest player ever to pull on a Wales shirt (17 years 332 days, set in 1991) was broken when namesake Ryan Green took the field against Malta in May 1998, aged 17 years 226 days.

WORLD CUP RECORD

1930/38	Did not enter
1950/54	Did not qualify
1958	Quarter-finals
1962/98	Did not qualify

JACK WALKER

Born: Blackburn 29.5.29

JACK WALKER is the Senior Vice-President of Blackburn Rovers, the man whose money has made it possible for Rovers to climb from second division hopefuls to Premiership champions in 1995.

● WALKER BECAME the club's benefactor after the sale of his Walker Steel empire for a colossal £330 million. The company's roots go back to 1945, when Jack's father, Charles Walker, began a tiny sheet metal and car body repair business with just £80 capital.

● A LIFE-LONG supporter of the club, Walker took control at Blackburn in season 1990/91. After the dismissal of Don Mackay at the start of the following season Walker installed Kenny Dalglish as the new

In perfect Welsh, Vinnie Jones lets rip with the famous anthem of the Valleys; 'You wot, you wot you wot you wot you wot?'

THE EIGHT CURRENT LEAGUE CLUBS WHO HAVE NEVER SUPPLIED A FULL INTERNATIONAL

Barnet
Colchester Utd
Darlington
Macclesfield
Rochdale
Scunthorpe United
Wigan Athletic
Wycombe Wanderers

manager, and gave him an open chequebook to sign players.

● AT THE SAME time the publicity-shy businessman has provided the funds to redevelop Ewood Park, turning it into one of the finest grounds in the country.

WALSALL

Year founded: 1888
Ground: Bescot Stadium (9,485)
Highest ever crowd: 10,628, 20th May 1990, England B v Switzerland B
Previous names: Walsall Swifts, Walsall Town and Walsall Town Swifts
Nickname: The Saddlers
Colours: Red shirts, black shorts and red socks

WALSALL'S BIGGEST win and worst defeat were against the same club. In 1899 The Saddlers thrashed Darwen 10–0 in a Second Division match, gaining revenge for a 0–12 reverse inflicted by the Lancastrians in 1896. Walsall also lost 0–12 to Small Heath in 1892.

● WALSALL'S MOST famous victory, though, was against Arsenal in the FA Cup in 1933. The Gunners were humbled 2–0 in one of the greatest giant-killing acts in the history of the competition.

● TWO PLAYERS share the honour of being Walsall's leading scorer. Tony Richards scored 184 league goals for the club between 1954–63, while his strike partner Colin Taylor matched that figure in three spells with the Midlands outfit between 1958–73.

● COLIN HARRISON is the club's longest-serving player, turning out in 467 league matches between 1964–82.

● IN THE eleven years between 1926 and 1937 Walsall had no fewer than nine managers: Joe Burchell, David Ashworth, Jack Torrance, James Kerr, S. Scholey, Peter O'Rourke, G. W. Slade, Andy Wilson and Tommy Lowes.

Roll of Honour

Div 4 champions 1960

WATFORD

Year founded: 1891
Ground: Vicarage Road (20,000)
Highest ever crowd: 34,099, 3rd February 1969 v Manchester United (FA Cup rd 4 replay)
Previous name: West Herts
Nickname: The Hornets
Colours: Yellow shirts, black shorts, black socks

WATFORD WERE struggling in the old Fourth Division when singer Elton John took over the chairmanship of his hometown club in 1978 and invested a substantial part of his personal wealth in the team. The club, under future England manager Graham Taylor, went on to enjoy a golden era, rising to the First Division and reaching The FA Cup Final in 1984. Both Taylor and John are now back at the club.

● ONE OF THE star players from that era, Luther Blissett, is Watford's record appearance maker. In three spells at Vicarage Road the robust striker racked up a total of 415 league appearances. Blissett is The Hornets' leading scorer, with a career total of 158 league goals.

● BLISSETT is also Watford's most expensive signing. In 1984 he rejoined the club for £550,000, after an unhappy spell with Italian giants AC Milan.

● WATFORD ENJOYED their record win, 10–1, against Lowestoft in the FA Cup of 1926. The Hornets' worst defeat, 0–10, was inflicted by Wolves in 1912, in the same competition.

● THE HORNETS received their biggest incoming transfer cheque in 1994, when centre-forward Paul Furlong moved to Chelsea for £2.3 million.

● TWO PLAYERS have made 31 international appearances while with Watford, England 's John Barnes and Wales' Kenny Jackett.

Roll of Honour

Div 3 champions 1969
Div 4 champions 1978
Div 2 (new) champions 1998

Luther Blissett: two very successful spells at Watford sandwiched a rather unsuccessful one at AC Milan

GEORGE WEAH

Born: Liberia 1.10.66
Position: Striker
Club career:
Young Survivors of Claretown (Liberia)
Tonnerre of Yaounde (Cameroon)
1988–92 Monaco
1992–95 Paris St. Germain
1995– AC Milan

LIBERIAN STRIKER George Weah won a unique treble of awards in 1995 – he was voted FIFA World Player of the Year, African Player of the Year and European Player of the Year all in the space of a month.

● WEAH IS the first world-class player to come out of Liberia. He started playing with the Young Survivors of Claretown in his own country, but soon moved to Cameroon to play for Tonnerre of Yaounde. In 1988 he moved to France to play for Monaco.

● AT THIS POINT he was still a winger – it wasn't until his move to Paris St. Germain in 1992 that he started playing a more central role. His 11 goals (in 32 games) helped PSG win the French title in 1994.

● AT THE BEGINNING of the 1995/96 season he moved to AC Milan (against whom he'd recently played in the European Cup semi-final) and helped them gain their 15th league win.

● IN JANUARY 1996 he starred in the African Nations tournament – ensuring his country could participate by paying for his teammates' expenses and buying a new kit (the entire team playing in red boots).

ARSENE WENGER

Born: Strasbourg 22.10.48

APTLY NAMED Arsenal boss Arsene Wenger became the first ever non-British manager to guide a team to the League Championship title when the Gunners lifted the Premiership trophy in 1998. Three weeks later he also became the first foreign coach to do the 'double' when Arsenal also won the FA Cup.

● WENGER, who Arsenal had been tracking for two years, brought with him one of the best coaching reputations in Europe. After coaching French club Cannes and Nancy, he had guided Monaco to the French Championship in 1987, the French Cup in 1991 and the European Cup Winners' Cup Final in 1992 (which they lost 2–0 to Werder Bremen of Germany). In 1995 he joined Grampus Eight and with them won the Japanese Cup in 1996.

● WENGER – a former player with Mutzig, Strasbourg and Cannes – has not endeared himself to all his fellow countrymen since arriving in England by plucking some of France's hottest young talent from French clubs and bringing them to Highbury. Patrick Viera, Remi Garde, Nicolas Anelka, Gilles Grimandi and Emmanuel Petit making up Arsenal's French Foreign Legion.

WEST BROMWICH ALBION

Year founded: 1879
Ground: The Hawthorns (25,500)
Highest ever crowd: 64,815, 6th March 1937 v Arsenal (FA Cup rd 6)
Previous name: West Bromwich Strollers
Nickname: The Baggies
Colours: Navy blue-and-white-striped shirts, white shorts, blue-and-white socks

THE BAGGIES were the first current league club to lose two consecutive FA Cup finals. They were runners up in 1886 and 1887, but finally won the Cup in 1888. The triumphant West Brom side was entirely made up of English players, which represented a first for a Cup-winning team.

● IN 1931 West Brom became the first and only team ever to win the FA Cup and promotion to the top flight in the same season.

● ALONG WITH Aston Villa, The Baggies can also claim another FA Cup record. The two clubs are the only cup finalists to have faced each other in three FA Cup finals (in 1887, 1892 and 1897).

● WEST BROM enjoyed their biggest ever win in 1892, overcoming Darwen 12–0. The score set a First Division record, only equalled since by Nottingham Forest. The Baggies' worst defeat, 3–10, was against Stoke City in 1937.

● TONY 'BOMBER' BROWN holds two important West Brom records. He is the club's longest-serving player, making 574 league appearances between 1963–80, and also their leading scorer with 218 goals.

● WEST BROM were the last winners of the League Cup under its old format of a two-legged final, overcoming West Ham 5–3 on aggregate in 1966. The following season they appeared in the first League Cup final to be played at Wembley, but lost 3–2 to Third Division QPR after leading 2–0.

● THE MIDLANDERS, though, returned to Wembley the following season and beat Everton in the FA Cup Final. Jeff Astle – now a member of TV's Fantasy Football League team – scored the only goal of the game, and in the process became one of only nine players in the history of the FA Cup to have scored in every round.

● WEST BROM'S record signing is Kevin Kilbane who cost £1.25 million from Preston North End in June 1997. Soccer legend Bryan Robson is the most expensive player to leave The Hawthorns, signing for Manchester United in 1981 for £1.5 million.

● BETWEEN 1975–88 successive West Brom managers had the following Christian names: Johnny, Ronnie, Ron, Ronnie, Ron, Johnny, Ron, Ron. Surely the most rhythmical order of succession in the game's history!

● WEST BROM's most famous fan is comedian Frank Skinner, star of Blue Heaven and Fantasy Football League.

Roll of Honour

Div 1 champions 1920
Div 2 champions 1902, 1911
FA Cup 1888, 1892, 1931, 1954, 1968
League Cup 1966

Did You Know?

In 1888 FA Cup Winners West Bromwich Albion played in what was dubbed the first ever 'world championship' match against Scottish Cup holders Renton. The Scots won 4-0 at Hampden Park.

WEST HAM UNITED

Year founded: 1895
Ground: Upton Park (26,014)
Highest ever crowd: 42,322, 17th October 1970 v Tottenham (Div 1)
Previous name: Thames Ironworks FC
Nickname: The Hammers
Colours: Claret shirts with blue sleeves, white shorts, claret-and-blue socks

DESPITE A strong cup tradition, East Londoners West Ham United have never won the league championship, though they have won the FA Cup on three occasions.

● THEY WERE the first club ever to taste defeat at Wembley, in the 1923 FA Cup Final. The match was the first game played at the ground, and produced remarkable scenes as thousands of spectators forced their way into the ground and onto the pitch. Eventually the fans were cleared away from

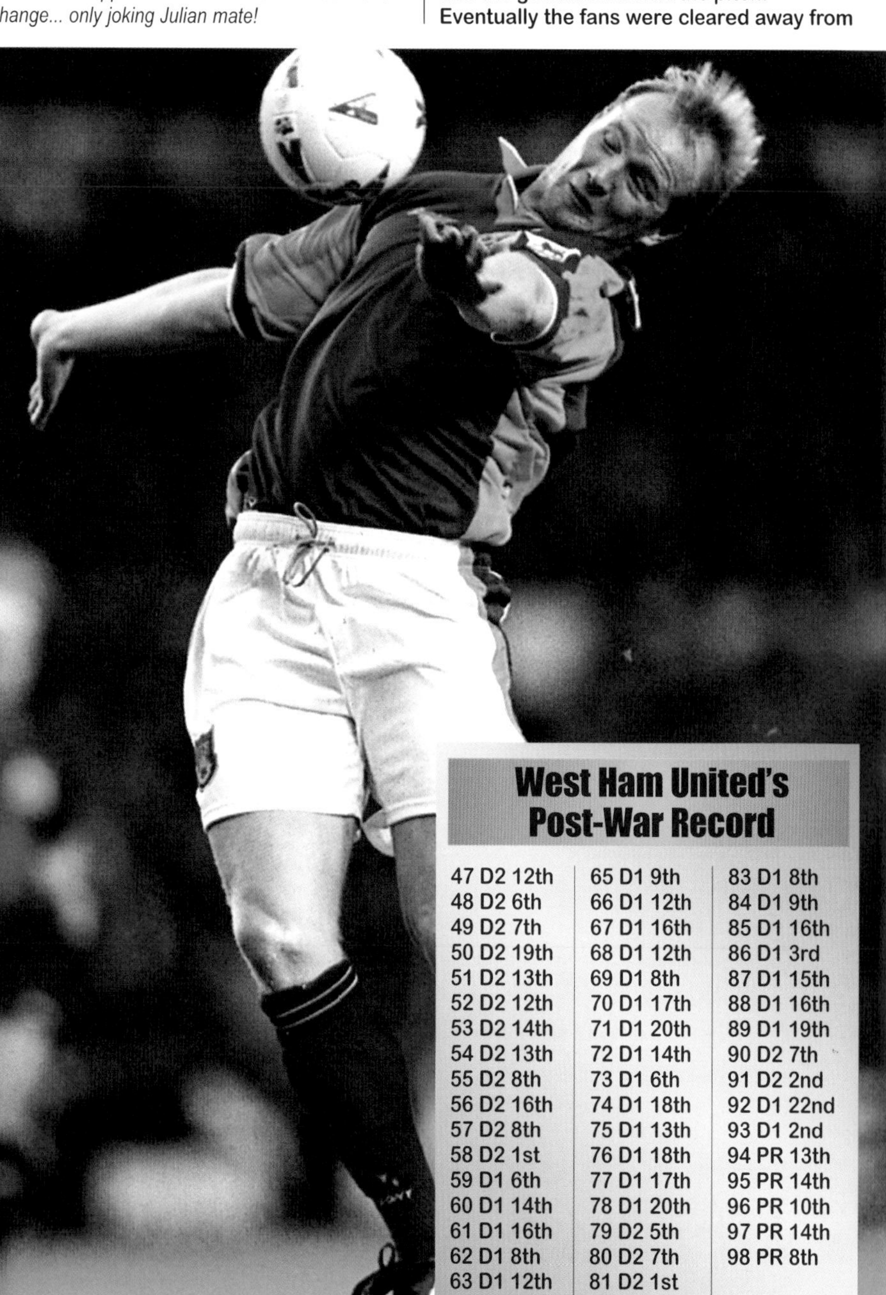

West Ham skipper Julian Dicks kicks the ball for a change... only joking Julian mate!

West Ham United's Post-War Record

47 D2 12th	65 D1 9th	83 D1 8th
48 D2 6th	66 D1 12th	84 D1 9th
49 D2 7th	67 D1 16th	85 D1 16th
50 D2 19th	68 D1 12th	86 D1 3rd
51 D2 13th	69 D1 8th	87 D1 15th
52 D2 12th	70 D1 17th	88 D1 16th
53 D2 14th	71 D1 20th	89 D1 19th
54 D2 13th	72 D1 14th	90 D2 7th
55 D2 8th	73 D1 6th	91 D2 2nd
56 D2 16th	74 D1 18th	92 D1 22nd
57 D2 8th	75 D1 13th	93 D1 2nd
58 D2 1st	76 D1 18th	94 PR 13th
59 D1 6th	77 D1 17th	95 PR 14th
60 D1 14th	78 D1 20th	96 PR 10th
61 D1 16th	79 D2 5th	97 PR 14th
62 D1 8th	80 D2 7th	98 PR 8th
63 D1 12th	81 D2 1st	
64 D1 14th	82 D1 9th	

the playing surface, the game kicked off nearly an hour late, and West Ham lost 2–0 to Bolton Wanderers.

● WEST HAM's biggest victory was against Bury in the League Cup of 1983. The Hammers thrashed the lower division team 10–0 to set a record score for the competition, which has only been equalled by Liverpool. West Ham suffered their worst defeat against Blackburn Rovers in 1963, going down 8–2.

● WEST HAM achieved another, and more enjoyable, Wembley first in 1965 when they beat Munich 1860 2–0 in the final of the European Cup Winners' Cup. It was only the second European final played at the home of English football… and West Ham's first and only European trophy.

● STRIKER VIC WATSON holds three goalscoring records for the club. He is the overall leading scorer for West Ham, with 298 league goals between 1920–35. In 1929/30 he notched 42 goals to set a record for a single season. In the same year Watson scored six goals in one match – a feat later equalled by Geoff Hurst against Sunderland in 1968.

● IN 1980 West Ham became the last side from outside the top division to win the FA Cup. The Hammers, then a Second Division outfit, beat Arsenal 1–0 in the final, with a rare headed goal by Trevor Brooking.

● NO WEST HAM player has appeared more often for the club than Billy Bonds. Between 1967–88 Bonds – affectionately known as 'Bonzo' to fans and teammates – played in a staggering 663 league games.

● IN 1966 West Ham were the only club side to provide three members – Bobby Moore, Geoff Hurst and Martin Peters – of the England World Cup-winning team. All four England goals in the final were scored by West Ham players.

● BOBBY MOORE is West Ham's most capped international. He played 108 games for England to set a record that has since been beaten only by Peter Shilton.

● WEST HAM won promotion from the Second Division in 1990/91, conceding just 34 goals in 46 matches, to set a divisional record for defensive meanness.

● IN THE 1960s West Ham had a schoolboy player on their books called David Cook. He failed to make the grade, but went on to achieve some success in the music industry under the name David Essex.

● WEST HAM's most famous fan is a fictional character. In the popular TV sitcom Till Death Us Do Part Alf Garnett was rarely seen without a claret-and-blue scarf around his neck. Real-life supporters include actor Nick Berry, comedian Phill Jupitus and various current cast members of East Enders.

● PAUL ALLEN is the youngest player to appear for West Ham. In 1979 he played against Burnley just one month after his 17th birthday. And in 1980 Allen became the youngest player ever to play in the FA Cup final, appearing against Arsenal at Wembley aged 17 years and 256 days.

Roll of Honour

Div 2 champions 1958, 1981
FA Cup 1964, 1975, 1980
European Cup Winners' Cup 1965

WIGAN ATHLETIC

Year founded: 1932
Ground: Springfield Park (6,674)
Highest ever crowd: 27,500, 12th December 1953 v Hereford (FA Cup rd 2)
Nickname: The Latics
Colours: Blue and white shirts, blue shorts and blue socks

FORMER SOVIET President Mikhail Gorbachev is Wigan's most famous fan. In the 1969/70 season Russian side Metallist Khartrov played a friendly against Wigan at Springfield Park, and included a young Gorbachev in the team party as "assistant secretary." The Russian politician has retained a soft spot for Wigan ever since.

● WIGAN ENJOYED their biggest victory in 1982, trouncing Scunthorpe 7–2 away from home. The Latics' worst defeat, 1–6, was inflicted by Bristol Rovers in 1990.

● KEVIN LANGLEY has Wigan's record appearances, with 317 league games in two spells at the club between 1981–94.

● PETER HOUGHTON is Wigan's leading goalscorer, with 62 strikes between 1978 and 1984. Graeme Jones holds the record for most goals in a season, with 31 in 1996/97.

● WIGAN HAVE had more managerial changes since the war than any other club in the Football League (although they didn't join until 1978), with no fewer than 30 managers taking the reins since 1945.

Roll of Honour

Freight Rover Trophy 1985
Div 3 champions 1997

RAY WILKINS

Born: Hillingdon 14.9.56
Height: 5ft 8ins Position: Midfielder
Club career:

1973–79	Chelsea 179 (30)
1979–84	Manchester United 160 (7)
1984–87	AC Milan 73 (2)
1987	Paris St. Germain
1987–89	Rangers 70 (2)
1989–94	QPR 154 (7)
1994	Crystal Palace 1 (0)
1994–96	QPR 21 (0)
1996–97	Hibernian 19 (0)
1997	Wycombe Wanderers 1 (0)
1997	Millwall 3 (0)
1997	Orient 3 (0)

International record:
1976–87 England 84 (3)

IN 1986 RAY WILKINS set the unenviable record of becoming the first Englishman to be sent off during a World Cup finals tournament. Wilkins threw the ball at the referee during England's frustrating 0–0 draw with Morocco. It was the second-last of 84 matches he played for his country.

● IT WAS very unlike Wilkins, who started his career as a talented teenager at Chelsea, becoming at 18 in 1975 the club's youngest ever captain.

● WILKINS MOVED to Manchester United in 1979 for a club record £825,000 and, after helping United to win the FA Cup in 1983 with a superb goal against Brighton, went on to Italian giants AC Milan for another club record (£1.5 million).

● HE HAD spells with Paris St Germain and Rangers before returning to England to play for QPR. After a very brief spell as player/coach at Crystal Palace (one game, which the Eagles lost 6-1 at home to Liverpool) he returned to QPR to become player-manager. His first full season in charge turned into a nightmare when Rangers were relegated the end of 1995/96. In 1997 he was appointed manager of Fulham by the club's new Director of Football Kevin Keegan, but was sacked by his former England colleague before the season had ended.

Once Chelsea's youngest captain, Ray Wilkins enjoys his hair while he can

HOWARD WILKINSON

Born: Sheffield 13.11.43

IN 1996 Howard Wilkinson was appointed the FA's Technical Director and entrusted with the enormous task of overhauling English football at every level, focusing particularly on the development of young players.

● IN 1992 WILKINSON became only the second man ever to manage Leeds United to the League Championship. The first, of course, was Don Revie.

● WILKINSON was the last manager to win the Football League championship before the top flight became known as the Premier League. Leeds pipped Manchester United in a thrilling run-in that went right to the wire, his master stroke ironically being the signing of Eric Cantona for the last third of the season.

● WILKINSON, one of the original long-ball managers, had previously managed Sheffield Wednesday. He started his career as a winger for Wednesday, before moving to Brighton & Hove Albion where he once scored the club's quickest goal ever, after 15 seconds. A modest player, Wilkinson knew early where his future lay: while at Brighton he got his coaching qualification from Lilleshall at the age of 25.

BOB WILSON

Born: Chesterfield 30.10.41
Position: Goalkeeper
Club career:
1964–73 Arsenal 243
International record:
1971 Scotland 2

BEFORE HE became a TV presenter, Bob Wilson was a goalkeeper who stood between the sticks for Arsenal and Scotland. Before that he was a qualified teacher, a job he decided to give up to concentrate full-time on a career in the Number 1 jersey.

● WILSON WAS the first and only Arsenal goalkeeper ever to win The Double: his scintillating form behind the defence helped Arsenal pinch the title from Leeds and beat Liverpool in the FA Cup Final in 1971.

● A YEAR EARLIER he had helped Arsenal win their first European trophy – The Gunners defeating Anderlecht 4–3 on aggregate in the Fairs Cup Final.

● WILSON only made two appearances for Scotland, both in 1971, against Portugal and Holland. Scotland lost both matches.

● Wilson went on to become the presenter of the BBC1 Saturday morning show Football Focus, until a shock transfer to ITV in 1994 when he became the station's main football presenter. He has also run a goalkeeping school and is still goalkeeping coach at Arsenal.

Bob Wilson makes a great save for Arsenal and turns to the TV cameras in mid-air, hoping to catch the eye of ITV's personnel officer

WIMBLEDON

Year founded: 1889
Ground: Selhurst Park (26,500)
Highest ever crowd: 30,115, 9th May 1993 v Manchester United (FA Premier League)
Nickname: The Dons
Colours: All navy blue with yellow trim

IN 1988, just 11 years after being elected to the Football League, Wimbledon sensationally won the FA Cup, beating red-hot favourites Liverpool 1–0 with a goal by Lawrie Sanchez, the greatest moment in the club's history.

● CAPTAIN DAVE BEASANT's second-half penalty save from John Aldridge in that match secured him a double entry in FA Cup history as the first goalkeeper to save a Cup final spot-kick, and the first keeper to captain his side to victory and lift the famous trophy.

● BALD-HEADED striker Alan Cork (the first man to be serenaded with the chant 'He's got no hair, but we don't care') holds a number of Wimbledon records. Between 1977–92 he played in 430 league games for the club, scoring 145 goals. Both figures are club records.

● CORK HAS also scored more goals, 29 in one season (1983/84), than any other Dons' player and is the only player ever to have scored in every division of the league (from Fourth to Premiership) with the same club... a record that cannot be equalled.

● CORK IS POSSIBLY the only player ever to play in an FA Cup final with a hangover. Manager Bobby Gould allowed the team to go to the pub on the night before the match and Cork claims he didn't get to bed until 2am. 'I had to wear my sunglasses on the coach,' he said.

● WIMBLEDON manager Joe Kinnear is the second-longest serving boss of a Premiership club, having been appointed back in January 1991. Only Alex Ferguson at Manchester United has been in charge of his club longer.

● WHILE he was at Wimbledon, Vinnie Jones held the record for being sent off more often than any other Premiership player. The hard-tackling midfielder was

Wimbledon's Post-War Record

Elected to the Football League from the Southern league, 1977

78 D4 13th	85 D2 12th	92 D1 13th
79 D4 3rd	86 D2 3rd	93 PR 12th
80 D3 24th	87 D1 6th	94 PR 6th
81 D4 4th	88 D1 7th	95 PR 9th
82 D3 21st	89 D1 12th	96 PR 14th
83 D4 1st	90 D1 8th	97 PR 8th
84 D3 2nd	91 D1 7th	98 PR 15th

'Let's go crazy': Vinnie Jones and Dean Holdsworth celebrate Wimbledon's unbroken run in the top flight

Did You Know?

In season 1992/93 Hartlepool set an English record when they went 13 League and Cup matches without scoring a goal. Strangely, the club's last goal before this depressing run had knocked Premier League Crystal Palace out of the FA Cup.

given his marching orders on 12 occasions in the top flight, although one red card was later reduced to a yellow.

● WIMBLEDON's remarkable success has been achieved despite attracting lower average crowds than any other Premiership club. In January 1993 Wimbledon's home fixture with Everton was watched by just 3,039 fans, the lowest ever gate at a Premiership match.

● WIMBLEDON's most famous fan is actress June Whitfield, best known for her starring role in the classic TV sitcom Terry and June.

● ALONG with Coventry, Wimbledon are the only team who have reached the top flight but have never been relegated.

● IN 1963 Wimbledon beat Sutton United in the FA Amateur Cup Final thanks to a remarkable four-goal spree by hotshot striker Eddie Reynolds. Scoring four goals at Wembley was remarkable enough, the fact that every one of them was a header makes it a truly unique double brace.

● WIMBLEDON's best ever win, 6–0, was against Newport County in 1983. The club's worst defeat, an 8–0 hammering, came at the hands of Everton in a League Cup match in 1980.

● THE CLUB's record signing is former Millwall defender Ben Thatcher who joined the Dons in 1996 for £1.7 million.

Roll of Honour

Div 4 champions 1983
FA Cup 1988
FA Amateur Cup 1963

SIR WALTER WINTERBOTTOM

Born: Oldham 31.3.13

WALTER WINTERBOTTOM was easily the longest-serving England manager of all time, holding the national reins between 1946–62 for a total of 139 games (29 more than Sir Alf Ramsey). He took control first as chief coach, then as manager.

● IN HIS REIGN he masterminded more England victories than any other manager (78) but also suffered more defeats (28). Winterbottom also saw England to a record four World Cup finals tournaments – in 1950, 1954, 1958 and 1962.

● WINTERBOTTOM, however, didn't have the power of a modern-day manager. The team, for example, was picked by an FA Committee, who once selected a man with a broken leg!

● WINTERBOTTOM was knighted in 1978 after (as FA Director of Coaching) setting up England's U23 team and launching a national system of coaching.

DENNIS WISE

Born: Kensington 15.12.66
Height: 5ft 6ins Position: Midfielder
Club career:
1983–84 Southampton
1984–90 Wimbledon 135 (27)
1990– Chelsea 244 (46)
International record:
1991– England 10 (1)

DENNIS WISE didn't have a very auspicious start at his first club Southampton – he was released from the club for being too small.

● SOUTHAMPTON's loss was Wimbledon's gain, however, and he joined the South London club in 1984. Within four years he had helped the Dons to their greatest moment, that FA Cup Final win over Liverpool in 1988.

● IN 1990 WISE became Chelsea's record signing and Wimbledon's record sale, when he crossed the Thames for £1.6 million.

● IN 1994 he was at Wembley again, but this time he had to settle for a runners-up medal as Chelsea lost the FA Cup Final 4–0 to Manchester United. He was back yet again in 1997, however, this time captaining the Blues to FA Cup success against Middlesbrough in a 2–0 win.

● AND THE FOLLOWING season those little arms were lifting yet another piece of silverware as Chelsea beat Middlesbrough 2–0 at Wembley once again... this time to win the Coca-Cola Cup. By the time Wise lifted the European Cup in Stockholm at the end of the season – after Chelsea's 1–0 win over VFB Stuttgart – he must have been exhausted.

● WISE MADE his debut for England in 1991. Eyebrows were raised when Wise was chosen by Graham Taylor over Chris Waddle to play in the vital European Championship qualifier against Turkey – but they soon came down again when he scored the only goal of the game.

● HOWEVER, he has since made only 10 international appearances, despite never being on the losing side with England. Even though he made him captain at Chelsea when he was manager at the club, Glenn Hoddle has never picked Wise for any of his England squads.

W

WOLVERHAMPTON WANDERERS

Year founded: 1877
Ground: Molineux (28,525)
Highest ever crowd: 61,315, 11th February 1939 v Liverpool (FA Cup rd 5)
Nickname: Wolves
Colours: Gold shirts, black shorts, gold socks

ONE OF THE most famous names in British football, Wolverhampton Wanderers enjoyed their heyday in the 1950s, when the British media's claims that they were the best side in the world (on the strength of a number of friendlies against foreign opposition) provoked the launch of the European Cup.

● IT WAS BACK in 1886, though, when Wolves enjoyed their biggest win, 14–0, against Crosswell's Brewery in the FA Cup. The club's worst defeat was a 10–0 humiliation at Newton Heath (who later became Manchester United) in 1892.

● WOLVES' most capped player is Billy Wright, who set a then record by appearing 105 times for England. Wright was the captain of Wolves (and England) during the 1950s when they enjoyed a long run of success under manager Stan Cullis, the pioneer of 'kick and rush' football.

Steve Bull, Wolverhampton's favourite son, whose first touch, according to former manager Graham Turner, 'isn't very good. But his second is bloody marvellous!'

● IN 1891 WOLVES player James Heath scored the Football League's first ever penalty against Accrington Stanley in 1891.

● DURING the 1937/38 season the club's 40-strong playing staff was entirely made up of unmarried men.

● WOLVES are one of only two clubs – the other being Burnley – to have won all four divisions of the football league. The club became the first to claim a 'full house' of titles in 1989 by winning the Third Division championship.

● Steve Bull is Wolves' record scorer with a fantastic haul of 249 goals since joining the Molineux club in 1986. Reliable defender Derek Parkin holds the club record for league appearances, turning out in 501 games between 1967 and 1982.

● IN 1972 WOLVES beat Dutch side Den Haag 7–1 on aggregate in the UEFA Cup. Den Haag had given them a helping hand, though, scoring three own goals in the away leg! In the final of that year's competition Wolves were beaten by Spurs in the only all-English European final ever.

● ONE OF Wolves' most famous fans is Robert Plant, formerly vocalist with hell-raising rock group Led Zeppelin.

Roll of Honour

Div 1 champions 1954, 1958, 1959
Div 2 champions 1932, 1977
Div 3 (N) champions 1924
Div 3 champions 1989
Div 4 champions 1988
FA Cup 1893, 1908, 1949, 1960
League Cup 1974, 1980

Funny Old Game

During World War I, women were allowed to play men in mixed teams. In 1917 a team of English men and women took on a similar Canadian team, and to even things up all the men played with their hands tied behind their backs (presumably that didn't include the goalkeeper)... the English team won 8–5.

Lisa Spry of Arsenal's women's team, on their way to winning the coveted League and FA Cup double in 1995, battles with Liverpool's Maria Harper

WOMEN'S FOOTBALL

THE FIRST Women's FA Cup Final took place in 1971, and Southampton beat Stewarton and Thistle in the final.

● THE FIRST British international match between women took place a year later in 1972 when England beat Scotland 3–2.

● ENGLAND WON the first edition of the Women's European Championship, beating Sweden 1–0 in 1984. It has since been dominated by Scandinavian nations – though Germany flexed their muscles for the first time in 1995, beating Sweden in the final.

● THERE HAVE been two Women's World Cup tournaments. The first took place in China in 1991 and saw the United States beat Norway 2–1 in the final. The second edition was in Sweden in 1995 when Norway beat Germany 2–0 to lift the trophy.

● THE WOMEN's FA was founded in 1969, and in 1992 a Premier League was formed. Leading sides include the Doncaster Belles, Millwall Lionesses and Arsenal Ladies. In 1995 Arsenal enjoyed a tremendous season, winning The League and Cup Double without losing a single match. Top players in the women's game include Debbie Bampton and Gillian Coulthard, both of whom have won over 90 caps for England.

W

THE WORLD CUP

THE FIRST WINNERS of the World Cup were Uruguay, who were also the first hosts. They beat neighbours and bitter rivals Argentina 4–2 in front of 93,000 fans in Montevideo in 1930.

● ITALY WON the second tournament in front of Mussolini and 54,999 other spectators in Rome in 1934. They beat Czechoslovakia 2–1 in extra time, after Argentinian import Orsi scored a crazy, curling equaliser for the Azzurri.

● THE 1938 EDITION, played in France in the shadow of a great deal of political upheaval, was also won by Italy, who beat Hungary 4–2 in the final. Brazil rested striker Leonidas for the semi against Italy, and paid for their overconfidence by losing 2–1 to the Italians.

● WORLD WAR II, and the upheaval that followed it, meant that there wasn't another World Cup tournament until 1950, played in Brazil. England, who had in the meantime finally joined FIFA, entered for the first time but were beaten 1–0 by the unfancied USA in one of the biggest shocks in the history of the competition. Uruguay were the eventual winners, beating Brazil 2–1 in the final after going a goal down.

● 1954 SAW SWITZERLAND hosting the fifth edition of the competition. The great Hungary side of that era were overwhelming favourites, but fell at the last hurdle to West Germany, who they had beaten 8–3 earlier in the tournament. The Germans were 0–2 down after eight minutes but fought back and, after 86 minutes, scored the winner. It was the only time Hungary lost between 1950–56.

● THE 1958 TOURNAMENT saw all four British teams in the tournament for the first and only time, but none managed to make it past the quarter-finals. This tournament was graced by the emergence of a 17-year-old called Pele, who inspired Brazil to a 5–2 win over hosts Sweden, scoring twice. This remains the biggest ever win in a World Cup final.

Only one player has played in as many World Cup matches as Diego Maradona. None has been as controversial

The most famous picture in English football, taken after England won the 1966 World Cup Final at Wembley. Unfortunately it's getting more and more faded

● BRAZIL WERE victorious again in 1962, despite losing Pele to a torn muscle in the second match. Brazil knocked England out in the quarter-finals before eventually facing Czechoslovakia in the final. Czech keeper Schroiff marred an otherwise faultless tournament with three mistakes and the South Americans ran out 3–1 winners.

● THE 1966 TOURNAMENT took place, of course, in England, and the hosts ended up winning the thing. Alf Ramsey, due to a shortage of top quality wingers, had to devise a 4-3-3 formation, which steamrollered any opposition it came across, although the West Germans were only beaten by an eagle-eyed Russian linesman (German fans would argue cross-eyed) in extra time in the final. Oh, and a thumper from Geoff Hurst, the first man to score a hat-trick in a World Cup final, when there were some people on the pitch who thought it was all over, and it was then.

● 1970 SAW THE Brazilians fielding what is usually considered to be the best team of all time,

Big bully Zinedine Zidane holds the World Cup up where French captain Didier Deschamps can't reach

including the likes of Pele (the only man ever to appear in three World Cup-winning sides), Jairzinho, Rivelino and Carlos Alberto, smashing Italy 4–1 in the final. They had beaten England 1–0 on the way through, in one of the best matches of all time, characterised by Gordon Banks's brilliant save from Pele, which is often deemed to be the best save of all time.

● 1974 WAS THE ERA of 'total football', played by the Dutch, who included the brilliant Johan Cruyff in their ranks. Holland made their way to the final, but came up against the West Germans, a pretty useful side themselves. It was the Germans who won 2–1, despite going down to the fastest World Cup final goal of all time, a first-minute penalty scored by Johan Neeskens.

● THE DUTCH got to the final again in 1978, but once more lost to the hosts. This time it was the Mario-Kempes-inspired Argentina, who beat them 3–1 after extra time on a huge wave of popular support and a carpet of ticker tape. It was the second time they had lost in the tournament: otherwise-dire Scotland had beaten them 3–2 in the qualifying round in a typical just-too-little-slightly-too-late cavalry charge.

● 1982 SAW WEST GERMANY in the final again in Spain, riding their luck against Italy, who missed an early penalty. There was no stopping Paolo Rossi that year, however: he scored Italy's first goal in a 3–1 win. England had qualified at last, but went out in the round robin quarter-finals despite not losing a match in the tournament.

● 1986 WAS FAMOUS for the 'Hand of God', but it was the feet of Diego Maradona which saw Argentina win the tournament, again held in Mexico, after controversially putting England out in the quarter-finals. West Germany were on the losing side in the final, beaten 3–2 by the South Americans.

● 1990 SAW ENGLAND's famous surge to the semi-finals, Gazza's tears, and West Germany beating a cynical Argentine side 1–0 in the dullest final in the history of the competition. Italy were hosts, but they were put out on penalties by Diego and co.

● 1994 WAS ANOTHER dull final after a sparkling competition in the United States. Brazil became the only team to win the competition four times, when they beat Italy on penalties (the first time ever in the final) after the first ever 0–0 draw.

● France 98 was the biggest ever World Cup tournament with 32 teams competing in a record 64 matches. And for the first time since Argentina in 1978 it was the turn of the host nation to taste victory, France reaching their first ever final before winning the trophy for the first time by beating favourites Brazil 3–0 in the final.

● Despite that disappointment Brazil are still the most successful World Cup team, having won the trophy four times. They are the only team to have appeared in every tournament and they have played the most matches (a total of 80) and scored more goals (171) than any other team.

● Germany are the most successful European team, and second in the world with three wins from a record six finals.

● Mexican goalkeeper Antonia Carbajal (1950-66) and German midfielder Lothar Matthaus (1982-98) are the only men to have appeared in five World Cup finals tournaments. Since France 98 Matthaus also holds the record number of appearances in World Cup finals, 25 matches.

● His compatriot Gerd Muller is the highest goalscorer in World Cup finals tournaments with 14, closely followed by French striker Just Fontaine (13, all scored in the 1958 finals making him the highest scorer in a single tournament), Pele (12) and Jürgen Klinsmann (11).

● All in all the competition has come a long way since the first ever World Cup match between France and Mexico at the Pocitios Stadium in Montevideo, Uruguay. France won 4–1 but only 1,000 people turned up.

World Cup Finals

1930	**Uruguay 4 Argentina 2** (Uruguay)
1934	**Italy 2 Czechoslovakia 1** (Italy)
1938	**Italy 4 Hungary 2** (France)
1950	**Uruguay 2 Brazil 1** (Brazil)
1954	**West Germany 3 Hungary 2** (Switzerland)
1958	**Brazil 5 Sweden 2** (Sweden)
1962	**Brazil 3 Czechoslovakia 1** (Chile)
1966	**England 4 West Germany 2** (England)
1970	**Brazil 4 Italy 1** (Mexico)
1974	**West Germany 2 Holland 1** (West Germany)
1978	**Argentina 3 Holland 1** (Argentina)
1982	**Italy 3 West Germany 1** (Spain)
1986	**Argentina 3 West Germany 2** (Mexico)
1990	**West Germany 1 Argentina 0** (Italy)
1994	**Brazil 0 Italy 0 – Brazil won 3–2 on penalties** (USA)
1998	**France 3 Brazil 0** (France)

Did You Know?

Iran beat The Maldives 17–0 in June 1997 in a World Cup qualifier, the biggest ever victory in the history of the competition.

THE WORLD CUP GOLDEN BOOT

THE WORLD CUP Golden Boot is awarded to the player who has scored most goals in a World Cup finals tournament: the top scorer in the first edition was Guillermo Stábile, whose eight goals helped Argentina to the final.

● THE MAN to score most goals in the World Cup finals is French striker Just Fontaine, who bagged an incredible 13 in the 1958 edition in Sweden. In 1962 in Chile nobody managed more than four goals in the competition, so the award was shared between six players.

● SIX GOALS have been enough to win the Golden Boot in the last four competitions. Among the winners is England's Gary Lineker, whose goals helped England get to the quarters of the 1986 edition in Mexico.

● AND SIX GOALS was enough again at France 98, although they came from an unlikely source... Croatia's Davor Suker.

Golden Boot Winners

1930 Guillermo Stábile (Argentina) 8
1934 Oldrich Nejeldy (Czechoslovakia) 5
1938 Leonidas da Silva (Brazil) 8
1950 Ademir Menezes (Brazil) 9
1954 Sandor Kocsis (Hungary) 11
1958 Just Fontaine (France) 13
1962 Florian Albert (Hungary), Garrincha (Brazil), Valentin Ivanov (USSR), Drazen Jerkovic (Yugoslavia) Leonel Sanchez (Chile), Vava (Brazil) all 4
1966 Eusebio (Portugal) 9
1970 Gerd Müller (West Germany) 10
1974 Grzegorz Lato (Poland) 7
1978 Mario Kempes (Argentina) 6
1982 Paolo Rossi (Italy) 6
1986 Gary Lineker (England) 6
1990 Toto Schillachi (Italy) 6
1994 Oleg Salenko (Russia), Hristo Stoichkov (Bulgaria) 6
1998 Davor Suker (Croatia) 6

WORLD FOOTBALLER OF THE YEAR

FIFA HAS BEEN running a World Footballer of the Year Award since 1991. The national coaches of over 100 countries vote for their top three players in 1-2-3 order.

● The first winner of the award was Germany's Lothar Matthaus in 1991 and in 1998 Ronaldo became the first player to win it two years in a row.

● READERS OF World Soccer Magazine have also been voting on their World Footballer of the Year, but for longer – since 1982, when Paolo Rossi won the award.

● SINCE THEN three men have won the award twice: Michel Platini (1984 and 1985), Ruud Gullit (1987 and 1989) and Marco Van Basten (1988 and 1992).

● MARCO VAN BASTEN and Roberto Baggio are the only men to have won both awards in the same year, in 1992 and 1993 respectively.

● NO BRITISH player has ever won the award.

FIFA World Footballer of the Year

1991 Lothar Matthaus (Germany)
1992 Marco Van Basten (Holland)
1993 Roberto Baggio (Italy)
1994 Romario (Brazil)
1995 George Weah (Liberia)
1997 Ronaldo (Brazil)
1998 Ronaldo (Brazil)

World Soccer Magazine World Footballer of the Year

1982 Paolo Rossi (Italy)
1983 Zico (Brazil)
1984 Michel Platini (France)
1985 Michel Platini (France)
1986 Diego Maradona (Argentina)
1987 Ruud Gullit (Holland)
1988 Marco Van Basten (Holland)
1989 Ruud Gullit (Holland)
1990 Lothar Matthaus (West Germany)
1991 Jean-Pierre Papin (France)
1992 Marco Van Basten (Holland)
1993 Roberto Baggio (Italy)
1994 Paolo Maldini (Italy)
1995 Gianluca Vialli (Italy)
1996 Ronaldo (Brazil)
1997 Ronaldo (Brazil)

WREXHAM

Year founded: 1873
Ground: Racehorse Ground (11,881)
Highest ever crowd: 34,445, 26th January 1957 v Manchester United (FA Cup rd 4)
Nickname: The Robins
Colours: Red shirts, white shorts, red socks

WREXHAM, the oldest surviving club in Wales, have appeared in more Welsh Cup finals (45) than any team, and no side has won the cup more often than The Robins (23 wins).

● TOM BAMFORD is the leading scorer in the club's history. Between 1928–34 he knocked in 175 goals, including a club record 44 strikes in 1933/34.

● THE CLUB enjoyed their biggest win in 1962, humbling Hartlepools 10–1. The Robins suffered their heaviest defeat the following year, when they crashed to a miserable 0–9 loss at Brentford.

● NO PLAYER has pulled on Wrexham's famous red shirt more often than Arfon Griffiths. In two spells at the club between 1959–79 he played in an amazing total of 592 league games.

● IN SEPTEMBER 1951 Ken Roberts made his debut for Wrexham at the age of 15 years and 158 days to become the second youngest player ever to play in a football league match.

Roll of Honour

Div 3 champions 1978
Welsh Cup 23 times

BILLY WRIGHT

Born: Ironbridge 6.2.24 Died: 3.9.94
Height: 5ft 9ins Position: Defender
Club career:
1946–59 Wolverhampton Wanderers 491 (13)
International record:
1947–59 England 105 (3)

BILLY WRIGHT became the first man to win 100 caps for England when he turned out against Scotland in 1959. Of those, 90 were as captain – a record only overtaken by Bobby Moore in 1973 – and 70 of them were in consecutive matches, a record which still stands. He remains England's fourth most capped player of all time.

● WRIGHT WAS also an extremely successful player for Wolverhampton Wanderers. Under the management of Stan Cullis (and with Wright as captain), Wolves won the League Championship three times in the 1950s – in 1954, 1958 and 1959 – and finished runners up – in 1950 and 1955.

● WRIGHT STARTED out with the club (and his country) as a wing-half, but will be remembered most for his performances after being converted to a centre-back.

● DESPITE HIS glorious achievements, there were some bad points. Wright captained England to three of their most humiliating experiences, defeat by the USA in 1950, and 6–3 and 7–1 drubbings by Hungary in 1953 and 1954.

● AFTER HANGING up his boots he tried his hand out at management – at Arsenal – then became a top TV executive.

Three lions on a shirt, and Tiddles still gleaming. Billy Wright celebrates his first England cat.

IAN WRIGHT

Born: Woolwich 3.11.63
Height: 5ft 9ins Position: Striker
Club career:
1985–91 Crystal Palace 225 (89)
1991–98 Arsenal 221 (127)
International record:
1991–95 England 31 (9)

IAN WRIGHT is Arsenal's highest scorer of all time. On 13th September 1997 his hat-trick against Bolton sent him past Cliff Bastin's record of 178 goals in all competitions. When he left the Gunners to join West Ham in July 1998 his total stood at 185.

● WHEN HE moved to Arsenal in September 1991 for £2.5 million he became the Gunners' most expensive signing – and the Eagles' most expensive sale. He was worth it, though, finishing top scorer at Highbury for six consecutive seasons. In January 1997 he scored his 200th goal in league football (against Middlesbrough).

● Wright has a terrible disciplinary record – at one point getting into trouble for calling referee Robbie Hart a 'muppet' – but he is the darling of the Highbury fans. He invents a new way of celebrating after scoring each of his goals, although when he removed his shirt to reveal a Nike t-shirt with 'Just Done It – 179', in fact he had only scored 178 and had equalled not broken the record.

● Wright's England days appeared to be over when he was overlooked by Terry Venables, but Glenn Hoddle resurrected his international career. Wright played a starring role in the crucial World Cup qualifier against Italy in Rome in October 1997, hitting the post, but injury cruelly ruled him out of the finals in France.

All Wright! Ian points out he's been Arsenal's top scorer for every season since he joined the Gunners from Crystal Palace in 1991

WYCOMBE WANDERERS

Year founded: 1884
Ground: Adams Park (9,650)
Highest ever crowd: 9,002, 7th January 1995 v West Ham United (FA Cup rd 3)
Nickname: The Chairboys
Colours: Light-and-dark-blue-quartered shirts, dark blue shorts, dark blue socks

IN 1993 WYCOMBE were promoted from the Vauxhall Conference, replacing Halifax Town in the Third Division.

● AND UNDER manager Martin O'Neill – now with Leicester City – they gained promotion to the Second Division in only their first season in the top flight.

● WYCOMBE recorded their best ever win in 1955, trouncing Witney Town 15–1 in an FA Cup preliminary round match. The club's worst defeat was an 8–0 humbling by Reading in 1899 at the same stage of the Cup.

● THE CLUB are known as The Chairboys because of High Wycombe's tradition of furniture-making.

● IN AUGUST 1956, while still a non-league side, Wycombe Wanderers became the first British team to play a touring Ugandan side, defeating their barefoot visitors 10–1 in a midweek match.

Roll of Honour

Vauxhall Conference champions 1993
FA Amateur Cup 1931

LEV YASHIN

Born: Moscow 22.11.29 Died: 1990
Position: Goalkeeper
Club career:
1951–70 Dynamo Moscow 326
International career:
1954–70 Soviet Union 78

IN 1968 THE LEGENDARY Lev Yashin became the only footballer to be awarded the ultimate honour of the Soviet state, the Order of Lenin.

● AND 'BY MARX' he deserved it. He is widely considered to be the best goalkeeper the world has ever seen, almost unbeatable in his 326 matches for Dynamo Moscow and his 78 international matches for the USSR.

● YASHIN, who wore a distinctive all-black outfit, won Olympic Gold in 1956 and helped the USSR win the first ever European Championship in 1960. He also won six league titles with Dynamo Moscow, as well as two Soviet Cups.

● IN 1963 YASHIN became the first Soviet player to win the European Footballer of the Year Award, and is to this day the only goalkeeper ever to have been given this honour.

● 'THE BLACK PANTHER', as he was known, saved more than 150 penalties in his career.

YORK CITY

Year founded: 1922
Ground: Bootham Crescent (9,534)
Highet ever crowd: 28,123, 5th March 1938 v Huddersfield Town (FA Cup rd 6)
Nickname: The Minstermen
Colours: Red shirts, navy blue shorts, red socks

YORK CREATED the biggest Cup shock of 1995/96, knocking Manchester United out of the Coca-Cola Cup. York's incredible 3–0 win at Old Trafford was the only home defeat the eventual Double winners suffered all season.

● YORK'S LESS famous but nevertheless record victory was a 9–1 hammering of Southport in 1957. In 1936 The Minstermen suffered their worst defeat, crashing 0–12 at Chester.

● BARRY JACKSON is York's record appearance maker, playing in 481 league matches between 1958–70. The club's leading scorer is Norman Wilkinson, with 125 goals between 1954–66.

● IN 1955 York City enjoyed their best ever run in the FA Cup, reaching the semi-finals as a Third Division club, before losing to Newcastle United. The run began with a 2–0 third round win over a Blackpool side containing Matthews and Mortensen – arguably York's best ever result.

Roll of Honour

Div 4 champions 1984

YUGOSLAVIA

First international: Yugoslavia 0 Czechoslovakia 7 (Antwerp, 1920)
First World Cup appearance: Yugoslavia 2 Brazil 1 (Uruguay, 1930)
Highest capped player: Dragan Dzajic (85)
Highest goalscorer: Stjepan Bobek (38)
Best win: 10-0 v Venezuela, 1972
Worst defeat: 0-7 v Czechoslovakia, 1920 and 1925
Colours: Blue shirts, white shorts, red socks

Yugoslavia were the first country to lose two European Championship Finals, going down 2-1 tot he Soviet Union in 1960 and 2-0 to Italy in a replay in 1968. At least they made it to the finals in those years, unlike in 1992 when civil war prevented the Yugoslavians from going to Sweden. Denmark filled in for them and promptly won the tournament!

● For such a talented footballing nation, Yugoslavia's record in the World Cup is disappointing, with appearances in the semi-finals in 1930 and 1962 the only highlights. However, the Balkan country did equal the then record – since surpassed by Hungary – for the biggest win in the competition with a 9-0 trouncing of Zaire in 1974.

● In the play-offs for France '98 Yugoslavia were easily the most comfortable victors. They thrashed Hungary 7-1 in Budapest making the second leg a formality. The Yugoslavs won it 5-0, anyway, with Real Madrid striker Predrag Mijatovic helping himself to seven goals over the two games. Slobodan Santrac's team made it to the second round of the tournament, where they met Holland. However, with the score at 1-1 Mijatovic became the first man to miss a non-shoot-out penalty in the World Cup finals since Belgium's Enzo Scifo in 1990 and a late Dutch goal sent the blues back to Belgrade.

WORLD CUP RECORD

1930 Semi-finals	1970 Did not qualify
1934 Did not qualify	1974 Round 2
1938 Did not qualify	1978 Did not qualify
1950 Round 1	1982 Round 1
1954 Quarter-finals	1986 Did not qualify
1958 Quarter-finals	1990 Quarter-finals
1962 Semi-finals	1994 Did not enter
1966 Did not qualify	1998 Round 2

ZICO

Born: Rio de Janeiro, Brazil 3.3.53
Position: Striker
Club career:

1969–83	Flamengo (Brazil)
1983–85	Udinese (Italy)
1985–93	Flamengo
1993–	Kashima Antlers (Japan)

International record:

1975–86	Brazil 88 (54)

ARTUR ANTUNES COIMBRA – or Zico – was so good on his day that he became known in Brazil as 'the White Pele'.

● ZICO'S speciality was the banana free-kick, and he scored one on his international debut in 1975 to prove it. It was the first of 54 goals for his country; only Pele himself has scored more times for Brazil.

● ZICO WAS deservedly voted South American Footballer of the Year an equal record three times, in 1977, 1981 and 1982. In 1983 he was voted World Footballer of the Year, to boot.

● IN 1981 ZICO helped his side Flamengo win the 1981 Copa Libertadores, and then the World Club Cup, in which they beat Liverpool 3–0 in Tokyo.

● HE WENT on to play for Udinese in Italy and became one of the first foreigners to play in Japan when he signed for the Kashima Antlers in the inaugural J League – but not before he had tried a spell in politics, as Brazil's Minister for Sport. Then in 1997 he was appointed technical co-ordinator of the Brazilian national team.

ZINEDINE ZIDANE

Born: Marseilles 23.6.72
Club Career:
1992–94 Cannes
1994–96 Bordeaux
1996– Juventus
International Career:
1994– France 39 (10)

On July 12th 1998 French midfield maestro Zinedine Zidane became the eighth man in football history to score more than one goal in a World Cup Final. Remarkably for a man known for his silky footwork he scored both his two strikes in the 3–0 win over Brazil at France 98 with his head (the first being the first World Cup Final goal in open play since 1986).

● Born in Marseilles of Algerian descent, Zidane began his professional career with Cannes before moving to Bordeaux in 1992. In 1994 he was voted the 'Best Young Footballer' in France and on August 17th of the same year he made his international debut against the Czech Republic.

● In 1996 he won a UEFA Cup runners-up medal with Bordeaux after the side had qualified for the competition via the Inter-Toto Cup. Then in 1996 he moved to Italian giants Juventus where, as the team's main playmaker, he has won the Scudetto twice – in 1997 and 1998 – but has also twice been on he losing side in European Cup Finals (against Borussia Dortmund in 1997 and Real Madrid in 1998).

● Winning the World Cup on home soil will have more than made up for that. It was a personal triumph for Zidane at the Stade De France on July 12th 1998, especially after he looked to have severely jeopardised his country's chances earlier in the tournament by getting himself sent off for stamping against Saudi Arabia in the first round and receiving a two match ban. After the victory a huge image of the French number 10 was projected onto the Arc De Triomphe.

DINO ZOFF

Born: Mariano del Friuli, Italy 28.2.42
Position: Goalkeeper
Club career:
1961–63 Udinese 4
1963–67 Mantova 93
1967–72 Napoli 143
1972–83 Juventus 330
International record:
1968–82 Italy 112

DINO ZOFF, Italy's most capped player with 112 appearances, holds the world record for international clean sheets. The legendary keeper went 1,143 minutes without conceding a goal between September 1973 and June 1974, a run which included 12 consecutive games.

● ZOFF LET IN five goals on his debut for hometown club Udinese, but things got better and better after that and, following several years at Napoli, he became Juventus's keeper and helped them to win seven league titles and the UEFA Cup.

● AT THE age of 40, amazingly he became the second Juventus goalkeeper to captain Italy to World Cup victory (the first was Gianpiero Combi in 1934) when the Azzurri beat West Germany 3–1 in the 1982 Final.

● HE WENT ON to manage Juventus, only to be told in 1990 that he would be sacked at the end of the season. Despite this setback, he guided the team to a UEFA and Italian Cup double.

Did You Know?

In 1983/84 York City became the first ever club to score 100 points (three points for a win was introduced in 1981/82) when they scored 101 points in the Fourth Division.

GIANFRANCO ZOLA

Born: Scicily 5.7.66
Ht: 5ft 5ins Position: Forward
Club career
1984–86 Nuorese 31 (10)
1986–89 Torres 88 (21)
1989–93 Napoli 105 (32)
1993–96 Parma
1996–Chelsea 60 (17)
International record
1991– Italy 36 (9)

In his first two seasons at Chelsea, pint-sized genius Gianfranco Zola won no fewer than three trophies - the 1997 FA Cup, the 1998 FA Cup and European Cup Winners Cup (in which he came of the substitutes bench to score the winner). His trophy laden 1997/98 season ended in heartbreak, however, when he was left out of the Italian squad for France '98.

● The previous season had ended better - he was voted Footballer of the Year. Ever modest, when he received the award he questioned how many of the illustrious journalists were sober when they cast their votes.

● ZOLA WAS born in Sicily but made a name for himself at Napoli, where he was understudy to the great Diego Maradona, whom he eventually replaced and who used to teach him how to take free kicks. Something definitely rubbed off, because an Italian newspaper recently worked out that statistically Zola is the most succesful free-kick taker ever to play in Serie A.

● AFTER NAPOLI (with whom he won the Italian league title in 1990) he moved to Parma where, alongside Faustino Asprilla, he was the focal point of a team which won the Italian Cup (1992), European Cup Winners' Cup (1993) and the UEFA Cup (1995) before Gullit lured him to West London.

NICKNAMES

By popular demand we have included two listings – an A-Z of nicknames for all the English and Scottish League clubs, with a brief word of explanation where necessary (NB we haven't included the blindingly obvious and uninventive Uniteds or Rovers), and an A–Z of grounds and stadiums for all the clubs included in this book.

- Accies – Hamilton Academical: the Academy is a school in the town.
- Addicks – Charlton Athletic, from the word 'haddock' – Charlton players used to take their opponents to a post-match fish-and-chip supper.
- Baggies – West Bromwich Albion, from the voluminous shorts the team used to wear, back in the days of Brylcreem and big ears.
- Bairns – Falkirk, from a Scottish saying 'Better meddle with the devil than the bairns of Falkirk'.
- Bankies – Clydebank
- Bantams – Bradford City: the club's claret and amber colours are apparently similar to a bantam chicken's colouring.
- Bees – Barnet, Brentford. Barnet from their amber and black kit, and the first letter of the club name. Brentford players in the 1920s used to play darts in a local pub called The Beehive.
- Bhoys – Celtic: the closest spelling to the Glaswegian-Irish pronunciation of 'boys'.
- Binos – Stirling Albion: a variation of the word 'Albion'.
- Blades – Sheffield United: Sheffield, the steel capital of England, was particularly noted for its knife production.
- Blue And Whites – Blackburn Rovers, from their strip.
- Bluebirds – Cardiff City, from their predominantly blue strip.
- Blues – Birmingham City, Carlisle United, Chelsea, Chester City,
- Chesterfield, Manchester City, Stranraer, from club colours.
- 'Boro – Middlesbrough
- The Boro – Scarborough
- Buddies – St. Mirren: a nickname for the inhabitants of Paisley, due to their penchant for crossing the Atlantic to North America.
- The Bully Wee – Clyde, either from Clyde bullying the Glasgow giants Rangers and Celtic, or from an old sea shanty about the River Clyde.
- Borderers – Berwick Rangers, from the town's position on the English side of the border with Scotland.
- Canaries – Norwich City, from their yellow strip.
- Cestrians – Chester City; a derivation of the Latin 'Castra', an early name of the city.
- Chairboys – Wycombe Wanderers: High Wycombe was a furniture-making centre.
- Cherries – Bolton Wanderers, from the red stripes on their shirts.
- Clarets – Burnley, from their shirt colour.
- Citizens – Manchester City
- Cobblers – Northampton Town: a lot of shoes have emerged from Northampton.
- Cockerels – Tottenham Hotspur, from the club badge: the cockerel is probably a reference to Spurs, as fighting cocks used to be equipped with tiny spurs.
- Cottagers – Fulham, from their ground Craven Cottage.
- Cumbrians – Carlisle United, the only Football League team in the area.
- The Dale – Rochdale
- Dark Blues – Dundee, from their strip.
- Diamonds – Airdrieonians, from the red diamond on their shirts.
- The Dee – Dundee
- Dons – Aberdeen, Wimbledon. Founder members of Aberdeen were professors at the local university, and the River Don flows through the city. Wimbledon's nickname is less high-brow, simply deriving from their name.
- Doonhamers – Queen of the South: a Gaelic variation of 'Down Homers'.
- Eagles – Crystal Palace, from Malcolm Allison's time at the club, when fans chanted 'Eagles' to echo their main rivals Brighton & Hove Albion's cry of 'Seagulls'.
- Fifers – East Fife
- Filberts – Leicester City, from the club ground Filbert Street.
- Foxes – Leicester City: once well known for its fox-hunting.
- Gable Endies – Montrose: a general nickname for Montrose-dwellers due to the large number of gables in the town.
- Gers – Rangers
- Gills – Gillingham, from their name, not a reference to their interest in the services of Fulchester United goalkeeper Billy the Fish.
- Glaziers – Crystal Palace, from the original exhibition building.
- Grecians – Exeter City, from a nearby Greek community.
- Gulls – Torquay United: a seaside reference.
- Gunners – Arsenal: the original players were workers at the Royal Arsenal, the state munitions factory.
- Hammers – West Ham United
- Hatters – Luton Town, Stockport County. Both Luton and Stockport were noted hat-making centres.
- Hearts – Heart of Midlothian
- Hibs or Hibees – Hibernian
- Honest Men – Ayr United, from Robert Burns' poem 'Tam O'Shanter' which claimed Ayr was full of 'honest men and bonnie lasses'. The Bonnie Lasses was not thought to be a sensible option.
- Hornets – Watford, from the club colours.
- Imps – Lincoln City, a reference to a carving at Lincoln Cathedral.
- The Iron – Scunthorpe United, from its steel industry.
- Ironsides – Middlesbrough, from its industrial past.
- Jags – Partick Thistle: 'jag' means thistle.
- Jammies – Heart of Midlothian, from rhyming slang (jam tarts = Hearts).
- Killie – Kilmarnock
- Latics – Oldham Athletic, Wigan Athletic: an abbreviation of Athletic.
- Lilywhites – Preston North End, from their white strip.
- Lions – Millwall, from the club badge.
- Loons – Forfar Athletic.
- Magpies – Newcastle United, Notts County: from their black and white strips.
- Mariners – Grimsby Town: a thriving sea port.
- Merry Millers – Rotherham United: the area boasts many mills. Why the team is merry is anybody's guess.
- Minstermen – York City, a reference to York's magnificent Minster.
- O's – Leyton Orient: the word Orient refers to Leyton's East End location.
- Owls – Sheffield Wednesday: the original name of the club's ground, Hillsborough, was the Owlerton Stadium.
- Pars – Dunfermline Athletic: various possibilities, including the suggestion that sailors from nearby Rosyth naval base used to attend matches with a banner for 'Plymouth Argyle Rosyth Supporters'. Alternatively the team's black and white strip resembles the parr fish.
- Pilgrims – Plymouth Argyle, whence the Pilgrim Fathers set sail.
- Pirates – Bristol Rovers, from the seafaring tradition of the city.
- Pompey – Portsmouth: the traditional nickname for the town.
- The Pool – Hartlepool United
- The Posh – Peterborough United: in 1934 Peterborough sported a brand-new strip in a game against Gainsborough Trinity which led to oohs and aahs from the crowd, and a brand-new nickname, too.
- Potters – Stoke City: the Stoke-on-Trent area, known as the Potteries because of the local industry.
- Quakers – Darlington: the area was a traditional Quaker stronghold.
- R's – Queens Park Rangers
- Railwaymen – Crewe Alexandra: Crewe has always been a railway hub.
- Rams – Derby County, from their club badge.
- Red Lichties – Arbroath, referring to the red light cast by Stevenson's famous Bell Rock lighthouse.
- Red Devils – Manchester United, from their colours rather than any on-pitch behaviour.
- Reds – Liverpool, pretty obvious.
- Robins – Bristol City, Charlton Athletic, Swindon Town: from shirt colours.
- Rokermen – Sunderland, from the club ground Roker Park.
- Royals – Reading, from its situation in 'Royal Berkshire'.
- Saddlers – Walsall, from the local leather-fashioning industry.
- Saints – St. Johnstone, Southampton. In Southampton's case, the club, originally a church side, were once called Southampton St. Mary's.
- Seagulls – Brighton & Hove Albion, from the town's location.
- Seasiders – Blackpool, for the same reason.
- Shakers – Bury, from a comment by the club chairman in 1891 – he expected his team to shake the opposition.
- The Shire – East Stirlingshire
- Shrews – Shrewsbury Town (often tamed, unfortunately).
- Shrimpers – Southend United, a memory of summers past.
- Silkmen – Macclesfield Town
- Sky Blues – Coventry City, Forfar Athletic. From their strips, in Coventry's case the Jimmy Hill-hyped version.
- Sons – Dumbarton, from the phrase 'the

sons of the rock', a reference to the hill on which Dumbarton's castle proudly stands.
- Spiders – Queen's Park, from their black-and-white-hooped shirts (Edinburgh spiders, it seems, are a different colour to other spiders).
- Spirites – Chesterfield, from its famous twisted spire.
- Spurs – Tottenham Hotspur, from Harry Percy, known as Harry Hotspur, son of the first Earl of Northumberland (made enduringly famous by Shakespeare's Henry IV Part 1), who bought land locally.
- Stags – Mansfield Town, from its proximity to nearby deer-rich Sherwood Forest.
- Tangerines – Blackpool, from the club's orange strip.
- Terriers – Huddersfield Town: a Yorkshire terrier adorns the club badge.
- Terrors – Dundee United, probably from the lion on the club badge, or simply an attempt to intimidate the opposition.
- Throstles: West Bromwich Albion: the club's emblem of a thrush (or throstle) commemorates the bird kept by the landlady of the club's original pub HQ.
- Tigers – Hull City, from their strip.
- Toffees – Everton: the club was founded in a house opposite a shop called 'Ye Ancient Everton Toffee House'.
- The Ton – Greenock Morton
- Trotters – Bolton Wanderers: in the 1880s the team were well known for their practical jokes. A 'trotter' is a practical joker.
- Tykes – Barnsley: Yorkshire dialect for 'the Yorkshiremen'.
- U's – Cambridge United, Colchester United, Oxford United, from United – although possibly also a reference to the universities.
- Valiants – Charlton Athletic, Port Vale. Charlton play at The Valley, Port Vale at Vale Park.
- Villans – Aston Villa
- Warriors – Stenhousemuir
- Wasps – Alloa, from their waspish team colours.
- Wee Jags – Livingston: a 'jag' is a Scottish word for a thistle – Livingston used to be called Meadowbank Thistle.
- Wee Rovers – Albion Rovers
- The Well – Motherwell
- Wolves – Wolverhampton Wanderers
- Wombles – Wimbledon, from the 1970s TV show.

GROUNDS

- Abbey Stadium – Cambridge United
- Adams Park – Wycombe Wanderers
- Ali Sami Yen – Galatasaray
- Almondvale Stadium – Livingston
- Amsterdam Arena – Ajax
- Anfield – Liverpool
- Ashton Gate – Bristol City
- Bayview Park – East Fife
- Belle Vue – Doncaster Rovers
- Bernabeu Stadium – Real Madrid
- Bescot Stadium – Walsall
- Bloomfield Road – Blackpool
- Blundell Park – Grimsby Town
- Boghead Park – Dumbarton
- Bombonera Stadium – Boca Juniors
- Bootham Crescent – York City
- Boothferry Park – Hull City
- Boundary Park – Oldham Athletic
- Bramall Lane – Sheffield United
- Brisbane Road – Leyton Orient
- Britannia Stadium – Stoke City
- Broadwood Stadium – Airdrieonians and Clyde (shared)
- Brockville Park – Falkirk
- Brunton Park – Carlisle United
- Bulgarska Armia – CSKA Sofia
- Cappielow Park – Greenock Morton
- Carrow Road – Norwich City
- Cellnet Riverside Stadium – Middlesbrough
- Celtic Park – Celtic
- Centenario Stadium – Penarol
- Central Park – Cowdenbeath
- The City Ground – Nottingham Forest
- Cliftonhill – Albion Rovers
- Constant Vanden Stock Stadium – Anderlecht
- County Ground – Swindon Town
- Craven Cottage – Fulham
- Crvena Svezda – Red Star Belgrade
- Dean Court – Bournemouth
- Deepdale – Preston North End
- The Dell – Southampton
- Dens Park – Dundee
- Deva Stadium – Chester City
- Dinamo Stadium – Dynamo Moscow
- Dos Antas Stadium – FC Porto
- East End Park – Dunfermline Athletic
- Easter Road – Hibernian
- Edgar Street – Hereford United
- Edgeley Park – Stockport County
- Elland Road – Leeds United
- Elm Park – Reading
- Estadio Da Luz – Benfica
- Ewood Park – Blackburn Rovers
- Feethams – Darlington
- Field Mill – Mansfield Town
- Filbert Street – Leicester City
- Firhill Park – Partick Thistle
- Firhill Stadium – Hamilton Academical
- Fir Park – Motherwell
- Firs Park – East Stirlingshire
- Forthbank Stadium – Stirling Albion
- Fratton Park – Portsmouth
- Gamla Ullevi – IFK Gothenburg
- Gay Meadow – Shrewsbury Town
- Gayfield Park – Arbroath
- Gigg Lane – Bury
- Glanford Park – Scunthorpe United
- Glebe Park – Brechin City
- Giuseppe Meazza (San Siro) – AC Milan and Inter Milan (shared)
- Goodison Park – Everton
- Gresty Road – Crewe Alexandra
- Griffin Park – Brentford
- Hampden Park – Queen's Park
- The Hawthorns – West Bromwich Albion
- Highbury Stadium – Arsenal
- Highfield Road – Coventry City
- Hillsborough – Sheffield Wednesday
- Home Park – Plymouth Argyle
- Ibrox Park – Rangers
- Kenilworth Road – Luton Town
- Kilbowie Park – Clydebank
- Layer Road – Colchester United
- Links Park – Montrose
- Loftus Road – Queens Park Rangers
- London Road – Peterborough United
- Love Street – St. Mirren
- McDiarmid Park – St. Johnstone
- Maine Road – Manchester City
- Manor Ground – Oxford United
- Meadow Lane – Notts County
- Millmoor – Rotherham United
- Molineux – Wolverhampton Wanderers
- Monumental Stadium – River Plate
- The New Den – Millwall
- Ninian Park – Cambridge United
- Nou Camp – Barcelona
- Oakwell – Barnsley
- Ochilview Park – Stenhousemuir
- Old Trafford – Manchester United
- Olympiastadion – Bayern Munich
- The Oval – Glentoran
- Palmerston Park – Queen of the South
- Parc Des Princes – Paris St. Germain
- Philips Stadium – PSV Eindhoven
- Pittodrie Stadium – Aberdeen
- Plainmoor – Torquay United
- Portman Road – Ipswich Town
- Prenton Park – Tranmere Rovers
- Pride Park – Derby County
- Priestfield Stadium – Gillingham
- Rangers Stadium – Queens Park Rangers
- Recreation Ground – Chesterfield
- Recreation Park – Alloa
- Reebok Stadium – Bolton Wanderers
- Riverside Park – Middlesbrough
- Roots Hall – Southend United
- Royal Dublin Society Showgrounds – Shamrock Rovers
- Rugby Park – Kilmarnock
- St. Andrews – Birmingham City
- St. James Park – Exeter City
- St. James' Park – Newcastle United
- San Siro – AC Milan and Inter Milan (shared)
- Selhurst Park – Crystal Palace and Wimbledon (shared)
- Shielfield Park – Berwick Rangers
- Sincil Bank – Lincoln City
- Sir Alfred McAlpine Stadium – Huddersfield Town
- Sixfields Stadium – Northampton Town
- Somerset Park – Ayr United
- Spotland – Rochdale
- Springfield Park – Wigan Athletic
- Stadio Delle Alpi – Juventus
- Stadio Olimpico – Lazio and Roma (shared)
- Stair Park – Stranraer
- Stamford Bridge – Chelsea
- Stark's Park – Raith Rovers
- Station Park – Forfar Athletic
- Steaua Stadium – Steaua Bucharest
- Tannadice Park – Dundee United
- Telford Street Park – Caledonian Thistle
- Turf Moor – Burnley
- Twerton Park – Bristol Rovers
- Tynecastle Park – Heart of Midlothian
- Underhill Stadium – Barnet
- Upton Park – West Ham United
- Vale Park – Port Vale
- The Valley – Charlton Athletic
- Valley Parade – Bradford City
- Vélodrome – Marseille
- Vicarage Road – Watford
- The Victoria Ground – Hartlepool United, Stoke City
- Victoria Park – Ross County
- Vila Belmiro Stadium – Santos
- Villa Park – Aston Villa
- White Hart Lane – Tottenham Hotspur
- Windsor Park – Linfield

AUTHOR ACKNOWLEDGMENTS

Special thanks to Clive 'Statto' Batty, super-sub Pete May, and Neil, Ian and Keith at Prima Creative Services. Plus much appreciated assistance from the population of Planet Football, especially David Barber and Mark Sudbury at the English FA, Ceri Stennet at the Welsh FA, Alison at the Scottish FA, Thomas Doran of the Deutscher Fussball-Bund, the Premier League press office, Ged O'Brien (Project Director of the SFA Museum Trust), Celtic View, Rangers News, Roger Harrison at Blackpool FC, Pete Rundall at Dundee United, Tom Wright at Hibernian FC, Dave Allen at Middlesbrough FC, Reg Davis at Wimbledon FC, Graham Courtley at Newcastle United FC, Brian Cambell at Ross County FC, Richard Harnwell of Stockport County FC, Andy Porter of Tottenham Hotspur FC, Anna Paula Godinho at Benfica, the press offices of FIFA, UEFA, AC Milan, BBC Sport, Blackburn Rovers, Manchester United, Juventus.

No thanks whatsoever to the Brazilian FA ('send another fax'), Colombian FA ('please hold the line for several weeks'), Zimbabwean FA and Nigerian FAs ('beep, beep, beep'), Brondby FC, Monaco FC, the Danish FA, Monaco FC and the man in a bad mood on reception at Bradford City.

PUBLISHER ACKNOWLEDGMENTS

The publishers would like to thank the following for their help and enthusiasm:
Roger Kean and everyone at Prima Creative Services
Rick Mayston for picture research
Lee Martin and the Allsport football squad (Marc, Mark and Paul)
Ray Driscoll for statistical and editorial support
Hal Norman for editorial back-up

PICTURE ACKNOWLEDGMENTS

All the photographs in this book were supplied by Allsport/Hulton Getty
A.Jones (Evening Standard), Alex Livesey, Anton Want, Aubrey Hart (Evening Standard), Ben Radford, Chris Cole, Claudio Villa, Clive Brunskill, Clive Mason, Craig Prentis, Dan Smith, David Cannon, David Leah, Gary. M. Prior, Graham Chadwick, Howard Boylan, James Meehan, Jeff Holmes, Julian Herbert, Mark Thompson, Mike Cooper, Mike Hewitt, Mike Powell, Pascal Rondeau, Phil Cole, Richard Martin, Richard Saker, Ross Kinnaird, Shaun Botterill, Simon Bruty, Steve Morton, Stu Forster